A NOTE FROM TH

Many books have been
nedy assassination. In A
undertook a project to pu
cause we were impressed
reporter had handled the Kennedy case in a *New Times* magazine article.

We had expected a solid, provocative treatment of the assassination, but when Robert Sam Anson's finished manuscript came into the house in August, we realized that he had given us much more: people who were completely uninterested in reading about the Kennedy case were unable to put the book down. Others who had read extensively on the controversy agreed that Anson's book was the first to present a complicated mystery in a thoroughly readable manner; that his theory of what really happened in Dallas was chillingly plausible. One of the earliest readers of the manuscript, a firm and knowledgeable believer in the Warren Commission Report, admitted that the book had turned him around.

As enthusiasm and respect for the manuscript grew, we knew we had to publish the book as quickly as possible. The topicality of the subject was a minor factor. The real urgency stemmed from the nature of the book itself: the most eloquent, persuasive plea for a new investigation of John F. Kennedy's murder.

"THEY'VE KILLED THE PRESIDENT!" does not name any specific individual as a member of any conspiracy concerning the assassination of John F. Kennedy.

TWELVE YEARS IS A LONG TIME

There were many versions of what happened that day in Dealey Plaza. The man charged with the crime denied any part in it. The wounded survivor clung stubbornly to his own interpretation of the gunfire. The investigating Commission seemed unanimous in its verdict. The President who called the Commission into being had doubts about its findings. And twelve years later America wondered if it would ever hear the full truth.

"I didn't shoot anybody, no sir."

—Lee Harvey Oswald to a reporter in the Dallas County Jail, November 22, 1963

"I knew it when I just looked down and I was covered with blood . . . The thought immediately passed through my mind that there were either two or three people involved or more in this."

—Governor John Connally testifying before the Warren Commission, 1964

TO HAVE BURIED THE TRUTH . . .

"On the basis of the evidence before the Commission, it concludes that Oswald acted alone."

–Report of the President's Commission on the Assassination of President John F. Kennedy, September 1964

"I don't think that they [Warren Commission] or me or anyone else is absolutely sure of everything that might have motivated Oswald or others that could have been involved."

–Lyndon Baines Johnson in an interview with Walter Cronkite, September 1969

"Up until a few months ago I was one who believed the Warren Commission conclusion that Lee Harvey Oswald acted alone. But all these new developments have caused me to question some of the Commission's assumptions. To me it's like a big, public boil that's going to burst."

–Senator Richard S. Schweiker, sponsor of a select committee resolution to take a new look at the Kennedy assassination, September 1975

ABOUT THE AUTHOR

ROBERT SAM ANSON went to work for *Time* as a correspondent in 1967, one of the youngest journalists ever to hold that position at the magazine. In the six years he worked for *Time*, Anson reported from Chicago, New York, Los Angeles and Indochina. In 1970, while on assignment in Cambodia, he was taken as prisoner of war by North Vietnamese troops and Cambodian guerrillas. His subsequent first-person account of his capture was the longest personal narrative ever to appear in *Time*.

Mr. Anson is currently Executive Producer for Special Events for public television station WNET in New York and the national political correspondent for *New Times* magazine. He has had two articles on the JFK assassination published in *New Times*. His articles have also appeared in *Harper's*, the *Atlantic*, *Columbia Journalism Review* and *Ms.* His first book, *McGovern: A Biography*, was described by the *Wall Street Journal* as "substantial, analytical, literate."

“They’ve Killed the President!”

The Search for the Murderers of John F. Kennedy

By Robert Sam Anson

"THEY'VE KILLED THE PRESIDENT!"
A Bantam Book / November 1975
2nd printing
3rd printing
4th printing
5th printing

Published simultaneously in the United States and Canada

Bantam Books are published by Bantam Books, Inc. Its trademark, consisting of the words "Bantam Books" and the portrayal of a bantam, is registered in the United States Patent Office and in other countries. Marca Registrada. Bantam Books, Inc., 666 Fifth Avenue, New York, New York 10019.

PRINTED IN THE UNITED STATES OF AMERICA

For Christian Kennedy Anson

Contents

Acknowledgments

A number of people have provided invaluable contributions to this book, and to my own thinking on the Kennedy assassination. For their generous assistance and friendship, I would like to thank in particular Jones Harris, Peter Dale Scott, and Sylvia Meagher.

I would also like to express my gratitude to Jerry Policoff, Carl Oglesby, Mark Lane, Frank McCulloch, and one very nice lady in Dallas.

The works of a number of authors have aided me greatly. They are: *Inquest* and *Counterplot* by Edward Jay Epstein; *The Fall and Rise of Jimmy Hoffa,* by Walter Sheridan; *Kennedy Justice,* by Victor Navasky; *Six Seconds in Dallas,* by Josiah Thompson; *Rush to Judgment* and *A Citizen's Dissent,* by Mark Lane; *Accessories After the Fact,* by Sylvia Meagher; *The Dallas Conspiracy* (unpublished), by Peter Dale Scott; *The Politics of Heroin in Southeast Asia,* by Alfred McCoy; *The Grim Reapers,* by Ed Reid; *American Grotesque,* by James Kirkwood; *Without Cloak or Dagger,* by Miles Copeland; *With Fidel,* by Frank Mankiewicz and Kirby Jones; *A Thousand Days,* by Arthur Schlesinger; *The Reds and the Blacks,* by William Attwood; *Compulsive Spy,* by Tad Szulc; *To Move a Nation,* by Roger Hilsman; *The Tentacles of Power,* by Clark Mollenhoff; *Legacy of Doubt,* by Peter Noyes; *The CIA and the Cult of Intelligence,* by Victor Marchetti and John Marks; *Inside the Company: CIA Diary,* by Philip Agee; *The Invisible Government,* by David Wise and Thomas Ross; *The Assassination Tapes,* by George O'Toole; *The Crime Confederation,* by Ralph Salerno and John Tompkins; *The Second Oswald,* by Richard Popkin; *Whitewash IV,* by Harold

Weisberg; and, of course, *The Enemy Within,* by Robert F. Kennedy. Sandy Smith's articles on organized crime in *Life* and *Time* were also of enormous use.

Jon Larsen and George Hirsch, the editor and publisher, respectively, of *New Times* magazine, provided the initial resources and encouragement that made this project possible. Thanks also to Jerry Toobin of WNET/13 in New York and to Linda Amster.

I also wish to extend my appreciation to Peter Shepherd, my agent and friend, and to Jean Highland, Joëlle Delbourgo, Mary Ann Rice, and Judy Knipe of Bantam Books, who saw me through the dark days to deadline.

And, finally, there is Maggie.

You must wonder when it is all going to end
And when we can come back home.
Well, it isn't going to end . . .
We have to stay at it.
We must not be fatigued.

—John Fitzgerald Kennedy
November 1963

DEALEY PLAZA

November 22, 1963   12:30 P.M.

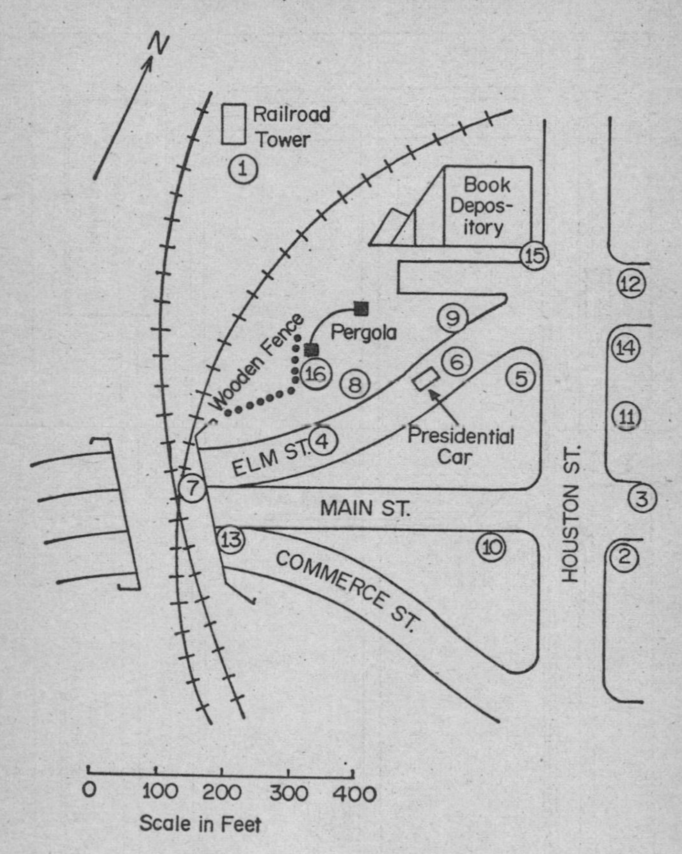

1. Lee E. Bowers, Jr.
2. Richard Randolph Carr
3. Roger D. Craig
4. Chief of Police
   Jesse E. Curry
5. Ronald B. Fischer
6. Bobby W. Hargis
7. S.M. Holland
8. (Mrs.) Gayle Newman
9. William Eugene Newman
10. Orville O. Nix
11. Arnold Lewis Rowland
12. Joe Marshall Smith
13. James Thomas Tague
14. (Mrs.) Carolyn Walther
15. James Richard Worrell
16. Abraham Zapruder

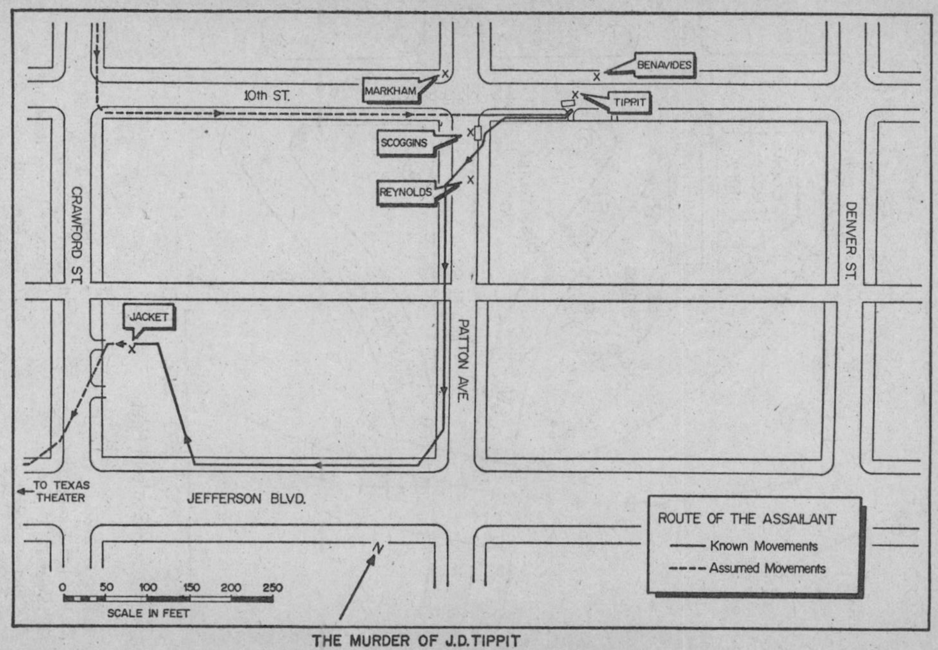

THE MURDER OF J.D.TIPPIT

"They've Killed the President!"

Introduction

Dallas Was Yesterday

THEY STILL COME to Dealey Plaza in Dallas, people by twos and threes, tugging along children who are too young to remember. Quietly they walk down the gentle curving slope that is Elm Street, now and again glancing over their shoulders at the squat red brick building with the Hertz Rent A Car sign on the top. The building is sealed off from the curious; the companies which once stored books there have long since moved away. Up on the sixth floor, in the extreme southeast corner, someone has painted a large black *X* on one of the windowpanes, the only surviving token of the specialness of the place. The people study the window, measuring the distance to an invisible spot in the middle of Elm. And then, inevitably, they turn toward the knoll. "It's funny," says one of the groundkeepers. "It's as if folks are looking for something. I don't know what. They just keep looking."

Maybe it is for a bit of their past. It seems like yesterday. And yet twelve years have slipped by since that sunny day in Dallas: a war, two presidents, changes without number, and still it is the moment no one will ever forget. Where were you on November 22, 1963? If you were alive that day, you will remember, even to the fine details, what you were doing when word came that John Kennedy had been murdered. There will always be the memory. And, for many, wonder and doubt.

The Commission appointed by President Lyndon Johnson and chaired by Chief Justice Earl Warren was supposed to end the questions. Its investigation was said to be the most thorough and exhaustive in American history, comprising more than 25,000 interviews, a full twenty-seven volumes of conclusions, testimony, and exhibits. There was no equivocation in the Report's central finding: a deranged young man named Lee Harvey Oswald, acting alone, shot and killed the President of the United States, and was himself killed two days later before a national television audience by an equally lone and deranged strip-joint operator named Jack Ruby.

And yet the doubts remained. In the months before his death, Lyndon Johnson told several reporters that he believed that his predecessor might have been the victim of a "Communist conspiracy," then asked the reporters to keep his remarks secret on grounds of "national security." [1] Then Governor John Connally was more public with his objections. Before the Warren Commission and later, he repeated his conviction that he had been wounded by a different bullet from the one which struck the President [2]—a crucial point, for as one Commission lawyer candidly put it, "To say that they were hit by separate bullets is synonymous with saying that there were two assassins." [3] Senator Richard Russell and Representative Hale Boggs, both members of the Commission, expressed disbelief in the report they had signed.[4] Henry Wade, still the district attorney of Dallas, said the assassin he indicted had been part of a larger conspiracy.[5] Jesse Curry, the Dallas police chief at the time of the assassination, admitted it would have been difficult if not impossible to convict Oswald on the basis of the evidence,[6] a sentiment a number of eyewitnesses evidently shared. Fifty-two of them claimed to have heard or seen shots coming from in front of the President; [7] the Warren Commission dismissed them all. The critics, however, didn't. Within a few years of the publication of the Commission Report, more than forty books had been published attacking virtually every one of its conclusions. They found an increasingly receptive audience. By 1966 both the Gallup and Harris polls found that 66 percent of the American people did not believe that Oswald was the lone assassin.[8] The same year, two bills were introduced on the floor of Congress, calling for a new investigation.

Then, in New Orleans, District Attorney Jim Garrison, a man of large ambition and unsavory reputation, announced that his office had solved the case and arrested a local businessman named Clay Shaw, charging him with conspiracy in the murder of John Kennedy. After a bizarre trial Shaw was acquitted, and Garrison was driven from office. The critics of the Warren Commission were scattered in disarray. The assassination became a subject for kooks and charlatans. For a time, the doubts went underground.

Now they have returned, deeper and more persistent than ever. New bills calling for a reopening of the case have been introduced in Congress. Two separate congressional subcommittees have begun probing Oswald's ties with American intelligence, and the withholding of evidence from the Warren Commission by both the CIA and FBI. Petition drives are being mounted. The assassination is once again on the lecture circuit. The long-suppressed Zapruder film of the assassination has been shown on national television. A raft of Freedom of Information Act lawsuits have dislodged thousands of pages of secret Warren Commission testimony and documents from the National Archives. According to a poll taken in the summer of 1975, the Americans who disbelieve the Warren Commission now number four in five.* [9]

The continuing fascination with John Kennedy's life and the violence of its taking can be ascribed to many causes: morbid curiosity, Americans' love of a great thriller, paranoia, the President's youth, his family, his style. Or simply a nostalgic longing for times that seemed simpler, somehow better. When matched against Vietnam and Richard Nixon and Watergate,

---

* The poll, which was conducted by Cambridge Survey Research as part of a general sampling of American attitudes on various issues, posed the simple question: Who do you think killed President Kennedy? The responses were as follows:

Lone, deranged assassin (the Commission finding)	18%
Foreign conspiracy	5%
Some sort of conspiracy	33%
Not sure, needs to be investigated	18%
Don't know, no opinion	13%
CIA conspiracy	13%

the explanations have a certain logic. The logic, however, cannot measure the loss, how it happened, or why.

John Kennedy's death defies simple rationality. Its impact is as much emotional as political, discerned better by psychologists than historians. The assassination, more than any other event, gave the succeeding decade its shape and form. For the generation that came to political consciousness in the sixties, the assassination is the seminal happening. It matters very little that it was John Kennedy who sent combat advisers to Vietnam, who encouraged newspapermen to investigate the private lives of his enemies, whose administration plotted the assassination of Fidel Castro; despite it all, somehow times were better when he was alive. Even today his death is the emotional demarcation between hope and promise and bitterness and despair. The polls confirm what the gut feels: never since Dallas have Americans invested so much trust in their government. Each year, from 1964 onward, the figures have become worse: declining confidence in government, in the church, in the family, in the inevitability of change for the better. The first spadeful of earth in what has come to be called the "credibility gap"—but is really the chasm we feel in ourselves—was turned over in Dealey Plaza.

A decade ago there was only the gnawing feeling that something was terribly wrong. Today many of the worst suspicions have become fact. Americans now know things about their government that, only a few short years ago, seemed the product of the worst paranoid delusions. Thanks to Vietnam and Watergate and disclosures about the Central Intelligence Agency, they realize not only how the government lies, but how it operates. That its intelligence agencies have spied on thousands of citizens,[10] opened their mail,[11] monitored their conversations,[12] probed their private lives;[13] that a secret police agency was created within the walls of the White House;[14] that the CIA entered into an alliance with organized crime;[15] that the United States plotted and executed the assassination of several foreign leaders.[16] Most important, we have learned how little we know about the CIA and the other members of the "intelligence community," a beneficent phrase that suggests a group of quiet families living off in the Washington suburbs. We know enough, however, to realize that our previous conception of the Agency as a repository for clipped-accented James Bonds, sworn to their country's protection, is a woeful misconception. Painfully, still disbelievingly, we are learning that many of the men who have served under the alert eagle of the CIA's crest have lied, cheated, stolen, suborned, maimed, and murdered to achieve their ends. We are finding also that there is no effective control over this "invisible government," that it defies not only Congress and its own director, but on numerous occasions the direct, explicit orders of the President of the United States. In a world where the CIA has "persistently, ingeniously and sometimes irresponsibly engaged in undertakings that confronted the nation with the possibility of war," [17] as Arthur Schlesinger has written, nothing is impossible, no undertaking unthinkable. Suddenly even the ultimate horror seems possible.

The time is gone when the Warren Commission was able to muster belief, if only because any other scenario of events seemed so wildly improbable. Conspiracy—the Latin root means "breathe together"—no longer seems so alien. The revelations of the past few years have shown that, on the contrary, conspiracy is as American as apple pie. It's something that General Electric does to fix prices;[18] Gulf and Northrup to bribe governments; [19] the President of the United States to obstruct justice.[20] When former Harvard deans can sit in the White House and discuss the pros and cons of assassination, as McGeorge Bundy did during the Kennedy administration; [21] when a senior presidential aide, in public questioning, refuses to rule out murder in the national interest, as John Ehrlichman did during the Watergate hearings,[22] it is clear that even at the highest levels anything can happen, and, given sufficient rationalization, the worst often does.

The temptation to which many have succumbed is to assume that because anything is possible, the worst is always true. Thus in recent years sensational charges have arisen, tales of gunmen in bushes, of Watergate burglars on the grassy knoll, of zombie assassins programmed by the CIA. There is a devil theory to fit every prejudice, from the Soviets to the Secret Service to Texas oil millionaires to Madame Nhu. Given the history of the last decade it is easy to see how such stories arise. Absurdity seems to demand an absurd explanation.

By contrast, the known facts of John Kennedy's murder are relatively dull, seemingly insignificant bits of detail and odd coincidence which when fitted together like pieces of a grand mosaic form a picture, only half complete. Year after year more pieces are collected, evaluated, and, more often than not, put aside. The crime is like an onion; one layer is peeled away only to reveal another and yet another. It is altogether possible that the full truth of the Kennedy assassination will never be known—a modern version of the legend of Judge Crater.

It need not be. There is at this moment a body of facts and scientific evidence, much of it newly disclosed, which when analyzed by reasonable men presents overwhelming evidence of conspiracy. When the critics began delving into the Warren Commission report eleven years ago, most of what they uncovered indicated what wasn't: that Oswald *wasn't* a good marksman, that his rifle *couldn't* have fired the shots, that the so-called "magic bullet" *didn't* pass through John Kennedy and into John Connally. The new information, secured only after lengthy lawsuits, adds to the mountain of negative data. But, more tantalizingly, it reveals part of what *was:* that Oswald *did* have numerous links to the intelligence community; that there *was* an Oswald look-alike; that the FBI and CIA *did* withhold and destroy vital evidence. Perhaps most importantly, the new evidence quotes verbatim hitherto secret discussions among the members of the Warren Commission expressing the same fears which, when coming from the critics, have officially been dismissed as paranoia.

One of the most dramatic developments is recent

public showings of a clear, bootlegged copy of the famous Zapruder film. Long suppressed by legal controversy, its content distorted by both the Warren Commission and the press, the film, in its horrifying entirety, has now been seen by millions of Americans. What emerges from the twenty-two-second 8-mm piece of color celluloid is irrefutable proof of the conspiracy that took John Kennedy's life. The arguments, the theories, the obscure nuances disappear before the horror one sees with one's very eyes: a man quite literally having the back of his head blown off.

This book is the story of those twenty-two seconds, the events that led up to them, the trauma that even today is being felt because of them. It is not intended as a point-by-point refutation of the Warren Commission or as a response to every unanswered question. The matter of Oswald's guilt or innocence in the conspiracy is left unresolved. How many assassins fired on the motorcade and where they were stationed is only suggested. You will find no conclusive solution in these pages; no assassins will be named.

What this book seeks to do, on the basis of the available evidence, is to establish a few core facts—that there was a conspiracy; that Oswald had numerous links to the intelligence community; that Oswald, whether he fired at the President or not, was implicated in the crime by the intentional use of a look-alike, a common practice in intelligence work; that vital information about Oswald's and Ruby's backgrounds was deliberately withheld from the Warren Commission by the CIA and the FBI—and, working from those facts, to present a reasonable explanation for the events in Dealey Plaza and the cover-up that followed. An accounting will be given, one which points in a certain direction, not at individuals but at groups, seemingly separate entities whose interests, in fact, make them one. Inevitably, theory will mingle with fact. Where they intersect each will be clearly identified. The final conclusions are left for you to draw.

This is a book about process: how people and events moved toward one moment, and how, because of it, they moved after. The moment, of course, is 12:30 p.m.

(Central Standard Time), November 22, 1963. But it is only one moment, and not the most important one at that. In the past the assassination has been looked on as an isolated event, a happening so unimaginable in its occurrence, so shocking in its impact, as to remove it somehow from normal time. It is as if November 22 is a day forever frozen. The Warren Commission and most of its critics are alike in the respect that they dwell on that moment, and the people involved with it, almost to the exclusion of all else. More than 20 million words have been devoted to the recounting of the events of November 22. Seemingly every scrap of evidence, however minute, has been gone over and gone over again. Apparently every conceivable question has been asked; every theory, however improbable, considered; every witness interviewed, if not by the Commission, then surely by the critics; every photograph studied, enlarged, and enhanced. Everything that could be done has been done. Except to ask one question: Why?

The answer to that question is not in Dealey Plaza. Ballistics tests and autopsy results will not provide a motive. Where the assassins were stationed—on the grassy knoll, atop the Triple Underpass, in adjoining buildings, even, as a few of the more lurid conspiriologists have suggested, in the sewer—may make for fascinating theorizing, but the guessing is an exercise in irrelevance. The fact is that, how many their number, wherever they were, they performed their task with fatal efficiency. Once again the question is: *Why* did they?

In a normal murder case, arriving at the answer is a straightforward process. The police investigate the victim's friends and family, check his history, list his enemies, and decide who among them had sufficient motive to kill him. The next step is evaluating whether they had the opportunity: Where were the enemies at the time of the shooting? And, if they had an alibi, could they have been in contact with professional killers? Finally, there is the matter of means: Did the victim's enemies have access to the weapon that killed him and the expertise to use it?

Motive, means, and opportunity: the three essentials

in any murder investigation. The fatal flaw in the Warren Commission's investigation is that they proceeded backward. They took a single suspect, who had neither the motive nor the means nor the opportunity, and constructed the facts in a fashion so that it seemed he did. This does not mean that the members of the Warren Commission were less than honorable men, or that they were accomplices in the conspiracy, or even that they actively sought to cover up the crime. They were none of these. The explanation is much simpler. They were just wrong.

Critics, Edward J. Epstein in particular, have detailed the basis for the Warren Commission's errors: its reliance on junior staff, the pressures to produce an explanation for the assassination in a hurry, the natural inefficiencies of all bureaucracies. The crucial error, though, was the unconscious substitution of "the national interest," that great catchall in whose name the worst crimes are committed, for the single-minded pursuit of truth, wherever the truth lay. Given the temper of the times in 1963—a period which seems so close, and yet, as we too often forget, was very different from the world in which we live today—the Warren Commission may very well have made the right choice. For the uncovering of the truth of John Kennedy's murder would have shaken an already weakened American government to its very core. The even larger danger would have been for the Commission to perceive the conspiracy, but, as would have been all too easy to do, misperceive the direction from which it had come. If Oswald had been found to be part of a Cuban or Soviet conspiracy, the country might very well have been plunged into World War III. It was that fear that led Lyndon Johnson to appoint the Warren Commission. In that sense, we ought to be thankful that he did.

There is no need to be afraid any longer. The danger now comes not from Cuba or from the Soviet Union, but from the cancer that is eating away at us from within, the malignancy of a decade of deceit.

If the truth of John Kennedy's death is to be known, the event must first be regarded for what it is: not an irrational tragedy, but a political event, a murder used as a means of policy, but a murder nonetheless. Then the questions can be asked: Who had the motive? Who had the means? Who had the opportunity? John Kennedy had many enemies. If we examine the past, however, we can see who among them had the most to gain from his death, the most to fear from his continued life. We can see who had the means to kill him: the murderous expertise at their disposal, the experience and disposition to use it. We can see, finally, who had the opportunity, not only to commit the crime, but to get away with it. The answers to these questions narrow the range of possible suspects dramatically. Indeed, they come down to one. To quote Sherlock Holmes: "When you have eliminated the impossible, whatever remains, *however improbable,* must be the truth." As it happens, the prime suspects in the murder of John Kennedy are not so improbable at all.

The correct perception of history is crucial. A barrier to understanding the Kennedy case is the commonly held assumption that although the President was murdered, his policies continued. If there was continuance, the argument goes, the motive for anyone but a lone, deranged assassin, with nothing to gain but a place in history, disappears. And, true enough, Lyndon Johnson did pledge: "Let us continue." Many of the members of the Kennedy administration did carry on, including for a time, the attorney general, Robert Kennedy. Some policies, notably in the field of civil rights and the elimination of poverty, were extended and enlarged under Johnson's leadership. Many others were not. In the midst of the relief that the system survived the assassin's bullet, there has been some notable forgetfulness. Events did turn in Dallas. The promising rapprochement of Castro, which was beginning to take on substance the last months of Kennedy's life, was terminated by his death. Ironically, Castro's acceptance of Kennedy's offer to begin informal discussions toward normalization of relations arrived at the White House one day after the President's murder.[23] By then it was too late. The project, McGeorge Bundy informed William Attwood, a friend of Kennedy's who had been handling the negotiations, would have to be put "on ice," where, as Attwood later noted, it has remained ever since.[24] The same was also true of Vietnam. In an insightful essay that was included in the Pentagon Papers, University of California professor Peter Dale Scott points to the fact that at the time of his death Kennedy had already begun the process of withdrawing American combat advisers, who then numbered 16,000.[25] One thousand were to be taken out of Vietnam by the end of the year. All would be gone by the end of 1965. The President was to have met with U.S. Ambassador to Saigon Henry Cabot Lodge on November 24, 1963, to nail down some of the final details.[26] The meeting, of course, never took place. Instead, a meeting of quite another kind took place on the Sunday following the President's death, where Lyndon Johnson was told that "if Vietnam was to be saved, hard decisions would have to be made." [27] Johnson made the decisions. The withdrawal of combat advisers was canceled. Instead, the new president took the first steps toward what would be an eventual commitment of half a million men in the most bitter and divisive war in the nation's history. There were other changes. Before going to Dallas the President told his aides that "the CIA will have to be dealt with."[28] A full-scale review of the Agency's covert operations would shortly be in the works.[29] It died in Dallas. Finally, there was the problem of crime. In the course of a thousand days the brothers Kennedy had done more to damage the structure of the organized crime conspiracy than any administration before or since. After disposing of James R. Hoffa, Robert Kennedy intended to go after crime in its own backyard, Las Vegas.[30] He would make the state of Nevada, he told his aides, a test case, a demonstration that, given the determination and the resources, organized crime could be rooted out. "If we do not . . . attack organized criminals with weapons and techniques as effective as their own," he wrote, "they will destroy us." [31] In that assessment he was all too prophetic.

Cui bono? asks the Latin phrase: Who benefits? A number of people profited by John Kennedy's murder, and the key beneficiaries were linked in a common cause. That cause was Cuba. The beneficiaries were organized crime and the Central Intelligence Agency. The plot did not succeed entirely. Oswald was, as the conspirators intended, arrested, and his background pointed straight to Castro. The key, however, was the discovery of a pro-Castro conspiracy. What the conspirators had not counted on was a Presidential Commission that would deny the obvious. In finding Oswald alone guilty, in deciding he had no rational motive, the Warren Commission not only butchered the truth, it snatched away the final reward of the conspiracy: the invasion of Cuba.

Such is the theory of the following pages. It is not a new one. Recently declassified documents reveal that the Warren Commission considered important parts of it, especially the possibility that Oswald was the witting or unwitting tool of anti-Castro exiles, and ultimately rejected all of it. To have admitted any of it would have been to accept the existence of a conspiracy, with the persons who planned and executed it unknown and still at large. It does not require a vivid imagination to guess the consequences of such a finding, in an America only a year after a brush with nuclear disaster over Cuba. Add to the death of Oswald the suspicions voiced even by the Commission that he had been an agent of a foreign power, or even worse, of American intelligence, and it is not surprising that, as the secret transcripts quoted in these pages will show, the Commission was determined from the very start not to uncover any evidence which would disturb the single-assassin theory. The problem the Commission faced was that the evidence of conspiracy was considerable. There were eyewitnesses to the other shots, not little old ladies in tennis shoes, but dozens of upright Dallasites. There were autopsy results which would not square with any thesis except conspiracy. There was physical evidence. There were government officials who swore that they saw what the Commission did not want them to have seen. There were even photographs and movies of the actual event. Seldom, in fact, has a crime been so publicly committed in the full view of so many eyewitnesses.

The Commission did, then, what it had to do: it ignored the witnesses, the testimony, the physical evidence, and instead concocted an explanation for the events in Dealey Plaza beside which the weirder theories for the assassination seem tame by comparison. To believe the Warren Commission you must believe that bullets pause in midair and make ninety-degree right-hand turns; that a poor marksman can do what experts cannot; that Newtonian laws of motion were not operating on November 22; that a man can be in two places at once; that atoms are able to change their structure; that everything in life is mere coincidence. The commissioners and their lawyers put on an extraordinary performance. Men of the highest probity were branded as liars. Known liars were taken at their word. The Report of the President's Commission on the Assassination of President Kennedy is a pathetic, sloppy, self-contradictory document, a repository of the most improbable fantasy. The real wonder is that anyone believed it.

There were those who never did. The critics like Mark Lane who came forward to challenge it. For their troubles, they were, as the records now show, subjected to surveillance, intimidation, and harassment ordered, as the records of the Warren Commission show, in the name of the chief justice of the United States.[32] At that, they were lucky. Many of the witnesses who kept insisting that they had seen something else that day in Dallas met a different fate. Within three years of the assassination, more than a dozen had died under violent or mysterious circumstances. In this case, as in others that would follow, the interests of crime and national security were identical.

It is not a pretty story. Decent, honorable men doing a dirty, dishonorable job never is. There are few heroes to be found—especially few among the press, the very people who should have been most suspicious, and instead were, for reasons which will be explained, most eager to accept the Warren Commission's conclusions. As it happens this writer is a reporter, with all a reporter's instincts and prejudices, someone who came to this story not only disbelieving, but not wanting to believe. A reporter who, after sifting through the facts, asking the questions, resolving the doubts, was finally forced to believe.

I, too, remember where I was on November 22, 1963, when the news came. I was getting books together for the next class at the University of Notre Dame. The radio was on and when the bulletin was read I caught only part of it, enough to hear that a "president" had been shot. I remember assuming that it must be somewhere in South America. Those kinds of things didn't happen in the United States. They were foreign. Two days later, a group of us were watching television as they brought Lee Harvey Oswald into the police basement. There was a shot, a scuffle and mass confusion, and the announcer was yelling, "Oswald has been shot! Oswald has been shot!" I remember that we all cheered. Perhaps that is what John Kennedy's killers were counting on.

Everything is so much changed today. To many Oswald has become the martyr, an innocent victim shot down in cold blood. It is Kennedy who is called upon to justify himself. For the extreme left, Dallas does not matter. Kennedy, they say, was no different from his successors. Only we know that he was, and that, because of him, we were as well. In that sense, his assassins killed a bit of all of us.

And so we look, searching for the part of us that is missing. The assassination of John Kennedy is no longer an intellectual parlor game to be played by esoteric buffs. Late, but hopefully not too late, the assassination has been recognized for what it is: a crime against the American people. A crime which demands solution.

1

One Sunny Day

I am sure that all but a handful of our citizens will cordially welcome the President of the United States to Dallas.

—Jesse Curry, chief of police
November 1963[1]

IT RAINED Friday morning in Dallas, the kind of sudden storm that sweeps over the Texas plains, and just as quickly disappears. That is how it was with this rain: quick, violent, gone. By 9:30 the clouds had disappeared, and a bright November sun was climbing in the sky.[2] It was a perfect day for a parade.

The city prepared. In slightly more than two hours, the President of the United States would arrive.

There had been no choice for John Kennedy. He had to make this trip. One reason had brought him to Texas: politics. There was none more compelling. In less than a year he would, by his calculation, as well as that of the political experts—and of his enemies—be elected to a second term with a handy majority. Only disaster could prevent it. But Kennedy was taking no chances. He wanted to run his vote total as high as he could. The paper-thin margin of his first victory had cramped his style, made him unaccustomedly cautious, had helped him blunder into mistakes. Now the worst errors were behind him. He was gaining confidence. There was much, however, that was left to do, and many who would seek, who had already sought to block him. Kennedy would need all the strength he could muster. Which is why he had come to Texas. Because Texas was important. And Texas was a problem.

The state's Democratic party was, as usual, badly split, between the dominant conservatives of the Connally-Johnson wing of the party, and the small but noisy group of liberals led by Senator Ralph Yarborough. Yarborough and Connally were not even on speaking terms. There were other problems. Kennedy's brand of liberalism did not go down well in conservative Texas. Cuba, the test-ban treaty, the administration's initiatives in civil rights, and now the move to repeal the sacrosanct 27½ percent oil depletion allowance were, to say the least, not popular in this, the largest oil-producing state in the nation, which had one of the most massive defense establishments.[3] If the election were held this November, Kennedy would probably lose Texas. And he knew it.

There had been talk of coming to Texas for more than a year, but the decision was finally pinned down in early June, at a meeting between Kennedy, Connally, and Johnson in El Paso. It was agreed: the President would come to Texas in late November.[4] One of his stops would be Dallas. By mid-September the President's upcoming trip was already well known in the city.[5] In October a motorcade was added to the schedule.[6] In early November the planning of the exact motorcade route, and the selection of the site where the President would speak, began.[7] By and large, it was an exercise in irrelevance. Once it became known that the President would come to Dallas and speak to a large luncheon crowd there was, for all practical purposes, only one site that made sense. That was the spanking new Trade Mart, west of downtown, out on the Stemmons Freeway. And since the President would be driving downtown so that a maximum number of people could see him, there was only one route the motorcade could travel: through the suburbs, then downtown on Main Street, right onto Houston, then left onto Elm and through the Triple Underpass that led to Stemmons Freeway and the Trade Mart beyond.[8]

Everything had been set, and so far all had gone well. On Thursday the President had arrived in San Antonio, then gone on to Houston, and finally to Fort Worth to spend the night. The crowds had been large and friendly, the reception uniformly warm. The Kennedy magic was working. Even Connally and Yarborough had begun talking to each other. Friday morning the President spoke to a prayer breakfast of the Fort Worth Chamber of Commerce. Now, there was only one stop left before heading home. Dallas.

The city was a worry. A week before Kennedy's visit, Ambassador Adlai Stevenson had come to Dallas to speak to a local UN Association luncheon. When Stevenson emerged from the Adolphus Hotel, where the luncheon had been held, a group of noisy right-wing protesters were waiting for him. At the sight of Stevenson there was a small riot. The demonstrators shoved and spat on and cursed Stevenson.[9] At least one picket hit him on the head with a sign. Stevenson was left shaken by the incident. He called Arthur Schlesinger and asked him to warn Kennedy not to go to Dallas.[10] The city seemed to foster extremists. But Adlai Stevenson was not taken seriously by John Kennedy, or his aides. He had a record, after all, of shrinking from confrontation. During the missile crisis, it had been he who had urged accommodation with the Russians most forcefully. Besides, not visiting Dallas, the most important city in the state, was unthinkable.

When Kennedy picked up the *Dallas Morning News* in his hotel room Friday morning he saw that Stevenson was not kidding. There, emblazoned in bold black type, was a full-page advertisement suggesting in so many words that the President was a Communist and a traitor. The ad was signed: "American Fact–Finding Committee"[11] Kennedy was appalled, and angry. "How can people write such things?"[12] he demanded. Then he began to reflect on the ultimate extremism. If people wanted to badly enough, if they hated him sufficiently, they could kill him. He mused on how it could be done. Put a man in a high building; give him a high-powered rifle with a telescopic sight; ensure that he was willing to trade his life for the President's, and then—well, all the security in the world couldn't save the President. Kennedy was not worried.[13] He had an Irish sense of fatalism. Danger was one of the things that went with the job.

Lee Harvey Oswald was up and dressed while his wife, Marina, still lay in bed.[14] Their marriage had not been going well. They had been quarreling for more than a year, almost from the moment Lee brought her to the United States from her home in Russia.[15] The couple had separated for long periods at a time, but always Lee came drifting back. This time, though, they seemed to be heading for divorce. Lee was talking of going back to Russia, where he had lived for two years after getting out of the Marine Corps.[16] Marina would hear none of it.[17] The rowing had gotten fiercer, and five weeks before, Lee had moved out again, this time into a rooming house in the Oak Cliff section of Dallas. Marina and the children had stayed in nearby Irving, Texas, living at the home of her friend Ruth Paine.[18] Lee continued to visit her on weekends. This week, though, he had broken his routine. He came to the Paine home Thursday night to pick up a package [19] to take to work the next day at the School Book Depository in downtown Dallas, where to his embarrassment, he labored as a stock boy for $1.25 per hour. The clock read 7:15 when Lee walked through the kitchen toward the back door.[20] In his right hand he carried the package that had brought him home to Irving, a long, bulky brown bag tapered at one end. Buell Frazier, a friend and coworker from the Book Depository, met him at the back door. They walked across the street and got into Frazier's car. Lee put the bag on the back seat. "What's the package, Lee?" Frazier asked. "Curtain rods," Oswald answered.* [21]

---

* This reconstruction of the events of November 22 is based on the testimony and public recollections of *credible* eyewitnesses. From this category the accounts of a number of witnesses, including some who support the single-assassin thesis as well as some who contradict it, are purposely excluded. Thus, for example, the testimony of Mrs. Helen Markham, who told the Commission she spoke to Officer Tippit *after* he had been instantly killed,[22] is omitted, as is that of nearsighted Howard Brennan, who claimed to have seen Oswald firing the rifle from the sixth-floor window, yet was unable to pick him out of a police lineup.[23] By the same token Julia Ann Mercer's account of a man carrying what appeared to be a gun case up the grassy knoll several hours before the assassination [24] is also passed over, since investigations by the Dallas police and the FBI found that no such man ever existed. Moreover, Mrs. Mercer raised serious doubts about her credibility when, during the Garrison trial, she put Jack Ruby near the grassy knoll as well.[25] The accounts which are included stand on their own even though some witnesses contradict each other. It is clear, for instance, that Oswald carried a package with him to work on November 22. It is not at all

The morning passed uneventfully at the Book Depository. As he did every day, Oswald worked filling orders, moving boxes and cartons back and forth to the shipping room. On the sixth floor a work crew labored to install a new flooring. They broke for lunch about 11:45 and, in a playful mood, ran to the building's two elevators. The game was to see which elevator could race the fastest to the ground floor. The workers climbed aboard the cars, slammed the gates, and started down.[26] As one of the elevators passed the fifth floor, some of the workers saw Oswald standing in the doorway, evidently getting ready to break for lunch. "Hey guys," he yelled as they passed by, "how about an elevator for me?" [27] As the car disappeared down the shaft, Oswald shouted after them: "When you get downstairs, close the gate!" [28] Lee Oswald didn't want to be kept waiting. If the gate wasn't closed, he couldn't call the car back up. It was a long walk down to the first-floor lunchroom.

At first it was just a dark speck in the brilliant blue Texas sky. The speck got larger and larger, the roar louder and louder, and at last the silver, red, white, and blue Boeing swooped down on the runway at Love Field. As the big plane emblazoned with the seal of the President of the United States rolled up to Gate 28I, a cheer went up from the waiting crowd. Excited schoolgirls waved tiny American flags.[29] Home-made signs bobbed above the welcomers. "We Love You Jack!" "Welcome to Texas, Mr. President!" "We Love *You,* Jackie!" The President and first lady were obviously pleased. Mrs. Kennedy, resplendent in a pink suit and pillbox hat, smiled widely when she was presented with a large bouquet of long-stemmed red roses. The President grinned and plunged into the crowd, shaking hands, touching, reaching out to the hands that reached after him.

---

certain that this package, despite the Commission's claims, contained the Mannlicher-Carcano. In the same vein, the cars which Lee Bowers saw cruising the area near the Book Depository before the assassination could have been doing so innocently. They may just as well have contained assassins. The conclusions are left for you to draw.

The plane had touched down at 11:37. Minutes slipped by and the President was still working the crowd. This, after all, is why he had come. But the Secret Service were getting anxious. The agents were worried by the chief executive's prolonged exposure in the open. Already they were late. By the time the motorcade wound through Dallas, they would be later still. Finally the President broke away from the crowd and waved one last time. The motorcycles roared to life. Red lights blinking and sirens screaming, the motorcade slowly rolled away, pilot car in the lead, then the motorcade lead car, then the presidential limousine, the Secret Service follow-up car immediately behind it, then cars containing the vice-president, local dignitaries, and the press.[30]

The crowds had long since been forming in downtown Dallas. By the time *Air Force One* touched down at Love Field they were stacked up on Main Street seven and eight deep. They were in a festive, buoyant mood. Earlier, some men had moved among the crowds passing out handbills with the President's picture on them. "Wanted for Treason," the headline read. The leaflet ticked off seven particulars, among them a charge that the President was appointing "anti-Christians to Federal office," that he had given "support and encouragement to Communist inspired racial riots," that he had been soft on Communists—"betraying our friends (Cuba, Katanga, Portugal) and befriending our enemies (Russia, Yugoslavia via Poland)."[31] Most people threw the leaflets in the street, with the other trash. Today, Dallas was friendly.

Toward 12:30 Mrs. R. E. Arnold, one of the secretaries in the Book Depository, got up from her desk to join the crowd outside waiting for the President. She went outside and stood in front of the doorway. She turned around for a moment and glimpsed one of the employees standing in the hallway between the front door and the double doors that led to the warehouse. She caught only a fleeting look at the man, and she could not be sure, but she thought it was one of the new boys. Lee was his name. Lee Harvey Oswald.[32]

The crowd in Dealey Plaza numbered several hundred, and more were coming by the minute. Dealey Plaza was a good place to catch a look. Unlike the downtown streets, now packed with people, the plaza was wide open. The several-acre-sized plaza, which had been named after the founder of the *Dallas Morning News,* was a gently sloping V-shaped bowl dissected by several main business arteries. The streets formed a pitchfork. On one side, curving away to the east, was Commerce Street. On the other, curving down toward the west, was Elm Street. Running down the middle was Main Street. All the streets came together at the base of the plaza beneath a railroad overpass. At the top of the plaza, two hundred yards away, ran Houston Street. On the right side of Houston, away from the plaza, were several tall buildings, the last of them, at the corner of Houston and Elm, the School Book Depository. Once the President's motorcade passed through Dealey Plaza, it would be out on the freeway. The plaza was the last chance to see the President up close.

Atop his tower in the Union Terminal railroad yards, Lee Bowers looked out to watch the motorcade. The time was nearly 12:30. The President would be passing at any moment. From his tower Bowers could see virtually everything that moved into, out of, or around the parking lot behind the grassy knoll atop Elm Street. Two and a half hours before, around 10:00, Bowers had spotted two cars moving into the area. The first had been a mud-smeared 1959 blue and white Oldsmobile station wagon. All that distinguished it was out-of-state plates and a Goldwater for President sticker on its bumper. The car drove in front of the School Book Depository, down across two or three sets of tracks, and then circled the area in front of his tower, as if searching for a way out.[33] A few moments later another car appeared, this one a 1957 black Ford. The driver, Bowers noticed, appeared to be holding a microphone to his mouth. After three or four minutes of cruising the area, the black car departed the same way the Olds had.[34] Now Bowers saw a third car. This one was a Chevrolet. But in many ways it was identical to the Oldsmobile Bowers had seen earlier. The Chevy had the same out-of-state plates, the same Goldwater bumper sticker; even the red mud that covered the car's sides was the same as that which had smeared the Olds. The car circled in front of Bowers and slowly cruised back toward the School Book Depository.[35]

Abraham Zapruder was nervous. He had bought his Bell and Howell 8-mm movie camera only the day before, for the express purpose of filming the motorcade, and Zapruder was worried that, what with the newness of it, something would go wrong. Zapruder, who ran a dressmaking company in the nearby Dal-Tex Building, was an unabashed admirer of John Kennedy's, which made him a distinct rarity among Dallasites. When Zapruder drove to work Friday morning the skies were dark and threatening. Figuring that the day would be poor for picture taking, he had left his camera at home. But as the sun broke through the clouds, Zapruder changed his mind. He hurried back home and grabbed his camera.[36] When he returned to Dealey Plaza the crowds had already lined Houston Street. With that vantage point gone, Zapruder next tried the window of his office, across the street from the Book Depository. But the camera angle there was too narrow. Finally, with Marilyn Sitzman, his receptionist, tagging along behind him, he walked outside and spotted the perfect position: a four-foot-high concrete pedestal on the pergola overlooking Elm Street. Shortly before 12:30, the motorcade pilot car hove into view. Zapruder could hear the cheering coming from Main Street. He set the lens selector on telephoto, brought the camera up to his eye, focused on the lead motorcycle, and pressed the shutter release.[37]

Carolyn Walther, too, had been waiting for the parade to come by. Standing across the street from the Book Depository, she cocked her head at the sound of the approaching motorcycles, and then absently gazed up at the building in front of her. To her surprise she saw two men standing in the corner window of one of the upper stories. Both were looking south up Houston Street, as if they were waiting too. The dirt on the windowpanes obscured her view of one man, but Mrs. Walther could see the other clearly. He was wearing a white shirt, and his hair was light or blond. And he was holding something. It was a rifle, that much Mrs. Walther could be sure of, but one like she had never seen before: a weapon with a short barrel and something that seemed large around the stock—just what she couldn't tell. She guessed that it was a machine gun, and that the men were in the window to protect the President. Before she could think more of it, someone in the crowd shouted, "Here they come." [38]

Moments before, Bob Edwards had seen a man in the Book Depository too, standing in the sixth-floor corner window, a low wall of cartons behind him. Edwards and a friend, Ronald Fischer, were standing near a reflecting pool on the southwest corner of Houston and Elm. Edwards had spotted the man in the window by chance, but there was something about him that captured his attention. The man, who wore a light-colored sport shirt, seemed uncomfortable.[39] Edwards poked Fischer and told him to look up at the window. Fischer saw the man, too. Oddly, the man in the window wasn't watching the parade. Instead, he was looking away toward the Triple Underpass. The man stared at it, seemingly transfixed.[40]

Arnold Rowland saw the man too, the same figure in a light-colored sport shirt open at the collar. From where he stood on Houston Street, midway between Main and Elm, Rowland could see something else as well: a rifle, mounted with a telescopic sight, cradled in the man's arms.[41]

The turn from Houston onto Elm was sharp and oblique. To negotiate it the long presidential limousine had to come almost to a dead halt directly beneath the sixth-floor window on the southeast corner of the School Book Depository. The car paused and began its turn. The Secret Service agents, some of them weary from a long night before, looked ahead, to the rear, and to both sides. Everywhere but up.[42]

As the presidential limousine rounded the sharp corner, a gust of wind caught the President's hair and he reached up with his right hand to pat it back into place. Nellie Connally, the governor's wife, turned to Mrs. Kennedy, pointed to the underpass and said, "We're almost through; it's just beyond that." [43] Jacqueline

Kennedy looked at the tunnel and smiled, thinking it would be cool inside, away from the Texas sun.[44] No one had guessed it would go so well. The crowds had been big, enthusiastic. Nellie was proud of the city. She smiled at Kennedy. "Well, Mr. President, you can't say Dallas doesn't love you."[45] There was no answer, only a sharp, popping noise, a sound, someone thought, like exploding firecrackers.

In the jump seat in front of Kennedy, John Connally sensed immediately what the sound meant. He turned to his right to look over his shoulder, and seeing nothing, faced around and was beginning to turn to his left when, all at once, what felt like a tremendous punch slammed into the right side of his back.[46] Connally's handsome tanned face contorted in pain, his cheeks puffed, and his hair flew askew. As he slumped into Nellie's arms, he yelled in pain, "Oh, my God, they are going to kill us all."[47]

Nellie Connally did not recognize the crack of a gunshot, only that the noise she heard was loud and frightening. She turned around and saw the President contort in pain. The expression on his face revealed nothing, only a trace of puzzlement. An instant later, her husband crumpled into her arms like a wounded animal. As she nestled him close to her chest, she heard a third and final shot, and felt a fine mist fall over her. For a moment, she thought it might be chaff from buckshot. Then she realized that the mist came from what had been John Kennedy's brains.[48]

Glen Bennett, one of the Secret Service men riding in the follow-up car behind the presidential limousine, had seen it all. They had just rounded the oblique corner at Houston and Elm when he heard the crack of rifle fire and saw the bullet go into the President's back, four inches beneath the right shoulder.[49] Then Connally had been hit.[50] Twenty yards ahead of him, much farther than it should have been, the limousine slowly coasted downhill. Bennett and the other agents watched, stunned, immobile.

In the car with them, Dave Powers watched too. Powers was the President's professional funny man, the Boston Irishman whose duty was making his chief relax. Powers always had a story or a quip. Even in the worst moments he could bring John Kennedy back to the easier days when John was a skinny U.S. representative from Brookline. What Dave Powers heard and saw now filled him with horror. As the motorcade swung down Elm, Powers heard what he thought was an exploding firecracker. He looked ahead and saw the President going down. There was a second pop, and Connally disappeared from view. Then the third shot. From the sound Powers thought the shots had come from overhead, and perhaps one from the front. The impact of the final round could be heard distinctly. To Powers it sounded like a grapefruit being splattered against a wall.[51]

On the fifth floor of the Depository three workers were spending their lunch hour watching the motorcade from the windows. As the presidential limousine cruised by beneath them, Harold Norman, one of the workers, thought he saw Kennedy bring up his right arm in a salute to the crowd.[52] Then he heard something that convinced him Kennedy wasn't waving. He turned to Jim Jarman and Bonnie Ray Williams, who were watching the parade with him, and exclaimed, "I believe someone is shooting at the President." [53] Then Norman heard another sound, the noise of shell casings dropping on the floor above him. There was another shot, and the whole building seemed to shake.[54] Jarman noticed that Williams had some kind of fine, white dust on his head. And then it dawned on him. It was plaster, shaken loose from the ceiling above.[55] He stuck his head out the window and looked up.

Bob Jackson, a photographer for the *Dallas Times Herald,* looked up from the motorcade and saw Norman and Williams standing in the window, craning to see something above them. Jackson's eyes panned up and he saw what they were looking for. "Look up in the window," he yelled to the reporters in the car with him. "There's the rifle." [56]

Zapruder had not seen the President being hit. The Stemmons Freeway sign to his left had blocked his view. But when the limousine emerged from behind the sign it was obvious that something was terribly wrong.

Kennedy was slumping forward, his face a mask of pain, his arms coming up to his throat. Connally had looked back, and then he too had gone down. Instinctively Zapruder followed the scene through the viewfinder. Only yards in front of him, the limousine glided down the hill. In the front seat the Secret Service agent driver turned and looked back at the President, turned forward, and then turned back again. Still the car coasted, as if frozen in time. The seconds slipped by . . . one one thousand . . . two one thousand . . . three one thousand . . . four one thousand . . . five one thousand. Then, behind him and to his right, Zapruder heard an awful roar and felt a bullet whistle past his right ear. What he saw through the viewfinder sickened him: an explosion of blood and brains completely obscuring the President's head. For an instant it jerked him forward, and then, like a blow from a giant sledgehammer, drove Kennedy's body backward into his wife's arms, only now the entire left portion of his skull was missing. "They killed him," Zapruder cried. "They've killed the President!" [57]

Riding in the lead car of the motorcade, Jesse Curry, the Dallas police chief, could hear but not see the shots. He grabbed at the microphone of his radio transmitter and barked an order: "Get a man on top of that triple underpass and see what happened up there." [58] In the Secret Service follow-up car, chief Dallas agent Forrest Sorrels had heard the shots as well, and turned to look to where he thought they had come—above and to the right, toward the knoll.[59] Several of the agents riding with Sorrels were sure that the final explosion had been a double impact, one shot followed instantly by another.[60] But only one agent moved.

Clint Hill was off the follow-up car and running at the sound of the final shots. A favorite of Mrs. Kennedy, Hill had not been scheduled to make the Dallas trip until, at the last moment, she had personally requested he come along. Now Hill could see Mrs. Kennedy's arm reach back, trying to grasp something that flew off the top of her husband's head. In a moment she was on the back of the car, crawling after it. Just then Hill reached the limousine. It lurched forward and he lunged after it, grabbing one of the handrails and vaulting in, pushing Mrs. Kennedy backward into the car. In the front seat, Secret Service Agent Roy Kellerman was yelling into the microphone to the lead car: "We are hit. Get us out of here." [61] Hill had only to glance at the form that lay on the seat before him, amid the blood and scattered roses, to know that now escape was too late. As the accelerating Lincoln emerged from beneath the underpass, agents in the car behind could see Hill beating his fists on the trunk, in anger and frustration.[62]

The impact of the final bullet spattered motorcycle officer Bobby Hargis with blood and sticky gray tissue, nearly knocking him off his bike. The force was so violent that for a moment Hargis thought he had been hit.[63] As it was, the windshield of the motorcycle he had been riding to the left and rear of the presidential limousine was covered with blood. He had no doubt where the shots had come from. Hargis jumped off his bike and, gun drawn, joined the crowd that was racing up the grassy knoll.

Bill and Gayle Newman were lying flat on the ground as Hargis charged by them. Newman, a decorated infantry officer in World War II, knew when he heard the shots ring out that somebody was firing from behind him, from behind and atop the knoll. He saw a bullet rip into Kennedy's right temple and blow out the back of his head. He yelled to his wife to get down and threw himself face forward so he would not be hit.[64]

James Tague was not as lucky. He had been standing nearly a hundred yards away from the presidential limousine, watching the motorcade from the right side of Commerce Street, at the mouth of the Triple Underpass, when the shots struck the President. Somehow Tague was struck too. A bullet had gone wild and hit the curb in front of him, chipping the concrete and sending a shard of stone into his face. The stone nicked him in the cheek and Tague was bleeding.[65] It had been a near thing. Tague was glad to be alive.

Atop the Triple Underpass, S. M. Holland and half a dozen workers from the railroad had been watching the motorcade pass. Holland heard four shots,[66] and after the report of the final round looked down and to his left, past the trees, to a stockade fence atop the knoll. The last shot had been as loud as the first three, and as Holland looked to the point from which he thought it had come he saw a puff of smoke wafting out from beneath the trees.[67] Some of the other workers saw the smoke too. Now, together, they ran into the parking lot behind the knoll. The lot was jammed with cars, and after a few moments of clambering over bumpers and hoods Holland and the other workers, joined by a deputy sheriff, finally reached the fence. Whoever had been there was gone. They saw only the traces: some footprints, a few crushed cigarette butts, a dirty car bumper smeared by someone cleaning mud off his shoes. The footprints seemed to belong to more than one man. They were in a tight grouping, as if people had been walking back and forth, pacing like tigers in a cage.[68]

As Holland and the other workers scrambled toward the fence, J. C. Price had seen someone running from it. Price had been watching the motorcade from the roof of the Terminal Annex Building, across Dealey Plaza from the knoll. After the shots he saw a young man in a dress white shirt and khaki trousers running toward the cars parked along the railroad siding. Price finally lost sight of him, but before he did he saw the running man was carrying something in his hand.[69]

Within moments the parking lot and the area behind the knoll were swarming with people. On Police Chief Curry's order, lawmen were checking cars, looking for a trace of the assassin. One of the police officers doing the searching was Joe Marshall Smith. Smith had been directing traffic at Houston and Elm when a woman ran to him, yelling, "They're shooting the President from the bushes." [70] When Smith got to the parking lot he could still smell spent gunpowder hanging in the air.[71] As he moved from car to car he encountered a stranger in a business suit. Smith leveled his gun and demanded identification. The stranger obligingly reached into his jacket and pulled out his credentials. They read: "United States Secret Service." [72] Feeling foolish, Smith lowered his weapon and moved on. Though he could not know it then, all the Secret Service men had gone on with the motorcade.[73]

Moments before, Lee Bowers had seen two men standing behind the fence atop the grassy knoll. His attention had been drawn to them because of all the people he could see from the railroad tower these were the only strangers. One was middle-aged and heavyset.[74] The other, who Bowers judged was in his mid-twenties, was wearing a plaid jacket.[75] Bowers's attention was then distracted by the approach of the motorcade. When the shots rang out Bowers looked and saw that the two men were still there. Something else caught his eye, something he could not identify, perhaps a flash of light.[76]

Orville Nix had seen something too, but at that moment he didn't know it. He had been standing on the greensward that divides Elm from Main, across the street from Zapruder. Like Zapruder, Nix had brought along a movie camera to record the motorcade. Later, when Nix's film was developed, a tiny white hump would appear behind a light-colored station wagon parked atop the grassy knoll. The FBI would decide that the hump was nothing more than shadows and light.[77] But careful blowups of the frame in Orville Nix's film would, to some, reveal something very different. Though the lines were grainy the outline was plain. It was the figure of a man, carefully sighting something in his hand.

Dealey Plaza was a scene of panic and confusion. Sirens were wailing. People were racing everywhere, or cowering on the ground, afraid that they too would be shot. In the midst of the chaos one man remained icily calm. He was dressed in a dark business suit and he seemed to be middle-aged. There was one other thing about him. On this sunny, windy day he was carrying a large black umbrella. The man had found the ideal vantage point from which to observe the President: on the curb along Elm Street, immediately behind the Stemmons Freeway sign. When the motorcade turned onto Houston, his umbrella stayed furled. But when it came down Elm, beneath the Depository and toward the grassy knoll, the man suddenly raised it up.[78] As the President emerged from behind the freeway sign, hit but not fatally wounded, the umbrella was clearly visible to anyone on the grassy knoll. It stayed there, almost like a marker, until the final, fatal shots. Then the man furled it again, paused for a moment, looked after the departing limousine, and unhurriedly began to walk up Elm toward the Depository.[79]

By now almost everyone else was running—policemen, guns at the ready, toward the knoll, others to the Triple Underpass, and still others to the Book Depository, where the Hertz time sign blinked 12:32. Marrion Baker was the first police officer to reach the building. Baker had been riding a motorcycle in the middle of the motorcade. At the sound of the shots he looked up and saw pigeons scattering from their roosts in the Book Depository. He wheeled his bike around and gunned it toward the building. Arriving, he found Roy Truly, the building manager, and together they raced up the stairs toward the upper floors, where people had already reported shots fired. On the second-floor landing Baker encountered a thin young man wearing a white shirt, leaning against a soft-drink machine, calmly sipping a Coke.[80] Less than two minutes had elapsed since the final shots. Baker poked his gun in the young man's stomach. Baker turned to Truly. "Do you know this man, does he work here?" "Yes," Truly answered.[81] Baker lowered his pistol and rushed by. Lee Harvey Oswald finished drinking his Coke and slowly walked downstairs and outside, looking for a bus.[82]

He found one within moments. But the shooting had tied up traffic. The bus was hopelessly enmeshed in cars. Oswald waited for a few minutes, then got up and left the bus and walked to the nearby Greyhound Bus Terminal.[83] There he hailed a cab. But as the cab pulled up to the curb Oswald saw that an elderly woman was waiting for a ride too, and he graciously offered his cab to her.[84] The lady declined, Oswald got in, and they headed off toward Oak Cliff. The cab drove off. Oswald was gone.[85] Within fifteen minutes, police would issue an alert for a suspect matching his description as the perpetrator of the crime of the century.[86]

As Oswald strolled away, attention was turning to the Dal-Tex Building, behind and across the street from the Book Depository. Here too, police were conducting a floor-by-floor search, looking for anything suspicious, anyone out of place. In the course of their hunt they discovered two people. One was a boy, who had been in the building, as the police report later put it, "without a good excuse."[87] No one would ever know anything more about him. After his arrest and transfer to the sheriff's office, he simply disappeared.[88]

Quite a lot was known about the other suspect. The name he gave the officers who arrested him on the second floor of the Dal-Tex Building was his alias, Jim Braden; he was better known to the police as Eugene Hale Brading.[89] A self-described oilman, Braden told police he had merely happened to be in the area at the time of the assassination, and had gone into the Dal-Tex Building in search of a phone.[90] The cops, not knowing that the files of the Los Angeles police department listed him as a long-time associate of organized crime,* [91] took him at his word. Within hours of his arrest Braden was released.[92]

Across the street in the School Book Depository, the search was beginning to turn up clues. On the sixth floor in the extreme southeast corner, behind a shield of packing cases, the police had found three shell cases scattered around the floor.[93] Not long after the shell cases were found a high-powered rifle, mounted with a telescopic scope, was discovered near an opposite wall, wedged between some packing cases.[94] The Book Depository was quickly sealed, trapping three men who were not employees inside. Two were newsmen.[95] The other was Captain James W. Powell, an army intelligence officer.[96]

There was action outside the Depository as well. Like many witnesses to the assassination, James Worrell was frightened, worried that perhaps the shooting was not over. He ran from Elm, where he had watched

* The information on Brading's criminal background and police record throughout is reported by Peter Noyes, *Legacy of Doubt*.

the motorcade, past the Depository onto Houston. He did not stop until he reached the corner of Pacific Street, a hundred yards from the Depository. As he paused to catch his breath, he saw a man burst from the back door of the Depository. From where Worrell stood the man seemed to be young, dark-haired, medium height and build, wearing light pants and a dark sport jacket. That was all that Worrell could see. The man was running away.[97]

Richard Carr saw someone leaving the Depository too. Carr thought he had seen him before; in fact, only moments before, in one of the upper windows of the Book Depository.[98] From his perch on a metal stairway of the new county courthouse then a-building at the corner of Houston and Commerce, Carr could now see him more clearly. He was heavy-set, wore a hat, horn-rimmed glasses, and a tan coat.[99] As Carr watched, the man walked very fast south along Houston Street. He turned east on Commerce and walked a block to Record Street. There he got into a late model gray Rambler station wagon, parked just north of Commerce on Record. The car bore Texas plates, and a dark young man was at the wheel. The station wagon pulled away, heading north.[100]

Marvin Robinson saw the car again when it stopped on Elm, down from the Depository at the base of the grassy knoll. At the time, Robinson himself had been driving south on Elm. He had just crossed the intersection at Houston, directly in front of the Depository, when he spotted the station wagon. It paused only for a moment, just long enough for a man to come down the grassy knoll and climb inside. The station wagon then drove off, heading in the direction of Oak Cliff.[101]

By now John Kennedy's motorcade had come to its final destination, the emergency entrance of Parkland Memorial Hospital. Inside the building, a frantic call went out for doctors to report to trauma room 1. A foul-up in police communications had sidetracked the message that the gravely wounded President would soon be reaching the hospital.[102] It was too late in any case. In the limousine, Jacqueline Kennedy pulled her husband's shattered body close to her. Clint Hill's suit jacket had been draped over the President's head to keep the curious from viewing the hideous wound.[103] Now Hill told Mrs. Kennedy that the President would have to be brought inside. "You know he's dead, Mr. Hill," [104] she replied, and pulled his body even closer. Gently, other arms pulled him from her grasp and lifted his limp body onto a stretcher. In the jump seat John Connally, still conscious, tried to rise, but collapsed from excruciating pain.[105] There was a large jagged wound in his chest. His lung had collapsed and his right wrist had been smashed.[106] Finally the attendants succeeded in lifting him from the car and placing him on a stretcher.

In trauma room 1, Dr. William Kemp Clark, the young physician on duty, took one look at his patient and knew that the prognosis was terminal. It did not stop him. Quickly but methodically he examined the President's wounds. There were two that he could see: a gaping gash on the right side of the head, from which oozed blood and brain matter,[107] and a small neat hole just over the Adam's apple.[108] The heartbeat and pulse were faint and irregular, but still there was life. The President needed air. The bullet that Clark judged had entered the President's throat had punctured his windpipe. Taking a scalpel, Clark cut into the throat wound and enlarged it, providing an air passage.[109] Other resuscitory measures were taken. A blood transfusion was begun. As Kennedy's heart began to fail, Malcolm Perry, another one of the doctors, desperately began pumping his chest to keep the rhythm going.[110] Other doctors inserted tubes in Kennedy's chest and in his leg. They did everything. Everything was not enough. After twenty minutes one of the doctors turned to Perry and said, "It's too late, Mac."[111] Perry brought up his hands from John Kennedy's chest. A priest was summoned to perform the last rites of the Catholic Church. At 1:00 p.m. (CST) the President of the United States was pronounced dead.[112]

Outside, in the hospital corridors, the Secret Service were struggling to maintain a semblance of security, for the new president had been taken to Parkland as well. With each passing moment the crowds around the hospital grew larger. The White House press corps had also arrived. One of the first reporters on the scene was Seth Kantor, a writer for the *Dallas Times Herald*. At 1:30 Kantor was hurrying to a briefing by Assistant White House Press Secretary Malcolm Kilduff, who would announce that John Kennedy was dead. As Kantor walked through the hospital corridor he felt a tug on the back of his jacket and turned to face an old acquaintance. Kantor was tempted to keep going, but the friend stuck out his hand. "Isn't this a terrible thing?" the friend asked the reporter. Kantor agreed gravely that it was, and anxiously started to pull away. But the friend had another question: "Should I close my place for the next three nights, do you think?" Kantor said he had to go, that he was late for the briefing, leaving his friend, Jack Ruby, to ponder his own question.[113]

As John Kennedy lay dying, Lee Oswald was hurrying home. He walked through the front door, brushed past his housekeeper, Earlene Roberts, and disappeared into his room. In a few moments he emerged, now wearing a dark zippered jacket.[114] Beneath it, tucked in his pants, was a .38 caliber revolver. Without speaking to Mrs. Roberts, he went back through the front door and walked to the street. He lingered there for a few moments, looking down the street as if he were waiting for something.[115] Then he started pacing briskly up the street in the direction of a local movie theater. A few moments later Mrs. Roberts heard a car horn toot outside, looked through the window, and saw a Dallas police cruiser parked at the curb. The car idled a few minutes as if it too were waiting for someone, and then drove off.[116] Later, authorities would be able to find no record of a police cruiser going to the Beckley Avenue address.[117]

There was at least one policeman in the area, however. His name was J. D. Tippit. At the time of the assassination, Tippit, a veteran of eleven undistinguished years on the force, had been on patrol on the outskirts of Dallas. At 12:45 his radio crackled to life. The police dispatcher told him to proceed to central Oak Cliff, miles from his position, and "be at large for any emergency that might arise." [118] At 12:54 Tippit radioed that he was moving into position.[119] At 1:00, as Oswald prepared to leave his rooming house, the dispatcher tried to raise Tippit again.[120] This time there was no answer. Eight minutes later, as Oswald was walking away from his home, Tippit tried twice to signal the dispatcher.[121] Now the dispatcher was silent. Tippit cruised on. He had just begun to head east on East 10th Street when something he saw caused him to pull to the curb.[122]

Acquila Clemmons, who was walking nearby, saw Tippit get out of the cruiser. She also saw two men, one short and somewhat heavy, the other tall and thin. The thin man was wearing light khaki trousers and a white shirt.[123] As Tippit walked to the front of his car the short, heavy-set man pulled out a pistol and fired several times. Four of the bullets struck Tippit in the head, and the officer fell to the pavement, killed instantly. The killer then waved to the other man, and they ran off in different directions.[124]

A few minutes earlier, Domingo Benavides, a mechanic at Dootch Motors, had driven off in the company pickup truck to bring back a part from an auto supply dealer. He was driving west on 10th when he saw Tippit's police cruiser pull to the curb.[125] When the shots rang out, Benavides was only fifteen feet away.[126] He saw the killer standing on the right side of the car. The man was wearing a light-colored zippered jacket and dark slacks.[127] After the shots Tippit's killer walked back to the sidewalk, unloaded his gun, and threw the shells on the ground.[128] He then started off toward Patton Street at a trot, the gun still in his hand.[129]

William Scoggins witnessed the murder, too. A cab-driver, Scoggins had just finished having lunch in a restaurant at the corner of Patton and 10th, and was getting back into his cab, when he saw Tippit's car drive slowly down 10th.[130] Scoggins headed that way as well. He saw Tippit stop his car, get out, and begin to walk to the front of the cruiser when a man in a light jacket fired at the officer several times.[131] Tippit went down, clutching at his stomach. Scoggins pulled his cab over and got out. For an instant the killer glanced over at him, and Scoggins ducked, afraid that he would be seen.[132] The killer then began to run away in the direction from which Scoggins had come. As he rushed by, Scoggins heard him mutter, "Poor dumb cop." [133]

Just then T. F. Bowley turned his car east onto 10th Street. He saw Tippit's body lying in the road and pulled over. Inside the cruiser Benavides was trying to work Tippit's police radio with no success. Bowley grabbed the mike and turned in the alarm.[134] It was 1:16 p.m. Blocks away, Lee Harvey Oswald was heading toward a rendezvous at the Texas Theatre.

Warren Reynolds was in his used-car dealership on Patton Street, just a block from where Tippit had fallen. Reynolds heard the shots and ran outside to see what happened. He saw a man with a pistol in his hand running south on Patton toward Jefferson.[135] Reynolds loped along behind him, but lost him when the man disappeared behind some buildings.[136]

The shots had brought many people into the streets. A number of them had seen a man fleeing the scene. One of the witnesses eventually found another police officer, H. W. Summers, cruising by. At 1:22, Summers relayed the witness's description of the killer to police headquarters. "I got an eyeball witness to the get away man, that suspect in this shooting," Summers reported. "He is a white male, twenty-seven, five feet eleven inches, 165, black wavy hair, fair-complected, wearing light grey Eisenhower-type jacket, dark trousers and a white shirt . . . apparently armed with a .32 calibre dark finish, automatic pistol which he had in his right hand." [137]

Within minutes police cars were converging on the area. There were several reports of suspicious men. First they surrounded the fundamentalist church where Reynolds had seen the man with the gun disappear. But before they could go in they were called off,[138] and sent in pursuit of yet another suspicious man, this one at a local library. This time a man was found, but he explained he had run inside to tell the people in the library that the President had been shot.[139] The police were satisfied. In any case, they had no time to linger. For there was another report. A man had rushed into the nearby Texas Theatre without paying.[140]

Johnny Brewer saw him first. Brewer was the manager of Hardy's Shoestore on West Jefferson, a few doors east of the Texas Theatre, and eight blocks away from the spot where J. D. Tippit had been murdered. On the afternoon of November 22 Brewer was in his shop listening to the radio reports on the assassination of the President when suddenly a bulletin cut in that a police officer had been shot in his neighborhood. Almost at that moment Brewer heard the first wail of police sirens. As he looked out to the street he saw a man duck into his doorway. The man appeared to be about 5′9″. His hair was brown, and he wore a brown sport shirt, partly unbuttoned.[141] For some reason Brewer thought he looked funny.[142] As the police sirens died away, the man walked away from Brewer's store and toward the theater. Brewer followed him and saw him walk inside without paying.[143] By now Brewer was highly suspicious. When he had first seen the man he looked as if he had been running. His shirt was untucked and his hair was disarranged. He had a scared look.[144] Entering the theater without buying a ticket completed the picture. Brewer informed the ticket taker, who called the police.[145] Brewer, meanwhile, walked inside, told his story to an usher, and together they proceeded to check the exits. None appeared to have been used.[146] He asked the operator of the concession stand if he had seen a man in a brown sport shirt enter the theater. He hadn't.[147] The concession stand man and Brewer then searched the balcony. A dozen, perhaps two dozen people were in the theater. In the dark, Brewer could not pick out the man he had seen by his store.[148] By now it didn't matter. The police were arriving.

The call about the theater had drawn everyone's attention. Jerry Hill, the police sergeant who had commanded the search on the sixth floor of the Book Depository, was there. So apparently was Bill Alexander,[148a] the assistant district attorney who would later want to charge Oswald with being part of an "international Communist conspiracy,"[149] and later still would successfully prosecute Jack Ruby. Now Alexander and several other officers, guns drawn, waited outside the building,[150] covering the exits, while still more officers went inside.

The house lights went up. For a few moments the movie, a war picture, played on, dancing across the figures in dark blue who strode across the stage.[151] N. M. McDonald, one of the officers, looked out over the rows of seats. There were twelve or fifteen people sitting on the lower level.[152] McDonald couldn't be sure who he was supposed to be looking for.[153] As McDonald scanned the theater, a man sitting near the front spoke up quietly. The man the police were looking for, he said, was sitting on the ground floor, in the center, about three rows from the back.[154] McDonald unholstered his pistol, climbed down from the stage, and started walking slowly toward the back, his eyes fixed on the suspect. He stopped after about ten rows and told two men who were sitting there to get up.[155] McDonald searched them for weapons and found none. All the while, he never took his eyes off the man in the rear. The man looked back, his face expressionless.[156] McDonald moved toward him in a crouch.[157] As he got to the row, Lee Harvey Oswald, the man he had been staring at, suddenly got up, and said, "It's all over now." [158] McDonald pounced on him. As he did Oswald struck him in the face and reached down for the revolver in his trousers.[159] McDonald grappled for it. The other officers closed in. Both Oswald's and McDonald's hands were on the gun. There was a click as a hammer fell down on a defective round.[160] Now the other officers were swarming over Oswald, punching and grabbing him. "Kill the President, will you," [161] one of them shouted as Oswald went down beneath his seat. When they yanked him up he was twisting and squirming. In a loud voice, so that everyone in the theater heard him, Oswald said: "I am not resisting arrest! I am not resisting arrest!" [162]

The police had their man. As they led him away the man in the front row who had fingered him rose from his seat, walked outside, and quietly disappeared.

2

The Blue-Ribbon Cover-up

> MC CLOY: The Commission is going to be criticized . . . no matter what we do, but I think we would be more criticized if we were simply posed before the world as something that is evaluating government agencies' reports, who themselves may be culpable.
>
> —John J. McCloy
> Transcript, First meeting of the Warren Commission, December 5, 1963

THE IRONY would always be that Earl Warren had not wanted the job.

How could he? The commission that Lyndon Johnson was determined to create to investigate the death of his predecessor would, despite the trimmings, be nothing more than a grand jury, and, like all grand juries, a prosecutor's weapon. Warren worried over the seemliness of the nation's chief justice being cast in such a role. Whatever the commission found, Warren figured, there would always be the doubters, the critics who would charge "cover-up," who would challenge the probity of the men who sat on the commission. Warren's fellow justices were anxious too. They had the same fears for the Court. Already the chief justice's picture was on billboards across the country, accompanied by demands that he be impeached, thinly veiled suggestions that somehow Warren and the men who worked with him were part of an insidious Communist conspiracy. At such a moment the Court needed every scintilla of credibility. For Warren to chair a commission on the assassination of President Kennedy, they firmly if politely told the chief justice, would not help the Court or the country.[1] Warren heeded their advice. He declined.

Then a call came from the White House. The President wondered if the chief justice could take time out of his busy schedule to see him on a matter of the gravest urgency. When Warren emerged from the meeting, some reports later had it, there were tears in his eyes. He had just accepted the chairmanship of the President's Commission on the Assassination of President Kennedy.[2]

On January 20, 1964, in his first meeting with the staff of the Commission, Warren explained why he had accepted the job. "The President stated that rumors of the most exaggerated kind were circulating in this country and overseas," Melvin Eisenberg, a staff lawyer, quoted Warren as saying. "Some rumors went as far as attributing the assassination to a faction within the government wishing the Presidency assumed by President Johnson. Others, if not quenched, could conceivably lead the country into a war which would cost 40 million lives. No one could refuse to do something which might help prevent such a possibility. The President convinced him that this was an occasion on which actual conditions had to override general principles." [3]

Warren went on to discuss the role of the Commission. As Eisenberg remembered: "He placed emphasis on the quenching of rumors, and precluding further speculation. . . . He emphasized that the Commission had to determine the truth, whatever that might be." [4]

Those who joined Earl Warren to seek the truth and quench the rumors were men who could be counted on. There was Hale Boggs, a representative from Louisiana, an old friend of Johnson's and the House majority whip; John J. McCloy, former military governor of Germany and chief of disarmament in the Kennedy administration; John Sherman Cooper, senator from Kentucky, Republican, and former county judge; Allen W. Dulles, the director of the Central Intelligence Agency whom Kennedy had ousted after the Bay of Pigs; Richard B. Russell, senator from Georgia, chairman of the Armed Services Committee and perhaps the single most powerful man in the Senate; and finally, the least senior of all of them, the Republican representative from Grand Rapids, Michigan, Gerald R. Ford.[5]

They were steady, disciplined men, cautious and conservative. There was not a born dissenter among them. If they reflected established attitudes, it was only natural. They were, in large measure, the establishment itself.

The commissioners shared Warren's determination to put an end to rumors. Shortly after his appointment to the Commission, Dulles told columnist Murray Kempton he was confident that the Commission would discover no evidence of conspiracy.[6] The atmosphere of rumors and suspicion was interfering with the functioning of government, especially abroad, Dulles said, and one of the main tasks of the Commission was dispelling those rumors. At the Commission's first executive session, Dulles presented each of his fellow commissioners with a paperback guide for their future deliberations. It was a study of how American assassinations were always the work of lone, demented men.[7] Later, after the Commission had finished its work, several other commissioners concurred with Dulles's assessment in interviews with Edward Jay Epstein, author of the most exhaustive study of the Commission's workings. McCloy told Epstein it had been of paramount importance to "show the world that America is not a banana republic, where government can be changed by conspiracy." [8] John Sherman Cooper added that a vital purpose of the Commission was "to lift the cloud of doubts that had been cast over American institutions." [9]

However noble that task, the commissioners did little to further it. They were important, busy men, and being busy they could invest comparatively little time sifting through the evidence and questioning witnesses. The bulk of these tasks were delegated to a staff of lawyers, under the directorship of New York attorney J. Lee Rankin, a transplanted Nebraskan who had served as solicitor general of the United States. But for the name that appeared on the Report's cover, it was far more Rankin's commission than it was Earl

Warren's. Rankin hired the staff and mediated the differences that arose among them. He funneled the messages from the staff to the commissioners, and from the commissioners to the staff. He questioned all the major witnesses, and when it came time to write the final report Rankin oversaw its creation.[10]

The team of lawyers Rankin assembled was, like the commission it served, composed of important, busy men. Included in their number were some names which would later become familiar. From Texas, there was Leon Jaworski, the future Watergate special prosecutor; from Indiana, Albert Jenner, who would later serve as minority counsel on the House Judiciary Committee's impeachment proceedings against Richard Nixon; from Iowa, David Belin, who would later turn up as executive director of the Rockefeller commission on the CIA; from Pennsylvania, Arlen Specter, who came to be known as the father of the "magic-bullet" theory, and would later become district attorney of Philadelphia, and still later emerge as one of Richard Nixon's lawyers; and William Coleman, the only black man on the Commission staff, and who would be named to the cabinet of President Gerald R. Ford.[11] These men, too, had limited time to spend on an investigation.

So at their second formal meeting the Warren Commission, on Rankin's recommendation, made a fateful decision. It would leave the bulk of its investigative work to federal agencies already established for that purpose, namely the FBI and the CIA. Dulles, the former CIA director, assured his colleagues that the choice was a wise one. Otherwise, he said, there would be needless friction in dealing with other government agencies, and the security problem would be vastly complicated. The commissioners took Dulles at his word.[12]

Hardly a month had gone by when the consequences of that decision became startlingly apparent. On January 22 Rankin got a telephone call from Texas Attorney General Waggoner Carr reporting that his office had picked up a story that Oswald was an informer for the FBI.[13] There had been similar rumors linking Oswald to the FBI and the CIA ever since the assassination, but what made this one so disturbing was its source and its specificity. The story had come from Alonzo Hudkins, a Houston reporter who was well known to Carr as well as to Dallas District Attorney Henry Wade. They thought Hudkins trustworthy. Moreover, the reporter had details to back up his story. Oswald supposedly had been paid $200 a month since September 1962, and his information identification number was 179. Rankin thanked Carr for his information, asked him to come with Wade to Washington, and hung up.[14] His next call was to Warren, urgently requesting a secret, emergency meeting of the Commission later that day.[15]

For years, even the existence of that meeting was shrouded in TOP SECRET classification. Once its existence became known, federal authorities at first claimed that no record had been taken. But Harold Weisberg, a former reporter, OSS man, and charter assassination buff, kept pressing. Finally, in 1975, years after Weisberg's first request for information, a partial transcript arrived in the mail. Some parts were garbled, and many voices were unidentified, but the meaning of the meeting was clear. So was the concern.

> RANKIN: . . . It was being rumored that he was an undercover agent. Now it is something that is very difficult to prove out. There are events in connection with this that are curious, in that they might make it possible to check some of it out in time. I assume that the FBI records would never show it, and if it is true, and of course we don't know, but we thought you should have the information.
>
> UNIDENTIFIED (presumably WARREN): Lee, would you tell the gentlemen the circumstances under which this story was told?

Rankin then related how the story came to his attention, saying finally: "I did talk to [Leon] Jaworski and he said he didn't think Wade would say anything like this unless he had some substantial information back of it, and thought he could prove it, because he thought it would ruin many in politics, in Texas, to be making such a claim, and then have it shown that there was nothing to it."

COOPER: How would you test this kind of thing?

UNIDENTIFIED (apparently RANKIN): It is going to be very difficult for us to be able to establish the fact in it. I am confident that the FBI would never admit it, and I presume their records will never show it, or if their records do show anything, I would think their records would show some kind of a number that could be assigned to a dozen different people according to how they want to describe them. So that it seemed to me if it truly happened, he [Oswald] did use postal boxes practically every place that he went, and that would be an ideal way to get money to anyone that you wanted as an undercover agent, or anybody else that you wanted to do business that way with without having any particular transaction.

The discussion then turned to the FBI.

UNIDENTIFIED: Mr. [FBI Assistant Director ALAN] Belmont would know every undercover agent.

UNIDENTIFIED: Belmont?

UNIDENTIFIED: Yes.

UNIDENTIFIED: An informer also, would you say?

UNIDENTIFIED: Yes, I would think so. He is the special security, of the division.

DULLES: Yes, I know.

UNIDENTIFIED (apparently RANKIN): And he is an able man. But when the Chief Justice and I were just briefly reflecting on this we said if that was true and it ever came out and could be established, then you would have people think that there was a conspiracy to accomplish this assassination that nothing the Commission did or anybody could dissipate.

BOGGS: You are right.

DULLES: Oh, terrible.

BOGGS: Its implications of this are fantastic, don't you think so?

UNIDENTIFIED: Terrific.

RANKIN: To have anybody admit to it, even if it was the fact, I am sure that there wouldn't at this point be anything to prove it.

DULLES: Lee, if this were true, why would it be particularly in their interest—I could see it would be in their interest to get rid of this man but why would it be in their interest to say he is clearly the only guilty one? I mean I don't see that argument that you raise particularly shows an interest.

BOGGS: I can immediately—

UNIDENTIFIED: They would have us fold up and quit.

BOGGS: This closes the case, you see. Don't you see?

DULLES: Yes, I see that.

RANKIN: They found the man. There is nothing more to do. The Commission supports their conclusions, and we can go on home and that is the end of it.

DULLES: But that puts the man right on them. If he was not the killer and they employed him, they are already it, you see. So your argument is correct if they are sure that this is going to close the case, but if it doesn't close the case, they are worse off than ever by doing this.

BOGGS: Yes, I would think so. And, of course, we are all even gaining in the realm of speculation. I don't even like to see this being taken down.

DULLES: Yes, I think this record ought to be destroyed. Do you think we need a record of this? [16]

The discussion continued for a few moments more on whether the transcript of the meeting ought to be destroyed. Finally, Boggs said: "I would hope that none of these records are circulated to anybody." A few lines later, the transcript ends.[17]

But it was not the end of the Commission's problem. At another closed-door meeting five days later, the subject of Oswald's having been an FBI man, and what to do to prove or disprove it, again came up. By now the commissioners were desperate to put an end to what Rankin called "this dirty rumor." But how?

RUSSELL: What steps, if any, have we taken to clear up this matter, Mr. Rankin, if it can be cleared up, to determine whether there is anything to this or not?

RANKIN: . . . I suggested the possibility for the Commission to consider that I should go over and see Edgar Hoover myself, and tell him this problem. . . .

BOGGS: What other alternatives are there?

RANKIN: Well, the other alternative would be to examine Hudkins, the reporter, to examine [Allan] Sweatt . . . to examine Hosty, the FBI agent who was working in that area, and to examine the special agent in charge of that area, and to examine Mr. Hoover, under oath, right up the line. . . .

We do have a dirty rumor that is very bad for the Commission, the problem and it is very damaging to the agencies that are involved in it and it must be wiped out insofar as it is possible to do so by this Commission. . . .

WARREN: . . . I said to Lee [Rankin] that if I were in the position of the FBI, and I was asked to respond to a rumor, just a plain rumor of this kind, that I would be inclined to ask for what facts, what the facts were and what they were based on before I was obliged to make a statement. . . .

Lee, on the other hand, felt it would be the better part of cooperation to go over and see Mr. Hoover and tell him frankly what the rumor was, state that it was pure rumor, we haven't evaluated the facts, but ask him, first, if it is true, and secondly if he can supply us with information to establish that these facts are not true, and they are inconsistent with what would be the way of operation of their bureau. . . .

MC CLOY: This is going to build up. In New York, I am already beginning to hear about it. I got a call from Time-Life about it. . . .

DULLES: There is a terribly hard thing to disprove, you know. How do you disprove a fellow was not your agent? How do you disprove it?

BOGGS: You could disprove it, couldn't you?

DULLES: No. . . .

BOGGS: . . . Did you have agents about whom you had no record whatsoever?

DULLES: The record might not be on paper. But on paper would have hieroglyphics that only two people knew what they meant, and nobody outside of the agency would know and you could say this meant the agent and somebody else could say this meant another agent. . . .

BOGGS: . . . Let's say [U-2 pilot Francis Gary] Powers did not have a signed contract, but he was recruited by someone in CIA. The man who recruited him would know, wouldn't he?

DULLES: Yes, but he wouldn't tell.

WARREN: Wouldn't tell it under oath?

DULLES: I wouldn't think he would tell it under oath, no.

WARREN: Why?

DULLES: He ought not tell it under oath. Maybe not tell it to his own government, but wouldn't tell it any other way.

MC CLOY: Wouldn't he tell it to his own chief?

DULLES: He might or might not. If he was a bad one, then he wouldn't.

BOGGS: What you do is you make out a problem if this be true, make our problem utterly impossible because you say this rumor can't be dissipated under any circumstances.

DULLES: I don't think it can unless you believe Mr. Hoover, and so forth and so on, which probably most of the people will. . . . What I was getting at, I think under any circumstances, I think Mr. Hoover would say certainly he didn't have anything to do with this fellow. . . . You can't prove what the facts are. There are no external evidences.* [18] [Emphasis added.]

Despite the caveat from Dulles, the commissioners concluded that they had no other choice but to rely on Hoover's assurances. The meeting adjourned with Ran-

---

* A considerably sanitized version of this colloquy appeared in Gerald Ford's *Portrait of the Assassin.* Aside from the pains Ford took to delete the most unflattering references to the FBI, and the trauma of the commissioner's own dilemma, Ford's use of the then top secret transcript was notable in one other respect: it was a violation of federal law, the same law under which Daniel Ellsberg would later be prosecuted for release of the Pentagon Papers. The incident came up during Ford's confirmation hearings as vice-president before the Senate Judiciary Committee in November 1973.

CHAIRMAN: Now, Mr. Ford, it has been stated that as a member of the Warren Commission you voluntarily accepted the constraints which all the members of the commission accepted, providing that you would not publish or release any of the proceedings of the Commission.

You did, however, in association with another, publish a book and provide material for a *Life* magazine article on the proceedings of the Commission. Do you feel this was a violation of your agreement?

FORD: To the best of my recollection, Mr. Chairman, there was no such agreement, but, even if there was, the book I published in in conjunction with a member of my staff . . . we wrote the book, but we did not use in that book any material other than the material that was in the 26 volumes of testimony and exhibits that were subsequently made public and sold to the public generally.[19]

This, of course, was not true. The transcript Ford used was not declassified and released to the public until 1974. Later, when a member of a House committee suggested to the vice-president-designate that he might have committed perjury before the Senate, Ford said that he had not understood the meaning of the chairman's question.[20]

kin, an old friend of Hoover's, being instructed to visit the FBI director and ask whether the rumor was true. Hoover, predictably, said there was nothing to it.

Five months later, in early May, the question of Oswald's possible involvement with the FBI came up once more, this time with the appearance of Alan Belmont, the Bureau's assistant director. The FBI now seemed willing, even anxious to cooperate with the Commission. Belmont went so far as offering to leave Oswald's FBI file with the commissioners so they could study it at their leisure.[21] Rankin was eager to accept what, coming from the Bureau which guarded its files like Holy Writ, was an extraordinary offer. As Rankin pointed out, if the commissioners looked at Oswald's file, "the Commission could say in its report, 'We have seen everything that they have.' "[22] Warren, however, was wary, finally deciding to decline the offer. "Well," the chief justice explained, "the same people who would demand that we see everything of this kind would also demand that they be entitled to see it, and if it is a security matter, we can't let them see it."[23]

Earl Warren and his commissioners were neither naive nor malicious men. Their problem, as Epstein adroitly summed it up, was that the truth they sought was of a special, rarefied kind, a kind often at variance with the facts. Epstein called it "political truth."[24] He explained:

> There was thus a dualism in purpose. If the explicit purpose of the Commission was to ascertain and expose the facts, the implicit purpose was to protect the national interest by dispelling rumors.
>
> These two purposes were compatible so long as the damaging rumors were untrue. But what if a rumor damaging to the national interest proved to be true? The Commission's explicit purpose would dictate that the information be exposed regardless of the consequences, while the Commission's implicit purpose would dictate that the rumor be dispelled regardless of the fact that it was true. In a conflict of this sort, one of the Commission's purposes would emerge as dominant.[25]

The investigation showed which purpose did. Soon after the staff was organized it was broken into teams, each team pursuing a separate aspect of the case. The blueprint for the investigation was set out in the beginning. All the ballistics evidence was grouped under the subheading: The Shots from the Texas School Book Depository. The information about Oswald was collected under the heading: The Assassin. In a separate section there was also an exhaustive biography of Oswald, from his birth to his death in the basement of the Dallas jail, November 24, 1963. Consciously or not, the Commission was playing with a loaded deck.[26]

Even so, the Commission kept running into difficulties. One of the most serious came from the least likely of sources, the FBI. The Bureau's Summary Report on the Assassination was completed less than a month after the assassination. This report stated that Oswald was the assassin, but went on to present a scenario for the assassination which ruled out anything but a conspiracy. According to the FBI report President Kennedy was struck by the initial shot fired from the School Book Depository, Governor Connally by a second shot, and then, a few seconds later, President Kennedy by a third and fatal bullet.[27]

This account of the assassination caused consternation within the Commission staff. For after calculating the time of the shots from the Zapruder film and matching the findings with the known speed of Oswald's bolt-action rifle, the staff determined that it would have been physically impossible for Oswald to shoot the President, work the bolt, and shoot Governor Connally in anything less than 2.3 seconds.[28] And, as the Zapruder film clearly showed, Connally was wounded no more than 1.6 seconds after the President.[29]

The task of resolving this conundrum fell to Assistant Counsel Arlen Specter. He devised an ingenious, if unlikely solution. After consulting with doctors and staging an elaborate re-creation of the assassination in Dallas, complete with camera-mounted rifle and FBI agents as stand-ins for the President and governor, Specter concluded that one rather than two bullets struck Kennedy and Connally.[30] In time, this hypothesis, on which the entire single-assassin scenario rested, came to be called "the magic bullet."

The thesis had a number of problems. Oswald, as the Commission learned from a check of his service records with the Marine Corps, was something less than a crack shot. During his service with the marines he had barely qualified as a "marksman," the lowest shooting grade in the corps.[31] In the Soviet Union, where Oswald belonged to a hunting club (a fact that the Commission took as indication that he was honing his shooting skills), Oswald was such a poor shot that, according to his KGB file, "it was necessary for persons who accompanied him on hunts to provide him with game."[32] The shots that hit Kennedy and Connally were difficult ones: three bull's-eyes with an awkward, clumsy rifle at a target moving constantly down and away from the shooter, all within 5.6 seconds. To clear up the doubts the Commission staged another reenactment, though with some important qualifications. Three "expert" marksmen—the *highest* shooting qualification—were selected from the National Rifle Association.[33] They were to shoot at a *stationary* target,[34] taking all the time they wished to line up their first shot[35] (unlike Oswald, whose view of the motorcade as it began moving down Elm Street was blocked by the foliage of a large oak tree in front of the Depository).[36] Amid great fanfare the test was arranged. Before it could be conducted, however, three metal shims had to be placed beneath the scope to align the sights.[37] Otherwise the scope—the same one Oswald allegedly used—would be worse than useless. Finally the appointed day arrived, and, Mannlicher-Carcano in hand, the experts had their try. As the saying goes, they should have stayed in bed. None of them could score three bull's-eyes in the allotted time.[38]

The more tests the Commission ran, the more unhappy the results, though none more unhappy than the wound ballistics experiments. At the Commission's direction, ballistics experts fired a round from the Mannlicher-Carcano into the wrist bone of a cadaver.[39] The demonstration was important because Commission

Exhibit 399—the bullet which allegedly wounded both Kennedy and Connally—had been recovered from a stretcher at Parkland Hospital virtually intact. To the Commission's considerable distress, the test bullet which struck the cadaver was severely flattened.[40]

Unwittingly, the Commission seemed to be stumbling from one evidentiary disaster to the next. Like the sorcerer's apprentice, the Commission cleaned up one mess only to have others appear, some bigger and messier than others. That is how it was with the wounding of John Connally, who, along with *all* the other eyewitnesses, stoutly insisted that separate bullets had wounded him and the President. The Zapruder film seemed to back Connally up. In the film, Connally, immediately after the first shot, displayed no pain, while behind him the President contorted in agony.[41] This, Specter, with the concurrence of several doctors, wrote off to a "delayed reaction" [42] to the impact of a 6.5-mm high-powered rifle bullet slamming into his back, smashing his rib, exiting his chest, and continuing down to shatter his wristbone, finally burrowing into his thigh.[43] There was also the matter of the Secret Service testimony. Two agents had already sworn that the President's wound was several inches down from the collar line.[44] Moreover, the FBI produced photographs taken by its crime lab of the President's bloodstained suit jacket and shirt; both clearly showed a bullet hole nearly half a foot below the collar line.[45] Most damning of all, the diagram of the wound on the official autopsy report was also beneath the shoulder.[46] Specter resolved the inconsistencies by dismissing them. The Secret Service agents and the autopsy diagram were simply mistaken, he declared. As for the jacket and shirt, defenders of the Commission later argued that it was possible that they had become "hunched up" [47] on the President's shoulders during the motorcade—something neither the witnesses nor the Zapruder film recorded.

Specter's hypotheses were the heart of the single-assassin case. If any one of them was wrong the whole creaky edifice would come tumbling down. And, it was obvious, even to the commissioners, that the structure

Specter had erected had, to say the least, a very serious list. Three commissioners—nearly half the membership—were unhappy with the single-bullet hypothesis; two of them, Russell and Cooper, vehemently so.[48] Russell flatly threatened not to sign the Report if it stated that both Kennedy and Connally had been wounded by the same bullet.[49] The commissioners decided to resolve their dilemma in time-tested political fashion: they compromised. After all, they reasoned, it was only a matter of wording. Epstein, who studied the proceedings closely, records: "Ford wanted to state that there was 'compelling' evidence that both men were hit by the same bullet, while Russell wanted to state merely that there was only 'credible' evidence. McCloy finally suggested that the adjective 'persuasive' be used, and this word was agreed upon." [50] As the Report finally put it:

> Although it is not necessary to any essential findings of the Commission to determine just which shot hit Governor Connally, there is very persuasive evidence from the experts to indicate that the same bullet which pierced the President's throat also caused Governor Connally's wounds. However, Governor Connally's testimony and certain other factors have given rise to some difference of opinion as to this probability but there is no question in the mind of any member of the Commission that all the shots which caused the President's and Governor Connally's wounds were fired from the sixth floor window of the Texas School Book Depository.[51]

In reaching this carefully phrased conclusion, as with others, the Commission merely ignored conflicting testimony, even when there was substantial corroboration. Certainly the idea of shots coming from the grassy knoll was not the product of one or two crazed imaginations. Of the ninety persons asked (either by the police, the FBI, the Secret Service, or the Commission itself) where the shots had come from, fifty-eight stated they were from the direction of the grassy knoll.[52] The Warren Commission said all of them were mistaken.

In other instances Commission lawyers cut off key witnesses before they were able to finish their answers, or failed to ask relevant questions. Thus, for instance, Lee Bowers, the railroad towerman, was in the midst of describing the movement that caught his eye at the moment the shots were fired when the Commission lawyer interjected with a question off the subject.[53] Other witnesses found that their testimony did not match what appeared in the Report. A classic case, discovered by Mark Lane, involved S. M. Holland, a railroad man who had been watching the motorcade from above the Triple Underpass. As the shots rang out Holland looked to his left, toward the wooden fence on the grassy knoll, and saw "a puff of smoke come out from under those trees." [54] Holland, with a number of his coworkers, ran to the area, and together with a dozen policemen searched it for shell casings. They found nonc, but did discover a number of footprints, along with a mud-covered station wagon.[55] Holland told his story to the Warren Commission, and if one takes the trouble to look up his testimony in the supplementary volumes, the account jibes with the version he gave Lane and others. The Report, however, uses Holland's testimony in an entirely different way. As the Report puts it: "Holland, for example, immediately after the shots, ran off the underpass to see if there was anyone behind the picket fence on the north side of Elm Street, but he did not see anyone among the parked cars." [56]

In some cases the Commission lawyers were openly hostile toward witnesses whose recollections disturbed the Report's preconceptions. Much of their hostility, though, was concealed in off-the-record exchanges, such as one which occurred between Commission lawyer Burt Griffin and Patrick Dean, a Dallas police sergeant who interrogated Ruby immediately after he shot Oswald. In the course of that interrogation, according to Dean, Ruby said that he had been plotting to kill Oswald for two days, a clear admission of premeditation.[57] The Commission, however, insisted that Ruby murdered Oswald on a spur-of-the-moment impulse.

Just how much Dean's testimony upset Griffin became obvious when Dean insisted on recounting on the record what had deliberately been left off the record:

> Well, after the court reporter left, Mr. Griffin started talking to me in a manner of gaining my confidence in that he would help me and that he felt that I would probably need some help in the future.
>
> My not knowing what he was building up to, I asked Mr. Griffin to go ahead and ask me what he was going to ask me. He continued to advise me that he wanted me to listen to what he had to say before he asked me whatever question he was going to ask me. I finally told him that whatever he wanted to ask me he could just ask me, and if I knew I would tell the truth or if I didn't know, I would tell him I didn't know.
>
> Mr. Griffin took my reports, one dated February 18, the subject of it was an interview with Jack Ruby, and one dated November 26, which was my assignment in the basement.
>
> He said there were things in these statements which were not true and, in fact, that both these statements, he said there were particular things in there that were not true, and I asked him what portions did he consider not true, and then very dogmatically he said that, "Jack Ruby didn't tell you that he entered the basement via the Main Street ramp."
>
> And of course I was shocked at this. This is what I testified to, in fact, I was cross-examined on this, and he, Mr. Griffin, further said, "Jack Ruby did not tell you that he had thought or planned to kill Oswald two nights prior."
>
> And he said, "Your testimony was false, and these reports to your chief of police are false. . . ."
>
> I quoted Ruby just about verbatim, and since he didn't believe me, and I was saying they were true, we might as well terminate the interview.
>
> Mr. Griffin then got back on the record, or before he did get back on the record, he said, "Well, now Sergeant Dean, I respect you as a witness, I respect you in your professions, but I have offered my help and assistance, and I again will offer you my help and assistance, and that I don't feel you will be subjecting yourself to loss of your job," or words to that effect, "If you will go ahead and tell me the truth about it." [58]

To this thinly veiled threat Griffin added that Dean might be well advised to get the services of a lawyer, since possible perjury had been committed. Dean nonetheless stuck to his story.[59]

At that, at least Dean testified. A number of witnesses were not even called. Fifty-five persons whose names were known and who were present at the assassination apparently were never interviewed by local or federal authorities.[60] Sixty-eight of the witnesses who were interviewed were not asked the direction from which they thought the shots had come.[61] There were some startling omissions. Julia Mercer, a woman driving to work who, several hours before the assassination, had seen a man with what she thought was a gun case walking up the grassy knoll, was never called as a witness, nor does her name even appear in the Report.[62] Similarly, Mrs. Eric Walther, the woman who had seen the two men standing in the window of the Book Depository, one of them holding a rifle, was never called before the Commission.[63] Apparently she was simply overlooked.

This was not true of Abraham Bolden. Bolden, the first black man to be appointed to the Secret Service White House detail, was publicly pressing to testify before the Commission about the failure of the Secret Service's security precautions. There had indeed been some notable, even suspicious gaps. Oswald's presence in Dallas, while well known to the FBI, had not been reported to the Secret Service, though other far less likely assassins in the Dallas area had been.[64] FBI agent James Hosty explained that omission to the Commission by saying he had no reason to believe Oswald "was capable or potentially an assassin of the President of the United States." [65] However, Police Lieutenant Jack Revill contradicted Hosty, and swore under oath that, within hours of the assassination, Hosty not only told him that Oswald had been under FBI surveillance, but that the Bureau considered him "capable of committing this assassination." [66] In any case, the Secret Service itself had been incredibly lax. The motorcade route had not been inspected for possible snipers' nests.[67] Windows overlooking the parade had not been sealed,[68] nor were any agents stationed on rooftops looking out for assassins.[69] The chief of the Secret Service told the Commission that "it has not been the practice of the Secret Service to make surveys or checks of buildings along the route of a Presidential motorcade." [70] The Commission found the Secret Service's statement "not persuasive." [71] It noted:

> The danger from a concealed sniper on the Dallas trip was of concern to those who had considered the problem. President Kennedy himself had mentioned it that morning, as had Agent Sorrels [the chief of the Secret Service's Dallas office] when he and Agent Lawson [the Secret Service White House agent who planned the route of the presidential motorcade] were fixing the motorcade route. . . . An attempt to cover only the most obvious points of possible ambush along the route in Dallas might well have included the Texas School Book Depository Building.[72]

Not only was the statement of the Secret Service not persuasive, it was a lie. The Secret Service *did* check the route of presidential motorcades in advance; windows *were* sealed; agents *were* stationed on rooftops. Retired Air Force Colonel Fletcher Prouty, who helped arrange the security precautions for President Eisenhower's trip to Mexico City in 1956, recalls:

> We walked over every foot of that route. We noted all the high buildings, all the possible sniper's posts. We even took down the position of all the manhole covers the President's limousine would pass by. And before it did, we made damn well sure that they were sealed. If there was an open window overlooking the parade route, we had an agent on that floor watching it. Listen, we leave nothing to chance.[73]

Except in Dallas. Dallas was special. The night before the assassination, while the presidential party was in Fort Worth, a number of agents in the presidential detail went out drinking. Several of them did not return to their hotel until 3:00 a.m.[74] One was up as late as 5:00 a.m.[75] All of them violated specific Secret Service regulations that forbade the use of any intoxicating beverages.[76] Their performance the next day showed it. As the motorcade turned on to Houston Street, the Secret Service follow-up car was right where it should have been, almost touching the back bumper of the presidential limousine.[77] But when the limousine turned onto Elm to drive past the Book Depository and the grassy knoll, the Secret Service follow-up car was nearly twenty yards behind the presidential limousine.[78] After the first shots the agents in the follow-up car were immobilized for several crucial seconds.[79] Only Clint Hill ran after the presidential car, and by then it was too late. Inside the presidential limousine the Secret Service driver and agent riding in the front seat made no attempt to shield the President after he was wounded in the back. Both agents later testified that they were unaware of what was going on.[80] But the Zapruder film clearly showed that William Greer, the driver of the car, looked back at the President not once, but twice.[81] The first time was after the President had been hit in the back. The second time was at the very moment the President was struck in the head. Then, and only then, Greer accelerated the limousine.[82]

Perhaps this is what was on Bolden's mind when he asked to testify before the Commission. The Commission would never know. Rankin stated that the Commission "hasn't had time to consider" Bolden's request, but that "the matter is being considered and the Commission will decide whether he [Bolden] or anyone else will be called." [83] Bolden never was. Later he was indicted and subsequently convicted and imprisoned on a charge of trying to sell government files.[84]

A number of witnesses the Commission did interrogate were dubious sources at best. One of the worst instances revolved around the circumstances of the Tippit shooting, an event of such importance that Belin later called it "the rosetta stone of the case." [85] However, the Commission failed to call some ten witnesses, including Acquila Clemmons, and instead relied on the testimony of thirteen others, only two of whom claimed to have seen the actual shooting.[86] One of those witnesses was Mrs. Helen Markham, who swore that she saw Oswald shoot the police officer.

By all accounts Mrs. Markham was a remarkable witness. She testified that after the shooting she kneeled on the ground and talked to Tippit, who had in fact been killed instantly.[87] She also said that before the shooting Oswald had leaned through an open window on the right side of the police cruiser and had chatted with Tippit; [88] the other witnesses, along with photographs taken at the scene, confirmed that the car window was *closed*.[89] In one recollection she described the assailant as "dark and bushy haired." [90] Yet an hour and a half after the shooting, after going to the police station in what the police report described as a "quite hysterical" condition,[91] she picked pale, thinning-haired Lee Harvey Oswald out of a lineup.[92] Mrs Markham was such an improbable character, her testimony so muddled and contradictory, that one Commission lawyer publicly characterized her as an "utter screwball." [93] The Commission itself dryly noted that Mrs. Markham was "uncertain and inconsistent in her recollection of the exact time of the slaying" [94] (a crucial point, since she placed Oswald at the scene at a time when it would have been physically impossible for him to have been there), yet nonetheless relied heavily on her testimony to establish Oswald as the slayer of Tippit.[95]

Charles Givens was an entirely different case. A black man with a police record (C.E. 705, p. 30),[96] * Givens was one of Oswald's coworkers at the Book Depository. On the afternoon of November 22, Givens told the FBI he had seen Oswald on the first floor of the Book Depository forty minutes before the assassination.[97] He repeated the story during the next six months without significant changes in detail.[98] Then, on April 8, 1964, Givens was interrogated by Warren Commission lawyer David Belin. Suddenly Givens's memory freshened. He remembered that shortly before noon on the day of the assassination he had forgotten his cigarettes, and had gone to the sixth floor of the

* All references to "C.E." or "C.D.," both in the text and end notes, indicate that the text is reporting information contained in an exhibit or a document placed before the Warren Commission.

Book Depository to retrieve them. There he saw Oswald.[99] Givens's latest recollection was crucial in building the case against Oswald, for no other credible witness had been able to place him on the sixth floor at a time anywhere near the assassination. Only Givens, a man who, according to a Dallas police official, "would change his story for money," (C.D. 735) had.[100] The Warren Commission believed him.

Still, the case against Oswald was largely circumstantial, and porously so at that. The Commission needed a star witness if Oswald's guilt were to be nailed down. It found her in his wife, Marina Prusakova.

Lee had met Marina in Minsk in 1961, during the period of his alleged defection to the Soviet Union. She was a strong-willed, attractive girl who had spent the last few years in Minsk with her uncle Ilya, a colonel in the MVD, the ministry that houses the Soviet Secret Police.[101] As a teenager Marina had been a member of Komsomol, the youth apparatus of the Communist party [102]—a fact she denied when it came time to apply for her visa to go to America.[103] It was not her first lie, nor, as the Commission would discover, her last.

Marina testified before the Commission nearly a dozen times. She was its first witness as well as its last. Each time she appeared there were new details, anecdotes, and stories, often contradicting the details, anecdotes, and stories she had told before. Her initial recollection of Lee was that he had been a good husband,[104] later that he had been bad.[105] Once she identified the Mannlicher-Carcano as "the fateful rifle of Lee Oswald," [106] another time, shown the same weapon, could not be sure.[107] In her testimony she talked of the pistol her husband owned.[108] Later on she said she never knew he owned one.[109] It was Marina who revealed that before the assassination Oswald had planned to kill two other public figures—General Edwin Walker,[110] who was indeed shot at and missed, and Richard Nixon.[111] And it was Marina who provided the Commission with the answer to the question that would always puzzle them: Oswald's motive. As Marina put it: "I came to the conclusion that he wanted in any—by any means, good or bad, to get into history." [112] It was a stunning turnabout for a woman who had earlier stated that her husband was innocent and had killed no one,[113] but not nearly as stunning as the testimony she gave the Commission in early September 1964, in Dallas. Said Marina: "I feel in my own mind that Lee did not have President Kennedy as a prime target when he assassinated him." "Well," Boggs asked, "who was it?" Answered Marina: "I think it was Connally. That's my personal opinion that he perhaps was shooting at Governor Connally, the Governor of Texas." [114]

Throughout it all the commissioners were the soul of politeness to the bereaved widow, never boring in, never expressing more than mild exasperation at the twists and turns of her convoluted tale. They showed such good manners that in time some of the Commission staff took to calling Marina and her inquisitors "Snow White and the Seven Dwarfs." [115] Some of the other staff were not so amused. Wesley Liebeler, a staff lawyer, said she was telling "approximately the truth," [116] tailoring her responses to what she thought the Commission wanted to hear. Joseph Ball, another lawyer quoted by Epstein, charged that Marina "left too many questions unanswered," [117] and still another lawyer, William Coleman, offered to prepare a "trappy deposition" for her.[118] But the harshest judgment came from lawyer Norman Redlich. "Marina Oswald," he wrote, "has lied to the Secret Service, the FBI and this Commission repeatedly on matters which are of vital concern to the people of this country and the world." [119] Redlich and his colawyers demanded that the Commission subject Marina to intensive grilling, but Rankin would hear none of it. The chief justice, he informed his staff, considered himself "a judge of human beings," and he and the other members of the Commission fully believed Mrs. Oswald's testimony.[120]

The omissions and inconsistencies—what Mark Lane would later call a *Rush to Judgment*—bothered some of the staff lawyers, especially Wesley Liebeler. Liebeler had worked on area four, the most crucial in the Report, the identity of the assassin. But the task of drafting the actual chapter had fallen to Norman Redlich, then professor and later to become dean of the New York University Law School.[121] Liebeler read Redlich's galley proofs the weekend of September 5, put them down, and spent the rest of the weekend composing a twenty-six-page single-spaced rebuttal.[122] In a gentlemanly way Liebeler demolished the entire substance of the chapter, raising most of the points the critics of the Commission would subsequently use to attack the Report. Liebeler contended that Redlich had not conclusively proven that the supposed assassination weapon was even in Oswald's possession the day of the shooting.[123] He was especially dubious of Oswald's capabilities as a rifleman—"a fairy tale," as he put it [124] —and said that the testimony Redlich had selected to prove Oswald was possessed of sufficient marksmanship distorted many of the known facts. At one point Liebeler noted: "Gaps cannot be filled in by ignoring them." [125] Redlich's methods had already made Joseph Ball, another one of the lawyers, uneasy as well. Ball was particularly troubled by the great credence Redlich lent to the testimony of Howard Brennan, who, so far as the Commission had been able to determine, was the only eyewitness who could identify Oswald as the assassin.[126] The trouble was that Brennan's identification had not come until March, five months after the assassination.[127] The day of the assassination itself, Brennan, who suffered from poor eyesight, had been unable to pick Oswald out of the police lineup.[128] Redlich, however, had written, "The record indicates Brennan was an accurate observer." [129] Joseph Ball scored Redlich heavily on this point.[130] Redlich was under attack on almost all fronts. Previously Liebeler had challenged his heavy reliance on the testimony of Mrs. Helen Markham, the woman who had managed to converse with the dead police officer in the street.[131] To this Redlich replied: "The Commission wants to believe Mrs. Markham and that's all there is to it." [132] It was not Redlich's conclusions that Liebeler disputed, but the way he arrived at them. "To put it bluntly," he wrote in his memo, "the sort of selection from the record could seriously affect the integrity and credibility of the entire report." [133]

When Liebeler presented his memorandum to Rankin, Rankin initially wanted no part of it, saying "No more memorandums. The Report has to be published." [134] Ultimately Redlich toned down a few of his adjectives, but on the question of Oswald's marksmanship he stood firm.[135] "The Commission judged it an easy shot," he said hotly. "And I work for the Commission." [136]

If the Commission was certain that Oswald had killed Kennedy (even if there were some doubts about how he managed to do it), it was not at all sure why. What was his motive? The question could have been answered easily enough if, like so many Americans, Oswald hated Kennedy. That was the catch. The President's accused assassin *liked* his supposed victim. Oswald had publicly said so a number of times, once during a radio debate in New Orleans a few months before the assassination, when he conceded that while Kennedy had "made some mistakes" in regard to Cuba, on the whole "he is doing a pretty good job." [137] Just one month before the assassination, Oswald attended a meeting of the Dallas Civil Liberties Union, and used the occasion to denounce the President's right-wing enemies, especially the John Birch Society. Michael Paine, a friend of Oswald's who attended the meeting with him, later recalled Oswald's performance:

> Lee . . . got up, speaking loud and clear and coherently, saying that . . . he had been to this meeting of the right wing group the night before . . . and how that people on the platform speaking for the John Birch Society had said anti-Semitic things and anti-Catholic statements or spoke against the Pope. . . . He said something very similar to, "I can't agree with what had just been said." . . . That was good speaking . . . it made sense.[138]

To explain why this man who liked the President decided one day to blow his head off, the commissioners had to go through some tortured reasoning. They had interviewed psychiatrists, talked to Oswald's friends, pressed Marina for a reason (she, disconcertingly, confirmed that her husband had been rather fond of the President),[139] and still the question was left hanging. The commissioners decided to answer it for themselves. Each of them seemed to have his own theory: Gerald Ford because Oswald was a Communist,[140] McCloy because of Oswald's "killer instinct."[141] In the end, the Report was a blend of all of them. Commission lawyer Joseph Ball later told Epstein that the Commission's recounting of Oswald's motivation was filled with "cliches that belonged in a television script."[142] Judge for yourself:

> Many factors were undoubtedly involved in Oswald's motivation for the assassination, and the Commission does not believe that it can ascribe to him any one motive or group of motives. It is apparent, however, that Oswald was moved by an overriding hostility to his environment. He does not appear to have been able to establish meaningful relationships with other people. He was perpetually discontented with the world around him. Long before the assassination he expressed his hatred for American society and acted in protest against it. Oswald's search for what he conceived to be the perfect society was doomed from the start. He sought for himself a place in history—a role as the "great man" who would be recognized as having been in advance of his times. His commitment to Marxism and communism appears to have been another important factor in his motivation. He also had demonstrated a capacity to act decisively and without regard to the consequences when such an action would further his aims of the moment. Out of these and many other factors which may have molded the character of Lee Harvey Oswald there emerged a man capable of assassinating President Kennedy.[143]

There were manifest troubles with this scenario, as the Commission itself conceded. The assassin who wanted to be a great man in history did little to assure his place. In fact, for two days after his arrest, Oswald vehemently insisted that he wanted no part of the role, that, as he put it to reporters, "I didn't shoot anybody, no sir."[144] Even the Commission was struck by Oswald's "considerable composure during his questioning."[145] "He admitted nothing,"[146] the Report conceded; he was so cocksure of his innocence that, to the Commission, his behavior seemed "arrogant and overbearing." [147] The commissioners didn't consider one other possibility. Namely, that Oswald was telling the truth.

The only other way to account for Oswald's performance was to assume that he had been insane. The Commission hinted at this without coming out and saying so. That was left for later accounts, such as that of William Manchester, who in *The Death of a President* wrote of Oswald's watching television the night before the assassination. "Apparently," wrote Manchester, Oswald "was intent upon the flickering Zenith screen. In fact, he was going mad. . . . [And] it seems clear that a total eclipse of his reason occurred shortly before 9 p.m." [148] Whatever their eloquence, the Commission and its defenders could only surmise that Oswald was crazy, and then only in disregard of the facts. For the facts, troublesome as they were, showed Oswald not only to be sane, but sober, bright, and confident of his eventual vindication. The only emotion he displayed out of the ordinary was anger and amazement that he had been arrested at all.

Prior to Oswald's arrest none of the medical examinations and psychiatric evaluations that he had undergone had revealed any severe disturbance. Dr. Renatus Hartogs, a psychiatrist who examined Oswald when he was thirteen, and who later became his chief psychiatric accuser, found in his original evaluation: "no retardation despite truancy; no psychotic mental changes." [149] That was also the impression Oswald left on people later. Sylvia Meagher put their recollections together. The picture they form was of someone who was far from crazy—or violent. Lieutenant Francis Martello, a police officer who interviewed Oswald at length after his arrest in New Orleans for "creating a scene," said Oswald liked President Kennedy and was not violent—"not at all. Not in any way, shape or form violent . . . as far as ever dreaming or thinking that Oswald would do what it is alleged that he has done, I would bet my head on a chopping block that he wouldn't do it." [150] J. Edgar Hoover admitted that there was "no indication at all that Oswald was a man addicted to violence," or a man who was mentally unsound.[151]

Police Chief Curry assured the television audience (while Oswald was still alive) that he was "mentally right"[152] and "not off his rocker." District Attorney Wade said repeatedly, before Oswald was murdered, that he was "not a nut," and that "he was sane."[153] Police Captain Glen King said on Dallas television station WFAA-TV on November 23 that Oswald was mentally competent and not deranged.[154] The president of the Dallas Bar Association, H. Louis Nichols, emerged from an interview with Oswald on Saturday saying that he "did not appear to be irrational."[155-56]

A man who was not crazy. A man with no rational motive. A man who did not seem capable of violence. A man who in any case was a poor marksman. A man who swore he was innocent. A man who was unseen by any credible eyewitnesses during the shooting. This was Lee Harvey Oswald, the lone murderer, the Commission said, of the President of the United States. The evidence might be lacking, but Oswald had been arrested for the crime, and now he was dead. There was no one to defend him. And he had, after all, been a Marxist.

The trouble the Commission faced was that if Oswald was not the lone assassin, who committed the crime? Who else could have pulled the trigger? Where were the other conspirators? No one had been able to find them, not the Dallas police, not the FBI, not the CIA. If there were others, they had vanished.

The Commission might dismiss their testimony, but many witnesses *had* seen someone else, both on the grassy knoll and in the School Book Depository, as well as before and after the killing of Officer Tippit. Only now the witnesses, too, were beginning to disappear one after another, with staggering rapidity, by threat, violence, or mysterious death.

First there was Acquila Clemmons. She had seen Tippit shot, and two men running from the scene. Neither of them was Oswald. She told her story to the Dallas police. They told her to keep quiet about it. If she didn't, she quoted them as saying, she might be killed.[157]

Then there was Warren Reynolds. He too had seen a man running from the scene of the Tippit shooting, gun in hand. It had not been Oswald. Two days after he was interviewed by the FBI Reynolds was shot in the back of the head. He recovered from his wound. His assailant was never found.[158]

Next there was Nancy Jane Mooney, a former stripper in Jack Ruby's bar. She had provided an alibi for one of the suspects in the Reynolds shooting. A week later she was arrested for disturbing the peace. Two hours later she was found hanging in her cell, with a noose made from her toreador pants wrapped tightly around her neck.[159]

Then there was Eddy Benavides, the look-alike brother of Domingo Benavides, one of the witnesses to the Tippit shooting. In February 1964 he too was shot in the head. His killer was never found.[160]

Then there was Hank Killam, the husband of one of Ruby's strippers and a friend of one of Oswald's fellow roomers. The month after Benavides was shot, he was found with his throat cut. The killer escaped.[161]

Then there was Bill Chesher. He was said to have information linking Oswald and Ruby. In March he died of a heart attack. He had had no history of heart trouble.[162]

Next there was Bill Hunter, one of the reporters who went to Jack Ruby's apartment the night of November 24. In April he was shot to death in the Long Beach, California, police station. His killer was a police officer.[163]

Then there was Teresa Norton, another one of Ruby's dancers. In August she was found shot to death in a motel room.[164]

Then there was Jim Koethe, the other reporter who had gone to Ruby's apartment. In September he was killed by a karate chop to the neck as he stepped from his shower.[165]

Then there was Tom Howard. He was one of Ruby's lawyers. The morning Oswald was shot, a policeman saw him in the police basement. In March 1965 Howard died of a heart attack.[166]

Then there was William Whaley, the cabdriver who took Oswald to Oak Cliff. In December he was killed in an automobile accident.[167]

Then there was Earlene Roberts, Oswald's housekeeper, who saw the Dallas police car parked by the curb, seemingly waiting for him. In January 1966 she died of a heart attack.[168]

Then there was Lee Bowers, the railroad towerman who had seen the cars moving into the area behind the grassy knoll before the assassination. In August Bowers's car rammed a bridge abutment and he was killed.[169]

Then there was Marilyn "Delilah" Walle, yet another of Ruby's strippers. In September she was shot to death a month after her marriage.[170]

Then there was James Worrell. He witnessed the assassination, and saw a man running from the Book Depository. In November he was killed in an automobile accident.[171]

And finally there was Harold Russell. He had seen Tippit's killer escaping. In February, he was killed by a policeman in a brawl in a bar.* [172]

As all this was going on, the Commission lawyers were hard at work in Washington, apparently unaware that witnesses were dying like flies. The Commission had a purpose and momentum of its own, and as spring

---

* In all there were some eighteen witnesses who died or were killed within little more than three years after the assassination. Sylvia Meagher, who collected data on all of them, discovered some striking statistics. Of the eighteen, she reported in *Accessories After the Fact,* five died of natural causes, and thirteen were victims of accident, suicide, or murder. Two of the eighteen were eyewitnesses to the assassination whose testimony conflicted with the lone-assassin thesis. Two had contact with Oswald during the forty minutes following the assassination. Three had direct or indirect contact with the Tippit shooting. Ten had a known or probable connection with Ruby. Seven of the eighteen deaths involved "primary" witnesses; their testimony before Commission lawyers or members was included in the Commission's volumes. Six were "secondary" witnesses, interviewed by the FBI or the Dallas police. Five were not mentioned in the volumes at all, but their stories had circulated in the press. Eight of the deaths occurred during the Warren Commission's investigation. Ten occurred after the Commission was dissolved.[173] The Commission, in any case, investigated none of these deaths. An actuary who was asked by the *London Sunday Times* to compute the likelihood of such a string of related deaths said the odds were 100,000 *trillion* to one against.[174]

turned into summer the purpose was to get out the Report. Because the Commission was late, June 1, 1964, the original deadline for completing the report, came and went with only partial drafts completed.[175] The Commission had already made up its mind; it was merely a matter of making the facts fit the conclusions. Since many of them didn't, obviously the drafting took time. As if to reassure the waiting country, the Commission leaked a long preview of its upcoming report to the *New York Times.* In a page one story in the newspaper's June 1 edition, Anthony Lewis reported that the Commission had considered the various conspiracy theories and had discarded all of them. "The Commission will unequivocally reject these theories," Lewis reported.

> . . . it has no credible evidence of any conspiracy. . . . A spokesman for the Commission said that none of these critical works, both foreign and domestic, had come up with any factual information. He said the Commission had found "just a rehash of the same material, the same questions which each man had presented before." . . . In some cases, the skeptics have raised questions about the number of shots fired. The Commission's data has shown that there were three, one that hit Mr. Kennedy in the back, wounding him, probably not fatally, the fatal shot followed. A third bullet, fired either before or after these two went wild. A Commission spokesman expressed conviction that the Report when issued would rebut such theories as presented by Mr. [Thomas] Buchanan [a Commission critic]. He said that "not even the authors of the theories will stand by them. We'll knock them out of their positions," he said.[176]

Meanwhile the deadline was pushed back to mid-July.[177] When that deadline, too, came and went with much work remaining to be done, the White House started to get restless. Telephone calls came in from McGeorge Bundy, urging all possible speed.[178] The country was anxious for answers. Besides, there was an election coming up in the fall, and the President did not want the assassination to become a campaign issue. The work pushed on. A number of Commission lawyers were worried over the incompleteness of the investigation.[179] Many questions remained outstanding. Many doubts were unresolved. The massive and thorough investigation by the FBI was not nearly so thorough and as massive as originally advertised. Indeed, it contained huge, gaping holes. The CIA was even worse. Many questions the Commission had asked the Agency to answer had remained unanswered. In some cases a Commission lawyer could not even get an agent to call him back.[180] The CIA was ducking and no one knew why. And after a while, few people cared. The deadline became everything. A third deadline was missed,[181] and then a fourth.[182] Finally, on September 24, 1964, ten months after the Commission began its work, the final Report was submitted to President Johnson.[183] At a farewell dinner for the commissioners and staff, the chief justice suggested to his former colleagues that they keep their deliberations in confidence.[184] Warren was also opposed to making public the testimony and evidence presented to the Commission but, two months after the submission of the report, twenty-six volumes of it were published.[185] Much evidence, though, including the most sensitive aspects of the case and Oswald's possible intelligence background, was classified and sealed away in the National Archives, where some of it was scheduled to remain for the next seventy-five years.[186]

The Commission had served its purpose. For the moment, at least, the dirty rumors had all been swept away. Lyndon Johnson could be satisfied. The assassination would not become a campaign issue. It would become something much worse. The Commission's work might well be over. The doubts were just beginning.

3

The Critics Respond

WHATEVER the Warren Commission's faults, lack of popularity was not one of them. The Report was an instant paperback bestseller. Within days of its release more than a million copies had been rushed into print.[1] The Government Printing Office sold out its entire first printing within twenty-four hours, then went to a second printing, both of which were quickly snapped up.[2] The three thousand sets of the accompanying twenty-six volumes of testimony and exhibits went nearly as fast, mostly to libraries, but many to persons with a special interest: the critics, who in the coming months and years would turn virtually every one of the Commission's words back on it. Earl Warren's fears had been proved correct. Whatever the Commission would uncover, there would always be the doubters. What he could not have guessed at was their number and intensity.

Some of the critics had not even waited for the release of the Report. Thomas Buchanan, an expatriate American living in Europe, had already suggested that a Texas oil millionaire he identified as "Mr. X" had masterminded the murder to protect the oil depletion allowance.[3] Joachim Joesten, a concentration camp survivor, elaborated on Buchanan's theme, adding the FBI, the CIA, and the army to the list of conspirators.[4] Leo Sauvage, a writer for *Le Figaro,* asserted that Kennedy's killers were drawn from the police, gangsters, and right-wingers.[5] The right, meanwhile, was blaming the left, especially the Communists. The John Birch Society immediately pronounced the assassination a Communist conspiracy, and found it more than passing strange that a "known Communist" like

Earl Warren had been chosen to head up the investigation.[6] In England the doubters were drawn from the intellectual establishment. A number of them, including Lord Boyd Orr, former director general of the United Nations Food Organization, Sir Compton Mackenzie, J. B. Priestley, Professor Hugh Trevor-Roper, Kingsley Martin, former editor of *The New Statesman,* and Michael Foot, joined with Bertrand Russell in a "Who Killed Kennedy Committee." [7] "Why were all the members of the Warren Commission closely connected with the U.S. government?" Lord Russell demanded. "If, as we are told, Oswald was the lone assassin, where is the issue of national security? If the government is so certain of its case why has it conducted all its inquiries in the strictest secrecy?" There had never been a "more subversive, conspiratorial, unpatriotic or endangering course for the security of the United States and the world." Russell concluded, "than the attempt by the United States government to hide the murderer of its recent President." [8]

Some went further than that. In the national tabloids, the most sensational charge of all appeared: that John Kennedy, a hideously wounded "human vegetable," was in fact still alive, living in closely guarded isolation in a remote wing of Parkland Hospital.

John Kennedy's murder brought them all out of the woodwork: the leftists, rightists, do-gooders, and plain crazies, united for once in their disbelief.

And then there was Mark Lane.

He had always been troublesome. As a state assemblyman from Manhattan, the liberal Lane had given the legislature fits. It was Lane who had burrowed into the state-financed bomb shelter project, then Nelson Rockefeller's personal baby, and exposed questions of conflict of interest involving prominent politicians.[9] It was Lane who went against the rules of the legislative game and threatened a filibuster if the assembly, as was it wont at the tail end of every session, voted on a package of bills it had not so much as read.[10] Lane retired from the legislature in 1960 and plunged into civil rights work. Bright, driven, and, to some, arrogant and self-righteous, Lane was heading toward a court case at the moment John Kennedy, a personal hero, was murdered in Dallas. Late that afternoon, as he was emerging from court, Lane encountered an old trial judge on the steps of the courthouse. "Well, Lane, do you think he did it alone?" the judge asked.

"Who, sir, did what?" Lane replied.

"Do you think this Oswald killed the President?" the judge said.

"I'm afraid that I don't know anything about it," Lane answered. "I just heard that the President was killed. I haven't heard any of the details."

The judge turned to walk away, and then looked back at Lane. "He couldn't very well shoot him in the back and cause an entrance wound in his throat, could he? The doctors said the throat wound was an entrance wound. It'll be an interesting trial. I want to see how they answer that question." [11]

Within weeks of the assassination Lane was in Dallas, visiting with the accused assassin's mother, Mrs. Marguerite Oswald. Not long afterward it was announced that Lane had been secured to defend the accused assassin's interests.[12] That association did not last long—Marguerite, an eccentric, quirksome woman, soon fired him from the case—but it was the beginning of a bitter, sometimes bizarre adversary relationship between Mark Lane and the government of the United States.

Lane formed a "Citizens Commission of Inquiry" as a counter to the Warren Commission. He roamed the country, interviewing witnesses, collecting evidence, picking out flaws in the case the Warren Commission was building. One of the witnesses Lane interviewed by telephone was Mrs. Helen Markham. During their conversation, which Lane thoughtfully tape-recorded, Mrs. Markham described the man she had supposedly seen shoot Tippit as short, somewhat on the heavy side, with slightly bushy hair.[13] Two days later, during his own appearance before the Commission, Lane repeated the substance of his conversation with Mrs. Markham. Mrs. Markham herself appeared before the Commission a few weeks after that and denied not only describing Tippit's killer the way Lane had quoted her, but having talked by phone about the killing with Lane.[14] Lane was thereupon summoned back to the Commission, where Warren told him: "We have every reason to doubt your truthfulness." [15] The Bar Association of the City of New York thereupon commenced an official inquiry into Lane's conduct.[16]

The Bar Association found enthusiastic supporters. The president-elect of the American Bar Association, who as it happened had been selected by the Commission to protect Oswald's legal interests, wrote privately to Rankin, inquiring if perhaps "there isn't some way the Bar can take disciplinary action against Lane." [17] The president-elect was Lewis W. Powell, later to be appointed by Richard Nixon as an associate justice of the United States Supreme Court.

The steps to disbar Lane continued even after Lane produced the tape recording, which when matched against Mrs. Markham's testimony to the Commission clearly showed that Lane was telling the truth.[18] Lane and several of the more prominent critics also found that they were being shadowed. At each of Lane's increasingly frequent public appearances, a couple of conspicuously dressed men would be sitting in the rear of the hall, taking notes on the proceedings. The notes were turned into reports, one of which went to the Warren Commission, the other to the FBI.[19]

The Commission also requested the CIA's dossier on Commission critic Joachim Joesten, which in turn had come from old records of the Nazis. It seemed that the Gestapo, too, had found Herr Joesten "politically unreliable." As the critics grew in influence, the moves to counter them got uglier. The FBI quietly circulated pictures among friendly members of the press, showing one of the most prominent of the critics engaged in kinky sex with two prostitutes.[21] One critic discovered a bug in his telephone.[22] Another found that the belongings he had been keeping in storage, including all his materials on the case, had been "mistakenly" sold at auction to an unknown bidder.[23]

All of which only convinced the critics that they were on the right track. In August 1966, less than two years after the release of the Warren Commission Report, Lane's *Rush to Judgment* was published. Pilloried by most of the major reviewers, and in fact deeply flawed, it nonetheless shot onto the *New York Times* bestseller list and stayed there for six consecutive months, for much of that time in the number one position.[24] Edward J. Epstein's *Inquest*, published shortly before Lane's book, had even more impact. Unlike Lane, who went to extraordinary lengths to suggest Oswald was innocent, Epstein seemed to have no particular ax to grind. He had in fact begun his study of the Warren Commission because it seemed an interesting topic for a master's thesis he was then completing at Cornell University.[25] Charming, often ingratiating, Epstein won the confidence of several members of the Commission's legal staff. The documents they provided him, especially Wesley Liebeler's twenty-six-page memorandum attacking the "Assassin" section of the Report, were convincing evidence that the Commission's labors were not as massive and thorough as originally advertised. Where Lane and the other critics attacked the Commission's findings, Epstein, in the most mild-mannered sort of way, undermined the Commission itself.

The effect was electric. The press, which had dropped its inquiries into the assassination after the release of the Commission's report, began digging into the facts once more. In Congress there was increasing talk of the need for a new investigation. More articles and books appeared, the most noteworthy of them Josiah Thompson's *Six Seconds in Dallas*, which offered a three-assassin theory based on a frame-by-frame study of the Zapruder film, and Sylvia Meagher's *Accessories After the Fact*. The study by Mrs. Meagher, a health organization official, was the most exhaustive work of all, a deliberately sober 475-page tome that rebutted the Commission's findings point by point, line by line.

Ironically, one of the weaknesses of the critics' arguments was that, taken as a whole, the points they raised were so numerous and complex, so carefully honed to the nth degree, that to many laymen the arguments seemed hopelessly dense. They were especially so when contrasted to the Warren Commission, whose scenario of events was simple, straightforward, and, if one disregarded the testimony and evidence that underpinned it, eminently reasonable. But if one picked one's way through the thicket a few key points stood out.

The Weapon

The rifle Lee Harvey Oswald allegedly used to murder the President of the United States was an odd choice for so awesome a task. According to the Report, Oswald purchased the rifle in March 1963 [26] from a mail-order house in Chicago. The total cost, including a four-power scope,[27] was $21.45, including postage and handling.[28] At that, the price was no bargain. In lots of twenty-five, the rifle could be purchased as cheaply as $3.00.[29]

Mannlicher-Carcano number C2766 [30] was described by a firearms expert for the FBI, as "a cheap old weapon." [31] Among the Italians, who manufactured them by the hundreds of thousands before and during World War II, the Mannlicher-Carcano had a reputation for being notoriously inaccurate. In honor of its properties the Italians dubbed it "the humanitarian rifle," since it was never known to injure anyone on purpose.[32] The feeling about the rifle was shared by American gun buffs. Jack O'Connor, writing in *The Rifle Book,* noted that the Mannlicher-Carcano had "a coy habit of blowing the firing pin out in the shooter's face." [33] As it happened, the Mannlicher-Carcano that supposedly murdered Kennedy was also discovered by the FBI to have "wear and rust." [34] It was in such bad shape that the experts who later test-fired it for the Commission declined to practice with it "because of concern with breaking the firing pin." [35]

Oswald's Mannlicher-Carcano had been manufactured in 1940, some twenty-three years before the assassination.[36] The ammunition he allegedly loaded on November 22 had last been manufactured in 1944,[37] and the company that made it wrote the Commission warning that "the reliability of such ammunition would be questionable today." [38]

The Commission had also been informed about the

Mannlicher-Carcano's defective scope—"the telescopic sight could not be properly aligned with the target," is how J. Edgar Hoover had put it in a letter[39]—but disregarded his information, and, indeed, insisted that the scope's misalignment might actually have *aided* Oswald in hitting his target.[40] The Commission neither mentioned nor explained at all that the scope was installed for a left-handed person. Oswald was *right-handed.*[41]

The Commission nonetheless insisted that the gun had to have been Oswald's for a number of reasons. One was the serial number: C2766. Weapons of American manufacture bear a unique serial number. The trouble was that Italian firearms do not. Hoover informed the Commission that a *number* of Mannlicher-Carcanos could have borne the legend C2766.[42] Moreover, the rifle that "A. Hidell" (Oswald's alias) had ordered from Klein's Sporting Goods in Chicago was thirty-six inches in length.[43] The Mannlicher-Carcano found in the Book Depository was *forty* inches in length.[44] Marina Oswald could not be sure that the rifle the Commission showed her was Lee's.[45] Ruth Paine, a friend of the Oswalds who had seen the rifle, testified that the sling on the Mannlicher-Carcano was unlike the sling she had seen on Oswald's rifle.[46] All the same, there was the palm print taken from the underside of the rifle barrel; it *had* matched Oswald's.[47] The Commission, however, was forced to take on faith the fact that it had come from the rifle. The Dallas police, who discovered the print, did not photograph it before lifting it (a violation of standard police procedure, even standard Dallas police procedure), and by the time the rifle arrived at the presumably more trustworthy FBI, all evidence of the palm print had disappeared.[48]

Even if the rifle were Oswald's, it would not have been any good to him without ammunition. But he had not bought any from the sporting goods store in Chicago.[49] Marina said that she could not remember that her husband owned any ammunition.[50] The FBI thereupon canvassed all the sporting goods stores in the Dallas area and found that none of them had sold any ammunition to Oswald.[51] When Oswald was arrested he was carrying no rifle ammunition.[52] Nor was there any ammunition among his personal belongings.[53] The police were able to find only one other round—still in the chamber of the Mannlicher-Carcano.[54] Added to the three spent shell casings, that makes four rounds. Oswald was evidently so confident of his shooting skills that he only loaded four rounds into the Mannlicher-Carcano's seven-round clip (which was never found in the School Book Depository), and even then didn't bother firing the fourth shot. Moreover, one of the shell casings from a bullet he allegedly did fire was dented at the upper lip.[55] The flaw was such that the casing could *not* have contained a slug on November 22.[56] The casing also lacked chambering marks characteristic of Oswald's rifle.[57] Two explanations could account for the condition of the shell casing: either Oswald removed the slug from the casing, dented it, and finally planted the casing on the sixth floor of the Book Depository to implicate himself in the crime, or someone else did.

There were even doubts about the murder weapon's identity. Deputy Sheriff Seymour Weitzman, who had discovered the rifle on the sixth floor of the Depository within an hour after the assassination, immediately identified it as a 7.65-mm German Mauser,[58] and later that day confirmed his identification in a signed affidavit, as did another police officer.* [59] For Weitzman to have been so mistaken was unlikely. He had formerly managed a sporting goods store, was familiar with most types of firearms [60]—and, more to the point, the Mannlicher-Carcano was clearly stamped on the barrel with

---

* Confirmation that the rifle was indeed a Mauser later came from Deputy Sheriff Roger D. Craig, who was present on the sixth floor during the search. In a March 17, 1975 letter written to Edward Tatro, a Commission critic living in Massachusetts, Craig said: "Deputy Eugene Boone and I found the rifle, which I might add was a 7.65 Mauser, so stamped on the barrel." In another letter to Tatro, dated April 9, 1975, Craig added another piece of interesting news: "As to the photograph of the shells, they were in uniform [position] lying on the floor no more than two inches apart all facing the same direction when I found them." If Craig was telling the truth, the implications of his story are ominous. Shell casings lined up neatly in a row suggest a plant. Moreover, police photographs of the scene show the shell casings to be scattered around the floor, as they would have been if naturally ejected from a bolt-action rifle.

the legend "MADE ITALY" and "CAL 6.5." [61] What makes the transmogrification of a large-caliber German carbine to a smaller-bore Italian bolt action especially intriguing is that in the assassination attempt against General Edwin Walker, which Marina had laid at the feet of her husband,[62] the bullet, which was later declared too mangled for positive identification,[63] was originally identified as a 30.06—the same caliber as a 7.65-mm rifle bullet.[64]

The Incriminating Pictures

On November 22, while gathering up Oswald's belongings from the garage of Mrs. Ruth Paine, a friend of the Oswalds', police came across two photographic prints of Oswald holding a rifle in one hand and socialist literature in the other.[65] Around his waist was strapped a pistol. The Commission stated that the rifle Oswald was hefting was the Mannlicher-Carcano,[66] and the photographs played an important part in establishing Oswald's guilt in the public mind. On February 21, 1964, one of the pictures appeared on the cover of *Life* with the headlined caption: "Armed for Murder." [67]

The more the critics studied the pictures, the more they asked the question: Just *who* was armed?

Oswald himself had provided one answer. When police showed the pictures during his interrogation on November 23, he had insisted that they were fakes; "that the face in the picture was his, but that the body was not," [68] and, in time, that he would be able to prove it.[68a]

Marina, however, stated that it was her husband in the picture and, what was more, that she had taken the photographs on March 31, 1963, in the backyard of their home in Irving, Texas.[69] The date was the first problem. The pictures show a yard bathed in brilliant sunlight, causing strong shadows on the ground and on Oswald's face. Yet a check of records of the weather bureau revealed that March 31, 1963, was a cloudy day in Dallas, with touches of rain.[70] One enterprising critic, noting that the bush behind Oswald was in bloom, discovered that such bushes not only are not in flower in late March, but do not bloom until September and October, a time when Oswald was in New Orleans and Mexico City.[71]

From there a whole torrent of questions were unleashed. In the first picture, for instance, Oswald's head is erect, but he seems to be standing oddly out of kilter. If a perpendicular line is drawn downward from the middle of his head, it ends nearly a foot to the right of his right shoe. When one attempts to stand at such an angle, one invariably falls over. Oswald's pose, the critic charged, was a physical impossibility.[72] The shadows beneath his nose were also suspicious. In the first picture, where Oswald's head is erect, his nose casts a shadow in the shape of a perfect V, as it should. In the second picture, Oswald's head is slightly cocked. The shadow, too, should change. Yet it retains the identical V shape.[73] Close examination of the area between Oswald's chin and his nose also reveals a fine line, the possible result of placing a picture of Oswald's head atop the body, neck, and chin of another man. Adding to that possibility is that the chin in the pictures is broad and squarish.[74] Oswald's booking photos, by contrast, show him to have a narrow, pointed, cleft chin.[75]

There was, finally, an explicable anomaly of height. The first picture is obviously taken at a somewhat closer range than the second, and it follows, then, that the figure in the first picture should be somewhat larger than the second, as indeed it is. But, when the heads are measured from just above the chin up, their size is *identical*.[76] One of two conclusions is possible: the pictures are forgeries, planted to implicate Oswald in the assassination, or Oswald grew several inches in the moments between the taking of the first picture and the taking of the second. Other calculations from Oswald's height showed that the rifle in the picture was 2.4 inches longer than the known length of the Mannlicher-Carcano.[77] From that the critics deduced that either the rifle was *not* the Mannlicher-Carcano, or, more probably, the man holding it was *shorter* than Oswald.[78]

In any case the implications of the pictures being forgeries (the FBI assured the Commission they were authentic)[79] are explosive. Quite simply, the photos constitute evidence of an artfully constructed frame.

C.E. 399

The most crucial piece of physical evidence in the assassination was the bullet which, according to the Commission, wounded President Kennedy and Governor Connally—the famous "magic bullet," Commission Exhibit 399.[80] The entire single-assassin thesis rests on this small piece of metal. If 399 did not wound *both* President Kennedy and Governor Connally, then Connally must have been hit by a separate shot, fired within a second after the first shot hit Kennedy. But Oswald's rifle could not fire that fast.[81] Ergo, there had to be a second assassin. From the critics' point of view, C.E. 399 shows precisely that. The bullet, they contend, is prima facie evidence of conspiracy. To argue the case either way, you must first account for 399.

According to the Commission, the bullet was discovered the afternoon of November 22 in a corridor of Parkland Hospital by Darrell C. Tomlinson, the hospital's chief engineer.[82] Tomlinson found the bullet after it rolled out onto the floor, while he was moving emergency room stretchers from an elevator.[83] Then and later, Tomlinson said that the stretcher from which the bullet had come had not been Governor Connally's.[84] The Commission, however, decided that the stretcher *had* to have been Connally's.[85] The most persuasive argument for this conclusion was that it was the only way the magic-bullet theory could work.

In either case the real dispute was not which man's body it had entered, but whether it had entered anyone's body at all.

The Commission, of course, insisted that it had, striking the President in the back of the neck, emerging from his throat, continuing on to hit the governor in the back, shatter his fifth rib, come out his chest plunging downward through his right wrist, smashing his wristbone, before it finally came to rest in the Governor's left thigh.[88] In short, one shot, seven holes, two broken bones.

High-powered rifle bullets are capable of such feats, and a bullet coming into contact with flesh or bone can take some amazing twists and turns. The journey of 399, however, was truly remarkable. For to judge from the position of the bodies of the two men as shown in the Zapruder film, C.E. 399, after it emerged from the President's throat, evidently stopped in midair, made a ninety-degree right-hand turn, traveled on a few inches, stopped again, made a ninety-degree left-hand turn, and then plunged into Governor Connally's body.[87] More remarkably still, it accomplished all this maneuvering and bone smashing and remained incredibly, one might even say miraculously intact. When it was discovered, 399 gave the appearance of being only slightly pinched, about the same distortion a ballistics expert might expect from a bullet which had been test-fired into cotton wadding.[88] The total weight loss, experts testified, was no more than 2.5 grains, slightly more than 1 percent of its original maximum weight.[89]

The Warren Commission's own witnesses were among the most dubious. All three autopsy doctors, along with Connally's doctors, and the doctor who had conducted the firing test on the goat, said they could not see how 399 could have been the bullet which had shattered Connally's wrist, much less having done all the other damage that the Commission attributed to it. For one thing the radial or wristbone is one of the strongest in the body. A bullet coming into contact with it, as the Commission's own tests had demonstrated[90] (see chapter 2), would inevitably have been deformed; 399 was not. Another equally if not more compelling reason to doubt the authenticity of 399 was the bullet fragments left in Connally's wrist. *All* of the doctors agreed that they weighed *more* than the fragments missing from 399 (there were also fragments left in Connally's chest and thigh).[91] The bullet, Dr. James Humes had explained in his testimony, is "basically intact; its jacket appears to me to be intact, and I do not understand how it could possibly have left fragments in the wrist."[92]

Moreover, for 399 to strike Connally, it first had to pass through the President's throat. And, though some of the Dallas doctors later changed their stories when they appeared before the Commission, their original impression was that the small hole in the President's throat was an *entrance* wound.[93] Dr Ronald Jones, one of the Dallas doctors who observed the throat wound never changed his mind. Jones told the Commission: "The hole was very small and relatively clean-cut as you would see in a bullet that is entering rather than exiting a patient." [94] If that were true, of course, 399 did not have the velocity to inflict the wounds on Connally. Indeed, it would never have reached him.

And then there was the President's cry of pain: "My God, I am hit." [95] Roy Kellerman, one of the Secret Service agents riding in the front of the limousine, distinctly heard those words from the President.[96] If Kellerman's recollection is accurate, Kennedy could not have been struck by 399, because in going through his throat, the magic bullet also punctured the President's windpipe. The throat wound had to have come later, either from a separate bullet (in which case, the question becomes, where did it go?) or, far more probably, from a bullet fragment.

All the conclusions were ominous for the report. They demolished the magic-bullet and with it the single-assassin theory. Lee Harvey Oswald, if he acted at all, was not alone.

The Z Film

Lawyers, prosecutors, and defense attorneys alike are uncomfortable with eyewitness testimony. A crime is an emotional event, capable of distorting perceptions. At that, the first impressions of an eyewitness are invariably the most accurate. As the months slip by, important details fade from memory. Details are often unconsciously added which, in fact, the witness did not see. There is nothing malevolent about it. All people are eager to please. If they want to please a prosecutor or a defense counsel, well, memory isn't perfect.

Scores of people witnessed the assassination, and while their recollections of it differed in many details, there was agreement among many of them on a number of important points, though none more vital than the shots which came from the grassy knoll. Still, the Warren Commission could dismiss them, even explain away much of the questionable physical evidence, if it had not been for the presence of one relentlessly impartial eyewitness: the movie camera of Abraham Zapruder.

But for the twenty-two seconds of film exposed through its lens, the Warren Commission would never have had to resort to impossible turns of logic like the magic-bullet theory, "delayed reactions" to the impact of high-powered rifle bullets, neurological spasms that defied the laws of Newton. A reasonable hypothesis could have been offered explaining how Oswald was in fact the single assassin. Doubts would have remained. But there would not be overwhelming disbelief. The Z film changed all of it.

Zapruder knew what he had on film. Soon after the assassination he took his film to a commercial photo studio in Dallas for rush developing. When the processed print was ready a few hours later, it was obvious that Zapruder had taken the most remarkable home movie in history. Word of the pictures Zapruder had soon spread. Within hours a number of major news organizations had contacted him. He finally sold the film to Richard Stolley of *Life* magazine for a reported price of $25,000,[97] which, it was announced, Zapruder was turning over to charity. The story was only one of many deceptions connected to the events of November 22. In fact, the $25,000 was merely a first payment on a total sales price of $150,000, the balance to be delivered in five yearly installments of $25,000 each.[98]

Time Inc. kept the original film locked in a vault in New York, after striking off several prints for the Secret Service and the FBI. Later the original was damaged when an inexperienced photo technician broke the film in two places while rewinding it.[99] A total of six frames were lost, none of them vital.[100] In any case, excellent prints existed in their entirety, along with slides made from the original.[101]

In January 1964 a print of the film and a full set of slides were turned over to the Warren Commission. The staff lawyers of the Commission viewed the film a number of times. When the Report was published it devoted considerable space to findings gleaned from the film, but omitted mention of the film's most dramatic moment of all, the final head snap that sends Kennedy's body hurtling backward at 100.3 feet per second per second.[102] Instead, as the Report calmly put it: "A second, fatal shot hit the President in the head and he fell into his wife's lap." [103] Those who went to the trouble of checking the volumes where the frames of the Z film were reproduced found confirmation for the Report's statement. The two critical frames showing the head snap—numbers 313 and 314—had been placed in reverse order so it appeared that the final bullet pushed the President's head *forward,* rather than as actually had been the case, violently *backward.* Later, J. Edgar Hoover attributed the frame reversal to a "printing error." [104]

For years afterward the Z film was seen by only a comparative handful of people. One of the few who viewed it was Josiah Thompson, a philosophy professor at Haverford College in Pennsylvania, who was then working with *Life* on its investigation of the assassination. According to Thompson's thesis, when Kennedy's car turned on to Elm it drove the President into a fatal cross fire. Thompson asserted that there were three gunmen firing onto Dealey Plaza in a coordinated, triangular pattern: one from the upper stories of the School Book Depository; another, also firing from the rear, probably from the County Records Building; and a third stationed behind the grassy knoll. The first shot, from the rear, struck Kennedy in the back. Within seconds a second shot, also from the rear, hit Connally. Then a third wild shot. And finally the mortal double impact: the first shot from the rear, striking Kennedy in the head, for an instant pushing him forward, directly into the path of yet another bullet aimed from behind the grassy knoll.[105]

The virtue of Thompson's scenario was its tidiness. It required no magic bullet, no delayed reaction, no confusion over autopsy results. It explained the almost imperceptible movement of the President's head forward, followed by the massive jolt back. It accounted for the witnesses who heard or saw firing from both the rear and the grassy knoll.

Thompson's findings, however, did not please the editors of *Life*. He finally turned them into an article for the *Saturday Evening Post,* and eventually published his speculations in a book called *Six Seconds in Dallas*. The book suffered from the absence of the relevant Zapruder frames. Time Inc. had refused to let Thompson reproduce them, even after Thompson offered to turn over to *Time* all the profits from his book.[106] Nor, for years, could anyone reproduce them. The only extant copies outside Time Inc.'s possession were scratched, dirty, blurred, almost impossible to see.

Finally, in 1966, a young New York optics technician named Robert Groden secured a bootlegged clear copy of the film. For the next few years Groden painstakingly worked with the film, studying each frame, enlarging it, enhancing the images, running it in slow motion, stop action, and backward. By 1975 Groden was showing his copy of the Z film to audiences all over the country.[107]

Those twenty-two seconds are the most horrifying moments ever captured on film. We see the lead motorcycles turning onto Elm Street, and behind them the President's dark blue Lincoln. Kennedy is smiling, waving to the crowds. Then, for a few seconds, the car disappears from view behind a freeway sign. When it emerges, Kennedy has been hit. His hands are clenched and he is bringing his arms up to his throat. Connally, apparently unhurt, turns back to his right, trying to see what has happened. He turns around and is beginning to turn to his left when his cheeks suddenly puff, his hair goes askew, and he is driven downward into the car. In the rear seat Mrs. Kennedy has now begun to lean over her stricken husband, who is slowly falling forward and to his left. The car continues on, almost coasting down the hill (its actual speed, calculated from the film, was slightly more than 11 miles per hour). Seconds pass. And then, for a fraction of an instant, the President's head is thrown forward a few inches, a blur, lost in the sudden violent impact that tears away the right side of his head in a shower of blood and brains, literally lifts him out of his seat and throws him backward and to the right with much more than the acceleration that could be caused by gravity.

The emotion one feels looking at this scene is overwhelming. Only cold, arithmetic logic, however, can explain what is happening and why.

First, some figures. The FBI calculated that Zapruder's film moved through his camera at a speed of 18.3 frames per second.[108] Knowing this it is possible to figure the speed of the car as well as the order of the shots. Tests also revealed that to work the bolt on Oswald's rifle and squeeze off a round required a minimum of 2.3 seconds, with *no* time allowance made for aiming.[109] Finally, the Warren Commission determined that the time span of the shots was no less than 4.8 seconds and in excess of 7 seconds.[110] In short, three shots were theoretically possible. According to the Warren Commission, those shots were one that struck President Kennedy and Governor Connally, another shot that killed the President, and a third, wild shot.[111]

The problem is timing.

While it was impossible, because of the freeway sign, to calculate the exact moment President Kennedy was hit the first time, the Warren Commission concluded that it was no earlier than frame 210 of the Zapruder film and no later than frame 225, an elapsed time of less than one second,[112] insufficient time for Oswald to work the bolt of the Mannlicher-Carcano and fire a second time. For there to have been a single assassin, the Warren Commission concluded, Kennedy and Connally had to have been wounded by the same bullet, C.E. 399.

Of course, there is another explanation: two marksmen, firing from behind, within split seconds of each other. This is what the Zapruder film clearly indicates. For in the film Connally shows no sign of being hurt, even as the President contorts in pain behind him. When Connally viewed the film, he picked out frame 234 as the moment a bullet went into him, slightly more than a second from the first possible moment Kennedy could have been wounded.[113] Looking at the same film, Connally's doctors concluded that the governor had been hit no earlier than frame 234 and no later than frame 238.[114] In other words, no more than one and a half seconds after the earliest moment Kennedy had been hit.

Connally himself had no doubt about what had happened. "I heard this noise, which I instinctively took to be a rifle shot," he said in 1966, after viewing slides made from *Life*'s original of the Zapruder film. "I instinctively turned to my right . . . but I did not catch the President in the corner of my eye. . . . Failing to see him, I was turning to look back over my left shoulder . . . but I never got that far in my turn. I got about in the position I am facing you, looking a little bit to the left of center, and then I felt like someone had hit me in the back. . . . They talk about the one-bullet or two-bullet theory, but as far as I am concerned, there is no theory. There is my absolute knowledge, and Nellie's too, that one bullet caused the President's first wound, and that an entirely separate shot struck me. . . . It's a certainty. I'll never change my mind."[115]

The only counterexplanation is that Connally did not know what had hit him, and that he shows no reaction in the Zapruder film because he is unaware that his chest has been torn open, his lung collapsed, and his wrist smashed by a high-powered rifle bullet.

Ludicrous as it seems, this is precisely what the Warren Commission chose to believe. Connally, the Report asserted, was conceivably suffering a "delayed reaction" to his wounds.[116] John Connally, however, wouldn't believe it. Nor would his doctors. While delayed reactions to gunshot wounds are not unknown, Connally's wounds, they pointed out, were "extremely painful."[117] The doctors based their conclusions not only on the Zapruder film and their patient's recollections, but on the nature of Connally's back wound: a small, elliptical hole, with rather clean-cut edges.[118] The neatness of the wound and the absence of any fibers in it from the governor's clothes suggested to the doctors that the bullet which caused it had not struck anything before hitting Connally.[119] If it hadn't, of course, then the magic-bullet argument was untenable, and the single-assassin thesis with it. From the instant the first shots rang out, John Connally was certain what was happening. "I knew it when I looked down and I was covered with blood; and the thought immediately passed through my mind that there were either two or three people involved."[120]

The Head Snap

Of the more than four hundred frames in the Zapruder film, frame 313 is the most graphic. It is at that moment that a bullet tears into John Kennedy's head. Frame 313 shows the impact as a yellowy-red corona around the President's head, a grotesque halo formed by blood and brain matter. Thompson laid a slide made from frame 313 alongside ones made from frames 312 and 314 and meticulously measured the movement of the President's head. He found between slide 312 and 313—a time frame of 1/18 second—an almost indistinguishable forward motion, no more than three inches, followed in the succeeding frames by a massive jolt backward not only of the head, but of Kennedy's entire upper body. The conclusion Thompson reached was that the frames showed Kennedy being hit not once but twice, the first time from behind, pushing his head suddenly forward at 69.6 feet per second, followed almost instantaneously by a second shot coming from the right front which drives him backward and to the left.[121]

The testimony of several witnesses who heard a final "double impact"[122] corroborates Thompson's findings, and perhaps more importantly, so do the Newtonian laws of motion. According to Newton's second law, bodies in motion stay in motion, or, more technically, the rate of change of momentum is proportional to the impressed force, and is in the direction in which the force acts.[123] Thus a bullet coming from the rear would push the head forward, while one coming from the front would push it backward.

Something caused Kennedy's body to topple backward. The first suspicion was that perhaps it was the sudden acceleration of the limousine. But the Zapruder film showed Mrs. Kennedy sitting on the edge of her seat, and *not* being pushed backward. Clint Hill, the Secret Service agent who ran after the car, did not lose his grip until well *after* the fatal head shot, by which time the President was lying on the back seat and Mrs. Kennedy was scrambling onto the trunk. Finally, a careful study of the film showed that the limousine did not speed up until after the head shot had been delivered. What was it then?

The Commission did not deal with this point in its report, but three years later, a doctor selected by the government to view the film and the autopsy results finally did. Dr. John K. Lattimer, a *urologist* from Columbia University Medical School, said that Kennedy toppled backward as the result of a "neurospasm" caused by massive injury to his brain.[124] A "neurospasm" is roughly akin to an involuntary bodily motion; a medical term for a reflex. Dr. Cyril Wecht, the coroner of Allegheny County (Pittsburgh), Pennsylvania, and one of the Commission's most respected critics, conceded that a neurospasm of the magnitude required to hurtle Kennedy backward was possible, though extremely unlikely.[125]

The questions about the head snap persisted. They grew in 1975 after the Zapruder film had been shown on national television. In an attempt to resolve them, the Rockefeller CIA commission, under the directorship of David Belin, a former staff lawyer for the Warren Commission, and author of an extensive work defending its findings, assembled a medical panel. The panel confirmed the Warren Report's findings that two bullets had killed the President, both of them fired from the rear. To explain the head snap, Belin offered the testimony of Alfred G. Olivier, a *veterinarian.* Olivier said that on the basis of his work with test animals, the head snap in the Zapruder film "could not possibly have been caused by the impact of a bullet." Instead, Olivier said, "a head wound such as that sustained by President Kennedy produces an 'explosion' of tissue at the area where the bullet exits from the head, causing a 'jet effect' which almost instantly moves the head back in the direction from which the bullet came." [126]

Thus the explanation for the Zapruder film moved forward: from a urologist to a veterinarian, from neurospasm to jet effect. All that remained to contradict it was Isaac Newton. And common sense.

The Bullets

Only one bullet was recovered intact after the assassination, the infamous C.E. 399. Ballistics tests conducted by the FBI established conclusively that it had been fired from the Mannlicher-Carcano.[127] In addition, mutilated bullet fragments were later recovered from the presidential limousine, along with several other shards of metal taken from Connally's wrist and the President's head.[128] The two largest fragments taken from the car were tested, and it was found only that they were similar in composition, not that they had come from the same bullet.[129] Which only left the fragments taken from the two men's bodies.

The question that aroused the curiosity of the critics was whether tests had been conducted on them, and, if so, whether they, too, matched.

Publicly the Warren Commission was silent on what amounted to one of the most important aspects of the entire case. For if the fragments taken from Connally didn't match 399, the governor, then, had to have been hit by a second bullet. And if that were the case, there was also a second assassin. The critics could only wonder. There seemed to be no evidence.

Not until more than ten years later did they find that there *was* evidence, and that it came from the unlikeliest of sources: J. Edgar Hoover. In a July 8, 1964, letter to the Commission not declassified until nine years later, Hoover reported that the bullet fragments recovered from Connally's body had, in fact, been subjected to spectrographic analysis, but that the tests had been inconclusive.[130] However, there was an additional test, NAA, a neutron activation analysis, a highly sophisticated technique that measures differences in material that has been bombarded with radiation down to parts per billion and sometimes even less. In his letter to the Commission, Hoover blandly reported that while "minor variations" were found between the fragments taken from Connally and 399, those differences were not judged to be "sufficient."[131] To the layman the explanation sounds fine, and certainly there is no record that the Commission ever questioned it. But when Hoover's letter fell into the hands of knowledgeable critics, bells started ringing.

At last it seemed as if there were a piece of conclusive evidence within reach, a document as irrefutable as the laws of atomic structure. For the beauty of the NAA was that its measurements were so precise that virtually any differences between materials subjected to its radiation were not only "sufficient" but absolute.[132] Several of the critics immediately filed a Freedom of Information Act lawsuit to secure the data on which Hoover had based his conclusions. There was a current of excitement among the researchers: the NAA test was the key they had been looking for. Why else had it been withheld from the twenty-six volumes of testimony and evidence? They were destined to be disappointed.

When the data finally became available in 1975, it neither proved nor disproved the existence of the single assassin. It was difficult, in fact, to figure out what the data proved at all. There was no report, no statement of conclusions, only seventy-three pages of raw lab notes. The final sorting out of what those notes showed awaited sophisticated computer analysis. But first indications were that Hoover was telling the truth; there were differences observed between the composition of the fragments and that of 399, but they were, as the Director had written "insufficient," falling somewhere in that great gray area scientists call "statistical error."[133] Moreover, the NAA test itself was crude by current standards. New tests *might* show differences that were absolute. As long, however, as the government held onto 399 and the fragments, there was no way new tests could be conducted.

All doubts would have been removed if another bullet had been recovered. But the bullet (or bullets) that struck President Kennedy's head disintegrated on impact. And that in itself was suspicious. For, according to the Commission, the bullets Oswald fired were "full-jacketed," military-type ammunition. The Commission summoned experts and conducted tests to prove that such bullets were capable of causing the kind of wound sustained by President Kennedy. But the tests, conducted on old, dried-out skulls filled with gelatin, did not nearly approximate an actual human head. Some pathologists and ballistics experts were also skeptical that full-jacketed ammunition would have disingrated—or caused such massive injury. In 1975 a young law student named Howard Roffman, after careful research with pathologists and ballistics experts, concluded that the bullet (or bullets) which killed the President was high-velocity, "soft" hunting ammunition—the kind that is ordinarily used to dispatch "varmints." Such ammunition could not have been fired from the Mannlicher-Carcano.[134] But what of the other bullets? If 399 was not the bullet that wounded both Kennedy and Connally, how did it wind up in Parkland Hospital? And where were the bullets that struck Kennedy and Connally?

Some of the critics, like Richard Popkin, author of *The Second Oswald,* which theorized that an Oswald look-alike was used to implicate him in the crime, argued that 399 was a plant, deliberately put in Parkland to increase the evidence of Oswald's guilt. While 399 was discovered most conveniently, and under somewhat suspicious circumstances, the difficulty with the plant thesis is that it suggested that conspirators were virtually everywhere in Dallas, even in the hospital. Moreover, it required a convoluted explanation for the bullet that did hit Kennedy, namely that it was buried with him, and that autopsy X rays that would have revealed its presence were "faked," which would extend the conspirators' reach to Bethesda. A much more reasonable explanation was one offered by the first FBI report on the President's assassination. According to the FBI, 399 came not from Connally's stretcher but from Kennedy's.[135] The bullet, the FBI report went on, struck Kennedy in the back, but did not penetrate his body deeply.[136] This squares with the autopsy performed at Bethesda, which found that the back wound extended to only a finger length.[137] Quoting from doctors, the FBI report concluded that the bullet "worked itself out" during external cardiac massage of the President, and thus wound up on the stretcher.[138] All of which seems to make good sense.

However, that still leaves two sets of wounds unaccounted for: those sustained by Connally, and the President's throat wound. Seemingly, if separate bullets had caused those wounds, they would have been found afterward either in the men themselves or in the limousine. An FBI ballistics expert, however, told the Commission that is not necessarily so. One or both of the bullets, he said, could have flown right out of the car: "I have seen bullets strike small twigs, small objects and ricochet for no apparent reason except that they hit and all the pressure is on one side and it turns the bullet and it goes off at an angle." [139]

Josiah Thompson offered a simpler explanation. The reason, he said, that no bullet was found in the President's throat is that the wound had been caused by a fragment. Thompson argued it was most likely that the fragment had been a piece of skull bone shattered by the final head shot. Such a bone fragment could cause a small, neat wound such as doctors saw in the President's throat.[140] Equally likely, a *bullet* fragment might have caused such a wound.

As for the bullet that hit Connally, Thompson noted that, like the bullet which struck the President in the back, it finally came to rest shallowly in skin tissue.[141] In Connally's case the final wound was in the thigh, though it was so minor that his doctors first overlooked it.[142] Thompson quoted Dr. Milton Helpern, who reasoned that this bullet, like the one which struck the President in the back, may have fallen out while Connally was being lifted from the limousine. As Helpern put it:

> It is not unusual at all for spent bullets that have passed through a human body to become lost. Most longtime homicide detectives can spin off several tales of cases of lost bullets. If I had to venture a guess as to what happened to the bullet that wounded Governor Connally, I would suggest that it fell out of his pants leg while he was being removed from the car and placed on the stretcher; or it could have fallen out at any stage of hospital experience.[143]

The Autopsy Results

Fine technical points, ballistics tests, eyewitness testimony, even movie films were, and perhaps would always be, open to dispute. If anything should have been clear about the assassination it should have been the wounds, how many and where they were. After all they had been seen, photographed, diagramed, and described by more than a dozen highly qualified experts. They should have answered all the questions, laid all the doubts to rest. Instead, it was the autopsy that aroused the single most bitter controversy of all the events of November 22.

When the dying President was wheeled into trauma room 1 of Parkland Memorial, two wounds were readily apparent: a gaping hole in his skull, and a neat, small circle over his Adam's apple.[144] Dr. Malcolm Perry, one of the attending physicians, judged the lesion in the neck to be the *entrance* wound of a bullet, a judgment in which the two colleagues assisting him consequently concurred.[145] However, by the time the President's body reached Bethesda Naval Hospital that night, what was once a small, neat hole had become a surgical gash, cut open during a tracheotomy to give the President air.[146] The doctors at Bethesda also discovered a wound the doctors in Dallas, in their struggle to save the President's life, had missed entirely: an entrance wound of a bullet in the President's back. Just where on the President's back was a question which, even a dozen years later, would provoke considerable argument.

Three military doctors conducted the autopsy of President Kennedy. Incredibly, none of the men selected for this awesome assignment had had extensive experience in performing autopsies.* The results of their work showed it. Henry Wade, the Dallas district attorney, later called the autopsy "the worst" he had seen in more than thirty years of law enforcement.[150] Dr. Milton Helpern, the former medical examiner of New York and widely regarded as the most competent pathologist in the country, privately said that "any second year medical student could have done a better job." [151] The participation of such doctors, said Helpern, who had conducted more than 60,000 autopsies, 10,000 of them involving gunshot wounds, was akin to "sending a seven year old boy who has taken three lessons on the violin over to the New York Philharmonic and expecting him to perform a Tchaikovsky symphony. He knows how to hold the violin and the bow, but he has a long way to go before he can make music." [152] Dr. Cyril Wecht, the former president of the American Academy of Forensic Sciences, condemned the work done in Bethesda as "worse than no autopsy at all." [153]

The Bethesda doctors committed a number of blunders, but two were especially glaring. The first was failing to establish the track of the bullet which struck the President in the back. During the autopsy the surgeons probed the back wound "to a finger length," [154] but did not attempt to track the wound further. Since the entire single-assassin theory rested on the premise that the bullet which entered the President's back exited his throat, the doctors' omission was not only incomprehensible but devastating. Not until 1968 did Colonel Pierre Finck, one of the autopsy surgeons, reveal why he had not followed standard medical practice; a senior

* The chief surgeon at the autopsy was Commander James J. Humes. His experience in forensic pathology consisted of a single course at the Armed Forces Institute of Pathology.[147] Humes's first assistant, Navy Commander J. Thornton Boswell, had no special experience in medico-legal autopsies.[148] Lieutenant Colonel Pierre Finck of the Armed Forces Institute of Pathology was the most experienced man on the team, but most of his work up to November 22, 1963, had been administrative, reviewing files, pictures, and records of finished cases.[149]

officer in the room had *told* him not to probe the wound.[155]

In their testimony before the Warren Commission the autopsy doctors also said that the wound in the President's back was located at the base of his neck, which jibed neatly with the magic-bullet thesis. That was not, however, where Boswell, another of the autopsy doctors, placed the wound on the autopsy diagram he filled out the night of November 22. The diagram locates the wound beneath the right shoulder [156] at a spot which exactly corresponds to the holes in the President's suit jacket and shirt.[157] Three Secret Service agents also testified that the wound in the President's back was beneath his right shoulder,[158] and a fourth agent, Clint Hill, who was brought into the autopsy room for the express purpose of viewing the wounds, also placed the wound six inches below the President's neckline.[159] There were two FBI agents present at the autopsy too, and they also reported that the wound was situated "below the shoulders and to the right of the spinal column." [160]

The Commission evidently shared that belief. During their secret meeting of January 27, 1964, Rankin and the commissioners discussed the difficulties that the autopsy report in front of them presented. Rankin opened the discussion by saying:

> Then there is a great range of material in regard to the wounds, and the autopsy and this point of exit or entrance of the bullet in the front of the neck, and that all has to be developed much more than we have at the present time.
>
> We have an explanation there in the autopsy that probably a *fragment* came out the front of the neck, but with the elevation the shot must have come from, and the angle, it seems quite apparent now, since we have the *picture* of where the bullet entered in the back, that the *bullet entered below the shoulder blade to the right of the backbone*, which is below the place where the picture shows the bullet came out in the neckband of the shirt in front, and the bullet, according to the autopsy, didn't strike any bone at all, that particular bullet, and go through.
>
> So that how it could turn and—

> BOGGS: I thought I read that bullet just went in a finger's length.
>
> RANKIN: That is what they first said. They reached in and they could feel where it came, it didn't go any further than that, about part of the finger or something, part of the autopsy, and then they proceeded to reconstruct where they thought the bullet went, the path of it, and, which is, we have to go into considerable items and try to find out how they could reconstruct that when they first said that they couldn't even feel the path beyond the part of the finger.
>
> And then how it could become elevated; even so it raised rather than coming out at the sharp angle that it entered, all of that, we have to go into, too, and we are asking for help from the ballistics experts on that. . . .
>
> So the basic problem, what kind of a wound it is in the front of the neck is of great importance to the investigation.[161] [Emphasis added.]

At the time, no one could have imagined how crucial these observations would later become. Only months later, with the Commission deep into its investigation, did it become apparent how everything hinged on the testimony of a very few doctors. And it was then, and only then, that the stories began to change. Now the Dallas doctors claimed that the press, which had widely reported their comments of an entrance wound in the throat during a news conference the afternoon of November 22, had mistaken what they had said, twisted their meaning, quoted them out of context.[162] Boswell noted that while he had mistakenly diagramed the President's wound beneath his shoulders at the autopsy, his marginal notes accompanying the diagram placed it near the base of the neck.[163] One of the critics thereupon pointed out that, strangely, this was the only note about a wound the good doctor had included, and, what was more, he had done so in distinctly darker ink than had been used for the rest of his jottings.[164] Boswell could only confess, "If I had known at the time that this sketch would become public record, I would have been more careful." [165] Humes, for his part, admitted that on November 24, he had burned the notes and first draft of his autopsy report in his recreation room fireplace.[166] The wound that once all had seen at the base of the shoulders seemed possessed of the same magic qualities as the bullet that caused it. In a twinkling it was suddenly at the base of the President's neck. As for the confusion, Humes allowed as how the President's being very well muscled probably had something to do with it.[167]

It required no great knowledge of medicine to sense that something was smelly. To the credit of the medical profession, it was other doctors who were most suspicious. In the months that followed the release of the Report, the legal and medical journals were dotted with questions about the Commission's methods, especially the treatment of the autopsy results. The headline of one such article, in the journal *Current Medicine for Attorneys,* put the suspicions plainly enough: "The Warren Report: How to Murder the Medical Evidence." [168]

In February 1968, then Attorney General Ramsey Clark, hoping to dampen the criticism, invited three pathologists and one radiologist to come to Washington and examine the evidence for themselves. After viewing the available autopsy photographs and X rays the panel endorsed the Warren Commission's conclusions.[169] But the controversy stayed alive. For one thing, all the doctors who had been permitted the autopsy evidence were announced defenders of the Commission Report. The critics had been excluded.

Finally, four years later, the first—and to date, the only—critic of the Report was allowed to examine the autopsy evidence. Cyril Wecht, the Pittsburgh coroner and a former president of the American Academy of Forensic Sciences, as well as the author of several scholarly articles attacking the Report's findings, was admitted to the sealed evidence in the National Archives in late August 1972. For two days Wecht examined autopsy photographs and X-rays and on the basis of what he saw tentatively agreed that, in at least some respects, the Commission had been correct: Kennedy had been struck in the head and body by bullets fired from the rear.[170] There were still problems. Wecht judged the back wound to be higher than the critics insisted, lower than the Commission stated.[171] In either case, the magic-bullet theory still would not work. Moreover, the wound in the back of the President's head was four inches higher than the Commission had said it was.[172] Lower down on the skull, just above the hairline on the back left side of the President's head, Wecht observed a "little flap" of loose scalp, which might either have been an entrance or an exit wound.[173] Only if he examined the microscopic slides of tissue taken from the wounds, as well as the President's brain, which had been removed at the autopsy, and in accordance with accepted medical practice, "set" in formalin for future study, could Wecht be certain. Examination of the slides would determine conclusively which wounds were of entrance, which of exit. Sectioning the brain would once and for all settle the path of the bullet or bullets that took John Kennedy's life. Records at the archives indicated that both the slides and the brain had been received. But when Wecht asked to see them, he made a grisly discovery: the President's brain was missing, and the slides with it.[174]

The critics were thus in limbo. The autopsy results neither proved nor disproved the existence of a conspiracy. What the critics were left with was a string of bizarre coincidences and improbable happenings: pictures that apparently had been altered, testimony that had been changed, bullets that turned corners in air, bullet fragments that were different, yet how different no one seemed to know. The reasonable explanation for these phenomena was more than one assassin. In contrast, the single-assassin hypothesis was forced to rely on everything that was unreasonable: magic bullets, moving wounds, delayed reactions, facts so twisted and distorted out of shape that reality had long since lost its meaning. The critics had succeeded in discrediting the Warren Commission's major conclusions, but as yet lacked the one piece of hard evidence—the proverbial "smoking gun"—that would bring a new investigation. The Warren Commission had not proved its version of the truth, but it was the one which was on the record, with all the resources of the federal government determined to keep it there. The critics, ironically, were cast in the role of prosecutors: not only had they to disprove what was false, but prove what was true. Soon, defenders like Belin were demanding: If there were more bullets, where did they come from? Where did they go? Who had fired them? How had they escaped? What possible purpose or meaning could a conspiracy have? In sum, the very questions the Warren Commission was supposed to have answered and had ignored.

The answers were just out of reach. The fragments that could explode 399 were still in John Connally's body. At the moment the first shot hit the President, a freeway sign blocked Abraham Zapruder's view. The President's brain was missing. A puzzle within a puzzle within a puzzle.

The people who set out to solve it were amateurs mostly, housewives and lawyers and college professors, people who had loved John Kennedy and people who had hated him, would-be detectives and seekers of living-room adventure, along with other, simple folk who merely wanted the truth. It was a maddening, disheartening business, this search for the killers of John Fitzgerald Kennedy, and in time it took its toll. One of the earliest critics, who did some of the best research, kept repeating his findings for years with nobody listening, and finally went insane with paranoia. Others were unsound to begin with, people who claimed, as one prominent female critic did, that the CIA had planted fiendish mind control devices in the skulls of its opponents. Others saw the White House exterminating dissident secretaries. Still others revealed that they were in contact with visitors from outer space.

The real wonder is that they didn't all go mad. For in the years immediately following the assassination the critics were working almost entirely with their wits. Almost all their evidence came from what the Warren Commission, in the Report and twenty-six supplementary volumes, decided to give them. The Freedom of Information Act that would pry loose reams of additional material was still years away. The questions were still questions, and some of the best critics were frankly despairing that there would ever be answers. Congress was interested, yet it failed to act. If there was ever to be a solution, the critics would have to look outside themselves. Only official power, the power of subpoena and investigation, would supply the answers they sought.

Then on March 1, 1967, at the very height of the furor over the Warren Commission, a man with just those powers appeared and made a dramatic announcement. He had found the answers. He had solved the case.

4

Charade in New Orleans

> On that day . . . when crime dons the apparel of innocence, it is innocence that is called upon to justify its existence.
>
> —Albert Camus

THE PRESS CONFERENCE in the office of the district attorney of Orleans Parish was noisy and crowded, which suited D.A. Jim Garrison just fine. A handsome, hulking figure, 6′6″ and weighing well over 200 pounds, the "Jolly Green Giant," as he was known locally, liked his doings to be as big and as colorful as he was, and that was considerable. He had a flair for sensing what the press wanted, and he always came through, from taking reporters along on a bust of one of the gay bars in the French Quarter to ensuring that they were present for the bookings of the minor racketeers he was always arresting. Jim Garrison always delivered. And now he was about to deliver the biggest story of all. There was an expectant buzz in the room.

For months rumors had wafted through New Orleans that Big Jim was digging into the Kennedy case, that indeed he had cracked it, and that arrests were imminent. One of the local newspapers had even printed a story flatly stating that it was so.[1] But Garrison played coy: "I will neither confirm that nor deny that," the prosecutor said.[2] New Orleanians smirked and winked at one another. Garrison was on to something all right.

New Orleans was a natural place to look. In what would prove to be the last year of his life Oswald had spent six months in this, the city of his birth, arriving on the night bus from Dallas on April 25, 1963.

He drifted from job to job, telling his wife, who had briefly joined him, that he was involved in "photographic work," [3] when, in fact, he was greasing coffee machines down the block from the headquarters of a Cuban exile organization. In his spare time Oswald read works about communism and revolution, and *John F. Kennedy: A Political Profile* by William Manchester.[4] He also organized a chapter of the Fair Play for Cuba Committee. Oswald was its only member. Its chairman was listed as A. J. Hidell, Oswald's alias. Oswald devoted at least as much effort to infiltrating anti-Castro organizations. To one such group he claimed to have experience in guerrilla warfare and offered to train Cubans to fight Castro, suggesting how they might blow up the Huey P. Long Bridge, derail trains, and make zip guns and gunpowder.[5] When he was exposed as an infiltrator he got into a fight with some anti-Castro Cubans, was arrested, and on being hauled into jail, promptly asked to speak to an agent from the FBI. In the meantime he secured a new passport and applied for a visa to the Soviet Union.

Such activities would have raised anyone's eyebrows, even if Oswald had not been the accused assassin of the President of the United States. Both the Warren Commission and the FBI spent considerable time tracking Oswald's life, but after months of effort they came away with mere tracings. The substance of what lay behind Oswald's movements remained hidden. New Orleans was a puzzle.

The Mardi Gras city relished such intrigue, reveled in fantasy so black. Its prosecutor was no exception. He lusted after adventure. During World War II he had served as an artillery officer and as pilot of an unarmed spotter plane.[6] He joined the FBI after his discharge, became bored, and reenlisted, eventually rising to the rank of lieutenant colonel in the National Guard. Since his election as district attorney in 1961, Garrison had conducted a running battle with the city's judicial and legal establishment,[7] a pose that only raised him in the estimation of most New Orleanians. He was a scrapper, loud, reckless, two-fisted, and what New Orleans liked best, quick to call down damnation on whatever establishment faced him at a particular moment. Even before the Kennedy case his exploits had made him a local figure of legendary renown. What was not so well known was that in 1951 Garrison had been relieved from active duty, and discharged in 1952, for what the army doctors diagnosed as chronic, moderate anxiety reaction, manifested by chronic hypochondriasis, exhaustion syndrome, gastrointestinal discomfort, and an allergy to lint. *Look* magazine, which reported these findings after the Shaw trial, continued: "He was also found to have a mother dependency. He was diagnosed as totally incapacitated for military service and moderately impaired for civilian life. Long-term psychotherapy was recommended." [8]

Sick or not, there was no way anyone was going to keep Jim Garrison away from the Kennedy case. He was on it within two days after the assassination. Acting on a tip that a local man had been involved in the plot as a getaway pilot, Garrison arrested a pilot and private investigator—and alleged friend of Oswald's—named David William Ferrie and held him briefly for questioning.[9] Just two months before his announcement in March 1967 Garrison had brought in another man for questioning, Clay Shaw, one of the city's most prominent businessmen and the retired director of the New Orleans Trade Mart.[10] Then, only days before, Ferrie had been found dead at home,* [11] the victim, it was whispered, of suicide, or maybe worse. Garrison's investigation was boiling over.

At last it was time for the announcement. Garrison didn't mince any words. Arrested and taken into custody, he said, was Clay L. Shaw. The charge: "participation in the conspiracy to murder John F. Kennedy." There was a low whistle in the back of the room. "My staff and I solved the assassination weeks ago," Garrison went on. "I wouldn't say this if we

---

* The same day Ferrie died Elidia del Valle, his friend, employer, and fellow plotter against Castro, was found dead in a Miami parking lot. Del Valle had been shot in the heart. His murderer, apparently leaving nothing to chance, also split his head open with an ax.[12] The crime has never been solved.

didn't have evidence beyond a shadow of a doubt. We know the key individuals, the cities involved, and how it was done."[13]

Thus began one of the most bizarre episodes in American legal history, one which, by its end, would produce unprecedented rulings by a federal court, damage careers, shatter reputations, and drive the critics of the Warren Commission almost totally underground.

The Garrison trial proved nothing; two years to the day after his arrest an Orleans Parish jury acquitted Shaw of the charges. Shaw, drained and shattered from the experience, died not long afterward, and Garrison, after surviving trials of his own on charges of bribery and income-tax evasion, was driven from office.[14] It was nonetheless a watershed in the Kennedy investigation. Never before had any authorities taken seriously the notion of a conspiracy in the assassination. Thanks to the trial, it would be years before they would again.

The crime Clay Shaw was accused of was conspiracy, not murder. According to Garrison, who not only leaked details of his case but announced them on national television on the Johnny Carson show,[15] the men Shaw supposedly conspired with constituted a fair representation of the New Orleans lowlife. The dramatis personae of the plot included Ferrie; Oswald; a Cuban exile named Carlos Quiroga;[16] W. Guy Banister, a former FBI agent and private detective deeply involved in anti-Castro activities; and Edgar Eugene Bradley,[17] a Californian whose only apparent offense was having a name like Eugene Hale Brading, the reported organized crime associate who was found in the Dal-Tex Building after the assassination.[18]

It was Ferrie who had first attracted Garrison's notice. Under any circumstances David William Ferrie would have been hard to overlook. He was a character who seemed to have been taken from the comic strips: a would-be priest who was bounced out of two seminaries for erratic personal behavior, who finally wound up a self-ordained "bishop" in the Orthodox Old Catholic Church of North America, a church of his own creation;[19] a would-be fighter-pilot who had once written to the secretary of defense demanding, "There is nothing I would enjoy better than blowing the hell out of every damn Russian, Communist, Red or what-have-you. . . . Between my friends and I we can cook up a crew that can really blow them to hell. . . . I want to train killers, however bad that sounds. It is what we need";[20] a would-be cancer researcher who kept hundreds of white mice in his apartment;[21] a would-be soldier of fortune who worked as a private investigator, gunrunner, thief, and—at the controls of a private plane over Cuba—bomber pilot.[22] Completing the image was that Ferrie, a victim of alopecia,[23] had lost all his body hair, a deficiency he attempted to correct by wearing a red wig and gluing what appeared to be tufts of carpeting to what had once been his eyebrows. It was this man, Jim Garrison would say later, who would be remembered as "one of history's most important individuals."[24]

The day of the assassination Ferrie was in a federal courtroom in New Orleans,[25] looking on as his employer of the moment, Carlos Marcello, the organized crime boss of New Orleans, was being cleared of charges that had resulted in his temporary deportation two years before.[26] In "celebration" of Marcello's victory, Ferrie and two friends decided to drive a thousand miles to Texas to go ice-skating and do some "goose hunting."[27] They set off in the midst of a torrential thunderstorm, drove all night, and arrived at a Houston ice-skating rink midday on the twenty-third.[28] A witness later testified that neither Ferrie nor any of his companions did any ice-skating. Instead, Ferrie hung around a pay telephone at the rink for two hours. The phone finally rang and Ferrie picked it up. When he completed the call he and his companions left the rink.[29] If they were bound for goose hunting they would have a problem. They hadn't brought along any guns.[30]

Garrison learned of Ferrie's trip and the possibility that Ferrie might have been the pilot of a getaway plane for Oswald, from a New Orleans private detective who in a later interview with the FBI claimed he had invented the entire story.[31] The trip was real enough, but after two days of questioning Garrison was unable to shake Ferrie's story.[32] The Secret Service also interviewed Ferrie, and, for reasons which are still unexplained, pressed him about whether he had ever lent Oswald his library card.[33] Ferrie denied that he had, or that he even knew Oswald. If Ferrie had lent Oswald his library card, it was not listed among Oswald's personal possessions. Ferrie was released.

There the matter might have ended were it not for an airplane trip Garrison took from New Orleans to New York in November 1966 in the company of two distinguished passengers, Joseph M. Rault, Jr., a wealthy New Orleans oilman, and Louisiana Senator Russell B. Long. During the flight the conversation drifted to the Kennedy assassination, then very much in the news, and Long remarked that the Warren Commission's version of the truth was full of holes. "If I were investigating," he said, "I'd find the hundred best riflemen in the world and find the ones who were in Dallas that day." [34] Garrison needed no further coaxing. When he returned to New Orleans his investigation resumed in earnest.

Ferrie was put under round-the-clock surveillance and cameras were installed in front of his house.[35] Meanwhile Garrison set about checking out old leads. One of them was a story told by a New Orleans lawyer named Dean Adams Andrews. Shortly after the assassination Andrews informed the Secret Service that Oswald had come to his office several times during the summer of 1963 looking for help in converting his "undesirable" discharge from the Marine Corps to an honorable one. The day after the assassination, Andrews added, he received a phone call from a man he knew as "a lawyer without a briefcase" [36] for local homosexuals, requesting that he go to Dallas and defend Oswald. The lawyer's name, Andrews said, was "Clay Bertrand." [37]

That was one version of Andrews's story. In another, told to the FBI, he admitted the whole thing had been a hoax.[38] Finally, before the Warren Commission, he recalled recently seeing Bertrand in a bar, only now he was "a boy." [39]

Garrison chose to regard the first version of Andrews's story as the truth, and subsequently decided that the name "Clay Bertrand" was an alias for Clay Shaw, the director of the New Orleans Trade Mart. There was no evidence to substantiate such a conclusion—on the contrary, Andrews had testified that "Bertrand" was a "boy," 5′5″ to 5′8″ with sandy hair, while Shaw was in his mid-fifties, had white hair, and stood 6′4″—only Garrison's unique powers of deduction. Shaw spoke Spanish and so did Bertrand. Shaw was a homosexual and so was Bertrand. Shaw's first name was Clay, so was Bertrand's. Ergo, Clay Shaw had to be Clay Bertrand.[40]

From then on Garrison's efforts were directed at making his hypothesis stick. In his search he operated remarkably like the Warren Commission. Any evidence that led away from Shaw, however credible, was discarded, while any testimony pointing toward him, however improbable, was readily accepted as fact. Given those ground rules, it was not overly difficult to turn up leads. Ironically, some of them came from the Warren Commission itself, which had also, albeit briefly, looked into Ferrie's background, as well as that of Guy Banister.[41] One of the witnesses the Commission turned up was a man named Edward Voebel, who testified that as a teenager he had belonged to the Civil Air Patrol in New Orleans. Ferrie, Voebel testified, was the commander of the unit, and one of the young cadets was Lee Harvey Oswald.[42] Garrison seized on the link.

As Garrison's probe continued, even more startling informants appeared. David F. Lewis, a sometime private investigator, told Garrison that he had been present at a meeting in 1962 between Banister, Ferrie, Carlos Quiroga, and a person he remembered as "Leon" Oswald, whom he later thought he recognized as Lee Harvey Oswald.[43] Shortly after making these revelations Lewis dropped from sight.[44] There were, in any case, problems with his story. Quiroga flatly denied it, before he too disappeared from view.[45] Moreover, it was doubtful that "Leon" Oswald was the same man as Lee Harvey Oswald, who, according to the Warren

Commission, was living in Texas at the time of the supposed meeting.[46] Garrison nevertheless dispatched an investigator to Miami to blueprint the activities of the anti-Castro exiles, and how Ferrie, Banister, and Quiroga fitted into them.[47] Just as this trail turned cold another informant turned up, a self-proclaimed ex-CIA man and antieavesdropping specialist named Gordon Novel. Novel volunteered that in 1961 he, Ferrie, two unidentified Cubans, and an exile leader named Sergio Arcacha Smith had raided an arms locker in Houma, Louisiana, and had subsequently dropped off some of the arms at the office of none other than Guy Banister.[48] On the basis of this information Garrison hired Novel as one of his investigators. In time Novel turned against him, finally fleeing the state when Garrison began to suspect that he, Novel, was part of the plot.[49] Years later Novel turned up in Washington at the side of Charles Colson. Novel had lost none of his flair. To Colson, Novel suggested secretly erasing the White House tapes at long distance, using "laser cannon." Later still he moved to Dallas, confidently awaiting what he said was his imminent appointment to the directorship of CIA.[50]

Novel was mild-mannered in comparison to Garrison's star witness, a twenty-five-year-old Baton Rouge insurance salesman named Perry Raymond Russo. Garrison's first contact with Russo had come in a letter Russo wrote to the D.A. stating that he had known David Ferrie and possessed interesting information about him.[51] In late February 1967 Garrison sent his chief assistant to Baton Rouge to interview Russo.[52] During the two-hour interview Russo claimed that he and Ferrie had been partners in a deal to sell pornographic films to Cuba, but that Ferrie's principal interests lay in more exotic fields of endeavor.[52a] He quoted Ferrie as hinting how easy it would be to shoot a president and flee to Mexico or Brazil, and that one day he would "get" Kennedy.[53] Russo, however, made no mention of any plot.[54] That came only after Garrison had jogged his memory, first with truth serum, under whose influence he supposedly recalled meeting with a man named "Bertrand," [55] and later under hypnosis, when at long last the details of the alleged plot came spilling out.[56] During his trance Russo recalled having attended a party at Ferrie's apartment in September 1963. At the party three men discussed the details of the forthcoming assassination, the need for an appropriate scapegoat, and possible means of escape. The three men, according to Russo, were Ferrie, a tall, white-haired man named "Clem Bertrand," and the ubiquitous "Leon" Oswald, whom, at length, Russo identified as Lee Harvey Oswald.[57]

Only one of the alleged plotters was still alive. In mid-February Garrison had picked up Ferrie for "protective custody," and had grilled him for two days before finally releasing him.[58] On February 22, the day after his release, and three days before the arrival of Russo's fateful letter, Ferrie was found dead in his apartment, the result, the coroner later determined, of a cerebral hemorrhage caused by the rupture of a blood vessel.[59] Within the week Garrison placed Shaw under arrest and called his press conference.

The announcement that an arrest had been made in the Kennedy assassination set off pandemonium among the Commission's critics, a number of whom flocked to New Orleans, where they quickly found employment on Garrison's staff. There was such eagerness to believe that even some of the more respected critics overlooked the obvious holes in Garrison's case—the very sort of omissions and distortions for which they had lambasted the Warren Commission—and, minds determinedly closed, enlisted in his cause. Their decision, if inexcusable, was at least understandable. Garrison promised the answers they had all been searching for, the power they had always lacked. And there was something about the man himself, the charm he exuded, the quiet fervor of his voice, the flattery he dispensed to one and all, assuring each critic that it had been *his* work which had opened his eyes.[60] Most of all Jim Garrison told them what they wanted to hear. John Kennedy, he said, had been the victim of a right-wing cabal, a conspiracy involving anti-Castro Cubans, and yes, as they had suspected all along, elements of the Central Intelligence Agency.[61] When

Mark Lane, who had been one of the first to arrive in New Orleans, asked Garrison how he knew all this, the D.A. fixed him with a stare and shot back: "Which group do you think did it, retired circus clowns?" [62]

And so the true believers took the plunge, leaping into the sparkling pool of illusion that was Jim Garrison's case, not knowing that at its bottom was an open drain, sucking all of them down. Lane became Garrison's closest confidant, his guru,[63] many said, consulting with him on bits of evidence, informing the press that he too knew the identities of the killers,[64] and in his spare moments writing what Garrison called "an unofficial history" of the investigation.[65] Richard Popkin, author of *The Second Oswald,* flew into New Orleans from his teaching post in California, had dinner with Garrison, and came away proclaiming that "the case had been solved." * [66] Penn Jones, the Texas newspaper editor who had first noticed the mysterious deaths of the assassination witnesses (by 1975, he had logged more than fifty),[68] kept track of developments in the Lone Star state, while Harold Weisberg, author of the *Whitewash* books, pored through the Warren Commission volumes looking for new leads. Garrison welcomed them all. Indeed, he gave several of the critics, notably Jones Harris and Ed Epstein, the run of his files and access to all the "evidence," including Shaw's and Ferrie's personal belongings.[69] Eventually Harris and Epstein became suspicious of Garrison and his methods, and turned from supporters to critics.[70] Thomas Bethel, a young Englishmen who had come to New Orleans out of love for jazz and eventually wound up as custodian of the files, shared their fears to such an extent that before the trial began he turned over a xeroxed copy of virtually Garrison's entire case to Shaw and his attorneys.[71]

But for Bethel's defection Garrison, proof or no, might well have won a conviction, so totally did he

---

* Popkin's original judgment seemed to be infectious. In the summer of 1975, the philosophy professor, working with materials even more dubious than Garrison's, announced that he too had "cracked the case," and that the culprits were a group of "zombie assassins," programmed, a la Manchurian candidate, by the CIA.[67]

dominate New Orleans. He was a populist demagogue in the tradition of Huey Long, and like his mentor he was not about to let the niceties of due process interfere with a case that had already won him national recognition, and if successfully pursued would, it was said in New Orleans, bring Jim Garrison bigger things, a Senate seat, maybe even more. He played the press, at least in the beginning, masterfully. Knowing of journalists' constant hunger for access, Garrison sated it. After Shaw's arrest he offered to conduct "a joint investigation" with a team of reporters from *Life,* and for ten weeks did just that, the *Life* reporters, in effect, working as investigators for the D.A. in what Garrison termed "an exchange of information." [72] Not to be outdone, *Playboy* accorded Garrison the longest interview in the magazine's history. In the course of seventeen pages of questions and answers Garrison laid out the sum and substance of the case against Shaw, ignoring a court order which forbade him to discuss the case in public. "A number of the men who killed the President were former employees of the CIA involved in its anti-Castro underground activities in the New Orleans area," Garrison proclaimed. "The CIA knows their identity. So do I." [73] Copy like that was difficult to ignore. "Jim has a philosophy about national headlines," said William Gurvich, a Garrison investigator who left the D.A.'s staff and was promptly indicted for petty larceny on a charge that he had taken copies of files worth nineteen dollars. "He believes that everyone reads the headlines concerning arrests and charges but few people read denials or correcting statements." [74] Accusing the CIA thus suited Garrison perfectly. "They can't afford to answer," as Garrison himself once put it.[75] To Lane, Garrison boasted that the government would never dare let the case go to trial.[76] In fact, he was counting on it; it was the very heart of his strategy. Another tactic was to solidify his support in New Orleans by persuasion, and if need be by intimidation. With Garrison's blessing a group of wealthy businessmen formed a fund to support his investigation and thus spare Garrison the unpleasantness of complying with a law that required public disclosure of his expenses. A $5000 contributor to the fund, which was dubbed "Truth or Consequences, Inc.,"[77] turned out to be John McKeithen, Louisiana's governor. When reporters asked McKeithen if he had any criticism of Garrison's investigation, McKeithen said he had none —"and even if I did, I wouldn't voice it. I have learned that most of Garrison's enemies are buried—politically speaking—and I don't want to join the list of the deceased."[78]

As Garrison's pretenses were stripped away, his accusations grew wilder. Where once he had been content to blame an amorphous group of Cuban exiles and revanchist ex-CIA men, he continued to expand the list of plotters to include Minutemen, oil millionaires, munitions exporters, White Russians, the Dallas police, members of the Dallas establishment, and unidentified elements of "the invisible Nazi substructure."[79] He saw assassins everywhere: in the School Book Depository, in the Dal-Tex Building, on the grassy knoll, in the bushes, behind the picket fence, even in the storm drain by the side of Elm Street, until finally his list stretched to seventeen people in all.[80] If there was a witness or reporter with the temerity to challenge his investigation Garrison simply indicted him—more than a dozen by the time he was finished, including three newsmen and two former members of his own staff.[81] Garrison said all of them were joined in a plot against him, their coconspirators the United States Supreme Court, the White House, the CIA, the FBI, and the Kennedys.[82] "Judging from the careful coordination which the Establishment showed in its last offensive against the case," Garrison said at one point, "it is safe to expect that the other elements of the federal government and the national press will now follow up with a new effort to discredit the case and the prosecution."[83] Before long, Garrison began to talk of his own assassination: "There's a torpedo from Havana after me, but they always sleep late."[84]

In the midst of it all, serene, quietly genteel, still possessed of his sanity, and even more remarkably, his good humor, was the almost forgotten man, the defendant in the case, Clay L. Shaw. It was hard to imagine Shaw mixed up with the kind of characters Garrison placed in the plot to murder John F. Kennedy. He was a shy, retiring man, a connoisseur of fine antiques and Restoration period architecture. If there was one thing that stood out about him it was his utter civility. Even as Garrison hounded him, Shaw could only express pity for his persecutor, venturing the opinion that perhaps the poor man was "quite ill." [85]

A striking, imposing figure, 6′4″ with a great shock of white hair, Shaw had been an army officer during World War II, and dabbled in theater before turning to business in New Orleans. The building of the $14 million International Trade Mart had been his crowning achievement. Shaw was a liberal and enjoyed a good reputation among New Orleans blacks and Jews. He said he favored the Alliance for Progress, and had voted for John Kennedy in 1960. Five years later, Shaw retired from business to devote full time to his twin avocations: the restoring of homes in the French Quarter to their former elegance, and playwriting. He planned, he said, to write a play based on the life of Antonio de Ulloa, the first Spanish governor of Louisiana. But that was before he ran into Jim Garrison.[86]

Shaw's first encounter with Garrison had been two days before Christmas 1966. Shaw was invited down to the district attorney's office and asked if he would answer a few questions. Shaw willingly complied, and did not bother to bring an attorney with him. One of the assistant D.A.'s told him that Oswald had been observed passing out Fair Play for Cuba leaflets in front of the International Trade Mart, the building of which he, Shaw, was director. Did Shaw know Oswald? Did Shaw know anything about the Cuban consulate, which maintained offices in the building? Had Shaw ever been acquainted with David Ferrie? Shaw answered no to all the questions and went on to a Christmas party at City Hall.[87] Two months later Shaw noticed that there was a car sitting outside his house, with two men in it who looked like detectives. After a while the men came to the door and introduced themselves as insurance salesmen. They said they were taking a survey of people's insurance needs. In fact, one of the men was from Garrison's office. The other was Perry Raymond Russo, brought along to see if he could identify Shaw as the elusive Clay Bertrand.[88] A day later a friend of Shaw's called him and told him that she had heard on television that Garrison had issued a subpoena for him.[89] The news surprised Shaw but did not frighten him. Curious, he went down to the D.A.'s office, again not taking a lawyer with him. This time the interrogation was more pointed. Shaw was told that if he did not agree to take a lie detector test the D.A. would indict him for conspiracy in the assassination of President John F. Kennedy. Shaw was stunned. "You've got to be kidding," was all he could say. "You've *got* to be kidding." [90] But Garrison was not playing games. Later, Shaw told writer James Kirkwood, who covered his trial and became his friend, "I was always one who thought Kafka rather overstated things. . . . Boy, have I changed, what a fellow feeling I have for K. now!" [91]

In part it was Shaw's demeanor which helped convince the press that the Garrison investigation was a grotesque charade. Shaw simply didn't seem the type who could plot anything, much less murder. Initially much of the press had been, if not receptive to Garrison, at least intrigued by his case. But as reporters began to check out Garrison's facts and discover them to be fiction, the press turned on him with a vengeance. The first major blow came from James Phelan, a reporter and once one of Garrison's friends. Phelan made the hegira to New Orleans, examined the available evidence, and turned to his typewriter to excoriate Garrison and his staff in a long article in the *Saturday Evening Post* which revealed, among other things, that Russo had made no mention of meeting with the plotters during his first interview with Garrison's investigator.[92] The most serious damage to Garrison, however, came from a half-hour NBC news special entitled: "The J.F.K. Conspiracy: The Case of Jim Garrison." The main architect of the program was Walter Sheridan, a significant choice of reporters.[93] For Sheridan had served as an assistant to former Attorney General Robert Kennedy, and was instrumental in digging up the evidence that finally sent Teamster boss Jimmy Hoffa to jail on a jury-tampering charge. Sheridan had not been in New Orleans long before he was approached with an offer of "help" in his investigation. The offer came from Zachary "Red" Strate, a New Orleans builder who had been convicted with Jimmy Hoffa of defrauding the Teamsters' pension fund of more than a million dollars.[93a] When Sheridan inquired what Strate wanted in return for his "help," Strate replied: "That's easy. Hoffa out of prison. You two [Sheridan and Robert Kennedy] won the war—now, why don't you let him go?" [94] Sheridan did not need such assistance. He pursued the story on his own and eventually discovered that Garrison's investigators had tried to bribe three potential witnesses to testify against Shaw; that Garrison's staff had attempted to induce a burglar to plant false evidence in Shaw's home; and that Garrison had allowed two key witnesses, one of them Russo, to testify against Shaw even though they had failed lie detector tests.[95]

By the time Shaw finally came to trial, Garrison's case was in shreds. The D.A. himself rarely showed up at the courtroom, which was just as well, for the humiliation was far from over. The "secret evidence" that Garrison and his defenders like Lane promised would "shake the nation to its foundations" [96] was not forthcoming. Garrison seemed to have forgotten all about it. Instead his assistants called a parade of witnesses to the stand, many of whom proved more valuable to the defense. Perry Raymond Russo, the state's star witness, admitted that the conspiratorial meeting he had recalled with benefit of hypnosis could easily have been "an inconsequential bull session." [97] With that Shaw's lawyers bored in.

> Q. Isn't it a fact you didn't really take this seriously?
>
> A. Initially, you couldn't believe Ferrie, and you couldn't not believe him.
>
> Q. Didn't this have all the characteristics of a bull session?
>
> A. Every characteristic.[98]

A New Orleans police lieutenant then testified that before coming into court, Russo admitted to him that he planned to deliberately lie about Shaw because he didn't like Shaw's attorney.

"He said your questions 'turned him on' when you kept asking him whether he believed in God—which is a very sensitive point with him—and he decided he was going to bury you," the lieutenant informed Shaw's lawyer. "Bury me?" the lawyer asked. "Bury you," the lieutenant replied.[99]

It was all downhill from there. One would-be witness for the state appeared in court clad in a toga, and, when asked his identity, calmly replied, "Julius Caesar." [100] But the lowest ebb came when a mild-mannered New York businessman named Charles Speisel took the stand. All went well as long as Garrison's deputies examined him. Speisel testified that he had come to New Orleans in May 1963. During his visit, Speisel said, he bumped into an old chum from the air force who turned out to be David Ferrie.[101] Ferrie invited Speisel to a party in an apartment in the French Quarter, where he was introduced to the host, who was identified as Clay Shaw. As Speisel recalled: "Somebody brought up the name of President Kennedy and just about everybody began to criticize him. Then someone said that 'somebody ought to kill the son of a b!' " [102] The talk, Speisel continued, turned to the mechanics of such an operation, and someone suggested that "it would have to be done with a high-power rifle with a telescopic sight and about a mile away." Then, according to Speisel, Shaw piped up with the possibility that the killer could escape by plane, an idea he began to discuss with David Ferrie.[103]

Then the defense had their turn with Speisel, and within moments it was obvious that they had done their homework. "Isn't it true," one of Shaw's attorneys asked, "you filed a suit in New York in 1964 against a psychiatrist and the City of New York, claiming that over a period of several years the police and others have constantly hypnotized you and finally harassed you out of business?" [104] With that the once composed

Mr. Speisel started to disintegrate. Yes, it was true, he admitted, and it was also true that his father had done undercover work for the FBI, and that the whole thing might just be a Communist conspiracy. And, yes, it was also true that a number of people had hypnotized him; maybe fifty or sixty, Speisel guessed.[105] Finally, as gently as he could, the defense attorney inquired how Speisel knew he was being hypnotized. Well, Speisel said, "When someone tries to get your attention —catch your eye. That's a clue right off." [106]

Amid such macabre testimony the prosecution team fashioned an equally macabre case for conspiracy. The Zapruder film was shown over and over again, until each gut-wrenching detail was burned into the memory of everyone in the courtroom. Autopsy results were pulled apart, angles of fire triangulated, FBI agents grilled over every fine point of detail. All the doubts, questions, and suspicions of the last five years made their appearance once more, like actors in a tragicomedy gone on the road a final time. None of it mattered. For it was not the existence of a conspiracy that the jury was deciding, but whether Clay Shaw had plotted to murder the President. And on the basis of the testimony and the evidence, a reasonable man could come to only one conclusion. Quite clearly, Shaw hadn't.

All that remained was the denouement. The jury was out only fifty minutes before it brought back its verdict. The foreman almost shouted it: "Not guilty!" Garrison's subsequent attempt to try Shaw on charges of perjury was blocked when a federal court, in a ruling unique in United States legal history, forbade his prosecution. Within months Judge Edward Haggerty, who had tried the case, was arrested in a raid on a stag party.[107] Shortly thereafter an item appeared in Jack Anderson's column reporting that Garrison had been accused of sexually molesting a young boy in the locker room of a New Orleans athletic club.[107a] Garrison beat that rap, but more trouble was in store. In 1973 he was indicted by a federal grand jury on charges of conspiring to protect illegal pinball machine operators.[108] He was acquitted of that charge as well as a subsequent indictment for income-tax evasion.[109] The charges left Garrison's already tattered reputation in ruins. In December 1973 he was beaten in the Democratic primary for renomination as district attorney.[110] Clay Shaw lived only long enough to see his vindication. A year after Garrison's defeat Shaw, drained and shattered, died quietly of cancer.[111]

For all practical purposes the serious investigation of John Kennedy's assassination was dead, too. Lane made a quixotic run for the vice-presidency on a ticket headed by comedian Dick Gregory, then drifted off to Vietnam protest and Indian rights struggles. The rest of the critics, broken and dispirited, scattered, some more paranoid than ever, convinced that the Garrison investigation had been the victim of a plot hatched by the CIA and the Kennedy family, others that it was Garrison himself who had been the plotter, trying Shaw only because he and those behind him knew it would end, once and for all, the clamor over the Warren Commission Report.

In fact, Jim Garrison undermined himself. He was a megalomaniac rather than a plotter. Asserting that he was somehow a part of a conscious cover-up might assuage the embarrassment of the critics who had been taken in by him, but Garrison's real motive was at the same time simpler and more complex. Stated starkly, it was furthering Jim Garrison. Politics to him was almost peripheral. Like a true demagogue, Garrison cared not for facts or ideology, merely for himself. It was ambition—and his own distorted view of the world—that drove him and crushed others beneath him. The critics were right in one sense, though. The trial of Clay Shaw did doom serious investigation of the Kennedy assassination. The bills in Congress asking for a new investigation were quietly shelved. The reporters who had spent months digging up leads put away their notebooks. Years would pass before anyone, save a hard-core band of diehards, would take the notion of conspiracy seriously again.

And yet, in the midst of the wreckage that had been the Garrison investigation, a few key facts remained unchallenged, a few key questions unanswered.

The testimony of Colonel Pierre Finck, one of the surgeons at Kennedy's autopsy (who ironically had been called as a defense witness), put into greater doubt than ever the medical findings that were so crucial to the single-assassin thesis. Under cross-examination by the prosecution Finck made some remarkable admissions. At one point one of Garrison's assistants asked Finck why, contrary to standard autopsy practice, none of the Bethesda doctors had called the doctors in Parkland before or during the autopsy. "I can't explain that," Finck conceded. "We had a wound of entry, and we had seen no exit and we knew there was no bullet in the cadaver. There was a very strong reason for inquiring [of the Parkland doctors] if there was another wound."[112] Finck also admitted that he and the other members of the autopsy team were not permitted to review the autopsy photographs and X rays before delivering their testimony to the Warren Commission.[113] But the most damning confession involved the President's back wound. At the autopsy the doctors had not fully probed it, and hence could not determine the track of the bullet. The track was vital to the single-assassin thesis, and for years the critics had puzzled why it had not been established. Now, under persistent questioning, Finck had an answer.

"I did not dissect the track in the neck," Finck began.[114] "Why?" the prosecutor pressed. "As I recall I didn't remove the organs of the neck," Finck answered.[115] Again the question came: Why? "We were told to examine the head wounds," Finck replied. "I was told that the family wanted the examination of the wounds of the neck and head."[116] Now the prosecutor was insistent: "Why didn't you trace the track of the neck wound?" Finally Finck answered: "As I recall I was told not to, but I don't recall by whom."[117] The next day the prosecutor again returned to the attack. "Doctor, you did take orders and didn't dissect the throat area?" "They were not orders," Finck said lamely. "They were suggestions."[118] The prosecutor shot back sarcastically: "Now, doctor, there were admirals and generals present, and you were only a lieutenant colonel."[119] To that the defense objected.

There were no more answers. Dr. Finck was excused from the stand.

Then there was the defendant himself. While no credible witness had been able to swear that Shaw had plotted with Ferrie, Oswald, or anyone else for that matter, a number of seemingly disinterested witnesses had testified to seeing Shaw, Ferrie, and Oswald together. These witnesses came to be known as "the Clinton people," the name coming from a little town where, in late August or early September 1963, a black Cadillac arrived bearing three strangers. Those strangers, various witnesses testified, were Shaw, Oswald, and Ferrie. The town barber remembered giving Oswald a haircut; [120] a state representative, telling him to register to vote; [121] the town marshal, speaking to the driver of the Cadillac,[122] whom he identified as Clay Shaw; the registrar of voters, spotting Ferrie and Shaw sitting in the parked car,[123] and later, Oswald standing in a registration line; [124] a CORE worker, also seeing Oswald, Shaw, and Ferrie in the car.[125] Though their testimony differed in some details, the Clinton people made compelling witnesses for the prosecution. They were diverse, plain, homespun, and, especially when compared to the other witnesses who appeared on the state's behalf, easy to believe.

The trouble was that one of Garrison's assistants had brought the Clinton people into court several days before their appearance on the stand for the express purpose of pointing Shaw out to them.[126] This coaching could well have influenced their identification of Shaw as the man they saw with Ferrie and Oswald. Moreover, Shaw bore a remarkable resemblance to Guy Banister. Both men were tall, middle-aged, and white-haired. Possibly, then, the Clinton people saw Banister and mistook him for Shaw.

In any case, the Clinton testimony did not prove the existence of a conspiracy. It did, however, put Oswald in odd company. If, in fact, Oswald knew Ferrie during his days in the Civil Air Patrol that might account for their relationship in New Orleans, and, of course, the friendship could have been altogether innocent. If Shaw knew Ferrie, their acquaintance might have well come as a result of their mutual prominence in New Orleans's homosexual community. One can speculate, then, that it was Ferrie who introduced Oswald to Shaw.

Garrison saw the machinations of the CIA behind their relationship, but he was never able to prove it. Shaw, it was true, had been the director of the International Trade Mart, reputed to be a center of intrigue in New Orleans. The CIA does maintain a sizable office in New Orleans from which it directs much of its operations in Latin America, and during the early sixties coordinated the activities of anti-Castro exiles;[127] the office, however, is not located in the International Trade Mart.[128] Garrison's evidence that Shaw either was or had been a CIA man seemed to consist of equal parts of rumor and wishful thinking. As it turns out the wishful thinking may have been right. For in early 1975 Victor Marchetti, the former executive assistant to then CIA Director Richard Helms, and coauthor of *The CIA and the Cult of Intelligence,* publicly quoted aides of Helms as saying that Shaw and Ferrie were former contract employees of the Agency.[129] According to Marchetti the Garrison investigation was of considerable interest at a number of Helms's morning staff meetings, with Helms asking his aides how the case was progressing, and according to Marchetti, encouraging them to do whatever they could on Shaw's behalf. After one such meeting, Marchetti later recounted, he asked another aide why there was so much interest in Shaw and was informed that the director of the International Trade Mart had been a former contract employee of the Agency, but that he was no longer, and that there was no evidence to suggest that he had been a part of a plot to murder the President.[130]

Marchetti's disclosure raises some provocative questions. If, as the CIA told the Warren Commission, the Agency was not in contact with Oswald after his return from the Soviet Union, why, then, were two of its employees squiring him around Louisiana in a Cadillac?

The answer possibly might be contained in the FBI's interrogation of Ferrie two days after the assassination. The bulk of that interview, some thirty-six pages, remains one of the last documents from the Warren Commission still classified and under seal at the National Archives.[131] One brief FBI report that is available mentions that Ferrie admitted being "publicly and privately" critical of Kennedy for withholding air cover from the Bay of Pigs, and had used expressions like "He ought to be shot." [132] The agents who questioned Ferrie decided, however, that he did not mean the threat literally.[133]

Anyone who came into contact with David Ferrie always found it difficult to sort out what he meant and what he didn't mean, who he was and what he wasn't. He seemed a fitting candidate for an asylum. Yet, many of his acquaintances counted him a genius—twisted, demonic, living in a fantasy world of his own creation, but a genius nonetheless. He was a man of many passions, for violence, for adventure, for young boys, and of course for flying. Ferrie was a crack pilot. Among the exploits attributed to him was the piloting of several incendiary bombing raids over Cuba,[134] as well as being at the controls of the plane that returned Carlos Marcello [135] home after the New Orleans Mafia boss, at Robert Kennedy's personal order, had been unceremoniously and illegally deported to Guatemala. Given his love of intrigue it is not surprising that Ferrie was also absorbed in Cuba, and had been since the mid-fifties. At first he worked on the side of the Castro cause, soliciting New Orleans businessmen for contributions to finance the Cuban revolution.[136] Ferrie turned against Castro once the revolution succeeded. He approached Sergio Arcacha Smith, the leader of the Cuban Revolutionary Democratic Front[136a]—a CIA-created and supported coalition of Cuban exiles, organized in 1961 by Watergate burglar E. Howard Hunt [137]—and volunteered to train exiles for an invasion of Cuba.[138] Apparently Arcacha Smith looked on Ferrie's request favorably. In 1962 Ferrie was reportedly instructing exiles in paramilitary tactics at a secret camp across Lake Ponchartrain from New Orleans.[139] If Marchetti is correct, Ferrie did this at the behest of the Central Intelligence Agency.

During that time Ferrie also worked on and off as

an investigator for Guy Banister.[140] They seem to have been remarkably close. In 1961, when Ferrie was dismissed from his job as a pilot for Eastern Airlines, Banister flew to Miami to appear at a hearing on his behalf.[141] Banister was a former FBI man and had once headed the Bureau's important Chicago office.[142] In New Orleans Banister operated out of 531 Lafayette Place, which was a side entrance to the building at 544 Camp Street, the headquarters of the Cuban Revolutionary Council.[143] Banister's proximity to anti-Castro Cubans was to be expected. He had a reputation for being one of the city's most vocal anti-Castro spokesmen.[144] Banister was also an extreme rightist, a reputed member of the Minutemen[145] and publisher of the racist *Louisiana Intelligence Digest,* which suggested that integration was a Communist plot.[146] In April 1967 a copyrighted story in the *New Orleans States-Item* reported that Banister had stored fifty to one hundred boxes of grenades, mines, and various munitions in his office in 1961, shortly before the Bay of Pigs invasion.[147] Such goings on at 544 Camp Street were the routine of the day for Banister. What made them, him, and 544 Camp Street interesting is that it was also the address Lee Harvey Oswald stamped on some of his Fair Play for Cuba literature. After Banister's death his wife, while going through his belongings, came across a file drawer full of Oswald's "Hands off Cuba" leaflets.[148]

There were even more interesting tales about Oswald, Banister, and Ferrie that surfaced during the Garrison investigation, none of which could be absolutely checked out. Hugh F. Ward, one of Banister's investigators, was also said to have been mixed up with the Minutemen.[149] But before he could be questioned, Ward, who reportedly had been taught to fly by David Ferrie, died in a plane crash.[150] Another of Banister's associates was said to be Maurice Brooks Gatlin, Sr., who talked of CIA money financing an assassination attempt against Charles de Gaulle in 1962.[151] He too was never questioned. In 1964 he either fell or was pushed from a hotel-room window in Panama.[152] Gatlin himself, according to one report, had been a leading figure in the Inter-American Confederation for the Defense of the Continent, a CIA-supported front which played a major role in overthrowing the left-wing regime of Jacobo Arbenz in Guatemala.[153] The connection became more interesting with the publication some years later of E. Howard Hunt's memoirs, a portion of which are devoted to detailing the major role *he* played in getting rid of the unfortunate Mr. Arbenz, including the creation of the confederation.[154] At the charter meeting of the confederation in Mexico City a number of professional anti-Communists were reported in attendance, including Gatlin and a lawyer for Mr. Carlos Marcello of New Orleans.[155] There were other stories of incriminating missing files,[156] of Ferrie schooling Oswald in the uses of a telescopic rifle,[157] of a man identifying himself as Oswald buying trucks for Cuba when the real Lee Oswald was said to be in the Soviet Union.[158] All of them went glimmering. Witnesses changed their minds, were discredited, died, or simply disappeared until finally the truth, if indeed there had ever been any, could only be guessed at.

Quite clearly the trial of Clay Shaw was a monstrous, grotesque hoax, a charade whose existence even now is difficult to believe. Quite clearly also, Garrison, by design or pure chance, had stumbled onto something. Even after the crazies had been accounted for, there were simply too many odd coincidences to write off to pure chance. There was no denying Oswald's involvement in Cuban politics, both left and right. There was no denying that he operated in a world where the interests of crime, Cuba, and the CIA overlapped as surely as did the careers of David Ferrie, Guy Banister, and various New Orleans exiles of Oswald's acquaintance. There is, finally, no denying that much of the time Oswald spent in New Orleans in those fateful months before the assassination remained a mystery not only to Garrison but to the FBI and the Warren Commission.

The investigation by Jim Garrison, rather than solving the mystery, made the prospect of its ultimate unraveling immeasurably dimmer. It was a classic case of what is known in the intelligence trade as "disinformation." Truth mixed with half truth, scrambled with no truth at all. The purpose of disinformation is to discredit the truth. It succeeded brilliantly in New Orleans. Garrison's methods were so outrageous, his assertions so preposterous that reasonable people not only wanted to have nothing to do with them, but were repelled by the case which seemed to have started it all. A whole new phrase entered the vocabulary: a "Garrison-style investigation," a synonym for the process of justice run amok.

And therein lay the most inscrutable puzzle: the Jolly Green Giant himself. Garrison's behavior seemed almost calculated to outrage. Significantly, he thought his case against Shaw would never come to trial and when it did he absented himself from nearly all the proceedings. Garrison seemed willing to pursue any theory, however fantastic, so long as it led to the CIA. The few pieces of hard evidence failed to arouse his curiosity. Ferrie's and Banister's connections to the mob were just as well established, if not more so, than their ties to the CIA. Both men had worked as investigators for Marcello. Ferrie had been his pilot. One of the calls Ferrie made from the ice-skating rink in Houston was to Marcello's lawyer. Ferrie's companions on the "goose-hunting" trip refused to talk to police until they had benefit of counsel—Carlos Marcello's counsel.[159] There were even indications that Marcello had financed a gas station that Ferrie operated in the early sixties.[160] Garrison, however, was singularly uninterested in pursuing these facts, telling Jones Harris, who had raised the matter with him, that Ferrie's connections to Marcello were "not important." Indeed, for a prosecutor, Garrison had a decidedly benign view of the mob. His chief investigator and closest friend was an old wartime buddy named Pershing Gervais. Gervais had been thrown out of the New Orleans police department after he twice stole payoff money that was awaiting distribution to other cops.[161] Later, Gervais admitted to frequent meetings with Carlos Marcello, and called himself a "counselor for people who get arrested." [162] Garrison repeatedly asserted that there was no organized crime in New Orleans, at a time when the scale of its yearly operations in the city was reckoned at over $1 billion.[163] "People worry about the crime 'syndicate,'" Garrison said once. "But the real danger is the political establishment, power massing against the individual."[164]

The flurry of vice arrests in the early sixties that won Garrison his reputation as a "racket buster" were all of low-level operators of prostitution and gambling. Their removal from the scene helped Marcello consolidate his hold over vice and narcotics in the city.[165] Garrison enjoyed considerably less success against Marcello. Between 1965 and 1969 Garrison managed just two convictions and five guilty pleas in cases the New Orleans police made against Marcello's associates. He dismissed eighty-four cases, including twenty-two gambling charges, one of attempted murder, three of kidnapping, and one of manslaughter.[166] At the time of the Shaw trial Marcello, a convicted dope peddler and associate of Meyer Lansky and Frank Costello, was regarded by law enforcement officials as one of the most powerful organized crime figures in the United States, with a domain that sprawled east and west from New Orleans, from the Florida Gulf Coast into Texas and beyond.[167] Garrison, however, told a national television audience that Marcello was a "respectable businessman."[168] Considering the subsequent disclosures in *Look* that Garrison had purchased his expensive home at a cut-rate price from a Marcello lieutenant,[169] and that a mob "button man" had picked up his expenses (including a $5000 line of credit at a casino) during a junket to Las Vegas,[170] Garrison's generous evaluation of a man whom the records of the New Orleans police characterized as "one of the most notorious underworld figures in the country" is not surprising. Garrison, according to *Life*, "even managed to hush up the fact that last June [1969], a Marcello bagman, Vic Carona, died after suffering a heart attack during a political meeting held in Garrison's own home."[171]

Jim Garrison was like that: hard to figure.

At the beginning of his investigation Garrison told reporters that "the key to the whole case is through the looking glass. Black is white. White is black."[172] Most of the reporters assumed that Garrison was merely indulging in one of the cryptic utterances for which he was famous. What they couldn't know was that, for once, Big Jim was telling them the truth.

5

One Story Away

ON NOVEMBER 22, 1963, Merriman Smith, the UP's veteran White House correspondent, was, as befitted his rank, riding in the press pool car less than 50 yards behind the presidential limousine. When the shots echoed over Dealey Plaza Smith lunged for the radiotelephone in the back seat of the car, and as fast as he could speak began dictating the details of the story that would win him the Pulitzer prize. Sitting in the seat beside him his competition, Jack Bell of the AP, bristled with anger. Smith kept talking as Bell demanded, finally shouted for him to give up the phone. When Smith finished his story he hugged the receiver to his chest, curling up in a ball, as Bell beat him on the shoulders, grabbing desperately for the phone. Finally he wrenched it away, only to find that the line had gone dead.[1] Smith had his exclusive. By 12:39 p.m. the news was flashing over the wires:

> FLASH
> Kennedy seriously wounded
> Perhaps seriously
> Perhaps fatally by assassin's bullet
> JT1239PCS.[2]

In the newsroom of the *New York Times* one of the editors read the dispatch and reflected, "The year 2000 will see men still years from now, arguing and writing about the President's death." [3]

The *New York Times*, and most of the press with it, would never become part of that argument. When it came to the Warren Commission, the press, traditionally the most skeptical segment of American society, became instead the most willing to accept its conclusion that Lee Harvey Oswald, acting alone, murdered the President, and was himself gunned down by another lone, equally crazed assassin. The press, the *Times* in particular, devoted most of its investigative talents to filling in and explaining the gaps left by the Warren Commission rather than questioning and probing them. On September 27, 1964, the day of the Report's release, a front-page story in the *Times* reported that "the Commission analyzed every issue in exhaustive, almost archeological detail,"[4] while an editorial commented, "the facts—exhaustively gathered, independently checked and cogently set forth—destroy the basis for conspiracy theories that have grown weedlike in this country and abroad."[5] The *Times* editorial set a tone that was reflected in newspapers and on television from coast to coast. It was, to say the least, an unusual pose for an "adversary relationship" to strike. But then, the assassination of John Fitzgerald Kennedy was not a usual story.

The reporting out of Dallas on November 22 was, as could be expected, emotional, fragmentary, often laced with rumor and half-truths that never checked out. There was on a few points, however, virtual unanimity of detail. One was that the President and Governor Connally had been struck by separate bullets. Another was that at least some of the shots had come from the front. They were easy conclusions to reach. Not only were a number of witnesses telling such stories, but the reporters riding in the motorcade's press bus could see people scrambling up the knoll immediately after the shots. Finally, and most importantly, the press had the word of the doctors who had treated the President to rely on; at a press conference the afternoon of November 22, Dr. Malcolm O. Perry told reporters that the hole in the President's neck appeared to be a wound of entry.[6] Tom Wicker's account of the shooting, the first to appear in the *Times*, was typical:

> . . . the President's car was almost ready to go underneath a "triple underpass" beneath three streets—Elm, Commerce and Main—when the first shot was fired.

> That shot apparently struck Mr. Kennedy. Governor Connally turned in his seat at the sound and appeared immediately to be hit in the chest.
>
> Mr. Kennedy was hit by a bullet in the throat, just below the Adam's apple, they [the doctors] said. This wound had the appearance of a bullet's entry.[7]

There was no diverging from that reconstruction until the appearance of the Warren Report, and its finding that one bullet, rather than two, struck the President and Connally, and that the wound in his throat was of exit rather than of entrance. In the meantime the press was forced into theoretical contortions to account for the wound in the President's throat. *Life,* having purchased the Zapruder film, was in the best position to state conclusively how many shots had hit the President and where they had struck him. But C. D. Jackson, then the magazine's publisher, was sickened by what he saw. Reporter Richard Stolley, who had handled the actual negotiations with Zapruder, later recalled: "Jackson was so upset by the head wound sequence that he proposed the company obtain all rights to the film and withhold it from public viewing at least until emotions had calmed."[8] Nonetheless, some of the Z frames, excluding the one showing the head explosion, appeared in the magazine's November 29, 1963, issue. In the next issue of *Life,* however, the frames which showed the President being driven violently backward in his seat disappeared. Instead, writer Paul Mandel described what the pictures supposedly showed. Mandel's account suffered from a number of inaccuracies, but none more grievous than his description of the first shot (which was actually hidden from view by the freeway sign). The film, according to Mandel, "shows the President turning his body far around to the right as he waves to someone in the crowd. His throat is exposed to the sniper's nest just before he clutches it."[9] Mandel's account ("An End to Nagging Rumors," the headline read) made for interesting reading; it was also totally fictitious.

The public could not know that, of course; they had to rely on *Life* and the few other reporters who had a chance to glimpse the film. One of those reporters was Dan Rather, then an obscure CBS correspondent based in New Orleans. Rather had come to Texas to coordinate the network's coverage of the President's trip. After the assassination, it was Rather who represented CBS in the bidding for the Zapruder film. CBS eventually lost out of *Life,* but not before Rather had a chance to view the film in the office of Zapruder's lawyer. The lawyer ran the film once, and once only, and Rather, absorbed in what he was witnessing, did not have a chance to take notes. At the time, he didn't think he needed any. He knew he had a story. When the film was over, Rather "almost ripped the door off the hinges trying to get out of there," and raced to the studios of the local CBS affiliate. He told his bosses in New York what he had witnessed and requested immediate air time to relate what he had seen. The air time was granted and Rather, speaking entirely from memory, proceeded to narrate what Zapruder had caught through his camera in remarkable detail. He made only one mistake, but, as Fiorello La Guardia would have put it, it was a "beaut." According to Rather's narrative, which was repeated several times throughout the assassination weekend, the final shot drove the President's head "violently *forward.*"[10] (Emphasis added.) In fact, the bullet drove Kennedy's head violently *backward,* as it might have been expected to do had it been fired from the front. The millions of Americans who listened to Rather, however, could not know that, and would not know it, until years later when the Zapruder film, in its entirety, was finally shown on national television. Later, Rather conceded he had made a mistake, though his conviction about Oswald being the lone assassin remained undisturbed.[11]

In time the stories petered out. There were occasional pieces in the *Times,* the *Washington Post,* and elsewhere, quoting official unnamed sources who revealed, inaccurately from the Commission's eventual point of view, details of the autopsy, and sketched in a bit more of Oswald's background. But by and large the digging stopped. The press, and the country with it, seemed confident that the Commission would bring in all the answers.

There were a few notable exceptions. Shortly after the assassination *Life* assigned a team of reporters to assemble a profile of the accused assassin. The result of their labors was published in the magazine's February 21, 1964 issue, with the famous suspicious photograph of Oswald hefting the Mannlicher-Carcano on the cover. The headlines atop each page summed up the story: "He didn't seem to miss having friends. . . . He looked like he was just lost. . . . Lee never came to the squadron parties. . . . Marina wondered if he was unbalanced. . . . On the rifle range, he was excellent. . . . He poked a rifle out that window."[12] Just as the Warren Commission would eight months later, *Life* played armchair psychoanalyst with its subject. One of the experts *Life* consulted was Renatus Hartogs, a New York psychiatrist and columnist for *Cosmopolitan* magazine who in 1975 lost a $350,000 judgment to a young woman who said that he had forced her to have sexual relations with him as part of her "therapy."[13] In 1953 Hartogs had a brief interview with Oswald, who was then living at the New York Youth House for boys. In his official report of that conversation Hartogs characterized Oswald as a lonely, withdrawn youngster, badly in need of friends, affection, and encouragement.[14] He considerably embellished those findings for *Life*'s benefit. "The psychiatrist said he was not surprised when Lee Oswald was arrested for the assassination of President Kennedy," *Life* wrote. " 'Psychologically,' he said, 'he had all the qualifications of being a potential assassin. Such a criminal is usually a person with paranoid ideas of grandiosity who can get satisfactory self-vindication only by shocking the entire world and not just a few people. He had to show the world he was not unknown, that he was someone with whom the world had to reckon. When he was 13, he reacted negatively, by withdrawing. It took him a whole lifetime to develop his courage, and then all the accumulated hate and resentment came out. A person like Oswald resents a lifetime of being pushed to the sidelines. He culminates his career of injustice-collecting by committing a supreme, catastrophic act of violence and power.' "[15]

Life concluded its "Evolution of an Assassin" with a captioned reproduction of the cover picture. Read the caption:

> ASSASSIN TO BE AT 23. Full version of the photograph which appears on LIFE's cover shows Oswald proudly holding a Trotskyite newspaper, *The Militant*, in one hand and the rifle he used to shoot President Kennedy in the other. Dallas police have confirmed that this is the rifle found in the School Book Depository. On Oswald's hip is the revolver which killed Dallas policeman J. D. Tippit. Oswald posed for the photograph in the spring of 1963 outside his home in Dallas. He set the camera and then, handing it to Marina, directed her to take the picture. Shortly after, Oswald shot at Major General Edwin Walker. Seven months later, he killed the President.[16]

Even assuming, as *Life* did, that in fact it was Oswald in the picture, that he did kill Tippit and the President, and shoot at Walker (none of which had been established by the time of the magazine's publication), the caption was riddled with errors. Oswald, for instance, was holding *two* newspapers, the other being a copy of the Communist daily *The Worker*, which, as Sylvia Meagher dryly noted, showed "astonishing catholicity of reading tastes";[17] there was considerable dispute over whether the rifle in the picture was the Mannlicher-Carcano[18] (and, in fact, *Life* later admitted retouching the telescopic scope in the picture so it would more clearly resemble that mounted atop the Mannlicher-Carcano);[19] the revolver on Oswald's hip was holstered, thus making it impossible to identify its caliber, much less whether it was the same gun that killed Tippit; and finally, the picture was taken at Oswald's home in Irving, Texas, not Dallas.[20]

All the same, the *Life* story had a considerable impact on public opinion. The February 21 issue was one of the year's biggest sellers and quickly became a collector's item.

Several months before the appearance of *Life*'s

"assassin" issue, the *Boston Globe* carried a similar evaluation of Oswald and his motives, also written by someone who had observed him at close range. The author was Priscilla Johnson, a former Moscow correspondent for NANA, the North American Newspaper Alliance. In November 1959, shortly after Oswald's arrival in the Soviet Union, Ms. Johnson interviewed him at Moscow's Metropol Hotel where they both were staying.[20a] Oswald went to Ms. Johnson's hotel room and submitted to a five-hour interview—the longest known interview given to any American reporter—during which she thoughtfully brewed him a pot of tea. In the story Ms. Johnson filed she drew a sympathetic portrait of a confused young American far from home. *After* the assassination she saw him as a far more sinister figure. She recalled:

> With his suit of charcoal gray flannel and tan cashmere sweater, Lee looked and sounded like Joe College with a slight southern drawl. But his life hadn't been that of a typical college boy. . . . As we sat in my hotel room that evening and into the early hours of morning, he talked quietly about his plans to defect to Russia. I soon came to feel that this boy was of the stuff of which fanatics are made. . . . I had a terrible feeling of futility. Disillusion, I was sure, awaited him.[21]

In April 1964 Ms. Johnson expanded her recollections into a long piece for *Harper's*. She recounted how she had come to meet Oswald:

> I had sought him out a few hours earlier on the advice of an American colleague in Moscow. A boy named Oswald was staying at my hotel, the Metropol, the friend remarked casually. He was angry at everything American and impatient to become an Russian citizen. "He won't talk to any of us," my colleague added, suggesting that, as a woman, I might have better luck.[22]

On December 5, 1963, before the chief legal officer of the State Department, and later before the Warren Commission, Ms. Johnson identified her American "colleague" as John A. McVickar, an assistant consul in the U.S. embassy. The "us" whom Oswald wouldn't talk to was the U.S. embassy. It was McVickar who first informed Ms. Johnson and other reporters of Oswald's presence in Moscow. According to Ms. Johnson, McVickar advised her that she see Oswald although he had shown a reluctance to talk to embassy officials and other correspondents. After the interview with Oswald, she recounted the substance of her conversation to McVickar.[23–24]

The interview established Ms. Johnson's bona fides as an Oswald expert, and after the assassination she signed a contract with Harper & Row to coauthor a biography with Marina Oswald. The reported advance was $100,000.[25] Twelve years after the assassination no manuscript had appeared, though Ms. Johnson's husband, writer George MacMillan, seemed close to publishing a book arguing that James Earl Ray was the lone assassin of Martin Luther King.[26] In the meantime Ms. Johnson had worked on a variety of interesting projects. One was the translation of the memoirs of Svetlana Stalin, whose defection to the West was widely reported to have been arranged by the Central Intelligency Agency.[27] She also wrote several commemorative pieces on the assassination for the op-ed page of the *New York Times*. In one of them she stated that, by murdering Kennedy, Oswald was symbolically killing his father, adding that everyone would like to do the same thing. "Today it is we who are challenged to be the executioners," Ms. Johnson put it. "The rifle and the bullet are missing, but the feelings underneath are the same: the primal wish to kill the father, guilt and horror over this, and, at last, a desire to protect him, and keep him in his place after all." [28] In another piece, after the incident at Chappaquiddick, she suggested that "what we were engaged in that year was the symbolic murder of Edward Kennedy. We were killing him ourselves. In that way, we could spare ourselves the horror of yet another, real-life Kennedy assassination." [29]

These musings might perhaps be written off as absurd, harmless poppycock. However, a declassified

FBI document raises some questions as to whether Ms. Johnson was only a reporter. The FBI's report (C.D. 49, p. 24) states in part that:

> On November 23, 1963, Mr. Jack Lynch, United States Department of State (USDS), Security Office, telephoncially advised Special Agent in Charge (SAC) Allen Gillies, Oswald had been contacted in Moscow by three employees of the State Department, whom he identified as John McVickar, Pricilla Johnson, and Mrs. G. Staney Brown. Lynch indicated each of the above persons had interviewed Oswald in Moscow.[30]

When recently interviewed neither Lynch nor Gillies had any recollection of this incident. Ms. Johnson denies having been an employee of the State Department or any other government agency and has requested that the State Department make a full investigation of the circumstances of this report.

While the public was digesting these theories, two reporters were pursuing another angle of the case, the mystery of Jack Ruby. On the night of November 24, hours after Ruby had shot Oswald, five men met in Ruby's apartment. One of them was George Senator, Ruby's roommate, two were attorneys, and the other two were reporters, Jim Koethe of the *Dallas Times Herald*, and Bill Hunter, a former Dallasite, who had flown in from California to cover the assassination for his paper, the *Long Beach Press-Telegram*. The purpose of the meeting or what was discussed was never made clear. It was, however, an extraordinary get-together; so little time had gone by since the slaying of Oswald that not even the Dallas police had arrived to go through Ruby's apartment. Shortly after the meeting Koethe decided to take a leave from the *Times Herald* to write a book about the case and Hunter returned to California.[31] They both would be dead within the year.

Hunter was the first to die. On the evening of April 22, 1964, he was sitting in the pressroom of the police station in Long Beach, reading a mystery novel, when two patrolmen going off duty walked in. One shot

Hunter through the heart at a range officially ruled to be "more than three feet." [32] The first story the policeman who had done the shooting told was that he had dropped his gun, and that it fired as he picked it up. When the angle of the bullet's entry made that explanation impossible he switched his story and said that he was practicing his "quick draw" when his weapon went off. The other policeman in the room said his back was turned at the time of the shooting. Both officers were eventually convicted of involuntary manslaughter and given suspended sentences.[33]

Koethe died four months later, killed by a karate chop to the neck as he stepped from his shower. When police arrived they found the apartment ransacked; among the missing items were notes Koethe had been keeping for his book on the assassination.[34] Within weeks police arrested a suspect in the killing, a twenty-two-year-old ex-con from Alabama who was picked up after he had been spotted selling some of Koethe's personal effects. The grand jury, however, refused to return an indictment.[35] The crime remains unsolved.

The deaths of Koethe and Hunter almost went unreported. After the publication in June 1964, three months before the release of the Warren Report, of an exclusive in the *New York Times* reporting that the Commission could find no evidence of conspiracy,[36] the press lost any lingering interest in plots. Efforts turned to explaining and marketing the Report. CBS geared up a two-hour special to air September 24, 1964, the evening of the Report's release, to tick off the Commission's conclusions—without critical comment —one by one.[37] *Life* dusted off the frames of the Zapruder film and commissioned Gerald Ford to author an exclusive account of how the Commission reached its conclusions. The magazine, however, encountered some difficulties. The story kept changing. There were some *six* versions of the magazine's October 2, 1964, issue, each reflecting what seemed to be minor alterations in copy and pictures.[38] The changes were sufficiently important, however, to justify hundreds of thousands of dollars in additional costs for replating and printing delays. Paul Hoch, a San Francisco physicist and assassination researcher, collected all the editions and matched them against one another. He discovered some startling changes. In one edition *Life* reprinted eight frames from the Zapruder film with caption material underneath each. In the first version, the sixth slide was frame 324, which showed the President slumped back against the seat a half second after his head had been struck by a bullet. The caption read: "The assassin's shot struck the right rear portion of the President's skull, causing a massive wound and snapping his head to one side." [39] The slide and the caption disappeared in the next edition. Instead, frame 313, the famous explosion frame, was substituted, though the caption from 324 remained.[40] This error was corrected in the next edition of *Life,* so that now the caption read: "The direction from which the shots came was established by this picture taken at the instant the bullet struck the rear of the President's head, and, passing through, caused the front part of his skull to explode forward." [41] That, in fact, was not what the Zapruder film showed at all, but this explanation did have the virtue of conforming to the Warren Commission's version of events.

The *Times,* meanwhile, was rushing into print a special edition of the Commission Report. Within a week, more than a million copies of the *Times* edition of the Report were on bookstands from coast to coast. A long introductory essay by Harrison E. Salisbury, the *Times* assistant managing editor, heaped scorn on the critics and praise on the several-hundred-thousand-word Report, which Salisbury had had only days to examine. "The quest for truth in the Kennedy assassination has been long and arduous," Salisbury wrote. "The Warren Commission spent the better part of a year in exhaustive examination of every particle of evidence it could discover. . . . No material question now remains unresolved so far as the death of President Kennedy is concerned. True there is no confession. But the evidence of Oswald's single-handed guilt is overwhelming." [42] America had a tradition of single assassins, Salisbury noted; conspiracy was a foreign notion. As for the critics who insisted otherwise, Salisbury questioned not only motives but their sanity, as well as their patriotism. "In part," he said, referring to the work of the critics, "it is the deliberate product of widely-differing political forces and tendencies—including *tendencies of dangerous implication to the American system.*" [43] (Italics added.)

The *Times* followed up its edition of the Report with a volume entitled *The Witnesses,* culled from the testimony before the Commission. Jerry Policoff, a New York advertising salesman and one of the most careful students of the press and the assassination, compared *The Witnesses* with the volumes of testimony before the Commission and found that the *Times* had been careful in making its selection of what was relevant testimony. *The Witnesses,* Policoff noted, included the affidavit of Arnold Rowland, who said that he had observed a man with a rifle on the sixth floor of the School Book Depository, but not his testimony that he had actually seen *two* men, and that the FBI had told him to "forget it," or his opinion under oath that the shots had come from the railroad yards in front of the President.[44]

In a little noticed article in the underground magazine *The Realist,* Policoff went on:

> Omitted from the testimony of amateur photographer Abraham Zapruder was his statement that his immediate reaction was that the shots had come from behind (in *front* of the President). Similar statements relating an immediate impression that the shots had come from in front were deleted from the excerpted testimony of David F. Powers, a special assistant to the President, and Secret Service agent Forrest V. Sorrels, as it appeared in *The Witnesses.* Deleted from the testimony of Secret Service Agents William Greer, Clinton Hill and Roy Kellerman was the description each gave of a bullet wound in the President's back beneath the shoulder. Also omitted from agent Hill's excerpted testimony was his statement that he was not certain that all of the shots had come from the rear, and that they did not all sound alike. Autopsy surgeon Commander James J. Humes's excerpted testimony in *The Witnesses* omitted his statement that he had destroyed the first draft of the autopsy, as well as his

verbal gymnastics in reconciling the location of the bullet hole six inches below the collar in the President's shirt and jacket with the officially-designated location of the wound in the neck. Both Humes and Colonel Pierre Finck, a second autopsy surgeon, were skeptical that the nearly pristine bullet found on a stretcher in Parkland Hospital could have hit both Kennedy and Governor Connally, but these exchanges were also omitted from *The Witnesses,* as was the portion of the testimony of Nelson Delgado, a friend of Oswald's from his Marine Corps days, in which he referred to Oswald's extremely poor marksmanship. Testimony left out of *The Witnesses* altogether included numerous witnesses who reported at least some shots fired from the front, including Jean Hill, who reported seeing a man fleeing from the area of the "grassy knoll" after the shooting. Also left out was the testimony of Wilma Tice and Seth Kantor who reported seeing (and later conversing with) Jack Ruby at Parkland Hospital, as well as many others who gave relevant but inconvenient testimony before the Warren Commission.[45]

The pronunciamentos from the *Times* did not deter the doubters. They grew in number with the publication of Lane's and Epstein's critiques of the Commission Report, along with the continuing stream of magazine articles, both major and small, questioning many of the key findings. The reaction from much of the press was not to evaluate the evidence cited by the critics but to attack the critics themselves. As the most visible of the critics, Lane received the brunt of the abuse. An editorial in the international edition of the *New York Herald Tribune* termed critics like Lane "The Ghouls," and charged that they "seem motivated by a hunger for a buck, a drive for circulation at all costs."[46] Meanwhile, the *Tribune*'s New York parent, the *World Journal Tribune,* was advertising an upcoming article of its own on the assassination. Charles Roberts, who defended the Warren Commission for *Newsweek,* later published his own book, much of which was devoted to an assault on Lane. "With royalties from his book, his 'documentary film', and lecture fees rolling in," Roberts said of Lane, "he can chuckle all the way to the bank." [47] The fact was that, then as now, Lane was hardly growing rich on the assassination. He received no royalties from the film, and for two years after the assassination he lectured at universities and churches across the country for no fee. When Lane was asked to lecture in Denmark he paid his own air fare. He turned his fee over to the John F. Kennedy fund for retarded children.[48]

It was easy for the press to take potshots at critics like Lane, but by 1966 a number of establishmentarians had joined the doubters. Cardinal Cushing, Arthur Schlesinger, William F. Buckley, Richard Goodwin, and the American Academy of Forensic Sciences all called for a new investigation.[49] As public opinion mounted against the Warren Commission, the *New York Times,* in early November 1966, quietly undertook its own investigation. The first tip-off of the *Times*'s unease came in a November 25 editorial headed "Unanswered Questions." [50] To answer them, the *Times* assembled a small task force of reporters under the leadership of the selfsame Mr. Salisbury, who had expressed his own reservations in a recent issue of the *Progressive,* in what proved to be the first of several Salisbury flip-flops on the case.

The *Times* investigation was supposed to be thorough. "We will go over all the areas of doubt," Salisbury promised *Newsweek,* "and hope to eliminate them." [51] But the probe ended in less than a month. Salisbury, who had for some time been seeking permission to go to North Vietnam, suddenly received a visa. His departure left the *Times* task force without a leader, and the investigation sputtered and died. Gene Roberts, a member of the *Times* team, told Policoff: "We found no evidence that the Warren Commission was wrong, which was not to say that the Warren Report was right." [52] Years later Martin Waldron, another member of the *Times* team, provided a fuller explanation. He and his colleagues, he told a reporter, had, like the critics, come up with "a lot of unanswered questions." [53] The questions, however, were never answered. As Waldron put it: "I'd be off on a good lead and then somebody would call me off and send me out to California on another story or something. We never really detached anyone for this. We weren't really serious." [54]

CBS set out to answer the *Times*'s unanswered queries. The network assembled its own task force (the same team of reporters who had congratulated the Warren Commission three years before), interviewed witnesses, and, in a touch no one had considered, staged its own reenactment of the assassination, along with tests designed to explain what the Warren Commission and the critics had found inexplicable. The resulting four-part documentary that aired in June 1967 was breathtakingly misleading.

One of the tests CBS conducted, for instance, was to determine Oswald's capabilities with the Mannlicher-Carcano. Another Mannlicher-Carcano was secured and put in the hands of marksmen. The CBS Mannlicher-Carcano, however, was in significantly better condition than the rifle allegedly used by Oswald. For one thing it could fire much faster: two aimed shots in 4.1 seconds, versus two unaimed shots from the Oswald Mannlicher-Carcano in 4.6 seconds.[55] The scope was also in perfect condition, where Oswald's was defective.[56] Nonetheless CBS put the rifle into the hands of eleven *master* marksmen, who fired a total of thirty-seven three-round volleys.[57] Half of the shots CBS itself discarded because of "trouble with the rifle." [58] The average shooting time of the remaining volleys was 5.6 seconds, the maximum time the Commission said that Oswald had to get off his shots.[59] Evaluating the results, Walter Cronkite intoned gravely: "It seems reasonable to say that an expert could fire that rifle in five seconds. It seems equally reasonable to say that Oswald, under normal circumstances, would take longer. But these were not normal circumstances. Oswald was shooting at a President." [60]

To remove any doubts, CBS stated that Oswald had fired his first shot sooner than the Commission had determined, during a tenth-of-a-second break in the tree foliage that obscured his view. To prove its thesis CBS noted three distinct "blurs" in the Zapruder film, quoting a firearms expert as saying that the blurs had been caused by Zapruder's slight flinching at each of the shots.[61] *Life,* as it happened, had considered the blur theory in 1966 and rejected it, concluding that a flaw in the camera mechanism had caused them.[62] What CBS failed to mention, but what the ever alert Policoff noted, was that the Zapruder film was studded with blurs, proof, Policoff noted sarcastically, that "the assassin had employed a machine gun." [63]

The CBS documentaries were stocked with distortions and plain misstatements of fact. The network claimed that Zapruder's camera could have been operating as slowly as 15.3 frames per second, a figure which, extrapolated against the impact of the shots, would have allowed Oswald nearly three extra seconds to do his shooting.[64] The trouble was that FBI experts had concluded that Zapruder's camera ran at 18.3 frames per second, no more, no less.[65] CBS also shot out a number of light bulbs to simulate the bullet's explosive impact on the President's head, neglecting to consider that light bulbs are filled with air, while the human skull is composed of thick bone and brain tissue.[66] CBS showed how the single-bullet thesis was possible by setting up gelatin blocks to simulate Kennedy's neck and Connally's chest. A strip of masonite was used to simulate the far sturdier wristbone, but, at that, at least something was used. Connally's rib was not simulated at all.[67] Despite the weighting of the evidence, none of the CBS test rounds made it as far as the simulated thigh. All the same, CBS concluded that "a single bullet could indeed have wounded both men." [68] What CBS did not mention was the piece of physical evidence on which the critics based their refutation of the magic-bullet thesis: the nearly pristine condition of C.E. 399. CBS subsequently explained that the omission of 399 was an "oversight." [69] Robert Richter, a former CBS producer who helped put together the documentaries, said later: "From the material gathered for the program, someone could take the same raw footage and utilize the same tests, choose different excerpts from the same interviews, and give the audience a completely different, more objective impression of what the facts added up to." [70]

The viewers could not have known that, however. Outtakes from the program—nearly 85,000 feet of untelevised film (versus slightly more than 5000 feet that actually aired)—were destroyed within weeks of the program's airing.[71] The critics were outraged. One of them, Raymond Marcus, showed several photographs taken at the assassination site to Les Midgley, the documentaries' executive producer. In an enlargement of a section of one photograph, Marcus pointed out shapes behind a wall that could, Marcus said, be the head of a rifleman. Midgley pooh-poohed Marcus's suggestion, and then, picking up another photograph, exclaimed that he did see a man. Yes, said Midgley, thinking he was examining a photograph taken in Mississippi, "that's the man who shot [James] Meredith."[72] Midgley had made an embarrassing mistake. The photograph he was looking at was one taken of the grassy knoll in Dealey Plaza.

But by then it was too late. A veritable storm of self-congratulatory press releases was issuing from the CBS executive suite. CBS News President Richard Salant called his program "a truly great achievement,"[73] and in a public aside to Midgley said, "I have neither the eloquence nor the vocabulary to say properly how proud and grateful I am. . . . There are two words which are badly overused—'professional' and 'genius.' They are entirely applicable here."[74]

If the *Times* and CBS thought they had silenced the critics, they had miscalculated. The assassination made for good copy, and other news organizations pored through their files, looking for bits of evidence that would support or discredit the Warren Report's conclusions. *Life* resurrected the Zapruder film, showed it to Connally, and after the Governor repeated his oft-expressed conviction that he had been hit by a second bullet, editorially called for a new investigation.[75] United Press International, meanwhile, had been studying its own film of the assassination, which it had purchased from Orville Nix. Jones Harris had noted an odd shape behind a station wagon parked behind the grassy knoll in a number of the Nix frames and brought it to UPI's attention. To Harris the shape looked like the figure of a man. UPI was sufficiently intrigued to investigate.

The Nix film had had a curious history. After the assassination Nix returned to Dealey Plaza late in the afternoon, and with the original film still in the camera, filmed the Hertz time sign above the School Book Depository. Nix later gave the camera to his son, who used it to photograph Nix's daughter, a high-school majorette, performing at a local football game. Finally Nix sent the film to the developer. When it came back Nix looked at the results and immediately turned over the film to the FBI.[76] The Bureau was unimpressed. After screening, analyzing—and badly scratching—the film, agents returned the film to Nix.[77] Nix still thought he had something. Several news organizations agreed, and *Life* agreed to fly him to New York. Nix eventually accepted a bid from UPI of $5000, a good dinner, and a new hat, a trifle compared to the price for the Zapruder film.[78] But then, the Nix film was considerably less detailed than Zapruder's. Nix had been standing farther away from the presidential limousine, on the side opposite Zapruder. Moreover, one UPI executive described the film as "one of the cheapest brands of 8 mm color film, and either it had been underexposed or it had been underdeveloped at the lab: the colors were dark and contrasty, the grain structure was heavy, and the edges of the figures and shapes were fuzzy." [79] And, of course, it was also scratched.

Still, there were the mysterious shapes. UPI agreed to let Harris take some of the stills from the Nix film to a professional photooptician to have them enlarged and enhanced. The optician, Bernie Hoffman, a former *Life* photographer, worked on the project with painstaking thoroughness through the winter of 1965 and 1966. When his final blowup emerged it clearly showed what seemed to be the outline of a car, and a man standing behind it, shoulders fixed in the classic aiming position. UPI dispatched Jack Fox, one of its investigative reporters, to Dallas with a copy of the picture to see what he could come up with. Fox identified the car as a station wagon belonging to a local gun shop. Fox wrote that there might well be a gunman in the picture, or, just as probably, "a brown cow grazing." [80]

For the moment UPI was uninterested in proceeding further, but allowed Harris to take the film to *Life*. Richard Billings, *Life*'s chief investigative reporter, was interested in the pictures, but when he approached his superiors with the story was told that *Life* had already devoted sufficient attention to the Kennedy assassination. It was much the same story at *Newsweek*, Harris's next stop. Finally *Esquire* ran the picture in a long special report on the various assassination theories.

The shapes, however, were still just shapes. To be certain what they were UPI shopped around for an electronics firm which could run sophisticated "image enhancement" tests on the shapes, which would settle once and for all whether the shapes were substance or mere shadows. The film eventually wound up in Massachusetts at the offices of Itek, which studied the film for five months from January until May 1967. Itek's report concluded that the shapes were shadows and lights,[81] a finding seconded several years later by a team of researchers at the California Institute of Technology. As the Caltech study put it: "No errors were found in the Itek report and its conclusions remain the most likely. . . . However, in the light of the poor image quality and the availability of suitable hiding places, a grassy knoll assassin cannot positively be ruled out." [82] However, Caltech based its study not on the actual Nix film itself but on 35-mm color transparencies made from the film, in short, at least one generation away from the original. The Nix film was dim enough. The printing and enlargement to 35-mm slides obliterated almost all the detail. Later Alan Gillespie, one of the Caltech researchers who had studied the film, confessed: "The data . . . was so poor as to leave open questions concerning the disposition or existence of real or hypothetical assassins in the deep shadow, behind the picket fence. . . ." [83]

A final postscript to the Nix film appeared in 1975 in an article in the *Columbia Journalism Review*. Toward the end of his account of UPI's investigation

Maurice Schoenfeld, a former UPI executive who had a hand in analyzing the Nix film, mentioned almost casually that in 1967 he had discovered that Itek's president and one of the company's executives who handled the film were former agents for the CIA. "I love to tell the story on myself, and maybe on all of us," Schoenfeld wrote, "of how, in the end, the only people I could get to investigate a picture that might (by a stretch of conspiratorial imagination) involve the CIA were people who worked for the CIA." [84] Funny.

All of the news organizations that tried to investigate the Kennedy assassination had drawn blanks. The questions remained questions. As Gene Roberts had put it, they hadn't proved the Warren Commission wrong, nor had they proved it right. They hadn't, in fact, really tried.

Such efforts as there were, however, came to an end with the Garrison investigation. In a lengthy article in the *New York Times Magazine* published after Shaw's acquittal, Epstein now turned on the critics, suggesting that many of them were "demonologists." [85] He accepted the CBS documentary's conclusions as clearing up doubts about the single-assassin thesis. As for the remaining doubters, Epstein wrote: "The credibility of the evidence cannot be divorced from the credibility of the investigator who presents it." [86] Quite obviously Epstein thought the critics had none.

The pendulum now swung completely the other way. In 1973 Quadrangle Books, a subsidiary of the *New York Times,* published a massive defense of the Commission Report, *November 22, 1963: You Are the Jury,* by David Belin. The introduction was written by Harrison Salisbury, who noted enthusiastically: "For anyone who wishes to know how the crime of the century actually occurred . . . this work tells the story better than it has been told at any time before." [87] Belin's book was reviewed in the *Times* by George MacMillan and Priscilla Johnson MacMillan. They were more than up to the task. "It is as if Lee Harvey Oswald had lived and there had been a trial," they wrote. "Mr. Belin has done a better job of putting the evidence together than the one-volume Warren Commission Report . . . readable and fascinating." [88] When two books on the Garrison trial appeared, the job of reviewing them fell to John Leonard. Leonard concluded his review with a long paragraph headed "Mysteries Persist." Leonard reviewed the lingering questions of the critics, and added a few of his own. "Something stinks about this affair," he concluded.[89] That was how the review appeared in the *Times* first edition. In succeeding editions the headline of the review had been changed—from "Who Killed J. F. Kennedy?" to "The Shaw-Garrison Affair"—and the entire last paragraph, expressing Leonard's questions, deleted entirely.[90]

The *Times* could not be blamed. The Garrison fiasco had left all the press badly snakebitten. Even those publications which, like the *Times,* had been dubious about Garrison from the beginning came away from the trial sheepish, as if by the necessity of having even to cover the event they had somehow shared in its shame. *Life,* which had once been willing to invest considerable resources in the Kennedy story, was no longer. When Richard Billings approached the magazine's editors on a follow-up project, he was told: "It is not the function of *Life* to solve the Kennedy assassination." [91] Not long afterward, when Billings announced he was leaving the magazine, few tears were shed. Anyone who had had anything to do with conspiracies was just as soon forgotten.

The story thus passed into the hands of the national tabloids. They felt no such qualms. Hardly an issue went by in the *National Tattler* when some solution for the crime wasn't announced, each week's answer more fantastic than the last. Watergate burglars on the grassy knoll, Mafia men in the School Book Depository, assassins in storm drains—the *Tattler* welcomed them all. In a unique case of first-person journalism, the *Tattler* even reported on a séance with President Kennedy's ghost. The ghost informed the *Tattler*'s readers that he had committed many mistakes while he was alive and President, and that certain members of the United States Senate knew the identity of his killers.[92] A few weeks later the *Tattler* announced that its ace investigative reporters had cracked the case.[93] The pictures of the five supposed assassins were published on the front page. There was an accompanying story quoting Aristotle Onassis's butler as saying that Ari had investigated the case at his wife's behest, and had been forced to pull back when the lives of Caroline and John Kennedy, Jr., had been threatened.[94]

All of which only convinced the established media that their initial instincts were right. The Kennedy story was the province of freaks and weirdos, or as *Newsweek* put it in mid-1975, when interest in the assassination freshened: "They are back again . . . an odd-lot assortment of skeptics and ideologues, rationalists and fantasists." [95] John Lindsay, a respected *Newsweek* reporter who had a hand in putting together the magazine's rebuttal to the critics, said in exasperation: "I am sick and tired of being badgered by dilettantes. I'm sick of people who see shadows in bushes and gunmen under manhole covers. A whole generation of young people is being brainwashed." [96]

Everyone was sick of it; some more determined to put an end to the "brainwashing" than ever. In 1975, the CBS program *Sixty Minutes* began cranking up a final go at the assassination, based on the dubious thesis that Oswald and Ruby knew each other.* [97] A team of producers and researchers fanned out across the country, interviewing as many of Oswald's and Ruby's acquaintances as they could. They found little evidence that the men had ever known each other, though they did uncover new material that further discredited the Warren Commission. The fruits of their labors were supposed to appear in an hour-long documentary, "The Oswald-Ruby Connection." The project, however, was scrapped. The network had de-

---

* After the assassination, several witnesses did claim to have seen Oswald and Ruby together in Dallas, but on investigation their stories were discounted, and in the opinion of most of the critics, for good reason. The stories came to the attention of District Attorney Henry Wade, who tried Ruby in 1964. Wade too dismissed them, though he admitted in 1975: "I won't be hypocritical. If we hadn't had such a good case against Ruby, I would have thrown them in. What the hell." [98]

cided to take an entirely different tack. Reportedly CBS executives completed negotiations with Gerald Ford to purchase the rights to his book *Portrait of the Assassin,* and would produce it as a documentary after the presidential elections in 1976. The network also commissioned four half-hour documentaries on various assassinations during the sixties: John Kennedy's, Robert Kennedy's, Martin Luther King's, and the attempt on Alabama Governor George Wallace. The research the *Sixty Minutes* reporters had collected was turned over to the producers of the four new specials, the same producers who had turned out CBS's ill-starred defense of the Warren Commission Report in 1967.

The reaction of the press to the Kennedy assassination was understandable. The media was a part of no conspiracy. The mistakes it made, while grievous, were honest ones. It all had to do with the nature of the story, and what had become of it. Even the best reporters were put off. "Why don't you get into assassinations?" a reporter for *Rolling Stone* asked Seymour Hersh during a long interview in 1975. Hersh had a ready reply.

> I scrupulously avoid the assassination stories. I think its probably saved me about 350,000 years. I've read a lot of stuff about Jack Kennedy's assassination. . . . My feeling about the conspiracy theory is this: that if after the statute of limitations is up, if somebody doesn't write a book for a million dollars, then there was no conspiracy. I'll tell you what I have found; that the people who believe in conspiracy theories are the quickest to become extremely vituperative. One of these people calls you with a conspiracy theory and you say, "I don't buy it." And they say, "Sure, you don't buy it. It's because you're part of the conspiracy." It's a *gestalt* I don't like. So I really have avoided the conspiracy. I've also avoided flying saucers.[99]

Reporters, even reporters of the caliber of Seymour Hersh, are rather ordinary Americans, with the same desires as other Americans: getting ahead, looking good, and most important of all, keeping credibility.

The Kennedy assassination was a quagmire. More than one good reporter had been dragged down in it. One did not take such risks lightly. Indeed, one avoided them when he could.

Moreover, the story of John Kennedy's murder was damnably complicated. The Warren Commission had published more than 10 million words on the subject and still hadn't found the answer. The Commission had had the benefit of unlimited resources; the FBI and CIA were supposedly at its disposal. Only a few newspapers had the wherewithal to put a team of reporters on a single story. They chose their targets carefully. "I believe there was a conspiracy," said one prominent newspaper editor on the West Coast. "But how do you get a handle on it. If I were going to make a dent in the thing, I'd need twenty guys working on it full-time, with squads of lawyers and accountants to back them up. Just to get through the reading takes months. We don't have that kind of time. We don't have those bodies. Damn few people do."[100]

In fact, only one newspaper did: the *New York Times*. The *Times* was not known for chasing will-o'-the-wisps. The nation's newspaper of record, the gray lady, was cautious, even conservative. In many respects it was like the government it covered: big and powerful. It moved slowly, and when what seemed to be the nation's interest demanded it, sometimes not at all. More than once the *Times* had killed an exclusive at the request of the White House or the CIA. Weeks before the Bay of Pigs invasion Tad Szulc had put together the entire story. Yet his account did not run. President Kennedy asked the editors to hold off; later, he told them he regretted they had. If the story had run the disaster might have been avoided.[101]

There was nothing insidious about the *Times* coverage of the President's murder. On the contrary the pattern was all too familiar. For all the pious talk about the press and government being adversaries they were, when the stakes warranted, actually members of the same team. Certainly that was true of the *Times*'s attitude toward the Warren Commission. In a remarkably revealing letter to Commission Counsel J. Lee

Rankin, dated four months before the release of the Report, then *Times* Managing Editor Clifton Daniel wrote:

> We would certainly print in the international edition an extensive report of the Warren Commission findings, and substantial excerpts from the report, to the limits of our physical and financial capacity. We would also publish . . . a substantial advertisement, advising readers that they could order copies of the complete report from the Paris office of the New York Times for a modest fee. . . .
>
> It happens to be in our interest, as well as the interest of the Commission and the country, to obtain as wide a distribution of this document as we can.[102]

Daniel was only being candid. There was less excuse for one of his Pulitzer prizewinning reporters. "Nobody told us to stop," Harrison Salisbury said, explaining why the *Times* had ended its investigation of John Kennedy's murder. "We just felt that nobody cared." [103]

6

On Instructions of His Government

MC CLOY: Well, I can't say that I have run into a fellow comparable to Oswald, but I have run into some very limited mentalities in the CIA and FBI.

(laughter)

WARREN: Under agents, the regular agents, I think that would be all right, but they and all the other agencies do employ undercover men who are of terrible character.

DULLES: Terribly bad characters.

RUSSELL: Limited intelligence, even the city police departments do it.

WARREN: It almost takes that kind of man to do a lot of this intelligence work.

DULLES: They ought to be fairly smart. They may not be of high moral character, but they ought to be fairly smart.

—Executive Session of the Warren Commission January 27, 1964 [1]

TO THE WARREN COMMISSION it was "that dirty rumor." To the man who spread it, it was a harmless prank. To the critics it was merely confirmation of their worst suspicions. In the end no one could say for certain just what it was, only that the doubt had been planted, and all the assurances from the FBI and the CIA would never make it go away. Had in fact the President's accused assassin been an intelligence agent of the United States?

Stories that Lee Harvey Oswald was an agent of some sort spread almost from the moment of his arrest. The brief background provided by the Dallas police of the prime suspect in the murders of President Kennedy and Officer Tippit made such stories inevitable. Here was a young man, recently returned from a brief "defection" to the Soviet Union, married to a Russian woman (herself the niece of an official in the MVD), doing propaganda work for the Castro regime, using an alias, carrying phony identification and a notebook with the name, telephone, and license number of a Dallas-based FBI agent. One needn't have been paranoid to assume that Lee Oswald, a.k.a. Alek Hidell, a.k.a. O. H. Lee, was something more than a simple stock boy in a book depository.

The Alonzo Hudkins story brought the rumors to the surface. The possibility of Oswald's being an informer for the FBI plainly worried the Commission (see chapter 2), though not sufficiently to trace the story beyond a pro forma denial from J. Edgar Hoover. Hoover himself, in his testimony to the Commission, said it was a mystery to him how the story—as Hoover referred to it, "the lie"—got going.[2] His agents, Hoover reported, had questioned Hudkins, but the reporter refused to reveal his source.[3] The Secret Service had better luck. In an interview on December 17, 1963, Hudkins revealed that he had gotten the story from Allan Sweatt,[4] chief of the criminal division of the Dallas sheriff's office. Sweatt in turn said it had come from William Alexander,[5] the assistant Dallas D.A. who apparently had stood outside the Texas Theatre, gun drawn, waiting for Oswald to emerge, and later was keen to indict him as part of a "Communist conspiracy." [6]

If the allegation of Oswald's being a paid informant for the FBI did originate with Alexander or Hudkins, it would not be surprising. Before the assassination and after, Alexander made his dislike of the Bureau, and what he regarded as its stumble-footed incompetence, plainly known. "Lonnie" Hudkins, as he was known, was not a fan of the Bureau either, and in turn was no great favorite of the FBI's. Hudkins left Texas a few years after the assassination and eventually turned up in Baltimore as a reporter for the *News-American.* In 1973, Hudkins admitted to a reporter from the *Philadelphia Inquirer* that he and two of his pals had simply "invented" Oswald's supposed payroll numbers and leaked their existence by talking about them over a telephone they believed tapped.[7] Hudkins's latest explanation did not account for the newspaper story he had written in the *Houston Post* ten years before, reporting the numbers, or his interview with the Secret Service. In any case Hudkins told the *Inquirer:* "Oswald was either a stoolie for the FBI or CIA and turned out to be the greatest double agent of all time." [8]

The Commission Report, relying on the FBI and CIA, stated definitively that he was not. In an appendix entitled "Speculations and Rumors," the Report discounted statements by Marguerite Oswald that her son was an agent as baseless supicions, or simply malicious falsehood. "Investigation by the Commission," the Report concluded, "has revealed no evidence that Oswald was ever employed by the FBI or CIA in any capacity." [9] All that remains to contradict that statement is a collection of the most improbable coincidences.

They begin in the Marine Corps. Oswald enlisted in the Marine Corps on October 24, 1956, six days after his seventeenth birthday.[10] His life until then had been a lonely and unhappy one, growing up without a father, pulled from town to town by an indifferent mother, in and out of petty trouble, frequently truant from school, isolated for long periods of time in the hostile, alien world of a youth house or orphanage.[11] In short, a dreary background, though not unlike that of hundreds of thousands of children from broken homes. Lee's brother, Robert, had enlisted in the marines some years before [12] and had made a new life. The marines promised the same for Lee.

After basic training at San Diego and Camp Pendleton, California, Oswald reported to the Naval Air Technical Training Center in Jacksonville, Florida, for a six-week course in the basics of radar control.[13] Advanced instruction followed, and Oswald eventually was given an MOS (military occupational specialty) of Aviation Electronics Operator.[14] By mid-September Oswald was in Japan, assigned as a radar operator to the 1st Marine Aircraft Wing, based at Atsugi.[15] According to the Report, Oswald's job was "to direct aircraft to their targets by radar, communicating with the pilots by radio. The squadron also had the duty of scouting for incoming foreign aircraft, such as straying Russian or Chinese planes, which would be intercepted by American planes." [16]

The Report's straightforward prose makes the assignment seem routine. It wasn't. For Atsugi was more than an ordinary air station; it was also one of the largest CIA bases in the world.[17] From its runways U-2 reconnaissance planes of the kind flown by Francis Gary Powers over the Soviet Union were launched on spy missions over mainland China. Atsugi was also a launching pad for Chinese Nationalist agents who were parachuted onto the mainland. Deep in the honeycombed caverns that lie beneath the base, intelligence personnel monitored Communist communications traffic.[18] Minimum security clearance for the men in Oswald's unit, according to a marine who had served with him in California, was "secret." [19] Oswald had no trouble being cleared, despite the fact that he had twice been convicted by court-martial.[20]

Amid these exotic surroundings Oswald took up a new avocation. The boy with indifferent grades, who always had trouble passing tests, decided to study Russian, a Berlitz book his only reported guide.[21] He seems to have made remarkable progress. By the time he was transferred back to the States to a duty assignment at El Toro Air Station, California,[22] Oswald was reading Russian newspapers and impressing a Russian-speaking aunt with his skill.[23] Before long his buddies at El Toro kiddingly referred to him as "Oswaldskovich." [24] Oswald in turn sometimes addressed them as "comrade." [25]

Oswald was also knowledgeable about world affairs. The Report comments that "he appears to have been better informed than some of the officers, whose lack of knowledge amused and sometimes irritated him." [26] The Report quotes Lieutenant John E. Donovan, Oswald's commander and a graduate of the Georgetown University School of Foreign Service, as saying that Oswald was "truly interested in international affairs," and "very well versed, at least on the superficial facts of a given foreign situation." [27] Private Kerry Thornley, one of Oswald's fellow enlisted men, told the Commission that Oswald believed that "Marxist morality was the most rational morality to follow," that communism was "the best system in the world."[28] To Thornley, Oswald merely seemed to be toying with these ideas rather than holding any conviction. Thornley was so struck by the unusual young marine that he eventually wrote a novel based on Oswald's life.[29]

There is no record of the Marine Corps ever showing concern that one of its young radar operators, with access to secret information and stationed at one of its most sensitive bases, was talking of the joys of Marxism and the superiority of the Communist system to his fellows. In any case Oswald's active relationship with the marines came to an end on September 11, 1959, three months ahead of his scheduled discharge.[30] Oswald had applied for and received a "dependency discharge"[31] on the grounds that his mother had injured herself at work and could no longer support herself. All of which was a lie. True enough, Marguerite had been injured on the job when a jar fell on her head and struck her toe.[32] The accident had occurred nearly a year before,[33] however, and it had kept Marguerite from work less than a week. Coincidentally, Lee had been on leave in Fort Worth at the time of the accident, and had returned to duty without mentioning the incident.[34] All the same, Oswald's discharge was granted in less than a week, a speed which astounded his Marine Corps buddies.[35] Even the Commission was suspicious. An unpublished top secret Commission memo stated flatly, "He undoubtedly obtained the discharge fraudulently."[36]

There was also some funny business with Oswald's Marine Corps records. The Report, relying on a Defense Department chronology of Oswald's service, as well as his Marine service records, stated that Oswald spent a brief time on Taiwan beginning September 30, 1958, and then, with the rest of his unit, was transferred back to Atsugi.[37] Between October 6 and November 2, the records go on, Oswald was shuttled to another section of his unit on Japan, while awaiting shipment back to the United States.[38]

All this seemed routine until Oswald's pay records arrived at the Commission, slightly more than a week before submission of the final Report. They told an entirely different story. According to the pay records Oswald had been transferred out of his regular unit on August 29, 1958, and placed in a different unit with a new pay status between September 8 and October 17, 1958.[39] What this status was could not be determined. That part of the pay records was censored.[40] The pay records contained one other bit of interesting news. Oswald was not in Japan at all when the Report said he was but, along with his new unit, was on Taiwan.[41]

The questions are obvious: What was Oswald doing on Taiwan? What new job did he have? And why did the Defense Department and the marines go to such pains to conceal Oswald's status and exact whereabouts? One explanation for the determined obscurantism is that Oswald had been recruited for a covert assignment by the Office of Naval Intelligence. The Commission would never know. While it asked the CIA and FBI whether Oswald had been one of their agents, the Commission made no attempt to ask the same questions of the Department of Defense, the most logical organization to have recruited him.[42]

The odd happenings were beginning to stack up. They were nothing, though, in comparison with what occurred next. Three days after returning home to Fort Worth Oswald left for New Orleans, and immediately booked passage on a freighter bound for Le Havre,[43] on the first leg of a trip to the Soviet Union. From France he sailed to England, arriving in Southampton on October 9.[44] He informed British customs officials that he planned to stay in the country a week before proceeding on to Switzerland.[45] Instead he flew the next day to Helsinki, Finland.[46] On Monday, October 12, Oswald went to the Soviet consulate and applied for a visa.[47] It was granted two days later.[48] The next day he left Helsinki by train, crossing the Soviet frontier at Vainikkala.[49] By October 16 he was in Moscow.[50]

That, at least, is how the Report laid out Oswald's

itinerary. Given Oswald's interest in things Russian it is not surprising that he wound up in the Soviet Union, despite his stated intention to go to Switzerland. The problem is not *that* he went to Russia, but *how*.

How, for instance, did Oswald pay for a trip that at a bare minimum cost $1500? According to the Commission, Oswald, a frugal spender, saved the fare for his passage and expenses from his Marine Corps salary, which after deductions and taxes totaled $3000.[51] Yet Oswald's bank account before his departure for Europe showed a total balance of $203.[52] If Oswald didn't have another $1300 squirreled away in a mattress, someone had to have been extraordinarily generous. His friends and family reported giving him no money at all. Who did, then?

Oswald also managed to secure a Soviet visa in record time. The CIA told the Commission that under ordinary circumstances obtaining a visa in Finland took one or two weeks;[53] Oswald got his in two days.

He could have been lucky, of course; but luck would not explain how he managed to get from London to Helsinki in time to register at a hotel before midnight of the tenth. A CIA check found that the only available commercial flight would have gotten Oswald to Helsinki on the eleventh.[54] Yet Oswald's passport is stamped "Embarked 10 October, 1959."[55] Two explanations are possible. Oswald saved *all* his Marine Corps salary and used it to charter a private plane to take him to Finland, or—far more likely—someone with airplanes at his disposal flew him to Helsinki. The question, obviously, is who the someone is.

The day after Oswald's arrival in Moscow he went sightseeing with a young female Intourist guide. While she was pointing out Moscow's tourist attractions, Oswald informed her that he wanted to become a Soviet citizen.[56] Within a week he was visited in his hotel room by a man who introduced himself as a reporter for Radio Moscow, but whom the CIA deduced to be, in reality, an agent of the KGB.[57] Oswald repeated his story of wanting to give up his American citizenship and become a Soviet citizen.[58] The next day he was instructed to report to the Soviet Foreign Ministry's passport and visa department.[59] There an official listened unsympathetically to Oswald's request. Later that day the ministry sent word to Oswald in his hotel that his request had been denied and that he would have to leave Moscow within two hours.[60] Oswald thereupon slashed his left wrist.[61] Fortunately Oswald's friendly Intourist guide appeared in the nick of time and took him to the hospital.[62]

For the next three days, Oswald was confined to the hospital's psychiatric ward while the Soviets pondered what to make of him.[63] The day of his discharge Oswald was summoned before Soviet officials, who once again inquired what he wanted. Once more Oswald said he wished to become a Soviet citizen. The officials told him they would think it over.[64] For three days Oswald stayed in his hotel room, waiting for word. Finally, on October 31, he decided to take matters into his own hands. He went to the American embassy, and in the presence of two Foreign Service officers declared that he wanted to renounce his American citizenship.[65] Oswald denounced the United States and praised the Soviet Union, adding that he had offered to turn over to the Russians the secrets he had learned as a radar operator in the marines.[66] One of the officials was Richard E. Snyder, the embassy second secretary and a former State Department intelligence official.[67] Snyder seemed strangely unmoved by Oswald's threat. For nearly an hour he tried to talk Oswald out of his decision, and when he failed, told him to come back in two days to formally renounce his citizenship.[68] The other official, vice-consul John A. McVickar, who later advised Priscilla Johnson that she might want to interview Oswald, was far more skeptical. It seemed to him, McVickar told the Warren Commission, that Oswald possibly "was following a pattern of behavior in which he had been tutored by person or persons unknown . . . that he had been in contact with others before or during his Marine Corps tour who had guided him and encouraged him in his actions." [69]

Oswald failed to keep the appointment Snyder had suggested. Instead he wrote the embassy a letter, stating once again that he was renouncing his citizenship.[70] The State Department, over the vigorous objections of some of its own officials, eventually decided that neither Oswald's letter nor his verbal statements fully complied with the requirements for renunciation of citizenship.[71] The embassy kept Oswald's passport on file in case he changed his mind.[72]

The Russians, meanwhile, were still eyeing Oswald warily. Weeks went by and still action on his case was deferred. Oswald languished in his hotel and wrote several letters home, explaining his decision to his brother, Robert Oswald. In one letter Oswald wrote bitterly that the American system "exploits all its workers," that "art, culture and the sprit [sic] of man are subjected to commercial enterpraising [sic], [and] religion and education are used as a tool to surpress [sic] what would otherwise be a population questioning their government's unfair economic system and plans for war." Oswald continued: "Ask me and I will tell you I fight for *communism*. . . . I will not say your grandchildren will live under communism, look for yourself at history, look at a world map! America is a dieing [sic] country, I do not wish to be a part of it, nor do I ever again wish to be used as a tool in its military aggressions." Finally Oswald wrote: "In the event of war I would kill *any* american who put a uniform on in defence of the american government—any american. . . . I have no attachment's of any kind in the U.S. . . . I want to, and I shall, live a normal happy and peacful [sic] life here in the Soviet Union *for the rest of my life*." [73]

Whether or not these letters were written for the benefit of the Soviets (who presumably were intercepting Oswald's mail and reading it), the prose failed to impress. On January 4, 1960, Oswald was summoned to the Soviet Passport Office and informed that his request for Soviet citizenship was being denied.[74] He was issued an "identity document for stateless persons" and told that he was being sent to Minsk, an industrial city 450 miles southwest of Moscow, given a special stipend and a free apartment, and would be put to work in an electronics factory that manufactured radio parts.[75]

The Russians had good reason to be cautious about this young American who suddenly dropped in on them, spouting denunciations of capitalism and offering radar secrets. In the year before Oswald's arrival they had been fairly deluged with would-be American defectors, four of them in all, compared to almost none in the preceding thirty years.[76] Two more "defectors" would shortly follow Oswald.[77] Eventually all but one of them suffered a change of heart and returned to the United States.[78] Adding to the coincidence is that most of them had followed the same route of entry into the Soviet Union as had Oswald.[79] Up to now none of the "defectors" has been identified as an American intelligence agent. But the implications of their mysterious rush to the Soviet Union at the height of the cold war are obvious.

The Russians' fears were spelled out in 1964 with the arrival in the United States of a Soviet defector named Yuri Nosenko. Nosenko had been a senior Soviet intelligence officer before his flight to the West, and when he turned up in Geneva he had a batch of intelligence goodies with him, including the KGB's file on Lee Harvey Oswald.[80] The timing of Nosenko's defection was most convenient. He showed up in the West barely ten weeks after the assassination, at a time when there were real fears—shared by CIA and the staff of the Warren Commission—that Oswald might have been a Soviet intelligence agent. The documents Nosenko provided played a major role in putting those fears to rest. Privately, senior American intelligence officials were highly suspicious of Nosenko and the authenticity of his information on Oswald. Eleven years later, a former intelligence official finally admitted: "No doubt about it. Nosenko was a phony. Nosenko was a notorious deception—he really screwed up everything." [80a] Neither CIA nor FBI, however, bothered to convey these suspicions to the Warren

Commission, which continued to rely on what came to be called "the Nosenko file."* No mention of Nosenko appears in the Report, though, and the file was kept classified for several years after the publication of the Report. When the file was released in 1968 it revealed, among other things, that the Soviets were worried that Oswald was a "sleeper" American agent, a spy placed in their midst who could be activated on command, years, perhaps decades after his arrival and acceptance into Soviet society.[82] The Russians, according to the Nosenko file, decided to take no chances. They declined Oswald's offer of radar secrets and posted him off to an unimportant industrial center far from Moscow, where they continued to keep him under close observation until his departure from the Soviet Union in June 1962.

On the surface, at least, Oswald settled in to his new life. The stipend the Soviets had provided him, along with the free apartment, made his adjustment easier. He lived, he boasted, better than the foreman in his factory.[83] One night in mid-March 1961 Oswald attended a trade-union dance at the Palace of Culture for Professional Workers in Minsk.[84] A young girl caught his eye and Oswald asked one of his friends to introduce him. They danced, and when the evening was over, Oswald asked for her telephone number. Nineteen-year-old Marina Prusakova, the woman who was destined to be his wife, smiled and gave it to him.[85]

Marina had been living in Minsk for several years when she met Oswald.[86] She was a bright girl, ambitious, determined, and on occasion possessed of a slashing tongue. Her "freshness" had gotten her into trouble with her stepfather in Leningrad, and she

---

* According to the Nosenko file two Soviet psychiatrists who examined Oswald after his putative suicide attempt concluded that while he was not insane, he was quite abnormal and unstable. The KGB ordered that Oswald be watched closely, but not recruited for any intelligence assignment. It was on orders from the KGB that Oswald was denied a Soviet visa when he traveled to Mexico City in September 1963. After the assassination the KGB was reportedly terrified that, because of some slipup, Oswald *might* have been recruited for Soviet intelligence, and immediately dispatched a bomber to Minsk to retrieve Oswald's file. Nosenko recalled that the KGB examined the bulky dossier in terror, fearful as they turned each page that they would uncover evidence that Oswald had been a Soviet agent. They were enormously relieved when the file showed he was not.[81]

had come to live with her uncle Ilya Prusakov in Minsk.[87] Marina did well. She had a good job and several boyfriends. She had also made the politically wise move of joining Komsomol, the Communist Party's youth apparatus.[88] Her uncle may well have urged it on her. He was a party member himself, and an official in what the Warren Commission later categorized as a local bureau of the ministry of internal affairs, "concerned with lumber." [89] Ilya was not an ordinary bureaucrat. This "official" was actually a colonel in the MVD, the ministry which houses the feared Soviet secret police.[90]

Later the Warren Commission would worry about Marina and her background, but their fears would be kept secret. Rankin brought up the subject at one of the Commission's first executive sessions:

> RANKIN: The members of her family are a curious thing. She was apparently a child with a father unknown at the time she was born, and yet she acquired a name of a father in some of the registrations of the Soviet system. Well, according to the information we have, it is very rare that they would insert anything like that or would allow it, because their controls are so carefully made to try to identify people all their life and particularly where they were born so they can trace down through for the rest of the period, and that is an unexplained feature.
>
> Then the fact of her uncle and what his status was, apparently a part of the Interior government and not a part of the Intelligence. But nevertheless he had a telephone, and the style in which they lived, and the apartment and all were very unusual comparatively.
>
> RUSSELL: You mean while they were in Russia?
>
> RANKIN: Yes, I mean not only Oswald but this uncle, too, and it would appear that he was much more than just a person of the Interior government like she had said from what we have been able to get from the CIA and others about it.
>
> Then the fact that she was allowed to leave the country the way she was is not adequately explained by her testimony, her statements or anything.[91]

It remained unexplained. The Warren Commission, which had no way of independently verifying whether or not Oswald was an agent of the FBI or the CIA, could hardly determine whether his wife was an agent for Soviet intelligence. The suspicions, the unexplained questions merely lay there, tantalizing, worrying, waiting for answers that would never come.

Oswald himself revealed something of the nature of his activities in the Soviet Union during a radio debate in New Orleans with some anti-Castro Cubans on August 21, 1963.[92] When Carlos Bringuier, the leader of an exile organization Oswald had attempted to infiltrate, who later got into a fight with Oswald on the street,[92a] brought up the subject of Oswald's "defection," Oswald seemed startled, and reacted defensively. "Well, as I uh, well, I will answer that ques . . . uh question directly then, since you will not rest until you get your answer. I worked in Russia. I was under uh, the protection of the uh . . . American government. But that is I was at all times considered an American citizen." [93]

If Oswald was not under the embassy's "protection," he was certainly the recipient of the most unusual beneficence. In the bureaucratic scheme of things Oswald's announcement of "defection" in October 1959 should have resulted in the posting by the State Department of a "lookout card," warning embassies and passport offices against issuing Oswald a new passport. None, however, was prepared.[94] By March 1960 the embassy in Moscow had lost all trace of Oswald, and this time the State Department in Washington typed up, as it was directed to by law, a "refusal sheet," [95] the first stage in the issuance of a lookout card. Yet once again a lookout card was never prepared, the result, the State Department explained to the Commission, of a probable clerical error.[96] In June 1962 a *third* lookout card should have been prepared, preventing Oswald from obtaining a new passport until he repaid a $435 loan the State Department had made him so he could return home from the Soviet Union.[97] Once again, however, the lookout card never appeared, the victim apparently of yet another "clerical error." [98] When Oswald applied for a passport in New Orleans, he got it in twenty-four hours.[99]

No bureaucracy, especially one as large and complex as the State Department, functions perfectly; errors can and do happen. What makes the errors suspicious in Oswald's case is not only their frequency but the people who were making them. The State Department's passport office was, then as now, under the control of the stridently anti-Communist Miss Frances Knight. Among her lieutenants of the time was the legendary red-hunter Otto Otepka, whose zeal in ferreting out suspected Communists eventually cost him his job.[100] That Knight and Otepka, who were known to question the loyalty of ordinary citizens, should let a character like Oswald escape not once but *three* times through their bureaucratic net would seem to tax even the most innocent imagination. The explanation the Warren Commission chose to accept was that, in the unique case of Lee Harvey Oswald, the State Department functioned with the most appalling inefficiency.

Privately, though, the commissioners were highly suspicious. The question of the passport, and the ease with which Oswald obtained it, came up during the Commission's executive session of January 22, 1964. The now declassified top secret transcript reveals that the State Department found only one defender: Allen Dulles.

> UNIDENTIFIED: One of the strange things that happened, and it may have no bearing on this [whether Oswald was an FBI agent], at all, is the fact that this man who is a defector, and who was under observation at least by the FBI, they say they saw him frequently, could next day with a passport that permitted him to go to Russia. From my observations of the case that have come to us, such passports are not passed out with that ease.
>
> DULLES: Mr. . . . I think you are wrong on that.
>
> UNIDENTIFIED: I could be.
>
> DULLES: Because passports are issued valid for anywhere except specified countries. . . . But any American, practically any American, can get a passport that is good for anywhere. An American can travel and Russia is one of the countries that you can now travel to.
>
> UNIDENTIFIED: Well, maybe you can.

DULLES: You can get them quick.

UNIDENTIFIED (presumably WARREN): I think our general counsel and I both have some experiences in cases that have come before our Court which would indicate that that isn't exactly the fact.

DULLES: I think in the State Department . . .

UNIDENTIFIED (presumably WARREN): They have great difficulty, some of them, in getting a passport to go to Russia.

BOGGS: Particularly for someone who has any Communist . . .

UNIDENTIFIED: Oh, yes.

DULLES: Is there any evidence the State Department has that record in the files. I don't think that record has ever turned up.

COOPER: They admitted there wasn't any.

UNIDENTIFIED: What record, that he was a defector?

DULLES: Yes, I don't think the State Department or in the Passport Bureau, there was no record. It didn't get down to the passport offices. That is one of the things we ought to look into.

UNIDENTIFIED: The State Department knew he was a defector. They aranged for him to come back.

DULLES: But it don't get [words missing] passport files or the passport records. They are issuing hundreds and thousands of passports. They have their own particular system.[101]

The Commission let it go at that. Any other explanation—namely, that the ways were greased for Oswald because he was one of the government's own—was not even considered.

Oswald was not only lucky. In some instances, he seemed positively clairvoyant. A providential letter to his mother was a notable case. By March 1960 Marguerite Oswald had become worried. It had been months since her son's defection, and in all that time she had had no word from him. Mrs. Oswald was convinced that her son was on some mission for his government, but she wanted to be sure.[102] She wrote her representative expressing her concern about her son's well-being, and in due course the representative forwarded the letter to the State Department.[103] Mrs. Oswald herself showed up at the State Department on January 26, 1961, to inquire about Lee's whereabouts.[104] A week later the department requested the Moscow embassy to inform the Soviet Foreign Ministry of Mrs. Oswald's anxiety.[105] The request went by regular diplomatic pouch and arrived in Moscow February 10 or 11.[106] No action had been taken on the request by February 13, when a letter, postmarked Minsk, arrived at the embassy.[107] It was from Oswald, who asked for the return of his passport so he could return to the United States.[108] Another one of those coincidences.

The embassy handled Oswald's requested repatriation as a matter of routine. He was given a loan of several hundred dollars to pay for his passage home.[109] Marina, on the recommendation of the embassy, was exempted from the usual immigration quota and allowed to return with her husband to the United States.[110] Most generously of all, the embassy returned Oswald's passport months ahead of his scheduled departure, despite explicit, written instructions from the passport office in Washington that Oswald's passport be withheld until *after* he had finalized his travel plans, lest it fall into the hands of Soviet authorities.[111]

The Oswalds appeared at the American embassy in late May to fill out some forms and complete their travel plans to the United States.[112] Marina was also given a physical examination by the embassy doctor, Captain Alexis Davison, an Air Force flight surgeon.[113] Davison was uncommonly friendly. At one point he suggested to Oswald, the military turncoat, that if he were ever in Atlanta—Davison's hometown—he should look up his mother.[114] Oswald evidently intended to take the captain up on his invitation. After the assassination federal agents found Davison's mother's name written in Oswald's notebook.[114a]

Coincidentally, the Oswalds did stop in Atlanta on their way back to Dallas—not for a visit, but for their plane to discharge and pick up passengers.[115] What made the coincidence and Davison's offer of southern hospitality more striking was the captain's identity. He was apparently something more than an ordinary flight surgeon. On October 22, five months after the Oswalds' departure, the Soviets arrested Colonel Oleg

Penkovskiy and charged him with being a spy for British and American intelligence.[116] The Penkovskiy affair was one of the most sensational spy cases in Soviet history. Among the reams of secret information Penkovskiy passed to the West was the number and disposition of Soviet missile forces, data which played a key role in resolving the Cuban missile crisis.[117] The Soviets were understandably upset. Five months after his arrest, Penkovskiy was given a four-day trial, found guilty of treason, taken out, and shot [118]—but not before Soviet authorities named eight foreigners as Penkovskiy's contacts.[119] One of the eight was Alexis Davison.[120]

According to the Soviet prosecutor, Davison's phone number was found on Penkovskiy at the time of his arrest.[121] Davison was also said to have been observed picking up information left by Penkovskiy at a prearranged intelligence "drop" in Moscow.[122] On May 6, 1963, Davison left the Soviet Union. The next day, Penkovskiy's trial began.[123]

Davison's contact with Oswald could have all been by chance, of course—just another one of those coincidences. Everyone at the American embassy seemed most friendly to young Lee. And that was the trouble.

The Oswalds left Moscow on June 1, 1962, aboard a train bound for Holland.[124] "They crossed the Soviet frontier at Brest on June 2," the Report relates. "Two days later they departed from Holland on the SS *Maasdam*." [125] To read the Report, the Oswald's trip seems uneventful: a simple train ride and then a long voyage home, with the Oswalds staying by themselves, Marina not wanting to go on deck because as the commissioners report her testimony, "she was poorly dressed and Oswald was ashamed of her."

A check of the Oswalds' passports and a reading of Marina's own diary shows the trip to be something else. Lee's passport, in particular, contains unexplained anomalies. The Oswalds supposedly crossed the iron curtain at the railway station at Helmstedt, the tensest, most security conscious checkpoint along the border between East and West Berlin.[126] Yet there is no stamp on Lee's passport—as there *is* on Marina's—showing that he made the crossing.[127] Holland is also a puzzle. According to the Commission, the Oswalds stayed in Amsterdam two days before boarding a ship for America.[128] Marina's diary, however, talks of their staying in a "private apartment" for three days before taking ship.[129] The Commission itself noted the contradiction, and talked about it in executive session on January 27, 1964.

> RANKIN: . . . When they came back, they went to Amsterdam and were there for, I think, it was two days before they went to Rotterdam to take a boat, and it is unexplained why they happened to go there and stay, and got a place to live, some little apartment, and what they were doing in the interim, that entire period is just full of possibilities for training, for working with the Soviet, and its agents, and unusual compared with the experience of most Americans.
>
> Now, you recognize it is going to be very difficult to get all of that out of her no matter how well informed we are about her, what she has testified to, what she has given statements about, and she has given a good many of them, and what her written statement in Russian is, all of those things will be—we have, and we examined them in great detail and are prepared on them, but whenever she gets to these areas that might be enlightening for us, she is unable—[130]

At that point, the transcript records, another commissioner said he didn't understand what Rankin was talking about, and changed the subject. The Commission never did get a full explanation for the stopover in Amsterdam (the problems with Oswald's passport were missed entirely), from Marina or anyone else. And so they dealt with it as they had other questions for which there was no explanation: they ignored it.

The questions persist. How did Oswald pass from East Germany into West Germany? Why did the Oswalds choose to stay at an "apartment" rather than a hotel in Amsterdam? What did they do during those two unaccounted-for days?

Obviously Oswald would have found it difficult, if not impossible, to slip across the German border had he been an ordinary American. Moreover, if he were an ordinary American, there would have been no need for such derring-do. But suppose Oswald was an American agent. Then his actions become not only possible but logical. The apartment in Amsterdam might then have been an intelligence "safe house," and the three days spent in intensive debriefing.

What lends additional plausibility to this scenario is the otherwise implausible circumstances surrounding the Oswalds' entry into the United States. According to the Commission the Oswalds landed at Hoboken, New Jersey, on June 13, 1962.[131] They were met by Spas T. Raikin, whom the Report identifies as "a representative of the Traveler's Aid Society."[132] After clearing customs they went to New York, spent a night in the Times Square Hotel,[133] and left the next morning by plane for Dallas.[134] According to the Report, neither the FBI nor the CIA met Oswald on his arrival[135] —this at a time when the CIA was interviewing tourists returning from Yugoslavia. The Report would have its readers believe that the returning defector encountered no one more sinister than a social worker for Traveler's Aid.

The description of Mr. Raikin is correct—as far as it goes. It fails to mention his other credentials, however; namely, his reported position as former secretary general of the American Friends of the Anti-Bolshevik Nations, an anti-Communist lobby with numerous connections to intelligence services in the United States as well as in Europe and Asia.[136] Louis Johnson, the senior Immigration and Naturalization Service officer on the Hoboken pier, was decidedly reluctant to help Raikin track down Oswald,[137] but at length Raikin discovered Oswald waiting to claim his baggage, and most annoyed that his identity had been revealed.[138] The day of the assassination Raikin recognized Oswald and telephoned "a friend in the FBI in New York who had an interest in Bulgaria, and with whom I talked from time to time."[139]

The Bureau's interest in Oswald was certainly justified. He was, after all, a returning defector, and given his history, as far as the Bureau could surmise, a potential agent for Soviet intelligence. Raikin, in short, was doing the job he should have been doing. What is not so easily understood is the CIA's total lack of interest in Oswald; why the Agency claimed to have no contact with him either in the Soviet Union, in Europe, or on his return to the United States. The mystery, as Sherlock Holmes would have put it, is why the dog *didn't* bark.

The CIA was not the only agency which should have acted and didn't. On November 3, 1959, shortly after Oswald had flung down his passport on the desk of Richard Snyder, the U.S. naval attaché in Moscow cabled FBI, State, CIA, the Office of Naval Intelligence, and the Immigration and Naturalization Service, reporting that Oswald "has offered to furnish Soviets info he possesses on US radar." [140] This disclosure of possible treason and espionage provoked only mild reaction. The radar call signs and codes on the West Coast were switched,[141] and the marines downgraded Oswald's discharge from "honorable" to "undesirable" [142] (still a far cry from "dishonorable"), and then only on the grounds that Oswald had defected, not that he had committed espionage. One reasonably could have expected the pier at Hoboken to be crowded with representatives of various U.S. intelligence and law enforcement agencies, vying for the privilege of arresting the turncoat. None, however, appeared. The naval attaché's cable is noteworthy in one other respect. It identifies Oswald as "former Marine and . . ." The next forty-three spaces, describing whatever else Oswald was, are blanked out as secret.[143]

Apparently no one cared about Lee Oswald, the turncoat marine. What made the disinterest all the more remarkable was that Oswald was not just any marine, but one who had access to one of the United States's most sensitive intelligence programs: the U-2. Oswald had worked with the U-2's not only at Atsugi but also in the Philippines, where his unit was assigned to guard the aircraft in their hangers.[144] Moreover, one of Oswald's marine officers suspected that he was taking an uncommon interest in the planes.[145] The curiosity could have been innocent. All the same, on May 1, 1960, seven months after Oswald's arrival in the Soviet Union, the Russians, who had been bedeviled for years by the planes, finally managed to shoot one down.[146] The incident severely embarrassed the United States and led to the collapse of summit talks between Eisenhower and Khrushchev. Could there have been any connection between Oswald, the purveyor of radar secrets, and the Russians' unaccustomed accuracy? Francis Gary Powers, the pilot of the U-2 that was brought down, surely thought so. In his account of the mission, *Operation Overflight,* Powers pointed an accusing finger at Oswald. Oswald, he noted, had access to the new American MPS 16 height-finding radar. The Russians had never been able to shoot down a U-2 because it flew too high. Oswald arrives and suddenly the Russians' shooting skills improve. Concidence? Not to Powers it wasn't.[147]

The U-2 incident was all the more reason to question Oswald on his return to the United States. Instead, nothing. There would have been no need for the Agency to interview Oswald, of course, if they knew perfectly well who he was, why he had gone to the Soviet Union, and what he had done there—the things they would have known if he had been one of their agents. That would also explain why, at a time when the CIA has admitted conducting "mail covers" * on every letter going to and from the Soviet Union,[149]

---

* The CIA decided to start opening letters between the United States and the Soviet Union on September 30, 1952. According to the Rockefeller commission report:

> The Security Office requested the Deputy Director of Plans to inform the Director of Central Intelligence that Security planned to undertake activities to accumulate information on all letter envelopes or covers, passing through New York City, originating in the Soviet Union, or destined for the Soviet Union. . . . Both sides for all first class mail were to be photographed. . . . The mail opening project, which started in the early months of the operation with only a few letters, had expanded by 1959 to include the opening of nearly 13,000 letters a year. . . . Individuals or organizations of particular interest were specified in watch lists provided to the mail project by the Counterintelligence Staff, by other CIA components and by the FBI. The number of names on the watch list varied, from time to time, but on the average, the list included approximately 300 names, including about 100 furnished by the FBI. The watch list included the names of foreigners and of United States citizens.[148]

Oswald's recently declassified CIA file contains *no* letters.† [150]

Oswald did fly to Dallas the day after his arrival in New York. But the Eastern flight made one other stop en route: Atlanta, Georgia, the hometown of Captain Davison.[152] The stopover could well have been coin-

---

† One reason may be that the bulk of the Agency's material on Oswald is filed under another name. Recently University of California Professor Peter Dale Scott, a former Canadian diplomat, author of one of the Pentagon Papers, and one of the most respected assassination researchers, suggested that this "double filing" was, in fact, the case. According to Scott it would be a simple matter for the Agency to keep files on Oswald under two names: a "Lee Harvey Oswald" for open, cover material, and a "Harvey Lee Oswald" for covert, intelligence activity. The appealing aspect of Scott's hypothesis is that it is based on common intelligence practice, and more to the point, explains the recurring transposition of given names that invariably occurs when Oswald's activities are being monitored by an intelligence agency.

There are a number of such instances. The first appears in 1960, in a CIA response to a White House request for a report on recent defectors to the Soviet Union. The other defectors' names are listed correctly in the Agency's classified report, but Oswald's first two names are inexplicably transposed.

On the day of the assassination Lieutenant Jack Revill, the head of the Dallas police intelligence section, submitted a list of employees of the School Book Depository who were missing. The first name on the list was "Harvey Lee Oswald." The address given was 605 Elsbeth, a slightly falsified version of an address Oswald had used a year before the assassination, which was unknown to his employers. The Dallas police, however, claimed to have no information about Oswald, much less his old address, anywhere in their intelligence files. Where, then, did it come from?

Almost certainly, Scott feels, from the 112th Army Intelligence Group in Texas, which *did* carry a "Harvey Lee Oswald" residing at 605 Elsbeth Street. Revill and at least one of the officers under his command had contacts in the army intelligence group. Indeed, the day of the assassination Revill drove with an army agent from the School Book Depository.[150a] This partly explains a question that has intrigued critics since the assassination: Why did the police start looking for Oswald so quickly after the assassination when at least eleven other employees were missing from the Book Depository? But a more ominous question emerges: Why did army intelligence sic the cops on Oswald?

When the police arrived at Oswald's rooming house looking for him they asked the housekeeper, Mrs. Earlene Roberts, if she had a boarder named "Harvey Lee Oswald." Mrs. Roberts said no, because Oswald was registered under yet another reverse variant of his name, O. H. Lee.

"Harvey Lee Oswald" also crops up in a number of other intelligence reports. One from the FBI in Los Angeles on November 29, 1963, uses the alias, as does a Secret Service report from Austin dated February 28, 1964.

In April 1973, nearly ten years after the assassination, the Office of Naval Intelligence declassified a cable it had received from the U.S. naval attaché in Canberra two days after the assassination. The cable is less interesting for what it says than for the person it refers to: "Harvey Lee Oswald." In May 1973 army intelligence declassified another secret cable relating to the assassination. This one came from army intelligence in Texas on November 22, 1963. It reports false information from the Dallas police that Oswald was a card-carrying Communist and had been to Cuba. The cable concludes with "additional information on Oswald, Harvey Lee."

"By this simple device," Scott concludes, "the CIA could truthfully deny to FBI investigators shortly after the assassination that it had any CIA material in its files on Lee Harvey Oswald." [151] To get the right answers, apparently, you have to ask the right questions.

cidental, though it is hard to explain why the Oswalds would have chosen such a flight when a number of nonstops were available that day.[153] Or Oswald might have wanted to stop in Atlanta for a specific reason, a reason which will be discussed in the next chapter.

Once in Texas, the Oswalds were taken under the wing of Dallas-Fort Worth's large White Russian community. Most of the Russians had come to Dallas though the auspices of the Tolstoy Foundation, a right-wing lobby which, for a time, received yearly subsidies from the U.S. government (read: CIA) of $400,000 (9 H. 5).[154] * Life centered around the Orthodox Church, another recipient of the CIA's largesse.[155] The "godfather," patron, and leading ideological light of the community was Paul Raigorodsky, a millionaire oilman and director of the Tolstoy Foundation.[156] He was not one of Oswald's great admirers. He listened suspiciously to Oswald's tales of his life in the Soviet Union, with particular suspicion of the ease with which Marina had gained an exit visa. In Raigorodsky's experience such visas were unheard of. Russian-born wives were sometimes permitted to join their American husbands, but only long after their husbands had returned to the United States. Raigorodsky regarded Oswald's story as "unbelievable."[157] Oswald, however, found other friends, the best of them a petroleum engineer named George De Mohrenschildt.

De Mohrenschildt and his wife Jeanne were maverick outsiders as far as most of the other White Russians were concerned. Highborn (he was actually *Count* Sergei De Mohrenschildt),[158] sharp-tongued, and well connected (he was a friend of the Bouviers, Jacqueline Kennedy's family), De Mohrenschildt was, by his own admission, "highly individualistic."[159] De Mohrenschildt couldn't have cared less what his neighbors thought of him. He had his own way of doing and saying things, and no one was going to change him.

It was to this aristocratic descendant of Russian

---

* All references to "H.," both in the text and end notes, indicate that the text is reporting information contained in the twenty-six volumes of Warren Commission hearings, in this case, volume 9, page 5.

nobility that an unemployed high-school dropout and his wife were drawn. The De Mohrenschildts, in turn, lavished attention on the Oswalds. George took Lee to parties;[160] Jeanne chauffeured Marina on errands. When Lee's and Marina's marriage began to break up it was Jeanne and George who helped Marina move her things out of the house.[162] Yet the bond between Lee and De Mohrenschildt remained strong. Lee listed him as a reference on an employment application, boasted that he was his closest friend.[163] According to Larry Taylor, De Mohrenschildt's former son-in-law, "Whatever his [De Mohrenschildt's] suggestions were Lee grabbed them and took them, whether it was what time to go to bed or where to stay."[163a] They were close, all right; so tight that when Lee was dead his old friend George would provide some of the most damaging, controversial testimony against him.

After the assassination attention naturally settled on Oswald's friends. The De Mohrenschildts, George in particular, came under the most intense scrutiny. But in its Report the Commission found that their relationship was wholly innocent, De Mohrenschildt no more than a friend in need. The Report provided a brief background of De Mohrenschildt, noting that he had come to the United States in the late twenties, had studied to become a petroleum engineer, and had taken out citizenship in 1949.[164] No mention was made of any wartime service. The report also stated that "in 1960, after the death of his son, he and his wife made an 8-month hike from the United States-Mexican border to Panama over primitive jungle trails. *By happenstance they were in Guatemala City at the time of the Bay of Pigs invasion.* A lengthy film and complete log was prepared by De Mohrenschildt and a report of the trip was made to the United States Government." (Italics added.)[165] The Report does not mention which agency of the United States government, but it strains credibility to believe that it was not the CIA.

For good neighbor George was a spook. During World War II, or so he boasted, he worked as an intelligence agent for the French underground;[166] the FBI also had suspicions that De Mohrenschildt was a

German agent. What was not nearly so well known was that in June 1941 George De Mohrenschildt and a Mexican woman named Lilia Pardo Larin were picked up in Port Arthur, Texas, after they had reportedly sketched port facilities. The authorities searched and interrogated them, but did not arrest them. In September 1942 the authorities again had De Mohrenschildt under suspicion of being a German agent. (C.D. 777a; C.E. 537, 9 H. 184–86).[167–70]

None of which was mentioned in the Report. Instead, the Report concluded: "The Commission's investigation has developed no signs of subversive or disloyal conduct on the part of either of the De Mohrenschildts. Neither the FBI, CIA, nor any witness contacted by the Commission has provided any information linking the De Mohrenschildts to subversive or extremist organizations. Nor has there been any evidence linking them in any way with the assassination of President Kennedy."[171] The Commission's statement, if noteworthy merely for the fact of its inclusion in the Report, nonetheless begs the question, which is not whether George De Mohrenschildt assassinated President Kennedy, for quite clearly he didn't. It is rather why a man with such obvious, extensive background in intelligence work seemed to be "babysitting" Oswald.

Oswald remained in the Dallas-Fort Worth area ten months. They were not happy ones. Badgered by the FBI, he seemed incapable of holding a job, and his relationships with both Marina and their Russian friends were deteriorating. There were several loud arguments with Marina, apparently over sex and money[172] (Lee was not a good provider in either department), one of which climaxed with Lee striking Marina in the face and giving her a small shiner.[173] After a time, even the De Mohrenschildts stopped seeing them. In April 1963 Oswald decided a change of scene would cure his troubles. He boarded a night bus for the place of his birth, the city of New Orleans.[174]

It was in New Orleans that Oswald slipped into the shadow world of Cuban politics, with its petty deception and equally petty intrigue. Even now, which side he was playing (or, indeed, whether he was playing both) is impossible to say, for Oswald moved with equal facility among both pro- and anti-Castro Cubans. To the anti-Castro Cubans, many of whom were supported by the CIA, or as in the case of several of Oswald's contacts were its employees, he came on like a swaggering soldier of fortune, offering to blow up bridges and school them in the black arts of guerrilla warfare.[175] He was a classic provocateur, a forerunner of "Tommy the Traveler," the legendary FBI informant of nearly a decade later who wreaked havoc among the radical left. Oswald did Tommy one better. He obliged both left and right. After his overtures to the anti-Castro Cubans were rejected, Oswald created a fictitious chapter of the pro-Castro Fair Play for Cuba Committee, with himself the only member.[177] He boasted of his accomplishments in a letter to the New York headquarters of the Communist party,[178] an organization so thoroughly infiltrated with FBI men that Oswald would have done as well sending J. Edgar Hoover the note personally. Whether he sought its attention or not, Oswald was soon a red blip on the Bureau's radar screen. How closely the blip was followed is indicated by the letter Oswald wrote to the Communists on April 19, 1963: "I stood yesterday for the first time in my life, with a placard around my neck, passing out Fair Play for Cuba pamphlets," Oswald reported. "My home-made placard said; HANDS OFF CUBA! VIVA FIDEL!"[179] Two days later, the FBI filed the following report:

> Dallas confidential informant T-2 advised that Lee H. Oswald of Dallas, Texas, was in contact with the Fair Play for Cuba Committee. According to T-2, OSWALD had a placard around his neck reading, "Hands off Cuba Viva Fidel."[180]

Informant "T-2" was obviously reading Oswald's mail. Unless, of course, T-2 was Lee Harvey Oswald himself.

Oswald was a strange one, all right, stranger still for

someone supposedly enlisted in Castro's cause. A Marxist who, if the testimony of the numerous witnesses in Clinton is correct, spent much of his time in the company of two reported employees of the CIA, namely David Ferrie and Clay Shaw.[181] A left-wing activist who offered to train right-wing activists in how to make war on his hero.[182] An enemy of the FBI who, the moment he was arrested after a brief altercation with anti-Castro Cubans on a New Orleans street corner, demanded to see an FBI man.[183]

The last incident is especially puzzling. The "fight" Oswald was in, and for which he was arrested and convicted of disturbing the peace, was allegedly a one-blow affair,[183a] with Oswald, characteristically, on the receiving end of the punch. The man who reportedly threw it was Carlos Bringuier,[183b] a Cuban exile leader and the man whom Oswald had gone to see about joining the anti-Castro cause.[184] The New Orleans police complied with Oswald's request, and a local FBI man came to see him in jail. If the agent's report of his interview with Oswald is accurate, Oswald succeeded only in digging himself deeper into a hole. Oswald created an entirely new past for himself, saying he had been born in Cuba and was a major actor in the pro-Castro cause.[185] Why he lied, why he asked to talk to an FBI man in the first place, is another one of the unanswered questions. It could be, though, that Oswald was taking another step in establishing his bogus credentials as a Castro militant for an undefined future assignment.

He took the biggest step of all when he left New Orleans in September 1963 on a bus for Mexico City,[186] where he was to seek—and be denied—a visa for travel to Cuba. The Warren Commission reported the trip in detail, but never fully explained it even to its own satisfaction. The records of Oswald's trip were also left incomplete. The Commission, for instance, listed all the people who got Mexican travel visas the same day as Oswald, save one. The name of the person who received his visa immediately before Oswald was missing.[187] It was a small detail, but a nonetheless interesting omission. For years students of the assassination wondered who the missing man or woman could be. Finally, in 1975, nearly twelve years after the assassination, an inadvertently declassified FBI report revealed the identity of the man who had stood in line ahead of Lee Harvey Oswald. His name was William G. Gaudet, and he listed his occupation as editor of the *Latin American Traveller*, a small newsletter based in San Jose, Costa Rica.[188] What made Mr. Gaudet interesting was the fact that, by his own admission, he had been an employee of the Central Intelligence Agency.[189]

Gaudet had known Oswald and had seen him distributing his Fair Play for Cuba leaflets outside the International Trade Mart.[190] He denied, though, that their walking into the office of the Mexican consul was anything more than one of those coincidences that seem to have dogged Oswald the last years of his life.[191] Later, when he heard that Oswald had been charged as the President's assassin, Gaudet was incredulous. "He would have been the last person in the world I would have suspected ever could have been involved in this shooting," Gaudet remembered years later. ". . . He was a miserable creature . . . too nervous and . . . er . . . he was a very unstable person . . . and I don't think he knew exactly what he was distributing when he was distributing these pamphlets for the Fair Play for Cuba deal, which was *nothing but a front*."[192] (Italics added.)

Oswald's arrest may have surprised Gaudet; it left the Federal Bureau of Investigation thunderstruck. Within a hour of Oswald's pickup Dallas agent James Hosty had run up to Police Lieutenant Revill and blurted out, "Jack . . . a Communist killed President Kennedy. We know this guy. He is in our Communist file."[193] To this startling revelation Hosty added two others: that Oswald had been in touch with "two known foreign subversive agents"[194] within two weeks of the assassination, and most incredibly of all, that the Bureau "had information that this man was capable . . . of committing this assassination"[195]—information which FBI had withheld not only from the Dallas police but from the Secret Service. While Revill was digesting this news, Gordon Shanklin, the special agent in charge of the Dallas FBI office, was angrily phoning James Bookhout, another one of his agents, who had gone to the police station. Dallas homicide chief Will Fritz, who took the call, listened in on an extension and later reported the substance of the conversation:

> He said, "Is Hosty in that investigation?" Bookhout said no. He said, "I want him in that investigation right now because he knows those people he has been talking to," and he said some other things that I don't want to repeat, about what to do if he didn't do it right quick. So I didn't tell them that I even knew what Mr. Shanklin said. I walked out of there and called them in.[196]

The Bureau was worried by what Hosty had told Revill, especially after Curry repeated the substance of Hosty's conversation to the press later on November 22. Within minutes after Curry's statement, Shanklin cabled him. According to an account of the conversation Curry provided in a registered letter to Earl Warren (and which was concealed from the public until the *Houston Chronicle* uncovered a copy of the letter in September 1975), Shanklin "stated that the Bureau was extremely desirous that I retract my statement to the press." Curry complied, and told Revill to also keep his mouth shut.[197]

When Hosty himself joined the interrogation of the President's accused assassin, Oswald beat his fists on a desk in a rage. When Fritz asked Oswald why he was upset, Oswald told him that Hosty had twice mistreated Marina; the agent "practically accosted her," Fritz quoted Oswald as saying.[198]

Hosty, of course, had indeed seen Marina, and to judge from Oswald's accusation apparently had attempted to enlist her as an informer.[199] Now, however, the tables were turning. It was Hosty and the FBI who had cause to worry. For the accused presidential assassin was carrying a notebook at the time of his arrest. In that book was listed the name, auto license number, and telephone number of none other than James P. Hosty.[200]

The appearance of Hosty's name in Oswald's notebook, along with Hosty's announcement to Revill that the Bureau considered Oswald a potential assassin, did not do much for Hosty's career. He was suspended from the Bureau for thirty days without pay and transferred to Kansas City, where he has remained, buried, ever since.[201] At first the Bureau also neglected to include mention of Hosty in the report on Oswald's notebook it turned over to the Commission. Not until February 11, 1964, after the presence of the agent's name in the notebook became known by the press, did the Bureau turn over a "supplemental" report admitting that Hosty was mentioned.[202] Even then the Bureau's efforts to muddy the case did not stop. One key witness, Arnold Rowland, who saw a man running from the Book Depository immediately after the assassination, claimed that FBI agents told him to "forget about" what he had seen.[203] The most blatant intimidation, however, was of Marina Oswald.

In one of her first appearances before the Commission, Marina testified:

> Sometimes the FBI agents asked questions which had no bearing or relationship, and if I didn't want to answer they told me that if I wanted to live in this country, I would have to help in this matter, even though they were often irrelevant. . . .
>
> I think that the FBI agents knew that I was afraid that after everything that happened I could not remain to live in this country, and they somewhat exploited that for their own purposes, in a very polite form, so that you could not say anything after that. They cannot be accused of anything. They approached it in a very clever, contrived way.[204]

According to Robert Oswald, Marina's brother-in-law, the harassment began before the assassination.

> Marina did not want to speak to the FBI at that time. And she was refusing to. And they were insisting, sir. And they implied in so many words as I sat there . . . that if she did not cooperate with the FBI agent there . . . that they would perhaps deport her from the United States and back to Russia.[205]

The Bureau also seemed strangely determined to fix the guilt on Oswald and bring the case to a close. The FBI "Summary Report" on the assassination was completed and forwarded to the Warren Commission on December 9, 1963, breathtaking speed considering the complexities of the crime. The report minced no words in its central conclusion:

> Evidence developed in the investigation points conclusively to the assassination of President Kennedy by Lee Harvey Oswald, avowed Marxist, a former defector to the Soviet Union and self-appointed Secretary of the New Orleans Chapter of the Fair Play for Cuba Committee, a pro-Castro organization.[206]

The Bureau's utter certainty and the speed with which it reached its judgment made some Commission members suspicious, especially after they received what seemed to be a credible report that Oswald had been an FBI informer. They expressed their fears in private during a secret Commission meeting on January 22, 1964:

> UNIDENTIFIED: . . . The FBI is very explicit that Oswald is the assassin or was the assassin, and they are very explicit that there was no conspiracy, and they are also saying in the same place that they are continuing their investigation. Now in my experience of almost nine years, in the first place it is hard to get them to say when you think you have got a case tight enough to convict somebody, that that is the person that committed the crime. They claim they don't evaluate, and it is uniform prior experience that they don't do that. Secondly, they have not run out all kinds of leads in Mexico or in Russia and so forth which they could probably . . .
>
> DULLES: What is that?
>
> UNIDENTIFIED: They haven't run out all the leads on the information and they could probably say—that isn't our business.
>
> UNIDENTIFIED: Yes.
>
> UNIDENTIFIED: But they are concluding that there can't be a conspiracy without those being run out. Now that is not [words missing], from my experience with the FBI.

UNIDENTIFIED: It is not. You are quite right. I have seen a great many reports.

UNIDENTIFIED: Why are they so eager to make both of those conclusions, both in the original report and the supplemental report, which is such a departure. Now that is just circumstantial evidence, and it doesn't prove anything about this, but it raises questions. . . .

BOGGS: This closes the case, you see. Don't you see?

DULLES: Yes, I see that.

RANKIN: They found the man. There is nothing more to do. The Commission supports their conclusions, and we can go home and that is the end of it.[207]

The commissioners sensed that something strange was afoot. They could not know how strange. For the Bureau was not only failing to uncover, it was actively covering up as well. Two days after the assassination, and two hours after Oswald's own death, a note in Oswald's handwriting, and personally delivered by him to the Dallas office of the FBI three days *before* the assassination, was destroyed by Hosty.[207a] In the note, Oswald warned Hosty to stop harassing Marina. The existence of the note and the fact that the Bureau had destroyed it (in short, suppression of evidence) finally became known in August 1975 in a copyrighted story in the *Dallas Times-Herald*.[208] FBI Director Clarence Kelley admitted that the story was true and announced that the Bureau was "investigating" how the note came to be destroyed. The *New York Times*, quoting unnamed sources within the FBI, stated that the note had been destroyed at Hoover's personal command although later a Bureau official denied this.[209]

Ironically, two witnesses—Marina Oswald and Ruth Paine—told the Warren Commission that Lee had informed them of his visit to the FBI, as well as the warning he delivered, but both women discounted the story,[210] which, like so much of what Oswald said, turned out to be true. As Marina put it: "Lee had told me that supposedly he had visited their office or their building. But I didn't believe him. I thought he was a brave rabbit." [211]

The story says as much about Oswald as it does about the Bureau. It is hard to imagine even a "brave rabbit" going out of his way to provoke the Federal Bureau of Investigation three days before he planned to kill the President of the United States. He would have to be crazy or innocent. And there is not a shred of credible evidence that suggests he was crazy.

As for the Bureau, the most sinister explanation is that it had things to hide, that Oswald *was* one of their agents, perhaps even a part of a Bureau assassination plot. J. Edgar Hoover certainly had little love for either of the Kennedys—Robert especially, who was forever infringing on his prerogatives. The very day of the assassination, Hoover reportedly had the "hot line" Kennedy had installed in his office disconnected.[212] Henceforth, the Bureau's relationship with the Kennedy Justice Department was decidedly frosty.[213] Moreover, the Bureau was well aware of Oswald and his activities, and thus could conceivably be in a position to employ (or implicate) him in an assassination plot. Finally, there is, if not a mountain, at least a good-sized hill of circumstantial evidence (Hosty's name in the notebook, the failure to alert the Secret Service that Oswald was a threat to the President, the destruction of Oswald's note) that points in the Bureau's direction.

The theory, however, simply does not wash. While the Bureau has been implicated in numerous illegal acts over the last thirteen years, so far, at least, murder is not one of them. Unlike the CIA, which *has* committed murder numerous times, the Bureau was also well stocked with Kennedy partisans, including a number of senior officials. As for Hoover's dislike for the Kennedys, the fact is that the director didn't much care for *any* president or attorney general. The circumstantial evidence, while troublesome, can also be explained, though some items—notably, how Hosty's name wound up in Oswald's notebook—were never satisfactorily accounted for by the Commission. But the fact which tends most to clear the Bureau of complicity in the President's death is that its association with Oswald was so obvious. Only the Bureau raised sinister possibilities in Oswald's defection *before* the assassination[214] (see chapter 7). Only the Bureau took an interest in him when he returned from the Soviet Union.[215] Only the Bureau seemed anxious to find out just who this odd character was who had come back to Dallas. The Bureau left its fingerprints wherever it went. Report after report details its curiosity about Oswald *before* the assassination. Dozens, possibly hundreds, of agents, secretaries, and filing clerks saw these reports. If the Bureau truly did kill the President, presumably they would all have to be silenced, unless the plot were of even grander dimensions than the most paranoid imagination has so far been able to contemplate. The Bureau came on to Oswald like a big, curious dog, sniffing, sometimes knocking him over, sticking its nose into his pockets, and never being able to discover who he was or what he was up to.

The Bureau's first open contact with Oswald was on June 26, 1962, within weeks after his return to Texas from the Soviet Union. Oswald seemed somewhat suspicious and hostile, especially after agents asked him whether Soviet intelligence had tried to recruit him. After the interview the Fort Worth office of the Bureau noted that Oswald was an interesting character, one worth keeping tabs on.[216] Two months later the Bureau again approached Oswald, this time outside his home. Though Oswald invited the agents inside, they insisted on talking outside, in their car, saying it would be "more informal." [217] The interview went on for two hours, a time span that suggested to many Commission critics, as well as to members of the Commission itself, that the agents may have been persuading Oswald to become an informer.[218] The Bureau denied it, though an FBI account of the meeting does concede that Oswald promised to inform the Bureau if Soviet intelligence should attempt to contact him.[219] Oswald's next contact with the Bureau before the assassination was in New Orleans, after his arrest. Oswald and Special Agent John Quigley talked for an hour and a half. Oswald never told Quigley why he requested to see the FBI, and instead passed the time, according to Quigley's report, talking about his activities with Fair Play for Cuba and his association with the nonexistent A. J. Hidell, which of course was Oswald's alias.[220]

Commission critic George O'Toole,* a former CIA official, speculates that Oswald was indeed recruited as a Bureau informer, and that "Hidell" may have been his cover name with the Bureau.[223] O'Toole's theory, if correct, goes a long way toward explaining Oswald's use of an alias, the post-office boxes he kept under a fictitious name (presumably to be used as a pickup point for payoffs and instructions from the Bureau), the still unexplained anomalies of his finances, his attempted infiltration of the anti-Castro right, and why he requested to see an FBI man in New Orleans. It would also account for how Hosty's name happened to be in his notebook. The FBI had ample reason to want Oswald as an informer, either about pro- or anti-Castro operations. Oswald had access and credentials, and at the time, the Bureau itself was infiltrating both the pro- and anti-Castro movements in the United States. Even if O'Toole's assessment is correct, though, it does not automatically follow that the Bureau was involved in the assassination, or that Oswald did not remain an agent for someone else, namely the CIA. Agents frequently "double," even "triple."

The FBI wanting to cover up that relationship is understandable. Hoover was a man of legendary, neurotic sensitivity about bad publicity for his Bureau—"Don't embarrass the Bureau" was one of his chief

---

* O'Toole's main contribution to assassinology was the use of the highly controversial "psychological stress detector" to determine that Oswald was telling the truth when he said "I didn't shoot anybody, no sir." [221] The PSE measures differences in stress in the voice. A man, for instance, who is under emotional stress will provide the same readings as a man who is lying. Theoretically, though, a man who shows little or no stress, as Oswald did, is telling the truth. The fiendish beauty of the PSE is that it makes these measurements on sound, unlike a conventional polygraph machine, which has to be attached to its subject; the PSE is even supposed to be able to work from tape recordings. O'Toole fed a number of tapes into the PSE and discovered not only that Oswald was telling the truth, but that several of the major witnesses against him were lying, a finding which cheered critics of the Warren Commission, many of whom believe that Oswald was innocent. But innocent of what? O'Toole showed only that Oswald was innocent of firing the actual shots that killed the President, not that he wasn't part of a conspiracy. More to the point, the machine that provided all this information is highly suspect. Most major law enforcement agencies, including the FBI, will have nothing to do with it. The supposedly more reliable polygraph, or lie detector, is also subject to considerable error; hence, polygraph findings are inadmissible in most courts of law.[222]

maxims. One can imagine the embarrassment, and the anxiety to expunge it, after Oswald's arrest on November 22. The embarrassment must have become even more acute on November 24 when Oswald was shot down by Jack Ruby in the basement of the Dallas jail. For though few people knew it at the time, Jack Ruby too had served his country in the ranks of the FBI's legion of informers.[224] (See chapter 8.)

The Warren Commission was aware of Ruby's background, as it was aware of many of the details of Oswald's life. The commissioners were bothered by what they found, suspicious of the way both the Bureau and the Agency handled the Oswald case, and, in the end, powerless to do anything about their worries. The Commission's function was to deal in facts; in the face of inevitable denials from both the FBI and the CIA that Oswald had been an agent, they were left only with rumors which, as such, were discarded.

Looking back, the Commission's trust in both intelligence agencies seems incredibly naive. The world of 1963, however, was a very different one from the world of the mid-seventies. No one on the Commission—save Dulles—dreamed that the FBI and the CIA were anything but honorable, patriotic institutions, staffed by honorable, patriotic men, who on occasion were forced to employ "terribly bad characters." [225] Today we know differently. And yet even now we can only guess: Who was Lee Harvey Oswald?

Maybe the problem with understanding Oswald is that we think we know him so well. So ignore his name and then consider the facts: a man who works at a CIA base; has his records altered by the military; defects to Russia with no money; takes a plane when no planes are available; marries the niece of a high-ranking Soviet official; slips across the iron curtain without leaving a trace; threatens espionage and is not arrested; lives in a community infiltrated by intelligence agents; befriends a former spy; is seen in close contact with two intelligence agents; makes travel arrangements in the company of an employee of the CIA; uses an alias; keeps an office in a building with other agents; eludes detection by surveillance devices;

gets a passport when one should be denied; and is finally shot down in a room crowded with police by a former informer for the nation's chief investigative agency. Absorb these things, and then imagine that the man they happened to is named John Smith. Who do *you* think he is?

7

The Man Who Never Was

Everybody will know who I am now.
—Lee Harvey Oswald
November 22, 1963 [1]

ON SEPTEMBER 25, 1963, a young man walked into the offices of the Selective Service System in Austin, Texas, looking for help in upgrading his discharge. Mrs. Lee Dannelly, the assistant chief of the office's administrative section, listened to his tale of woe for nearly half an hour. He had been in the Marine Corps, the young man explained, and had gotten into a bit of trouble, trouble that finally resulted in his receiving an undesirable discharge. Ever since then he had had difficulty getting a good job. Employers just didn't want men whom the marines found undesirable. He was living in Fort Worth, the young man said, and he had a family to support. Perhaps, he thought, Selective Service might somehow help him out of his predicament. Mrs. Dannelly listened sympathetically and finally told the young man her office could be of no help. Selective Service just drafted men; it didn't discharge them. He ought to try the Veterans Administration. The young man thanked her and left the office. Later on that day the young man turned up at a print shop and a restaurant. Both the printer and the waitress remembered seeing him. On November 22 Mrs. Dannelly, the printer, and the waitress all saw the young man again. His picture was on television. The announcer said his name was Lee Harvey Oswald, and he had been arrested for murdering the President of the United States.[2]

There was only one trouble. On September 25, the day the young man was in Austin, Lee Harvey Oswald was eight hundred miles away in Mexico City.[3]

The report from Austin was one of hundreds that flowed in to the police, the Secret Service, and the FBI after the assassination from people who all claimed to have seen or known the troubled young loner who police said shot the President. Many of the calls were from ghouls looking for a ride on the coattails of history. Still others were from people who couldn't be sure, only *thought* that the man they had seen was Oswald. Others seemed unreliable sources. And then there was the small, final category: stable, reliable people who were sure what they had seen, who couldn't be shaken from their stories. This handful the Warren Commission considered, and worried about, to the very end of its investigation. When it came time to write the final Report, they too were discarded.

Albert Guy Bogard was one of these people. Bogard was a car salesman at a Lincoln-Mercury dealership in downtown Dallas. On November 9, 1963, a customer walked into his showroom and introduced himself as Lee Oswald. The man was interested in buying a used car, he said, and Bogard gladly offered to show him one. They walked into the lot, selected a model, and then, with "Oswald" at the wheel, took it for a test spin on the nearby Stemmons Freeway. Bogard could not forget that ride. His customer rocketed along at speeds up to seventy miles an hour. When they returned to the showroom they talked price and financing. "Oswald" said he didn't have enough money for a down payment, but would be coming into "a lot of money in the next two or three weeks." [4] To the credit manager Oswald said if financing could not be arranged, well, he might just "go back to Russia where they treat workers like men." [5] Other workers in the car dealership corroborated Bogard's story, and Bogard himself passed a lie detector test.[6]

Again there was a problem. On the day the man identifying himself as Oswald came into Bogard's car dealership, the real Lee Harvey Oswald was at home in Irving, Texas, composing a letter to the Soviet embassy in Washington.[7] Even if he had been in Dallas it is unlikely that he would have stopped in Bogard's dealership, or any other car showroom for that matter. Lee was always broke. More to the point, he didn't know how to drive.[8]

Two days before the incident at the car dealership a young man walked into a furniture and gun store looking for a part for a gun. The store didn't have the part, and the young man walked out to his car and brought his family in to look at furniture. Later two witnesses identified the man and wife as Lee and Marina Oswald. The Oswalds browsed for a while and then left, after Lee had been told where there was another gun store.[9]

The day after the assassination one of the clerks at the Irving Sports Shop, certain that he had seen the President's accused assassin somewhere before, rummaged through his receipts. Sure enough, there was the ticket. A man had come in several weeks before wanting to have two holes drilled in his rifle so he could mount his scope. The name on the ticket read "Oswald."[10]

A grocer in Irving had seen Oswald too. On the morning of November 8 Oswald had come in to cash a check for $189, payable to "*Harvey* Oswald."[11] (Italics added; see footnote on Harvey Lee Oswald, p. 175.) That was odd, because Lee Harvey Oswald never had checks that large. Nonetheless a barber a few doors down from the grocer saw Oswald the same day too. Oswald had come in for a haircut. The barber remembered him. He had a fourteen-year-old boy with him, and they had both made leftist remarks. The barber would remember that. He didn't like leftists.[12]

All the stories were puzzles. Marina said she had never been in the furniture shop with Lee.[13] The Mannlicher-Carcano Oswald ordered from Chicago came with the scope already mounted; moreover, it had not yet arrived when the other Carcano was brought into the gun shop.[14] On the day Oswald was supposedly getting a haircut, the real Lee Harvey

Oswald was at work at the Dallas School Book Depository.[15] Yet the witnesses were positive. Something definitely was strange.

And then there was the man on the rifle range. He first showed up on November 9, arriving at the Sports Drome Rifle Range with a foreign-made, scope-mounted carbine. He came several times after that as well. A number of people at the range were sure. A man like that was hard to forget. He fired rapidly, even though the range prohibited rapid fire. On occasion he also fired at other people's targets. He was loud and obnoxious, though what people remembered best was that he was a crack shot. One of the men on the range talked to him briefly and noticed the kind of weapon he was carrying. It was a 6.5-mm Italian carbine. After the assassination the people at the range were certain of the man they had seen. It had been Lee Harvey Oswald.[16] Only Lee Oswald could not have been there. He was either at home or at work.[17]

If people were trying to set Lee Oswald up they were doing a good job. There was a trail of clues that even an amateur could follow, left by a man who seemed to go out of his way to call attention to himself. Someone who was erratic and quarrelsome; who had been to Russia; who would be getting a lot of money very shortly; who was a deadly marksman. The question was who the someone was.

They called him "Leon" the night they introduced him to Sylvia Odio. Mrs. Odio was one of the leaders of Dallas's Cuban exile community. On the night of September 26 three men paid her a call, two Latins, "Angelo" and "Leopoldo," and a silent young American whom his companions called "Leon Oswald." Leopoldo did most of the talking. He said that he and his friends had just come from New Orleans and would shortly leave on another trip, to where and why Leopoldo would not say, but he hinted that violence on behalf of the Cuban cause was its purpose. Would Mrs. Odio, a daughter of Cuba, whose parents were even now in Castro's jails, give them some money? Mrs. Odio said she would not, that she disapproved of violence. With that, the men left her house.[18]

The next day Leopoldo called again. As Mrs. Odio subsequently recalled their conversation, Leopoldo said, "What do you think of the American?" Mrs. Odio replied: "I don't think anything." But Leopoldo kept pressing. "You know," he continued, "our idea is to introduce him to the underground in Cuba, because he is great, he is kind of nuts." Leopoldo mentioned that Oswald had been in the Marine Corps and that he was an excellent shot. Leopoldo chided Mrs. Odio for her lack of courage, telling her that Cubans "don't have any guts," that "Kennedy should have been assassinated after the Bay of Pigs," and that "Cubans should have done that." He concluded: "It is so easy to do it." [19]

The next time Mrs. Odio saw "Oswald" was when Lee Harvey Oswald's picture was flashed on a television screen on November 22. At the sight of the man who had been in her home she fainted.[20]

Sylvia Odio was stricken by the thought that the men who had murdered the President had once sought her help. Soon after the assassination she attempted suicide and was placed under a psychiatrist's care (C.D. 1553.)[21] The trauma had shaken her, but it did not shake her story. She repeated it confidently and without deviation to the Warren Commission. Several reputable sources, including her psychiatrist, vouched for her credibility.[22] Moreover, her sister had seen the men as well.[23]

The Commission could not help but be impressed —as well as worried. In late August 1964 Rankin wrote J. Edgar Hoover, stressing the volatility of the Odio story. "It is a matter of some importance to the Commission," Rankin warned, "that Mrs. Odio's allegations either be proved or disproved." [24] Within a month Hoover's men turned up a witness who claimed to have visited Mrs. Odio on the night in question with two other men, neither of whom was Oswald. The witness was Loran Eugene Hall. The men with him, he said, were Lawrence J. Howard and William Houston Seymour, who, according to Hall, bore a striking physical resemblance to Oswald.[25] The FBI showed pictures of all three men to Mrs. Odio; she failed to identify any of them.[26]

The Commission was anxious to leave the story at that. Mrs. Odio had to have been mistaken. Oswald could not have been in her house that evening, since he was on a bus that night heading to Mexico.[27] But Wesley Liebeler was still unsettled. Mrs. Odio's story coincided with facts she could not possibly have known; when Liebeler brought the matter to Rankin's attention the chief counsel reacted angrily.[28] "At this stage," he said, "we are supposed to be closing doors, not opening them." [29] The door on a possible conspiracy involving Oswald or an Oswald look-alike was thereupon slammed tightly.

Years later, a "top secret" Commission memorandum was declassified which lent further weight to the Odio story. The memo, written by two Commission lawyers assigned to check out "speculations and rumors" and released only in 1975, indicated that Mrs. Odio was telling the truth. "Mrs. Odio has checked out thoroughly through her psychiatrist and friends," the lawyers wrote. "And, with one exception—a layman who speculates that she may have subconscious tendencies to overdramatize and exaggerate—the evidence is unanimously favorable." The next six lines of the memo are censored. It picks up:

> Moreover, some of the details of Mrs. Odio's story, as it was first related to the FBI after the assassination—unfortunately, in a rather brief interview—check out with what we know about Oswald. For example, he was described as quiet and reticent, an impression Oswald usually gave; "Leopoldo" later told Mrs. Odio they had checked back on him in New Orleans, which is where in fact Oswald had come from; Leopoldo said he was told by New Orleans that "Leon" was "loco," a term Carlos Bringuier may very well have used to describe him; and, most importantly, of course, the name "Leon Oswald" is so close to "Lee Oswald" as to raise the strongest suspicions.[30]

Loran Eugene Hall, the man who came to the Commission's rescue, was an odd person to be helping the

United States do anything. For a time Hall had fought alongside Castro as a captain in the revolutionary army.[31] Then, in June 1959, Hall was arrested "in connection with an attempted armed expedition to Nicaragua." [31a] On July 8, 1959, Castro expelled Hall from Cuba.[32] It seemed to have been quite a day for housecleaning. Along with Hall, Castro bounced Santo Trafficante, Jr., the organized crime boss of Tampa, Florida,[33] and Henry Savaarda, a former employee of the mob-run Capri Hotel.[34] On his return to the U.S. Hall became "a participant in numerous anti-Castro activities," [35] according to the FBI. In mid-October 1963, Hall, while in the company of Seymour (the supposed Oswald look-alike who, in fact, did not look like Oswald at all), was, according to Harold Weisberg, arrested by the Dallas police on a charge of possession of dangerous drugs.[36] It was this man, Hall, on whom the Warren Commission relied to disprove the Odio story.

But the saga of Loran Eugene Hall did not end there. On October 2, 1964, nearly ten days after the Report had been presented to President Johnson, Hall retracted the original story he had told the FBI.[37] He now claimed he had never met Mrs. Odio. Subsequent checking revealed that the former Castro compatriot was closely allied with some of the most extremist exile organizations. Twice during the fall of 1963 Hall visited Dallas, first to raise funds for the exiles (reportedly for Frank Sturgis's International Anti-Communist Brigade),[38] a second time with a trailer full of arms destined for Cuban exiles in Miami.[39] Hall later redeemed a rifle he had pawned in Los Angeles with a check issued by the American Committee to Free Cuba, a Los Angeles group close to the Christian Anti-Communist Crusade of radio preacher Billy James Hargis.[40]

Still later Hall showed up during the Garrison investigation. It was Hall who accused Edgar Eugene Bradley, the unfortunately named Californian, of being part of an assassination plot. Hall told Garrison that Hall was at a meeting when the assassination was discussed, and also had contacts with the CIA. Garrison bought Hall's story completely, indicted Bradley,[40a] and absolved Hall from any responsibility in the assassination.[41]

The name "Leopoldo" had also come up before. He was one of fifteen "associates and employees" of Jack Ruby the Warren Commission asked the CIA to check out as "the most promising sources of contact between Ruby and politically-motivated groups interested in securing the assassination of President Kennedy." [42] The Warren Commission identified him as "Leopoldo Ramos Ducos," and reported to the CIA that his "life was threatened by a person suggesting that the same group that would kill Ducos had been responsible for getting rid of Kennedy." [43]

The CIA ignored the Warren Commission's request. The Agency ignored as well a book that identified one Leopoldo Ramos Duclos (correct spelling) as a Teamster official whom Jimmy Hoffa had installed as boss and trustee of the Union Gastronomica in Puerto Rico shortly after its headquarters had been blown up by five Molotov cocktails in February 1962.[44] The firebombing marked the climax of a long campaign by the Teamsters to take over the formerly independent Puerto Rican union. The spearheads of the Teamster campaign were Frank Chavez and Mike Singer.[45] Files of the Los Angeles Police Department revealed that Chavez had a long police record, including a charge of attempted murder by hurling a firebomb. Later he was implicated in two assassination plots against Robert Kennedy (see chapter 11). Singer was one of the most powerful Teamster bosses on the West Coast and, according to police intelligence sources, was heavily involved in organized crime, including a reported link to mob boss Meyer Lansky.[46]

The more one probed into the Odio story and the men who were so anxious to disprove it, the more ominous it seemed. The implications were clear. Men with a motive, means, and opportunity were plotting to kill the President of the United States. And Lee Harvey Oswald was not one of them. Oswald himself was sure of it. Hours before his death, he had put it succinctly: "I," he said, "am a patsy." [47]

MURDER ON FILM

Five key frames of the more than four hundred frames of 8mm movie film taken by Abraham Zapruder during twenty-two fateful seconds in Dealey Plaza.*

** The white areas on the left of each frame are sprocket holes.*

Z FRAME 225: President Kennedy emerges from behind the Stemmons Freeway sign. The President has clearly been wounded, though, as yet, not fatally. His face is contorted and he is beginning to bring his hands up to his throat. According to the Warren Commission, Governor Connally has also been wounded at this point, having been struck by a bullet which passed through the President's throat. But in this frame, Connally appears unhurt. He is facing forward, having already looked to his right to see what happened. The umbrella carried by the famous "umbrella man" is shown unfurled in the lower left center of the picture, immediately to the right of the Stemmons Freeway sign. The umbrella does not appear until after the President has been struck the first time.

Z FRAME 231: The President's hands are now almost to his throat. Mrs. Kennedy, aware that something has happened, has turned toward him. Connally, meanwhile, has turned to his left, apparently still unhurt. He holds his Stetson hat up in his right hand, seemingly with no difficulty. Yet, according to the Warren Commission, the wrist of this hand has already been shattered into a number of pieces by a high-powered rifle bullet.

Z FRAME 238: Connally is wounded. His righ shoulder is driven down, his cheeks are puffed, his hai is askew, and his face is contorted in pain. Connall and his doctors differed slightly on the precise momen when he was struck (Connally picked out Frame 23 as the moment, while his doctors concluded it was a many as four frames later), but this frame shows hi reaction most clearly. He could not have been woundec later than this frame. A second and a half has passec from the earliest moment Kennedy could have beer wounded. Without aiming, and in the hands of exper marksmen, the Mannlicher-Carcano could only be fired every 2.3 seconds. Oswald, then, would not have had sufficient time to wound Kennedy, reload, anc wound Connally. Therefore, there must have been a least one other assassin.

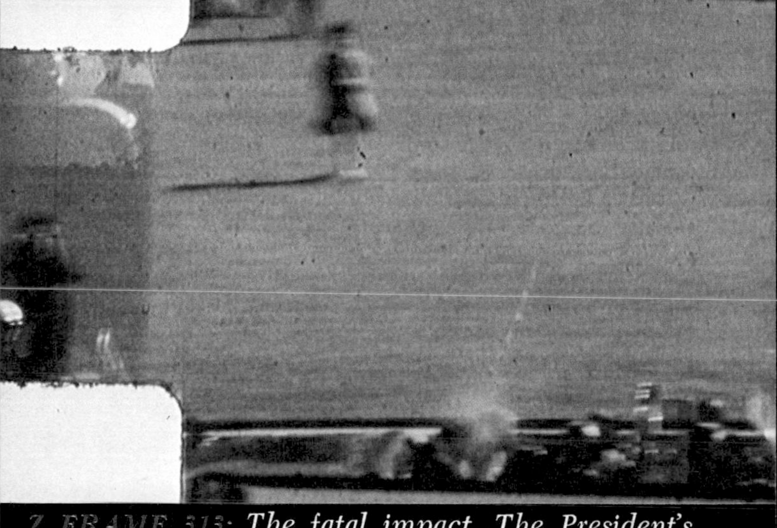

Z FRAME 313: The fatal impact. The President's head is obscured in a grotesque halo of blood and brains as a bullet slams into the right side of his skull. The bullet's explosive impact sends blood, brains, and skull fragments forward as well as down and rearward.

Z FRAME 323: The dying President, the right side of his head torn open, has been pitched backward and to the left, with sudden, violent force, as this frame, taken half a second after the fatal impact, clearly shows. Defenders of the Warren Commission suggest that the movement was caused by either a "neurospasm" or the "jet effect" of a bullet striking the President in the rear and exiting through the front of his head. Critics of the Commission, relying on Newtonian laws of motion, argue that the President was driven backward and to the left by the force of a bullet fired from the front and to the right.

THE EVIDENCE

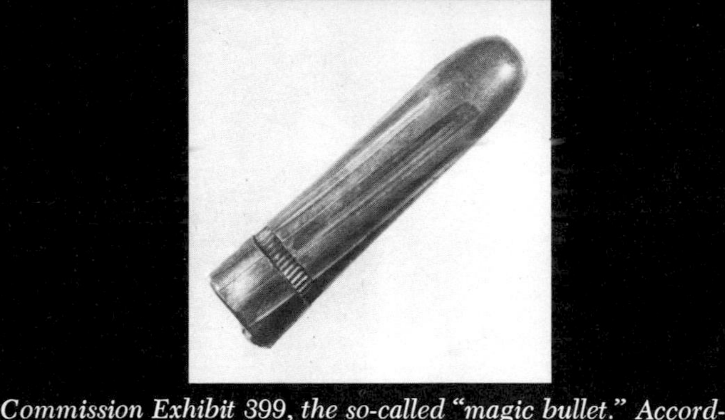

Commission Exhibit 399, the so-called "magic bullet." According to the Warren Commission, it was this bullet which first struck President Kennedy in the back of the neck and continued on to inflict all of Governor Connally's wounds. The bullet, however, is in virtually pristine condition, with only its tip slightly pinched, the total weight loss an estimated 2.5 grains. The nearly perfect condition of the bullet has led critics, forensic pathologists, and ballistics experts to conclude that the bullet could not *have wounded both Kennedy and Connally, making the single-assassin thesis untenable.* Wide World

This bullet was fired through a cadaver's wrist by Commission experts to duplicate the deformation suffered by C.E. 399 after smashing Connally's wrist bone. The test, however, succeeded only in proving the critics' point. Unlike C.E. 399, the tip of this bullet has been severely flattened and mangled, as the magic bullet should have been had it wounded Connally. UPI

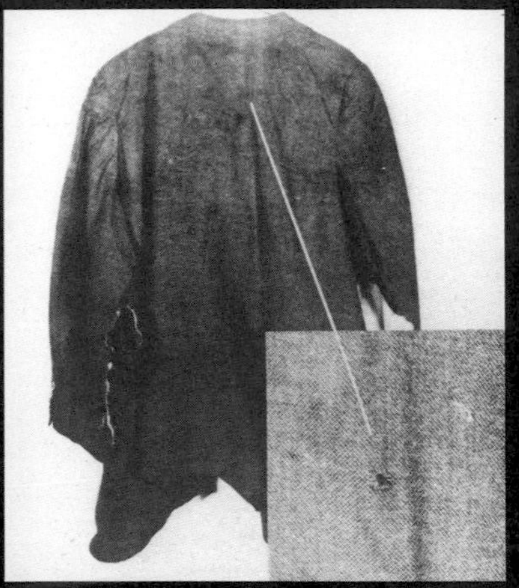

President Kennedy's suit jacket with bullet entrance hole (enlarged insert) in the back, to the right of the spinal column, and four inches below the collar line. Wide World

The back of President Kennedy's bloodstained shirt also locates the bullet entrance hole on the right side of the back and several inches below the collar line. The hole in the shirt and the suit jacket correspond exactly. If, as defenders of the Warren Commission argue, the President's shirt and jacket were "hunched-up" on his shoulders the bullet would have made two holes in both the jacket and the shirt. But the jacket and the shirt each contain only one hole—a hole well below where the Warren Commission stated the President was wounded. UPI

The President's tie and the front of his shirt collar. There is a small hole in the collar and a nick in the right side of the tie. According to the Warren Commission, these tears were caused by a bullet exiting the President's throat. A number of critics, pointing to the relative smallness and neatness of the tears, argue that they are further evidence that the wound in the President's throat was caused by a bullet fired from the front. Still other critics say that the tears were caused by bullet or bone fragments torn loose during the fatal head shot. UPI

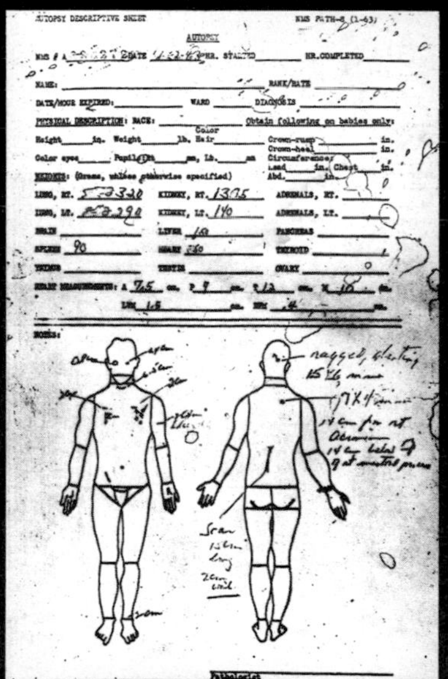
AUTOPSY DESCRIPTIVE SHEET NMS PATH-8 (1-63)

AUTOPSY

NMS # A 63-272 DATE 11-22-63 HR. STARTED ______ HR. COMPLETED ______

NAME: ______ RANK/RATE ______

DATE/HOUR EXPIRED: ______ WARD ______ DIAGNOSIS ______

PHYSICAL DESCRIPTION: RACE: ______ Obtain following on babies only:

Height ______ in. Weight ______ lb. Color Hair ______ Crown-rump ______ in. Crown-heel ______ in.

Color eyes ______ Pupil (Rt ______ mm, Lt. ______ mm Circumference: Head ______ in. Chest ______ in. Abd. ______ in.

WEIGHTS: (Grams, unless otherwise specified)

LUNG, RT.	320	KIDNEY, RT.	135	ADRENALS, RT.	
LUNG, LT.	290	KIDNEY, LT.	140	ADRENALS, LT.	
BRAIN		LIVER	1500	PANCREAS	
SPLEEN	90	HEART	350	THYROID	
THYMUS		TESTIS		OVARY	

HEART MEASUREMENTS: A 7.5 cm. P 7 cm. T 12 cm. M 10 cm.

LVM 1.5 cm. RVM .4 cm.

NOTES:

ragged, slanting

15 x 6 mm

7 x 4 mm

14 cm from rt acromion

14 cm below tip of rt mastoid process

Pathologist

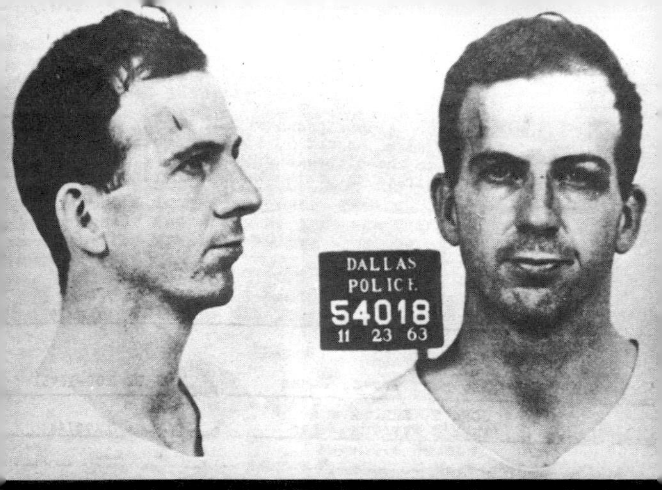

The Historical Oswald. Official booking photograph of Lee Harvey Oswald, taken after his arrest November 22, 1963

The Man Who Never Was. These, according to the Commission, are photographs of Lee Harvey Oswald taken while he was living in Minsk. Initially regarded by the Commission as "a problem," they are cited by critics as proof that Oswald never went to the Soviet Union, but was impersonated by an imposter on a mission for U.S. intelligence.

These two head shots of the Minsk "Oswald" show a man thicker of hair, fuller of face, and broader of chin than the Lee Harvey Oswald who was born in New Orleans and was arrested for the murder of President Kennedy and Dallas police officer J. D. Tippit.

The Minsk "Oswald" with Marina, the only known full-length picture of the Oswalds together in the Soviet Union. The problem here is height. Marina, according to Soviet records, stands a shade under 5′3″. Oswald, according to his passport, stood 5′11″. Yet, in this picture, "Oswald" seems only slightly taller than his diminutive wife.

The Minsk "Oswald" (left) with his arm around a friend in the Soviet Union. Again, "Oswald's" facial features seem strikingly different than those of the Oswald arrested in Dallas. The friend in the picture is identified by the Warren Commission as "Alfred (last name unknown), a Hungarian friend of Anita Ziger," (a Russian acquaintance of the Oswalds). In one of her letters to the Oswalds, however, Anita Ziger refers to the friend as "Alfred from Cuba."

The Incriminating Pictures. Marina Oswald testified to the Warren Commission that she took these two pictures of her husband in their backyard on March 31, 1963. They are the only pictures showing Oswald armed. There are a number of inexplicable inconsistencies in the photographs, however. In the pictures, the backyard appears to be bathed in sunlight. Yet, according to the Weather Bureau, the skies on March 31 in Dallas were cloudy and threatening, with a touch of rain. The bush beside Oswald is also in bloom. In March, such bushes have not yet begun to bud. The more serious problems, though, are with the man in the photograph. In the picture at left, "Oswald's" head is erect and his nose casts a V-shaped shadow. In the picture at right, Oswald's head is slightly cocked, yet the shadow remains the same. The posture of the man is also oddly out of kilter. When one attempts to stand at such an angle, one invariably falls over. Also, while the size of the bodies in both pictures differ, the size of the heads is the same. The chin of the "Oswald" in the photographs also seems broader and more squarish than the Oswald who was arrested in Dallas and who had a narrow, cleft chin. Finally, the weapon Oswald holds is longer than the known length of the Mannlicher-Carcano discovered in the School Book Depository. The conclusion some critics of the Warren Commission reach is that the pictures are forgeries, with Oswald's head cropped atop another man's body.

Was it possible that Oswald was telling the truth, that he had been framed, that an impostor had been used to implicate him in the crime of the century? And if one had been, why Oswald? Who, in fact, was Lee Harvey Oswald?

The impostor possibility was not new. In the face of all the Oswald look-alikes, the Warren Commission itself had reflected on the theory and finally rejected it, concluding that all the people who had seen Oswald when he was somewhere else were simply mistaken. The lawyers who investigated the charge did not know that they were not the first to ponder the chance that there might be more than one Oswald. On November 9, 1963, two weeks before the assassination, the Miami Police Department tape-recorded a conversation between one of its informants and an unidentified man who was an organizer for a segregationist political party. The man "said that a plan to kill the President was in the works. He said Kennedy would be shot with a high-power rifle from an office building, and he said that the gun would be disassembled, taken into the building, assembled and then used for the murder." He added: "They will pick up somebody within hours afterwards . . . just to throw the public off." [48] The Miami PD immediately alerted the Secret Service, since the President was scheduled to visit the city on the eighteenth.[49] The visit went ahead but the Secret Service took extraordinary security precautions. A planned motorcade downtown was abandoned, and at the Secret Service's insistence the President helicoptered into the city instead. No such precautions were taken in Dallas. After the assassination the tape-recorded conversation was given to the FBI, and the Bureau picked up the unidentified man for questioning on November 27.[50] Who he was and what he said remains a mystery. The entire incident was kept hidden from the Warren Commission. Finally the Miami police made the tape public in 1967.[51]

Back in 1960 when Oswald was a person known mainly to his family and the files of various intelligence agencies, J. Edgar Hoover himself had considered the possibility. The lawyers, however, could not know that.

The memo, reflecting Hoover's concern, had been withheld.* [52]

The impostor possibility had come to Hoover in a report filed by one of his Dallas agents. The agent had interviewed Marguerite Oswald, who was then very much worried about the safety of her son in the Soviet Union. During the interview Mrs. Oswald mentioned that Lee had taken his birth certificate with him.[56] To the ever suspicious Hoover that raised the possibility that the Russians, should they get their hands on Oswald's identification, would use it to create an identity for an agent who might then be infiltrated back to the United States. Accordingly, on June 3, 1960, Hoover sent a memorandum to the office of security of the Department of State. "Since there is a possibility that an impostor is using Oswald's birth certificate," Hoover wrote, "any current information the Department of State may have concerning the subject will be appreciated." [57]

Hoover's memorandum set the wheels of the State Department in motion. Warnings went out to various offices to be on the lookout for an Oswald impostor. Ten months later, on March 31, 1961, Edward J. Hickey, an official in the passport office, sent a memo to John T. White, an official in State's consular section, recommending that precautions be taken lest Oswald's passport fall into the wrong hands. Wrote Hickey:

> In view of the fact that this file contains information first, which indicates that mail from the mother

---

* The Hoover memorandum finally surfaced in 1975 at the National Archives. None of the Commission lawyers (including chief counsel J. Lee Rankin) charged with investigating the possibility of an Oswald impostor could recall seeing the memorandum.[53] Officials at the State Department and the FBI were similarly mystified. One former senior State Department official, Richard A. Frank, who acted as the department's legal liaison officer with the Bureau, suspected that "when the Oswald file suddenly became the object of the most intensive search and review, Mr. Hoover and his friends in the security operation at State simply made it disappear." [54] Former Warren Commission lawyer David Slawson, who should have seen the memo and didn't, was inclined to suspect the CIA. "It conceivably could have been something related to CIA. I can only speculate now, but a general CIA effort to take out anything that reflected on them may have covered this up." On the basis of the missing memorandum Slawson, while defending the Warren Commission's conclusions, called for a new investigation of the assassination.[55]

> of this boy is not being delivered to him and second, that it has been stated that there is an impostor using Oswald's identification data and that no doubt the Soviets would love to get hold of his valid passport, it is my opinion that the passport should be delivered to him only on a personal basis and after the Embassy is assured, to its complete satisfaction, that he is returning to the United States.[58]

A directive was flashed to the embassy in Moscow, instructing consular officials to withhold Oswald's passport until they had personally confirmed his identity. The embassy was also ordered not to give Oswald his passport until after his travel plans back to the U.S. had been completed.[59] The embassy complied with half the directions. Oswald was required to come in to the embassy to pick up his passport—a stipulation he stubbornly fought, but to which finally he was forced to yield—but the passport was given to him weeks *before* he had completed his travel plans.[60] What he did with it during that time, the embassy could not know. At least part of the time, however, it was in the hands of the Soviets.

In itself the embassy's failure to comply with the department's instructions seems insignificant. Oswald, or so the explanation went, was given his passport to make it easier for him to secure an exit visa from the Soviet Foreign Ministry.[61] All of which is true enough. Assuming that Lee Harvey Oswald went to the Soviet Union in the first place.

But did he?

Certainly Oswald's passport made the journey, that is clear. At least *someone's* passport made the journey, for inside the Commission there were suspicions that Oswald's passport was a forgery. The same Coleman/Slawson memorandum that backs up Mrs. Odio raises questions about the authenticity of Oswald's passport. The relevant section of the memo, however, is almost entirely censored. More than a dozen lines are blanked out, and then one sentence appears: "One other piece of evidence relating to the same point should be brought to the attention of the Commission." [62] Whatever that point and piece of evidence are only the secret keepers know for sure; for approximately the next eighteen lines are also blanked out. Finally the memo picks up: "All of the latter could be lies or forgeries, however, including even the American passport, since it was in Oswald's possession for about two weeks before he came into the American embassy—two weeks when he was in the hands of the KGB." [63]

Forged passports are a tool of the intelligence trade. No less than David Ferrie was once arrested with three *blank* passports in his possession.[64] What the Commission did not know (or at least failed to mention) was that Oswald himself had raised the possibility of his passport being a forgery in a letter he wrote from the Soviet Union to the marines, seeking restoration of his honorable discharge. The latter, dated March 22, 1962, but postmarked March 21 in Minsk, coincidentally followed by two days the reopening of Oswald's Office of Naval Intelligence file in Washington. The file was opened by the marines on March 19 on the grounds that Oswald might seek updating of his discharge in the near future.[65] As if on cue, Oswald made just such a request two days later. In his letter, Oswald asserted that the marines had "no moral or legal right" to downgrade his discharge to undesirable, since he had not violated Title 18, section 1544 of the U.S. Code.[66] Through the years, critics of the Warren Commission were suspicious of the letter, but for the wrong reason. What puzzled them was how, living in Minsk, Oswald could get his hands on a copy of the U.S. Code, and then burrow into it without careful coaching. It is an interesting question, but not nearly as interesting as the section of the code Oswald cites. Until 1975, critics took it for granted that the law to which Oswald referred must have had something to do with defection. It doesn't. Title 18, section 1544 of the U.S. Code is about the illegal use of passports. As the code puts it, "whoever willfully and knowingly uses or attempts to use any passport designed for the use of another" has violated the laws of the United States.[67] Here, then, was Lee Harvey Oswald stating that he had not broken a law which no one had accused him of violating. Was there a method to his madness? Or did the method belong to the man who was not Lee Harvey Oswald?

In any case a number of Americans also saw Oswald while he was in Moscow, and the Warren Commission published numerous photographs showing a man whom they identified as Oswald, including some taken in Minsk with Marina. For Oswald not to have gone to the Soviet Union would have required deception on a grand scale. Such deception is precisely what the evidence indicates.

The witnesses who saw Oswald, for instance, were all people who had never seen him before and would never see him again. Oswald seemed leery of witnesses who might provide independent verification. He brushed off the first three reporters who came to interview him in Moscow.[68] The journalist who spent thc most time with him at close range was Priscilla Johnson (see chapter 5).[69] She described the man she interviewed as "resembling a college boy with a southern drawl," clad in "flannel slacks and a tan cashmere sweater," [70] an image that contrasts sharply with the Oswald people knew in Dallas and New Orleans, a sloppy, slovenly dresser given to T-shirts and string ties.[71] Twice during his stay in the Soviet Union Oswald received telephone calls from home, one from his brother, Robert, the other from his mother, Marguerite. Oswald refused to even take the call from Robert,[72] and during his conversation with his mother, which lasted less than a minute, his responses consisted of grunts and "um-um's." When Mrs. Oswald put down the phone she said she could not be certain that the man on the other end of the line was her son.[73] For more than a year Oswald was out of touch with his family. He never wrote them, and their letters to him were returned unopened. Only after Mrs. Oswald went to the State Department, demanding that the government check on her son's well-being, did a first letter from Lee suddenly arrive.[74]

The letters themselves were suspicious, one in particular. What Lee wrote in one letter dated October 1959—thanks for recently delivered Christmas presents, a request that Marina be sent some American fashion magazines—is harmless enough. The problem is that he is referring to events that occurred during the winter of 1960–61.[75] In October 1959 Oswald had not yet been to Minsk or met Marina, much less married her.

In Oswald's letters, as in virtually all his writing, including the "Historic Diary" he kept after his arrival in Moscow, Oswald's spelling and syntax are atrocious, so bad that some psychologists who have read his letters have concluded that Oswald suffered from a neurological learning disorder.[76] Here, for instance, is a sample from the "Historic Diary," describing his wedding ceremony with Marina:

> two of Marinas girl friends act as bridesmaids. We are married. At her aunts home we have a dinner reception for about 20 friends and neboribos who wish us happiness (in spite of my origin and accept which was in general rather disquiting to any Russian since for. are very rare in the soviet Union even tourist. After an evening of eating and drinking in which . . . started a fright and the fuse blow on an overloaded circite we take our leave and walk the 15 minutes to our home. We lived near each other, at midnight we were home. [Neboribos = neighbors; accept = accent; for. = foreigners; ellipsis represents "Marina's uncle"; fright = fight; circite = circuit.] [77]

Compare this with a letter Oswald supposedly wrote in 1963 to the Fair Play for Cuba Committee in New York:

> Dear Mr. Lee
>
> I was glad to receive your advice concerning my try at starting a New Orleans F.P.C.C. chapter. I hope you won't be too disaproving at my inovations but I do think they are necessary for this area.
>
> As per your advice, I have decided to taken take a P.O. Box (no 30061).
>
> Against your advice, I have decided to take an office from the very beginning.
>
> I (sic) you see from the circular, I have jumped the gun on the charter business but I don't think its too important, you may think the circular is too provocative, but I want it too attract attention, even

if its the attention of the lunitic fringe. I had 2000 of them run off.

The major change in tactics you can see from the small membership blank, Is that I will charge $1.00 a month dues for the New Orleans chapter, only, and I intend to issue N.O. F.P.C.C. membership cards also.

This is without recourse to the $5.00 annual national F.P.C.C. membership fee.

However you will lose nothing in the long run because I will forward $5.00 to the national F.P.C.C. for every New Orleans chapter member who remains a dues paying member for 5 months in any year.

Its just that the people I am approching will not pay 5 dollars all at once to a committee in New York which they cannot see with their own eyes.

But they may pay a dollar a month to their own chapter, after having received their membership card from my hand to theirs.

Also I think such a dues system binds the members closer to the F.P.C.C.

I will promise only a membership card and a vote to future members, that is, I don't expect you to extend them national F.P.C.C. mailing for their one dollar a month.

As you will notice on the membership blank there is a place for those who *do* wish to subsribe to the national mailings' for the fee of $5.00, that fee will go directly to you in New York.

As soon as any member *has* paid dues adding up to five dollars in any year, I will forward that fee to you and then you may handle it as if it was a usual application for membership in the national F.P.C.C.

In any event I will keep you posted, and even if the office stays open for only 1 month more people will find out about the F.P.C.C. than if there had never been any office at all, don't you agree?

Please feel free to give advice and any other help.

Yours truly,
Lee H. Oswald [78]

The difference is indeed striking, and not only to assassination buffs, intent on proving the existence of a conspiracy. The Warren Commission itself noted the discrepancies (though it made no mention of them anywhere in the Report) and debated their meaning at the famous executive session of January 27, 1964. The TOP SECRET transcript of that meeting includes the following exchange:

> RANKIN: . . . It is very difficult to understand how anyone could write the letters he did from Russia and then write the other letters that he wrote in regard to the Fair Play for Cuba.
>
> BOGGS: Right, the spelling has changed.
>
> RANKIN: It is a world of difference. It is hardly believeable that anyone could have acquired such information during that period of time.
>
> BOGGS: . . . That letter has caused me a great deal of trouble. It is a much more literate and polished communication than any of his other writings.
>
> RANKIN: That is right.[79]

Since neither the Warren Commission nor its staff ever provided an explanation for the "unbelievable" difference in style, one can only guess what happened. All the choices involve forgery and deception. Either the letter to Fair Play for Cuba is a fake or the "Historic Diary" and Oswald's letters from Russia are counterfeit. Numerous witnesses swore that Oswald was indeed heavily involved in Fair Play for Cuba activities, whether that involvement, as seems likely, was a cover for other activities or not. So a third explanation has to be considered: Oswald wrote the Fair Play for Cuba letter (the handwriting was adjudged genuine), but copied word for word a text someone had provided him. Such an explanation makes sense if one assumes that Oswald was functioning in New Orleans as an undercover agent or informer for an intelligence service, a service which would naturally be anxious to establish his credentials as a sound, reliable devotee of the left. As for the "Historic Diary" and the correspondence from Russia, that too seems to be in Oswald's hand. What is not at all certain is *when* and *where* he wrote it. Two lawyers for the Warren Commission wondered about the same thing. In a TOP SECRET memo declassified in 1975 they expressed serious doubts about the diary's authenticity. "Even assuming that it is an authentic document," the memo argues, "[Oswald's diary] is not a good guide to the details of what occurred. He must have filled in most of the Diary entries for this period at a later time, possibly much later, and he seems not to have worried whether he was accurate or not on dates and even names." [80] Indeed, the lawyers were suspicious of *all* the records of what purported to be Oswald's trip to the Soviet Union. They noted:

> A high proportion of all the evidence on Lee Harvey Oswald which relates to his travel to and life in Russia derives from sources that could have been fabricated or otherwise falsified. The main sources of such evidence are his own statements after he returned to the United States. The letters he wrote from Russia to members of his family, Marina's statements to friends after she came to America and her testimony to the Commission, and all sorts of writings and documents dating from the Russian period or shortly thereafter. All of these sources *could* have been put together by the KGB, or be the result of its careful "coaching." [81]

The lawyers eventually concluded that Oswald was not a KGB agent. They did not consider another possibility: that he was an agent for the United States. Conceivably, Oswald's diary and letters could just as well have been written from the comfort of some undisclosed location in the United States as in Minsk.*

Oswald had to be somewhere else because, from most of the photographs taken of him in the Soviet Union, he does not seem to have been in Minsk. The "Oswald" who was in Minsk, and whose pictures appear numerous times in the Warren Commission's volumes,[83] seems thicker of hair, fuller of face, and broader of jaw and chin than does the Lee Harvey

* Novelist Gore Vidal presents an interesting, if wholly unproved explanation for the authorship of Oswald's "Historic Diary." Writing in the December 13, 1973, *New York Review of Books*, Vidal notes the coincidence that three accused assassins—Oswald, Sirhan, and Bremer—all kept diaries of their activities, and that in some respects, notably syntactical construction, the diaries sound remarkably alike. To Vidal this suggests that they may have been written by one man. The person Vidal selects for this assignment is a prolific fiction writer, and in the case of Ngo Dinh Diem, forger of assassination documents, that erstwhile spy and burglar E. Howard Hunt.[82]

Oswald who was born in New Orleans October 18, 1939, and was shot to death in the basement of the Dallas jail on November 24, 1963. Some members of the Warren Commission staff were also troubled by the photographs. The possibility that they were fakes, according to Alfred Goldberg, author of the "Speculations and Rumors" appendix to the Report, was briefly evaluated, but discarded as "a private rumor." [84] Most of the photographs are head shots, though there are several taken of "Oswald" full-length, including one widely reproduced photograph of "Oswald" standing alongside Marina on a bridge in Minsk.[85] The picture is so familiar that not until recently has it been closely examined. When studied the picture reveals an inexplicable and damning anomaly.

In the photograph Lee is standing half a pace in front of Marina, putting him closer to the camera, and thus increasing the height of his image ever so slightly. Marina is wearing low heels, almost certainly not more than an inch in height (at the time, taller heels were not sold in the Soviet Union). Side by side Lee appears to be an inch or two taller than Marina. Thanks to Soviet records we know that Marina's height is a fraction under 5′3″.[86] (Priscilla Johnson, who has seen her numerous times since the assassination, describes her as "a little bitty thing . . . five feet about.") [87] Add the inch from the heels and Marina stands 5′4″. Lee, then, would appear to be 5′5″ or 5′6″. Unfortunately the passport issued to Lee Harvey Oswald lists his height as 5′11″,[88] nearly half a foot taller than the man in the picture with Marina. (There is no question that the man in the picture is Marina's husband. Marina, for whatever her identification is worth, says it is; moreover, his face matches the faces in most of the other Russian pictures.)

The height listed on a passport, of course, is supplied by the person applying for it, so conceivably Oswald could have lied and stretched his height several inches. That, however, does not account for the other height anomalies recorded by medical doctors during physical examinations. Oswald's physical examination on his entrance into the Marine Corps in Octo-

The Incredible Shrinking Oswald—Physical Characteristics

DATE	DOCUMENT	HEIGHT	WEIGHT	EYE COLOR
Oct. 24, 1956	USMC Medical Examination Report	5′8″	131	Blue
Sept. 3, 1959	USMC Medical Examination Report	5′11″	150	Gray
Sept. 4, 1959	Passport Application	5′11″	n.s.	Gray
Nov. 16, 1959	Priscilla Johnson Interview	5′11″	150	Gray
Aug. 9, 1963	New Orleans Police Arrest Record	5′9″	136	Brown
Nov. 22, 1963	FBI File	5′9″	140	Blue-Gray
Nov. 24, 1963	Autopsy Report	5′9″	150 (est.)	Gray-Blue

This is a partial listing. There are more than a dozen other places where Oswald's description is listed, including files, employment applications, Selective Service cards, and reports of eyewitness identification. Only when the government (or, in the case of Ms. Johnson, someone connected with the government) provides the measuring does Oswald's height ever reach 5′11″. Independent medical examinations put him at 5′9″. Eyewitnesses who saw him when, according to the Warren Commission, he was somewhere else, say he was even shorter.

ber 1956 lists his height as 5′8″.[89] At his discharge, nearly three years later, marine doctors measured him again, and found him to stand 5′11″.[90] A growth of three inches in less than three years beginning at age seventeen is, according to medical experts, an exceedingly rare occurence, whatever the Marine Corps claims about "building men." [91] However, even if Oswald did manage to grow three inches, how does one account for the short man in the Minsk photograph? More dramatically, how does one account for the autopsy of Lee Harvy Oswald on November 24, 1963, an autopsy that listed his height as 5′9″? [92] Men do grow. They are not known to shrink.

When the incredible shrinking Oswald arrived in the United States, he was met by Spas Raikin, who saw him standing alongside Marina. "There was no significant difference between his [Oswald's] height and that of his wife," Raikin later recalled. "He was my height. I am certain of that." [93] Spas Raikin stands 5′6″,[94] about the same size as the photograph of the man in Minsk, and three inches shorter than the Oswald who was killed in Dallas.

The "Oswald" who walked into Albert Guy Bogard's car dealership was also short: "He was five feet nothing," recalled one of Bogard's coworkers.[95] Finally, on the night before the assassination, a man matching Oswald's description checked into a Fort Worth area motel. According to the motel operators, he went out of his way to call attention to himself. At one point he pulled out a revolver and checked to see if it was loaded. He also told the motel operators that, if they should hear he was in trouble the next day, they should contact the FBI. After the assassination, the motel operators did contact the FBI, and the Bureau picked up the man's registration records. Later, when the motel operators were interviewed by Jones Harris, they said that the man who had been their guest the night before the President's murder, looked just like Oswald but for one discrepancy. He was too short.[96]

Who were all these people?

On the face of it there seem to have been several Oswalds. One who entered the Marine Corps. Another who was discharged. A third who lived in the Soviet Union. A fourth who returned to Dallas to be murdered. A fifth who impersonated him at a car dealership. But for convenience's (if not sanity's) sake, assume that there were three: a historical Oswald—the man who was born in New Orleans and died in Dallas —a "secret agent" Oswald who went to the Soviet Union, presumably on a mission for the United States; and an impostor who was used to frame the historical Oswald for the murder of John Fitzgerald Kennedy.

This is not a happy solution; the mind recoils from anything that deviates from straight-line logic. We are comfortable with things that are simple, persons who are what they seem to be. Anything involving impostors and double agents and treachery and deception seems torn from a script of "Mission Impossible." It may well be. As it happens it is the way things work in the world of intelligence. Look-alikes are used. Identities are forged. Agents are planted. As Dwight Eisenhower, a man as plain as Kansas, said once of intelligence work, "These activities have their own rules and methods of concealment which seek to mislead and obscure." [97]

Concealing and obscuring is what seems to have happened to the identity of Lee Harvey Oswald. It might have worked like this: a rootless young marine, bright, with a keen interest in Russia and world affairs and an even keener sense of what he presumes are his own abilities, is recruited for an intelligence assignment. His job is a simple but important one: to stay out of sight, to go underground while a skilled agent borrows his identity for an assignment in the Soviet Union. He is in many ways an ideal candidate; for he has few friends to leave behind, a family he will not miss. The story of his defection will seem probable. He has already professed an admiration for Marxism and been in serious trouble with the marines. It would be unusual but not overly surprising if one day he turned up in Moscow, peddling radar secrets.

The second Oswald, whoever he is, is a trained professional, a practitioner of the craft of intelligence. Someone who knows what to look for and can keep his mouth shut. Superficially he resembles Oswald. He need not be identical to pass. All he requires is a birth certificate and a valid U.S. passport, a passport he will return to the United States government as soon as he reaches Moscow.

And so the plan begins. The "historical" Oswald goes into cold storage,* while the "intelligence" Oswald boards a ship for Europe. He arrives in England and is put aboard a "black" flight for Helsinki. From there it is a simple train ride across the border. The Russians, however, are supicious. They fear a "sleeper agent" has been planted in their midst, and they pack him off to Minsk and out of harm's way. After two years, his mission either completed or aborted, the intelligence Oswald departs the Soviet Union. A stopover in Berlin, debriefing in Amsterdam, and then it is home to the States. He boards a plane in New York, and following instructions gets off in Atlanta.[99] † Here the historical Oswald catches up with his identity. When the plane lands in Dallas, the historical Oswald deplanes to be met by family and friends. He talks about the Soviet Union, but is strangely vague about the details. When an unknowing FBI agent asks why he went to Russia, he can think of only one answer: "It is just something I did." [102]

---

* If, in fact, the historical Oswald did not go to the Soviet Union but remained somewhere in the United States, it would help explain the numerous sightings of Oswald (reported after the assassination) which were discounted by the Warren Commission because Oswald was supposed to be in the Soviet Union. While nearly all the reports lacked credible substantiation, one was especially noteworthy. That was in New Orleans on January 20, 1961. On that day Oscar Deslatte, the assistant manager of a local Ford agency, took an order for the purchase of ten Ford trucks. The two customers who bought them asked for a discount because the trucks were to be used by an organization called "Friends of a Democratic Cuba." Friends of a Democratic Cuba was a right-wing exile support group, one of whose founders was Guy Banister. That coincidence, however, was not nearly as interesting as one of the names that appeared on the order blank. It read: "Oswald." [98]

† A switch of the Oswalds somewhere between New York and Dallas would also account for a minor but intriguing problem: the case of the disappearing luggage. When the Oswalds arrived in the United States, one of the officials who met them noticed they were carrying seven pieces of luggage. The next morning when he took them to the airport, the same official noticed that two of the pieces were missing.[100] When he asked what happened to them, "Oswald" replied that he had sent them on ahead by Railway Express. That left "Oswald" with five pieces of luggage as the plane left New York. But when he arrived in Dallas, his brother Robert noted that he was carrying only *two* bags.[101] Either three pieces had been lost in transit (Lee never mentioned that it had) or someone had taken them off the plane when it stopped in Atlanta.

There are a number of catches. At least one photograph of Oswald taken in the Soviet Union with Marina does look like the Dallas Oswald. Also, it is possible that the doctors who measured Oswald could have been consistently wrong. But the biggest catch is Marina. What sort of woman would marry a stranger, bear his children, and keep silent when another man suddenly gets on a plane and takes his place? One answer is a woman with intelligence ties of her own, and here Marina's cloudy background and purposeful evasions seem strongly suggestive. But what kind of background? To guarantee her silence it would seem that she too had to have some connection to American intelligence. But all the signs point in the opposite direction. And how likely is it that the KGB and CIA would mount a joint operation? Tacit cooperation between rival intelligence services, even active cooperation on a case-by-case basis, is not unheard of. In one reported instance, CIA and KGB station chiefs "swapped" their respective embassies' diplomatic pouches—supposedly the one untouchable in the espionage game—long enough to allow each side to copy the entire contents.[103] The motive for the swap was patriotism laid over with not a little mutual careerism. The gaining of such information made both spies look good to their superiors. Nikita Khrushchev once startled Dwight Eisenhower with the jocular suggestion that the Soviets and Americans merge their intelligence services since, as Khrushchev slyly put it, "we are both paying the same people anyway."[104] But the sort of cooperation involved in infiltrating the Soviet Union with a known American agent boggles the imagination. What possible target would be worth such risk? How would the mutual interests of the United States and the Soviet Union be served?

Such is the dilemma. The story seems fantastic, but no more so than some of the astonishing happenings of the last decade, events of such profusion that they have lost the capacity to shock, and have become instead macabre, accepted commonplaces. In the end it comes down to a simple, bizarre choice: either Lee Harvey Oswald could increase and decrease his height and alter his appearance at will, or there was someone else using his identity.

Dallas, by contrast, is a far simpler matter. It would have been relatively easy to use an Oswald look-alike to implicate the real Oswald in the crime—especially if such deception had already been practiced once. One has to speculate, but possibly this is what might have happened:

Not the Agency, but someone close to the Agency, familiar with its workings and its weaknesses, discovers a young former marine who once served in an intelligence capacity and now works as a government informer. Again a double is used, but this time without Oswald's knowledge. A trail of incriminating clues is left, pointing straight at a pro-Castro activist. When Oswald is arrested and charged with the President's murder, there is no convincing way that either the FBI or CIA can explain that while he was once their man, he is no longer. After November 24, 1963, Oswald himself is in no position to talk. Confronted with such a conundrum, one fraught with peril for the security of the world, the United States government does what it has to do. It lets sleeping dogs lie.

If the theory is difficult to accept, the facts are more so. For by the fateful autumn of 1963 Oswald had become a shadow, a blur, now in focus, now out. He seems to have gone to Mexico in late September 1963 for the purpose of seeking a visa for travel to Cuba. Then or later, no one was able to accurately track his movements, much less divine what motive lay behind them. Hotel records show that a man named Lee Harvey Oswald was staying in Mexico City. Coincidentally the hotel where he lived during that time was a haunt for anti-Castro Cubans and their Agency patrons. Oswald visited two places where he was sure to leave a record. One was the Cuban mission, then under constant CIA electronic and photographic surveillance. Silvia Tirado de Duran was the secretary to the Cuban consul. In a sworn statement she provided on November 23, 1963, to the deputy director of Mexican Federal Security, she confirmed that Oswald had stopped by the mission to secure a visa to visit

Cuba on what he said was a planned trip to the Soviet Union.[105] The consul had told him that a visa would take time, and Oswald had argued with him.[106] When a Mexican reporter tried to interview Mrs. Duran in 1964 her husband stopped any questions, explaining that "she had suffered a nervous breakdown following her interrogation by the Mexican authorities and had been prohibited by her physician . . . from discussing the matter further." (C.D. 963.)[107]

The records, however, seem to confirm Mrs. Duran's recollections. There was a Cuban visa application with Oswald's photograph and signature; a letter written to the Soviet embassy in Washington referring to his visit; a notebook that included her name and telephone number. All these items, of course, could have been forged. The one conclusive piece of evidence would be a photograph of Oswald entering or leaving the mission. It just so happened that the CIA has several, taken not only at the Cuban mission but at the Soviet embassy as well.

The cameras had not been installed for Oswald's benefit. The Agency photographed *everyone* who entered or left either building. As former agent Philip Agee, who served in the Agency's Mexico City station, later described it in his diary, the surveillance of the Russian embassy was an elaborate operation.

> The station has two observation posts in front of the Soviet Embassy, which cover the entrances, plus a third observation post in back of the Embassy to provide coverage of the gardens. . . . From one of the front OP's [observation posts], radio contact is maintained with the . . . surveillance team for signalling when a particular Soviet surveillance target leaves the Embassy, his route and other data. Photos are regularly taken from all the OP's of Soviets and their families and all visitors to the Embassy. When visitors use vehicles, photographs are taken of their license plates for tracing.[108]

The cameras were in operation on October 1, 1963, one of the days when "Oswald" visited the Soviet embassy. The pictures were developed and a report sent to Washington. On October 10, the CIA sent the following teletype message to the FBI, the navy, and the Department of State:

> 1. On 1 October 1963 a reliable and sensitive source in Mexico reported that an American male, who identified himself as Lee OSWALD, contacted the Soviet Embassy in Mexico City inquiring whether the Embassy had received any news concerning a telegram which had been sent to Washington. The American was described as approximately 35 years old, with an athletic build, about six feet tall, with a receding hairline.
>
> 2. It is believed that OSWALD may be identical to Lee Henry [sic] Oswald, born on 18 October, 1939, in New Orleans, Louisiana. A former Marine who defected to the Soviet Union in October 1959 and later made arrangement through the United States embassy in Moscow to return to the United States with his Russian-born wife, Marina Nikolaevna Pusakova [sic], and their child.
>
> 3. The information in paragraph one is being disseminated to your representatives in Mexico City. Any further information received on this subject will be furnished you. This information is being made available to the Immigration and Naturalization Service.[109]

The CIA's description of a six-foot athletically built thirty-five-year-old did not jibe with the slightly built twenty-three-year-old who was Lee Harvey Oswald. Evidently the disparity bothered the CIA as well, for on October 23 the Agency requested that the navy immediately forward its two most recent photographs of Oswald so it could send the pictures to Mexico City to compare them with the pictures taken of the Oswald at the embassy.[110] The navy never sent the pictures. On November 22 the CIA turned over one of the pictures it had taken of "Oswald" in Mexico City to the FBI. There was a problem. Whoever the man was in the photograph, it was not Lee Harvey Oswald.

The CIA later admitted that the man in the photograph was not Oswald, that there had been a "mix-up,"[111] and that it would explain to the Warren Commission later how it occurred. The explanation was never forthcoming. The man who was not Oswald was never identified. The pictures of the real Lee Harvey Oswald were never found. Perhaps because they never existed.

The deception had worked. They had all been fooled: the CIA, the FBI, the Russians, the Cubans, the witnesses who saw the man who never was. Whoever the impostor was, he had carried off the masquerade exquisitely. No one would ever be sure what was real, what was unreal.

The impostor had one final assignment. A few minutes after the assassination a deputy sheriff named Roger Craig* was searching Dealey Plaza, looking for the place where the bullet that had missed the presidential limousine had struck. Suddenly he heard a whistle, looked up, and saw a man running from the Book Depository toward the Triple Underpass. Craig was sure it was Oswald. He ran after him but it was too late. The man got into a light-colored Rambler station wagon and disappeared beneath the underpass.[113] Later the Warren Commission would record:

> Although Craig may have seen someone enter a station wagon 15 minutes after the assassination, the person he saw was not Lee Harvey Oswald, who was far removed from the building at that time.[114]

---

* Craig, who was once named the "deputy sheriff of the year," later became embroiled in the Garrison investigation and ultimately lost his job with the sheriff's office. In 1967, he went to work for a Dallas bail bondsman. What he said were attempts and threats on his life also started that year. Once Craig claimed he was shot at. Another time an anonymous caller threatened his life and that of his family. In October 1970 his car engine exploded, injuring Craig seriously. In 1971 a car ran him off a mountain road, and his back was broken. After he recovered, he was wounded in the left shoulder by a shotgun blast. Few people, however, believed his stories. Finally, on May 15, 1975, Craig wrote a note to his father saying "I am tired of this pain," went into his bedroom, and according to the medical examiner's verdict, shot himself to death.[112]

8

The Grief-Stricken Mr. Ruby

> Then the other mystery is this other man—Ruby—who had no moral conditions, qualifications, no political ideals, no political passions, becomes so enraged by Kennedy's assassination that he kills the assassin right in front of the police. It was incredible, inconceivable. That does not happen even in the most mediocre movies.
>
> —Fidel Castro [1]

THE PRISONER WAS SCARED, anyone could see that.

Jack Ruby threw the pad on which he had been doodling on the table in front of him. In the interrogation room of the Dallas jail his distinguished visitors sat impassively.

"Gentlemen," Ruby said, "unless you get me to Washington, you can't get a fair shake out of me. If you understand my way of talking, you have got to bring me to Washington to get the tests. Do I sound dramatic? Off the beam?"

The chief justice tried to soothe him. "No; you are speaking very, very rationally."

But Ruby was nervous, insistent. "Unless you can get me to Washington, and I am not a crackpot, I have all my senses—I don't want to evade any crime I am guilty of."

His voice trailed off, and once again Warren was assuring him.

"Mr. Ruby, may I suggest this, that if we are to have any tests, either a lie detector or, as you suggest, maybe a truth serum . . . we have to have something to check against, and we would like to have the rest of your story as you started to tell us, because you are now getting down to the crucial part of it, and it wouldn't be fair to you to have this much of it and then not have the rest."

"Well," Ruby answered, "it is too bad, Chief Warren, that you didn't get me to your headquarters 6 months ago." The conversation rambled for a few minutes, and then Ruby asked again, pleading this time:

"If you request me to go back to Washington with you right now, that could be done, couldn't it?"

Now Warren was emphatic. "No; it could not be done. . . . the public attention that it would attract, and the people who would be around. We have no place there for you to be safe when we take you out, and we are not law enforcement officers, and it isn't our responsibility to go into anything of that kind."

"Gentlemen," Ruby said, "my life is in danger here." [2]

But Earl Warren ignored him. Jack Ruby would stay in Dallas. The questioning would go on. And the witness would tell them basically nothing.

Maybe it seemed that there was nothing to tell. The case was cut-and-dried. No arguments over ballistics or autopsy results, no impostors lurking in the background, and 20 million witnesses looking on while television cameras recorded the man who pushed through the crowd, stuck a revolver in Lee Harvey Oswald's stomach, and pulled the trigger one deadly time. "You know me," the murderer told the men who arrested him. "I'm Jack Ruby."

They knew Jack Ruby, all right. Half the Dallas police force knew Jack Ruby,[3] knew that he was good for a free drink and an occasional tip about low-level vice, knew that Jack was vicious and a bully, the sort who waited until a man was so drunk he could barely stand, and then beat him senseless.[4] The cruisers were always rolling up to the Carousel Club, the seedy strip joint that Ruby ran on the west side of town, called to cart away Jack's latest victim. Sometimes it was Jack himself they took away. Ruby had the proverbial arrest record as long as your arm; eight times he had been hauled in, twice on charges of carrying a concealed weapon.[5] If you knew Jack Ruby it didn't surprise you. Ruby played with the big boys. His friends were the mob.

The Warren Commission would record this—at least some of it—in detail. They would sketch his odd character, his temper, his violence, his friends, his trips to Cuba, even his love for dogs. And finally they would make nothing of them. He was, like the man he killed, a lone, deranged assassin, put in the police basement at exactly the right moment by, as his lawyer said, "the greatest coincidence in the history of the world." The Warren Commission would say that Ruby was unstable, unbalanced, incapable of the carefully coordinated action demanded by a conspiracy.[6] They would say that he killed out of love for the Kennedys. His motive, the Commission concluded, was irrational, overpowering, unfathomable grief.[7] They were right about one thing: Jack Ruby *was* the killer. The question—the one he seemed so anxious to answer that day with Earl Warren—was why.

The day of the assassination Ruby had been at the offices of the *Dallas Morning News,* checking on an ad for his club that would appear in the newspaper. When word reached the building that Kennedy had been shot Ruby, like nearly everyone else in the country, appeared, as one employee remembered, "obviously shaken . . . just very pale . . . and sat for a while with a dazed expression in his eyes." [8] Finally Ruby collected himself, made a couple of phone calls, and prepared to leave the building. As he did, he told John Newnam, an employee in the advertising department, "John, I will have to leave Dallas." [9] He did not leave, however. Instead, Ruby went to Parkland Hospital, where he encountered reporter Seth Kantor in one of the corridors. Kantor later remembered that there were tears brimming in Ruby's eyes.[10] Ruby's grief did not diminish his curiosity. From Parkland he went to the Dallas police station and for several hours loitered in the corridor close to the room where, at the moment, Lee Harvey Oswald was denying he had shot the President of the United States. At one point Captain Will Fritz, the chief of homicide, emerged and was surrounded by newsmen. Others wanted to know who was being interviewed. Ruby volunteered that it was Cap'n Fritz, as everyone knew him in Dallas, and then lest there be any mistake spelled out Fritz's name.[11] He went home to his apartment early in the evening, made some phone calls, and then headed out again, first to his temple, and finally to a delicatessen near one of his clubs. He bought some sandwiches and soft drinks and announced he was going to bring them to the police, or maybe the employees of a local radio station. He told one of the people in the restaurant that the assassination would be bad for Dallas's convention trade, then added pridefully that he had been the only club owner to close his doors in memoriam the President.[12]

With that Ruby went back to his car and headed downtown toward the police station. Once again he had no trouble getting straight to the heart of the action. District Attorney Henry Wade was holding an impromptu press conference for reporters. The DA announced that Oswald would probably be transferred to the county jail at the beginning of the next week. Then Wade began talking about Oswald, mentioning that the suspect had been a member of the "Free Cuba Committee"[13]—a serious slip of the tongue, since that was a right-wing *anti*-Castro organization—and a voice in the back of the room corrected him. "That's Fair Play for Cuba, Henry,"[14] the man said helpfully. One of the television cameras panned back to catch the face of the man who had made the correction. It was Jack Ruby.

When the press conference broke up Ruby introduced himself to Wade, put him on a telephone with a reporter, and finally left the police station, bound for the radio station, where he succeeded at last in giving away his soft drinks and sandwiches.[15] It was now long past midnight, but Ruby was highly charged, unable to sleep. He stopped by the Carousel Club, where he met one of his strippers and her boyfriend, a Dallas cop. They talked for an hour, the cop saying at one point, "They should cut this guy [Oswald] inch by inch into ribbons."[16] Ruby agreed and cursed Oswald. He went next to the *Dallas Times Herald* and talked with some of the pressmen on the late night shift about the President's assassination. He also joked with them, clownishly demonstrating his expertise in balancing atop an exercise toy.[17] At 4:30 a.m. Ruby drove home to his apartment and awakened his roommate, George Senator. At Ruby's insistence they went out, picked up Larry Crafard, one of Ruby's employees, and cruised around Dallas. It was past dawn before Ruby was home and in bed.[18] Larry Crafard did not sleep long. Hours after he left Ruby he started hitchhiking north. When the FBI found him several days later he was in Michigan with seven dollars in his pocket. He had heard that his employer had killed the accused presidential assassin, but hadn't thought of calling the police.[19]

On Saturday afternoon Ruby drove to Dealey Plaza. At television reporter saw him walking by the School Book Depository, out by the railroad yards. A police officer, noticing Ruby's interest, directed his gaze to the sixth-floor window from which the fatal shots had allegedly been fired. Ruby looked up solemnly, then walked to the greensward where wreaths had been laid in memoriam the President. He studied them briefly and then left.[20] He stopped in a garage to make some phone calls. The garage manager and one of the attendants couldn't help hearing them. They heard Ruby ask during one call about the whereabouts of the Dallas police chief. He also talked about the impending transfer of Oswald and told whoever he was speaking to, "You know I'll be there." [21]

That evening Ruby visited his sister, Eva Grant. They talked about the assassination and Ruby's feelings came pouring out. He was bitter, angry, sorrowful about the Kennedys. "Those poor people," he said. "Those poor people." [22] Eva urged him to calm himself, perhaps see a friend. But Jack started making more phone calls. One of them was to Ralph Paul, a business associate and restaurant owner. One of Paul's waitresses heard the call come in. She caught only fragments of Paul's conversation, hearing him exclaim at one point, "Are you crazy?" And then she remembered Paul talking about something else, something about a gun.[23]

His friends, the people who worked for him, his sister, the people he phoned that evening all knew that Jack Ruby was upset. He made no attempt to hide it. He talked of the unfairness of the killing, what it had done to the Kennedys, what it had done to Dallas, what, for some reason, it had done to the Jews. They paid no particular attention to him or what he said. Even at the best of times Ruby was high-strung. And that weekend they all had their private grief. Only Jack Ruby would do something about his.

Exhausted from the last day and a half Ruby did not rise until 9:00 Sunday morning. He watched television for a while and then made himself breakfast. When Ruby left the apartment at 11:00 he took his pet dachshund with him. Into his jacket pocket he slipped the .38 caliber revolver he usually carried in his car. He drove downtown past the School Book Depository, and parked his car not far from his destination, the Western Union Office, where he planned to send a $25 money order to one of his strippers. He would have no trouble coming up with the cash. There was more than $2000 of it in his pockets. At 11:17 the Western Union clerk gave Ruby a receipt for his money order.[24] Ruby walked out the door and headed down Main Street toward the police station. He was four minutes away from his rendezvous.

The basement of the Dallas jail the morning of November 24, 1963, was crowded with newsmen, police, and the plainly curious. They had come to see the show and they were getting impatient; it was already more than an hour late. The day before, the Dallas police had announced that they were transferring Oswald from his cell in the police building to the county jail, catercorner to the Book Depository, where they said, he would be more "secure." Already a number of death threats had come in. The tone, if not the exact words, had been the same. Lee Harvey Oswald would not live to stand trial.[25] Now in the basement of the jail the crowd mingled and murmured in expectation. The place was curiously loose. The police were making only a token attempt to check credentials.[26] People wandered in and out.

The police did not seem worried. They had worked out a decoy plan. An armored truck was parked on a ramp in the basement. When Oswald appeared the truck would drive away, and any potential assassin outside would be fooled into thinking Oswald had been driven away with it. In fact Oswald was to be placed in a police car and taken away by another route. But few people were fooled. The success of the decoy depended on secrecy. There could be no secrecy in front of live television cameras. To make matters worse, the police car that would drive Oswald away was not in place. Suddenly everything was going wrong.

It was too late. Captain Fritz was flashed the prearranged "high sign" and the elevator door opened onto the basement.[27] Handcuffed between two sheriff's deputies, Oswald was led into the crowd. The reporters could see him clearly; no one stood in front of him to block their view. Flashbulbs popped and reporters yelled questions. Then a man in a dark suit and a felt hat suddenly pushed forward, and before anyone could stop him, stuck out his arm. Oswald caught sight of him at the last moment. He looked startled, puzzled, and then all at once realized what was happening. Oswald's hands jerked back to protect himself from the blow. In that instant Jack Ruby's revolver exploded.

At his trial a few months later Ruby pleaded not guilty by reason of insanity. Considering the evidence, not to mention the 20 million potential witnesses against him, Ruby really didn't have much choice if he wanted to avoid the electric chair. Melvin Belli, Ruby's lawyer, produced a doctor who claimed that Ruby was a victim of psychomotor epilepsy, an affliction that brought on blackouts and uncontrolled spasms of rage.[28] Ruby was in the midst of such a spell, his lawyers contended, as he returned from his errand at Western Union. As luck would have it, the Dallas police chose that very moment to bring out their celebrated prisoner. Call it coincidence, call it fate—whatever it was, Ruby's lawyer said, his client didn't know what he was doing when he pumped a .38 slug into Oswald's stomach. However, the prosecution had a few doctors of its own, and they testified that the accused, albeit a bit odd, knew perfectly well what he was doing in the police basement, and if he were suffering from psychomotor epilepsy it was news to them.[29] The jury didn't have much trouble making up its mind. In expeditious Texas fashion, they found him guilty and Ruby was promptly sentenced to death.[30]

Ruby had a far easier time convincing the Warren Commission. The Commission took much of Ruby's testimony at face value, especially the parts about not being at Parkland Hospital (though two witnesses, including a distinguished member of the White House press corps, swore that they saw him),[31] or hanging around police headquarters (where, once again half a dozen credible witnesses, including police and reporters, contradicted him).[32] The Commission members were also more sympathetic to Ruby's supposed psychiatric ills. A psychiatric evaluation of Ruby, done when he was ten years old, was offered in support of the Commission's contention that Oswald's murder resulted in part from Ruby's "unusual craving to be recognized and relied on." [33] That plus Ruby's expressed desire to spare Mrs. Kennedy, "to save her the ordeal of coming back" [34] to Dallas for Oswald's trial were, as far as the Commission was concerned, the ingredients for homicide by chance, not conspiracy.

The Commission acknowledged that there had been "speculation" that Ruby "had acted on behalf of members of a conspiracy who had planned the killing of President Kennedy and wanted to silence Oswald," but after "thorough examination," concluded that the speculation was just that.[35] The Commission reported that it had studied Ruby's life in detail, including allegations that he was both a Communist and Bircher,[36] and had found there was nothing to either charge. On the contrary, the Commission said blandly, "Ruby considered himself a Democrat." [37] And one who loved dogs at that. "Ruby was extremely fond of dogs," the Commission reported. "Numerous persons stated that he was constantly accompanied by several of the dogs he owned. Testimony at Ruby's trial in March 1964 indicated that he referred to his dogs as his 'children.' He also became extremely incensed when he witnessed the maltreatment of any of his dogs." [38] The Commission allowed as how Ruby seemed to have an uncommon affection for police and criminals as well, but insisted that his favors for the police never went beyond providing them "free coffee and soft drinks," which, the Commission noted, "was not unusual for a Dallas nightclub operator." [39] As for Ruby's "underworld ties," as the Commission characterized them, they seemed nothing more sinister than a love for the ponies and a bit of "social gambling." [40]

The thoroughness of the investigation that underpinned these conclusions was indicated by one of the first facts the Commission reported about Ruby: his address. The Commission said that Ruby resided at 3929 Rawlins Street.[41] The Commission was partly right. A Ruby did live there, Jack's sister, whose name was Eva Grant. Ruby himself lived miles away at 233 South Ewing,[42] not far, as it happened, from the spot where Officer J. D. Tippit was gunned down.

The report contains other little nagging errors. There is a chronic problem about getting the names of some of Ruby's friends straight. Like "Frank Nitty," the associate of boxer Barney Ross, who according to an FBI report hired Ruby at the age of fifteen "to run innocuous errands." [43] It should be Nitti with an "y," as in Frank "the Enforcer" Nitti, cousin and heir to Al Capone. Or Dave "Yeres," who is mentioned by Ruby's sister only in passing, but on investigation turns out to be Dave Yaras, gambler, Cuban gunrunner, and member of the Chicago mob.[44] Or "Deutsch I. Maylor," a man whom Ruby mentions calling several days before the assassination, and who is better known to his chums in the Teamsters, where he heads the union's southern conference as "Dusty Miller." [45] Or one Murray "Humphries," [46] who actually spells his name with a *y*, as in Murray "the Camel" Humphreys, a Nitti mobster who, according to Ovid Demaris, was "perhaps the only kidnapper in history to have paid income tax on ransom money without being charged with the crime."[47]

The FBI, which checked out Ruby's reported ties to organized crime, missed some items entirely. There was a report, for instance, that Ruby was somehow involved in the 1939 murder of Leon Cooke, the financial secretary of local 20467 of the Scrap Iron and Junk Handlers Union in Chicago.[48] The FBI said they could find nothing about it. Perhaps they should have tried reading the newspapers. If they had looked on the front page of the *Chicago Tribune* of December 9, 1939,[49] they would have found the story of Cooke's shooting in an eight-column banner headline, and on the inside pages, pictures of two union officials who had been picked up for questioning by police. One of them was John Martin, the union president. The other was the union's secretary, one Jack Rubenstein, a.k.a. Jack Ruby.

The Warren Commission found nothing unusual about this or about Ruby's other "friends." He was, after all, in a tough business and there were times when he had to turn to unusual sources of help. During November 1963, for example, the Commission reported that Ruby was in the midst of a labor dispute with the American Guild of Variety Artists.[50] He needed help, and so he made a few calls. As Ruby himself explained to the Commission:

> . . . I had to make so many numerous calls that I am sure you know of. Am I right? Because of trying to survive in my business. . . .
>
> Every person I have called, and sometimes you may not even know a person intimately, you sort of tell them, well, you are stranded down here and you want some help.[51]

The people Ruby called the month John Kennedy was assassinated certainly could help. Besides Dusty Miller, he was also in touch with Paul "Red" Dorfman, a Hoffa intimate, boss of the Teamsters' Central States Pension Fund and one of the most powerful organized crime figures in the country;[52] Irwin S. Weiner,* [53] a senior Teamster bondsman who had close connections with the Chicago underworld;[53a] as well as Barney Baker,[55] whom Ruby called twice and who in turn called Dave Yaras on the eve of the assassination. None of them were interviewed by the Warren Commission. Baker, whose name also appeared in Ruby's notebook, would have made an especially interesting witness. He was, according to Robert Kennedy, "Hoffa's roving organizer and ambassador of violence," [56] and much more:

> An ex-convict (jailed three times in the 1930's), the 325 pound Baker was a former professional boxer, longshoreman, confidant of top hoodlums and bouncer before joining the Teamsters. His rise was rapid. . . . He boasted that he knew such sinister underworld figures as Joe Adonis, Meyer Lansky, the late Benjamin "Bugsy" Siegel, "Trigger Mike" Coppola, "Scarface" Joe Bommarito, Jimmy "Blue Eyes" Alo, Vincent "Piggy Mac" Marchesi and others. . . . Sometimes the mere threat of his presence in a room was enough to silence men who would otherwise have opposed Hoffa's reign . . . Hoffa testified: "Now Barney Baker works for the Central Conference of Teamsters under my direct orders." [57]

As attorney general, Kennedy managed to put Baker in jail. He was released not long before the assassination.[58]

And then there was Ruby's motive: grief, the Commission said, a desire to spare the Kennedys further sorrow. It was a laudable impulse, even for a man who had not bothered to watch his hero's motorcade come into Dallas—and past his front door. No doubt it was such sorrow that led Jack Ruby to joke and clown the night of the President's death, to worry how the as-

---

* In 1974 the federal government indicted Weiner for allegedly defrauding the Teamster pension fund of $1.4 million in a scheme to buy a plastics plant in New Mexico. Shortly before the case was to go to trial, the government's star witness was shotgunned to death in front of his wife and children. Weiner was acquitted.[54] This Irwin S. Weiner is not to be confused with the Irwin Weiner who is an officer of Walt Frazier Enterprises in New York City.[54a]

sassination would affect the tourist trade and whether his shuttered club would lose business to the other strip joints that had the tastelessness to stay open. And wanting to spare Mrs. Kennedy the pain of returning to Dallas to confront her husband's slayer, that was commendable too. What the Warren Commission neglected to mention was when these worthy impulses occurred. It was in his cell, months after the killing. During a visit with one of his lawyers, Ruby had written on a piece of paper, "Joe, you should know this. Tom Howard [another Ruby attorney] told me to say that I shot Oswald so that Caroline and Mrs. Kennedy wouldn't have to come to Dallas to testify. OK?" [59] Evidently it was, at least for the Warren Commission.

There were many things about Jack Ruby the Warren Commission flatly admitted it did not know. His whereabouts for five days during the two months before the assassination remained a puzzle.[60] The Commission could only deduce that he was in Dallas—doing what, they did not claim to know. Periods of several hours during the assassination weekend were only generally accounted for, and often the Commission's accounting was at variance with the testimony of reliable witnesses. The Commission could not even say for certain how Ruby had managed to slip into the police basement at precisely the right moment to shoot Oswald. The Main Street ramp, which the Commission concluded Ruby used to enter the basement,[61] was guarded by a police officer (one of the few who apparently was not a friend of Ruby), and several witnesses confirmed his statement that Ruby did not pass by him.[62] Apparently Ruby's appearance in the basement at 11:21 a.m. was merely another one of those unexplainable events that just had a way of happening in Dallas. In the end the Commission Report fell back on argument to prove what the facts could not:

> By striking in the city jail, Ruby was certain to be apprehended. An attempt to silence Oswald by having

> Ruby kill him would have presented exceptionally grave dangers to any other persons involved in the scheme. If the attempt had failed, Oswald might have been moved to disclose his confederates to the authorities. If it succeeded, as it did, the additional killing might itself have produced a trail to them. Moreover, Ruby was regarded by most persons who knew him as moody and unstable—hardly one to have encouraged the confidence of persons involved in a sensitive conspiracy.[63]

It was hard to fault at least part of the Commission's reasoning. The killing of Oswald did leave a trail. But you had to follow it back to its source.

It begins in Chicago, in the neighborhood where the stocky, tough kid they called "Sparky" was born, grew up, and before he reached voting age won a place in the mob.

In 1911, the West Side of Chicago was, as it is today, the toughest part of a very rough town. The 24th ward on the West Side was Jake Arvey's territory, home and battleground for the Jewish mob. Here, on March 19, 1911, the fifth child of immigrant Polish Jews named Joseph and Fannie Rubenstein was born. They called him Jacob—"Jack," for short.[64]

Life in the Rubenstein family was far from idyllic. Jack's father beat his mother frequently, so badly that several times the police were summoned to arrest him on charges of assault and battery.[65] Fannie Rubenstein suffered from delusions and eventually went insane and was committed to a state asylum, though well after Jack left home.[66] Jack himself was in and out of trouble, and more often in. At the age of eleven he was referred to the Institute for Juvenile Research by the Jewish Social Service Board for "truancy and [being] incorrigible at home."[67] A psychiatric evaluation was conducted and the agency concluded that Jack's problems (he was egocentric, undisciplined, and for an eleven-year-old had an extraordinary interest in sex) could be solved if he were placed in a "more wholesome environment."[68] He was accordingly packed off to a foster home. Before long, though, Ruby was in a gang out on the streets. He quickly won a reputation as a good man to know in a fight. One friend from the period is quoted in the Commission Report as saying that Sparky, as Ruby was known (both for his temper and his quick-wittedness) was "willing to accept any challenge without regard to the odds against him." [69]

Such qualities did not go without notice. Ruby and his pals, including boxer Barney Ross, were soon running what Ross described to the FBI as "innocuous errands" for a dollar a trip. The envelopes they delivered, according to Ross, "did not contain messages or anything of value." [70] Maybe so. It was the man who asked them to do these errands—"to keep them from hanging around the streets" [71]—who was not so innocuous. His name was Al Capone.[72]

Capone's efforts in keeping Ruby and his friends off the streets were not notably successful. In time many of them went on to bigger things. According to a congressional investigation, Dave Yaras and Lenny Patrick, two of Ruby's chums, graduated to become senior partners in the Capone syndicate.[73] In June 1946, shortly after Ruby's return to Chicago after service in the army, Yaras and Patrick were arrested for the murder of James Ragan, a Capone rival who had been operating a competing racing wire service. The indictments against both men were dropped after witnesses against them suffered a series of untoward events. One was murdered. Two changed their minds, and a fourth suddenly left town.* [74] When the Kefauver committee came to Chicago four years later to investigate the Ragan murder, two other witnesses were shot to death in gangland style.[75] Years later Yaras had a hand in the syndicate's gambling operations in Cuba, and according to statements made to the McClellan committee had "at least something to do with the setting up and establishing of [Teamsters] local 320 in Miami." [76] In 1964 Dave Yaras would be one of the people who would assure the Warren Commission that his old friend, "Sparky" Ruby, had no ties with the syndicate. But then the

---

* As reported by Ovid Demaris in *Captive City*.

FBI report in which this information was contained made no mention of Yaras's background either.* [77]

Nineteen thirty-three was not a vintage year for the Chicago mob. With Franklin Roosevelt's election to the White House, Prohibition ended, bringing what had been the mob's major source of revenue to that time to a halt. Ruby and several of his friends from the old neighborhood chose that year to move to the West Coast, first to Los Angeles, and later to San Francisco, where Ruby sold "tip sheets" at the Bay Meadows racetrack.[79] Ruby stayed four years before heading back to Chicago. Home again, Ruby "hustled" for a while, scalping tickets and peddling watches at suspiciously low prices.[80] Finally in 1937 he found steady employment as a negotiator for the Scrap Iron and Junk Handlers Union.[81]

At the time Ruby joined the union, Chicago's local 20467 already had a well-established reputation as "largely a shake-down operation," in the words of one FBI report.[82] There had already been numerous brawls, vandalism, and threats of worse to come. The union's leadership was splintered, with the "clean" faction being headed by Leon Cooke, the union's financial secretary, and supposedly Ruby's close friend.[83] The feud and simmering violence finally culminated at the union's headquarters on December 8, 1939, when Jack Martin, the union's president, already under indictment for racketeering, shot Cooke, who died nearly a month later.[84] Ruby was the only other union official present in the building at the time of the shooting. Police took both him and Martin in for

---

* Yaras was picked up in conversation in February 1962 by an FBI bug installed in a Miami mob hangout. His dialogue with Jackie Cerone, a member of the Chicago syndicate, provides a fair indication of the company Ruby kept. The transcript reads in part:

> YARAS: I wish . . . we were hitting him now, right now. We could have hit him the other night. We went to prowl the house . . . there was just Philly and he.
>
> CERONE: Yeah, that would have been a perfect spot to rub him out. . . .
>
> YARAS: Leave it to us. As soon as he walks in the . . . door, boom! We'll hit him with an . . . ax or something. He won't get away from us.

The particular victim Yaras and Cerone had in mind was tipped off before Yaras and Cerone could complete the contract.[78]

questioning. Ruby was released some hours later and Martin was formally charged with the murder. He was eventually acquitted on grounds of self-defense.[85] Ruby was later quoted as saying that he wanted to "take over" the union after Cooke's death.[86] Instead, for reasons which even now remain unclear, he left the union altogether three years later.[87] With Cooke removed from the scene, leadership passed totally into the hands of the mob. Paul Dorfman, later to become a key Teamster aide, assumed the union's presidency. He held the job until 1957 when, in the wake of investigations of labor racketeering by the McClellan committee, the AFL-CIO suspended Dorfman and placed the union in trusteeship.[88]

There is no hint anywhere in the Warren Commission report that Cooke's murder was anything more than an ordinary homicide, a violent falling out between rivals. But according to Robert Kennedy, who investigated the incident as chief counsel for the McClellan committee, in Cooke's killing lay the seeds to Jimmy Hoffa's ultimate rise to power and infamy. As Kennedy described it in *The Enemy Within*:

> For him [Hoffa], the key to the entire Midwest was Chicago. He needed a powerful ally there—and he found his man in Paul Dorfman. Dorfman, our testimony showed, was a big operator—a major figure in the Chicago underworld who also knew his way around in certain labor and political circles.
>
> A slight man with thinning red hair and an almost benign manner, Dorfman took over as head of the Chicago Waste Handlers Union in 1939 after its founder and head secretary-treasurer was murdered. In 1957, the AFL-CIO kicked him out for corruption.
>
> He has tied some strange knots in the strings he pulls. According to our testimony, he was closely linked with such underworld figures as Tony ["Big Tuna"] Accardo, who became head of the Chicago syndicate after the death of Al Capone, and with Abner (Longie) Zwillman—a top gangland leader in the United States . . .
>
> Hoffa made a trade with Dorfman. In return for an introduction to the Chicago underworld, the Com-

> mittee found, Hoffa turned over to him and his family the gigantic Central Conference of Teamsters Welfare Fund insurance. . . .
>
> Paul Dorfman and Jimmy Hoffa are now as one. Everywhere Hoffa goes, Dorfman is close by. Most important decisions by Hoffa are made only after consultation with Paul Dorfman.[89]

After the war Hoffa returned to Chicago, but only briefly. The war had revitalized organized crime, which thanks to a wartime alliance of necessity struck with the OSS, gained it a cloak of semirespectability. In the years immediately following the defeat of the Axis the Mafia moved into new areas—notably narcotics—and expanded its operations from its traditional bases on the East Coast and in the Midwest. One of the places the mob moved was to the American Southwest, to Nevada, Arizona, New Mexico, and Texas. Jack Ruby moved with it.

He arrived in Dallas in 1947, ostensibly to manage a supper club he and his sister had purchased with the help of loans from their brothers. It had been called the "Singapore Supper Club," but Jack changed the name to the "Silver Spur." [90] He also changed his own name from Rubenstein to Ruby.[91] Dallas that year was filling up with new arrivals from Chicago. One of them was a friend of Ruby's named Paul Roland Jones, whose previous convictions, according to Senate investigators, included ones for opium smuggling and murder of a state witness.[92]

In the best etiquette of the mob, Ruby and Jones had been introduced by mutual friends from the old neighborhood, all of them members in good standing of the Chicago syndicate's labor operations. One of the men was Paul "Needle Nose" Labriola; another, Jimmy Weinberg.[93] In 1954 they would both be found dead in the trunk of a car. It was a particularly messy leave-taking. Both men had been garroted.[94]

But in 1947, newly arrived in a strange town, there was business for Ruby and Jones to transact. And the first order of business was taking care of the law.

The Dallas sheriff of the time was Steve Guthrie, a lawman as tough as he was incorruptible. In May,

Jones approached Guthrie for the first time with a business proposal. In return for looking the other way while the mob moved gambling into Dallas, Guthrie would receive half of the take.[95] Guthrie mulled the offer over as the details of the bribe were spelled out during the course of twenty-two separate meetings. There were microphones listening too. Guthrie had thoughtfully installed them so that when it came time to present the evidence to the grand jury the case would be airtight. Jones and his friends, of course, did not know that everything they were saying was being recorded. And so they talked on, mentioning at one point that one of their friends from Chicago would operate a "fabulous" restaurant[96] as a cover for the gambling operation. The restaurant was the Silver Spur, née Singapore. The friend was Jack Ruby.

Jack was not the only Ruby to receive a share of the mob's largess. Hymie, Jack's brother, was asked by Jones if he wanted a share of a proposed scheme to smuggle whiskey into the United States from Canada. Subsequently two of Jones's men were caught smuggling, but opium, rather than whiskey, and from Mexico, not Canada. Two people Chicago police questioned in the case were Hymie Rubenstein and his brother Jack. (C.E. 1798, C.E. 1271, 23 H. 203–4, 374.)[97–98]

Guthrie reported all these events to the Warren Commission, but the Commission discounted them. Instead, it accepted the testimony of Lieutenant George E. Butler, who worked on the bribery case with Guthrie and later swore that Ruby's name had never been mentioned during any of the conversations with the mob.[99] That was not the story Butler told several months earlier to a reporter from the *Chicago Daily News*.[100] Then Butler confirmed that Ruby had been involved. Butler was also the source of an incredible tale that Oswald was Ruby's illegitimate son, and that Ruby had traveled to Mexico at the same time Oswald was in Mexico City seeking a visa for travel to Cuba.[101] The more that was found out about Butler the more puzzling he seemed. By his own admission he had been a close friend of Ruby's for fifteen years.[102] He was, according to one report, an extreme rightist. When Ruby shot Oswald in the police basement Butler was there looking on.[103] During the assassination weekend Butler was in the thick of the action. Thayer Waldo, a reporter for the *Fort Worth Star-Telegram,* talked to him several times during the weekend because, as Waldo put it, "he was always in on, apparently, high level information."[104] When everyone else was losing their head, Butler was keeping his. He had "this almost stolid poise, or perhaps phlegmatic poise . . . through even the most hectic times,"[105] Waldo said. But when Waldo bumped into Butler in the police basement, moments before Oswald was brought down, the poise had disappeared. To Waldo, Butler seemed "an extremely nervous man, so nervous that when I was standing asking him a question after I had entered the ramp and gotten down to the basement area . . . I noticed that his lips were trembling as he listened and waited for my answer. . . . I had by then spent enough hours talking to this man so that it struck me as something totally out of character."[106]

As for Jones, he eventually went to jail. But it did not end his friendship with Jack Ruby. He and the boys from Chicago continued to hang out in the Silver Spur. The last time Jones saw Ruby was one week before the assassination.[107]

Through the 1950s Ruby's luck went up and down. He would close one club, open another; make a pile, and just as quickly lose it. He drifted in and out of business and entertainment schemes, none of which seemed to click.[108] The hustling instinct had not deserted him, and neither had his friends. They had a distressing tendency, however, to wind up in jail or in the morgue. Or on the police force.

Ruby cultivated cops, seemed fascinated by them. Ruby said to one friend that he wished he had become a cop, and would have joined the force in Chicago had it not been for his height.[109] The police, in turn, cultivated Ruby. With his connections he was a natural source of information. Ruby was happy to oblige. The syndicate, growing more sophisticated in its ways, had long before concluded that the most efficacious way of dealing with upstart competitors was to turn them over to the police. This, evidently, was one of Ruby's main assignments. By the early sixties, he had become the "close friend" [110] of the chief of the special services bureau * of the Dallas police, who routinely dropped by the Carousel Club every night it was open. Later a detective would recall that Jack Ruby was a "source of information in connection with his investigatory activities," [112] activities that centered on the growing narcotics trade.

When it came to junk Ruby knew whereof he spoke. An FBI report quoted a Mrs. James Breen, an informer for the Federal Bureau of Narcotics, who said that she and her husband "had made connection with large narcotics setup operating between Mexico, Texas and the East." [113] The man who had cleared the deals was "Jack Ruby of Dallas."

The FBI report was filed in 1956, seven years *before* the assassination.[114] Understandably the Bureau was intrigued. A man with that sort of clout would be valuable to have on its own payroll. And so on March 11, 1959, the FBI recruited the same Jack Ruby of Dallas as an informer.[115] Charles W. Flynn, the FBI man who recruited Ruby and served as his contact man, later stated that he had approached Ruby on the assumption that he "might have knowledge of the criminal element in Dallas." [116] Ruby agreed to cooperate, and during the course of the next eight months he and Flynn met a total of nine times,[117] a frequency that, according to former agents, indicates that Ruby was a valuable source of information.[118] The Bureau, however, discontinued its relationship with Ruby on October 2, 1959, insisting that Ruby had not come up with any information.[119] After November 24, 1963, the Bureau's relationship with Ruby became acutely

---

* The special services bureau of the Dallas Police Department, Peter Dale Scott notes, was like many such bureaus in other police departments in that it had a number of responsibilities. One was organized crime and vice, where Ruby came in; another was subversive activities, where presumably Oswald came in (though the Dallas police denied that they had any information on Oswald prior to the assassination); and still another was providing protective intelligence for the visits of important government officials to Dallas, where Kennedy, Ruby, and Oswald all came in.[111]

embarrassing to J. Edgar Hoover, and the documents detailing it were omitted from the original Warren Commission volumes. They were finally declassified in the early seventies.

Actually the Bureau had no cause to be embarrassed. Ruby was a logical source of information, especially about narcotics, and it was only prudent to recruit him. Ruby knew dope, and he knew where it came from: Cuba.

Havana was the distribution center for the heroin that flowed into Dallas and other American cities.[120] After the war Mafia boss "Lucky" Luciano, the syndicate's heroin pioneer, designated Cuba to be the mob's base of operations in the Caribbean.[121] Cuba had much to recommend it. The island was close to the United States, a center for tourists—who dropped an estimated $100 million yearly at Havana's various mob-operated casinos[122]—and most important of all, blessed, from the mob's point of view, with a most benevolent dictator, Fulgencio Batista. Batista saw the mob as a business partner, a conservative, steadying influence with important connections of its own to American intelligence, which would help ensure his rule even as it lined his pockets. Tampa mobster Santo Trafficante, Sr., and Meyer Lansky (representing the syndicate's Jewish wing) struck a deal with Batista in 1933.[123] The syndicate would develop the island's tourist industry while the regime protected its heroin interests. Batista's payoff over the years was estimated by law enforcement agencies to be in the hundreds of millions of dollars.

Among the dozens of syndicate agents who flocked to Havana to oversee the operation was an old friend of Ruby's from Dallas, Lewis J. McWillie.[124] The Warren Report identified McWillie as "a known gambler."[125] McWillie (or any one of the three aliases by which he was known) was, according to one police report (C.E. 1693, p. 1), a murderer (the grand jury refused to indict him)[125a] as well as a gambler[126]—credentials which in any case seemed to ideally suit him for his job as manager of the Tropicana Casino in Havana. McWillie and Jack Ruby were more than ordinary friends. The Warren Commission said that Ruby "idolized" him;[127] McWillie described Ruby as "a brother."[128]

In August 1959, while still working as an FBI informer, Ruby visited McWillie in Havana and stayed for eight days.[129] McWillie later claimed to have invited him and paid all his expenses, saying he felt Ruby needed "a rest." Ruby returned to Cuba for another two-day visit with McWillie during the 1959 Labor Day weekend.[130] Ruby was lucky to have taken the rest when he could. Not long after Castro came to power the mob was tossed out, the casinos closed, and the heroin connection cut off. McWillie, according to the Report, became a "violent anti-Castroite"[131] and eventually turned up at the Thunderbird Hotel in Las Vegas.[132] He kept up his friendship with Ruby by long-distance telephone. Twice in the months before the assassination Ruby and McWillie spoke to each other by phone, and after one such call Ruby, at McWillie's request, sent him a pistol through the mail.[133] A month before the assassination, at a time when the Commission wasn't sure what Ruby was doing, several witnesses saw him in Vegas visiting with McWillie,[134] who was, then as before, reportedly in the employ of Meyer Lansky.[135]

The purpose of Ruby's visits to Cuba, according to the Warren Commission, was pleasure, mixed with a little business.[136] The business was gambling. Ruby claimed, however, that the "opportunities"[137] in Havana didn't seem promising, an opinion that all of the mob was coming to in 1959. Ruby thought the prospects might be brighter for selling war surplus material to the new Cuban government. Hearing that a large quantity of surplus jeeps were available, Ruby considered buying them up and selling them to Castro at what he imagined would be a handsome profit.[138] But the scheme, like so many others Ruby had embarked upon, fell through.

Robert McKeown, the man whom Ruby said he approached on the deal, remembered their discussions somewhat differently. McKeown had run guns to Castro when he and his guerrillas were still holed up in the Sierra Maestra.[139] After the revolution Castro remembered McKeown, and during a tour of the United States in 1959 stopped off in Houston and visited with him, telling the assembled reporters that if McKeown wanted it, a high position in the Cuban government would be his.[140] A week after Castro came to power McKeown was contacted by a local deputy sheriff who said a caller from Dallas was frantically looking for him on a "life and death matter." [141] Within an hour McKeown himself received a call from Dallas from a man who called himself "Rubenstein." [142] Rubenstein told McKeown that he wanted to get three people out of Cuba, and if McKeown could help he would be paid $5000 a head.[143] Rubenstein added that the operation was being financed by a party in Las Vegas.

Three weeks later an unidentified man showed up at the Houston drive-in where McKeown worked. The man said he had a business proposition for McKeown, one that could make him $25,000.[144] They went into a back room, and the man laid out the details. He needed a letter of introduction to Castro. The letter would have to clearly indicate that the man was responsible and reliable. If McKeown would write it, the man would pay him $25,000. McKeown said he would be glad to do it, but needed $5000 cash up front.[145] The man left and McKeown never heard from him again. He saw his picture, though, on November 24, 1963. It was Jack Ruby.

McKeown's story was convincing to law officers, if not to the Warren Commission. It jibed with Ruby's stated desire to make some sort of deal with Castro. And it made some sense of the so-called "pleasure" trips to McWillie's casino in Havana. What made it all the more interesting was the testimony of one of Ruby's employees, a female bartender named Nancy Perrin Rich. Mrs. Rich said that in 1962 she and her husband, Robert Perrin, an alleged gunrunner during the Spanish Civil War, attended several meetings in Dallas with an army colonel. There were others at the meetings too; Mrs. Perrin thought one of them was the son of Vito Genovese. The colonel was offering Perrin

$10,000—later increased to $15,000—to pilot a boat to Cuba. On the trip in the boat would carry guns; on the trip back to Miami, anti-Castro refugees. The Perrins and the colonel haggled over the price and the details of the proposed expedition. During one of their meetings there was a knock on the door, and to Mrs. Rich's astonishment, Jack Ruby appeared. He had a large bulge in his breast pocket. Ruby and the colonel went into another room to talk privately, and when they emerged the bulge in Ruby's pocket was missing. Mrs. Rich surmised that Ruby had been bringing the colonel money. She never found out. Fearing police entrapment, she and her husband later broke off the negotiations with the mysterious colonel.[146]

Nancy Perrin Rich was far from the most reliable witness in the world. She disliked Ruby, the story she told had no confirmation (her husband was dead), and by her own admission the life she had led the last couple of years had been filled with emotional disturbance.[147]

All the same, the story worried the Warren Commission. The Commission did not attempt to check out the truth of her statements, but two Commission lawyers did prepare a lengthy questionnaire for Richard Helms, then the CIA's deputy director of plans, on the basis of Mrs. Rich's testimony and other accounts of Ruby's Cuban activities. "It is possible," the memo said, "that Ruby could have been utilized by a politically motivated group either upon the promise of money or because of the influential character of the individual approaching Ruby." To support that thesis, the lawyers listed ten troublesome facts about Ruby:

1. He is known to have brutally beaten at least 25 different persons.
2. To generalize, it can be said that, while living in Dallas, Ruby has very carefully cultivated friendships with police officers and with other public officials.
3. At the same time, he was, peripherally, if not directly, connected with members of the underworld.
4. Ruby is also rumored to have been the tip-off man between the Dallas police and the Dallas underworld.

> 5. Ruby operated his businesses on a cash basis, keeping no record whatsoever—a strong indication that Ruby himself was involved in illicit operations of some sort.
>
> 6. When it suited his own purposes, he did not hesitate to call on underworld characters for assistance.
>
> 7. In about 1959, Ruby became interested in the possibility of selling war materials to the Cubans and in the possibility of opening a gambling casino in Havana.
>
> 8. Ruby is also rumored to have met in Dallas with an American Army Colonel (Last Name Unknown) and some Cubans concerning the sale of Arms.
>
> 9. A government informant in Chicago connected with the sale of arms to anti-Castro Cubans has reported that such Cubans were behind the Kennedy assassination. [See chapter 9.]
>
> 10. His primary technique in avoiding prosecution was the maintenance of friendships with police officers, public officials, and other influential friends in the Dallas community.[148]

The memo closed with a request that the Agency investigate possible ties "between Ruby and others who might have been interested in the assassination of President Kennedy," including "the Las Vegas gambling community." [149]

The memo, with a covering letter from Commission Counsel J. Lee Rankin, went to the CIA in February 1964. Eight months later, and nine days before the release of the Report, the Commission finally received a reply from Helms. It said:

> An examination of Central Intelligence Agency files has produced no information on Jack Ruby or his activities. The Central Intelligence Agency has no indication that Ruby and Lee Harvey Oswald ever knew each other, were associated, or might have been connected in any manner.[150]

Ruby was evidently just a man with strange friends. A troubled, vicious, deeply neurotic (though not insane, according to several psychiatrists and a Texas court) [151] loser, forever on the fringes of both official and criminal power. If he had been a grief-stricken milkman or insurance salesman, or anything except who he was, then the perfect timing that morning in the basement of the Dallas jail, however impossible, might have been ascribed to chance. Stranger things have happened. If his world had not overlapped with Lee Harvey Oswald's, if he had never been to Cuba, if he hadn't literally known half the policemen in the Dallas jail, fate might have been the killer. Destiny had intervened before. If the FBI had been able to spell a little better, if the CIA hadn't been so tardy, if the Dallas police had been willing to admit that he was their friend, then there would be no suspicion that there was something about Jack Ruby that no one wanted to find. If, if, if. The truth about Jack Ruby comes down to a single personal choice: How much is one willing to suspend disbelief? How many innocent coincidences is one man allowed before, finally, they become sinister calculation?

In one respect the Warren Commission's logic is hard to fault. Ruby does not match the cinematic image of the suavely calculating professional hit man. The fact that he happened to slip into the jail basement at exactly the right moment is extraordinary. And there was certainly no doubt that he would be caught. Why would any man take such a risk if he were not truly insane?

The simple answer is that Jack Ruby was not unique. Given an even bigger risk—namely, the possibility of Oswald's talking, or even more probably, the eventual discovery of his innocence—the gamble of trial and possible execution might be worth taking, especially if one had gone to the trouble, as Ruby had since the assassination, of creating an alibi of insane grief. Jack Ruby, moreover, was a gambler: he had been all his life. Here was an opportunity for the biggest play of all, the chance to make good on years of losses. Others have taken such a risk. On June 28, 1971, Joe Colombo, one of the organized crime bosses of New York, was shot down in the midst of an Italian-American rally in midtown New York.[152] At the time of his shooting Colombo was surrounded by bodyguards and police. There was no possibility that his assailant, a black man and minor syndicate figure, Jerome Johnson, could escape.[153] And in fact Johnson was cut down in a hail of gunfire seconds after he shot Colombo. Yet Johnson took the chance. Like Ruby, he gambled and lost. If the stakes are sufficiently large the mob can always find someone who will gamble.

And Ruby, for all his supposed instability, was the ideal choice for such an assignment. Someone who knew the territory. Someone who could slip in close without being detected. Someone whom the police trusted. Oswald on November 24 had already been alive—and talking—for two days after the assassination. If, as seems likely, he was supposed to have been silenced in the Texas Theatre (the click in the darkness of a misfired gun could just as well have come from a police revolver as it did from Oswald's weapon, which had supposedly functioned with deadly accuracy minutes before in the Tippit killing), one can imagine the panic when the job was botched. On November 24 Oswald was being moved to more secure quarters. The guard around him would be strengthened. There could be no certainty that there would ever again be so propitious an opportunity. And every moment he remained alive represented an increased danger to the President's killers. Time was of the essence. It was, in short, then or never.

Ruby need not have arrived in the basement by chance. Indeed, several witnesses saw him there earlier in the morning. He could have gone out and sent the money order, strengthening his alibi and still been assured of being in the right spot at the right time. Radio and television were providing a minute-by-minute account of Oswald's movements. Who is to say, finally, that Ruby arrived just as Oswald was being moved? It is equally possible that Oswald's movement was timed to *Ruby's* arrival. Considering the somewhat dubious integrity of the Dallas Police Department, there could have been an inside man.

The Warren Commission would never know. During the interview in the Dallas jail Ruby had warned them,

"Gentleman, if you don't take me to Washington, you will never see me again." [154] In that promise, he was prophetic. On January 3, 1967, weeks before a new trial that would in all likelihood leave him a free man, Jack Ruby died at Parkland Hospital from complications of cancer.[155] "His death," one of his lawyers said, "was a merciful release." [156]

9

The Cuban Connection

> A politician driven into banishment by a hostile faction generally sees the society he has quitted through a false medium. Every little discontent appears to him to portend a revolution. Every riot is a rebellion. He cannot be convinced that his country does not pine for him as he does for his country . . .
> This delusion becomes almost a madness when many exiles who suffer in the same cause herd together in a foreign country. . . . They become ripe for enterprises which would at once be pronounced hopeless by any man whose passions had not deprived him of the power of calculating chances.
> —Thomas Macaulay, on the followers of the Duke of Monmouth

CUBA.

It was everyone's obsession. The Kennedys', the Agency's, the mob's, the exiles', Ruby's, and, of course, a young Texan's named Lee Harvey Oswald. There was something special about the place long before anyone had ever heard of Fidel Castro. Back to Teddy Roosevelt's time Americans had felt protective of the island and its people in a way they never felt about Mexico or Canada or anywhere else in their hemisphere. The closeness was part of it: "ninety miles from home" is how people put it, whatever point they wanted to argue. But there was something more than that, maybe the romance of the island, the mystery, the forbidden pleasures, the Hemingwayesque intrigue. Cuba called up all the images. If you were a plotter or a grade B movie producer, Cuba was simply the place you went.

Thus it was not surprising that when a bearded young lawyer named Fidel Castro led a handful of rebels into the hills, his cause should find a warm spot in many American hearts. The *New York Times* and *Life* approvingly recounted the exploits of the young idealist battling against what seemed hopeless odds. Americans sent money and support. The more adventurous ran guns or went into the hills with him. Even the syndicate, hoping to hedge its bets, lent a small measure of quiet assistance. Cuba evoked that sort of emotion—the kind of feeling that could just as quickly flash to rage, when Castro, his revolution now a success, announced allegiance to Marxism. About things Cuban, Americans were as hot-tempered as the Cubans themselves.

John Kennedy was no exception. For years he waged war, open and covert, on Castro with stubborn Irish intensity. Before it was over the Kennedy crusade would shatter the Central Intelligence Agency, humiliate his own administration, and bring the United States to the precipice of nuclear war. Within moments of Kennedy's murder in Dallas the rumors were already spreading. Somehow, some way, Cuba was involved.

But which Cubans? Oswald, the accused assassin, was a supposed partisan of Castro. However, the Secret Service, shortly after the assassination, received a report from Chicago that a "revolutionary Cuban" negotiating an illegal arms deal had been overheard saying that his group would soon "take care of Kennedy." [1] The anti-Castro exile had made the statement on November 21.[2] The Secret Service investigated, but eventually discounted the report. The group to which the exile belonged—the "30th of November Group"—according to "other security agencies" [3] (presumably the CIA) was not the sort that "would be involved in illegal activities." [4] Had the Secret Service investigated further they would have found that, on the contrary, illegal activities were the 30th of November Group's specialty. The previous July, U.S. Customs had seized one of the group's leaders in the Florida Keys with an arsenal of arms. (C.D. 1085) [5] The 30th of November Group was allied with Alpha 66,[6] the most notoriously violent of the various exile factions.[6a] The FBI itself conceded that the 30th of November Group "supported revolutionary type activity within Cuba." [7] Not until 1975, however, was it revealed that the 30th of November Group's "revolutionary activities" included, according to a long statement issued by the Cuban government, participation in two assassination plots. The Cuban statement said that the first 30th of November Group plot was hatched in July 1961, and included explosives, mortars, high-powered rifles, and .30 caliber machine guns, reportedly provided by the CIA through the Guantanamo naval base.[8] Castro, the intended victim of the conspiracy, failed to arrive at a scheduled appointment and the plot fizzled. In mid-September 1961, the 30th of November Group was said to have been involved in an actual attempt on the life of a Cuban official. The weapons were said to have included handguns, machine guns, and a high-powered rifle with a telescopic sight, again allegedly supplied by the Agency.[9]

The Cuban connection, wherever it led, was indeed worrisome. The United States had already risked nuclear war once over the island. If the assassination pointed to Havana the risk might become reality. It was that concern, evidently, that prompted Clifton Carter, Lyndon B. Johnson's assistant, to call the Dallas district attorney twice the night of the assassination to ensure that no mention of "international Communist conspiracy" was made in Oswald's indictment.[10] The new president did not want to face the possibility of going to war over the murder of his predecessor. As Johnson put it in his memoirs:

> We were aware of stories that Castro . . . only lately accusing us of sending CIA agents into the country to assassinate him, was the perpetrator of the Oswald assassination plot. These rumors were another compelling reason that a thorough study had to be made of the Dallas tragedy at once. Out of the Nation's suspicions, out of the Nation's need for facts, the Warren Commission was born.[11]

It was a commendable motive. Somehow, though, Oswald had to be explained. Everything about him said Cuba.

Oswald's affair with Cuba, whatever it was, began in the Marine Corps. Lieutenant John E. Donovan, one of his officers, remembered later that in 1959, then Private Oswald took an extraordinary interest in international affairs, especially Latin America, and Cuba in particular. Oswald made an attempt to learn Spanish and expressed sympathy with Castro, but as Donovan noted, "what he said about Castro was not an unpopular belief at that time." [12]

When Oswald was discharged from the marines he stopped in Los Angeles to pick up a passport. Among the countries he listed as those he wished to visit was Cuba. He also made several visits to the Cuban consulate.[13] When Oswald left Texas a few days later his mother assumed that he was heading for the island. When he turned up, instead, in the Soviet Union, she was stunned.

Minsk, the Russian town where Oswald settled, was also the site of a Cuban training institute, and Oswald—despite the Commission's statement to the contrary—had at least one close Cuban friend. His name was "Alfred," [14] and his picture, with Oswald's arm around his shoulder, is contained in the Commission's volumes, though the Commission unaccountably identifies him as a "Hungarian friend of Anita Ziger." [15] But Mrs. Ziger, a friend the Oswalds made in Russia, wrote Marina and Lee in Texas reminding Lee of his friend "Alfred from *Cuba*." [16] (Italics added.)

The first public notice of Oswald's Cuban activities was in New Orleans, where Oswald organized a fictitious chapter of the Fair Play for Cuba Committee under the chairmanship of the equally fictitious A. J. Hidell.[17] Oswald distributed pro-Castro literature, had his picture shown on television, and debated on a local right-wing radio program with a Cuban exile leader, Carlos Bringuier.[18] By the time they appeared on the radio together in mid-August, Oswald and Bringuier were well acquainted. Only days before, in a scuffle that had landed Oswald in jail, Bringuier had allegedly punched him in the nose.[19] A week before that Oswald had gone to Bringuier and his group of exiles, offering to school them in the ways of guerrilla warfare.[20] The offer must have startled Bringuier and his compatriots, because at that moment a secret training camp for precisely that purpose was operating in New Orleans.[21] There was another coincidence to Oswald's visit. The week before, the FBI, on orders from Robert Kennedy, had raided a vacant house in Mandeville, Louisiana, outside New Orleans, and only a mile from the Cubans' training camp.[22] The agents had seized more than a ton of dynamite slated for use in exile operations. The house was reportedly owned by one William Julius McLaney,[23] a gambler who operated out of McWillie's Tropicana Hotel in Havana until Castro forced him to leave the island in 1960. Bringuier was aware of the FBI raid and of the exiles who escaped. Two of them visited his office three days before Oswald's sudden appearance. Small wonder then that Bringuier was suspicious that Oswald was a government plant, and dispatched one of his men to check on his background.[24]

Bringuier himself was a rightist, bitter not only at Castro but at Kennedy for failing to overthrow him. One of Bringuier's Cuban friends later told the Warren Commission: "He hates the United States as much as he hates Russia." [25] When Bringuier came to New Orleans in 1961, he published a right-wing Cuban newsletter with the support of the Crusade to Free Cuba Committee.[26] More commonly known as the Free Cuba Committee, the organization, like many embracing Cuban exiles, was under the patronage of the CIA.[27] It was to the Free Cuba Committee that Dallas District Attorney Henry Wade said Oswald belonged, until his mistake was corrected by Jack Ruby.[28] The organizer of the committee was Robert Caire, a New Orleans advertising man who later told the Secret Service that around 1963, he "seemed to recall Oswald applying for a job with his agency." [29] Another one of the committee's financial supporters was William Reily, Oswald's first employer in New Orleans.[30] At one time or another the committee attracted a number of interesting individuals, including David Ferrie, Sergio Arcacha Smith, and Gordon Novel of Garrison fame.[31]

As Kennedy curtailed and finally cracked down on exile raids against Cuba, Bringuier's politics grew more radical. In 1962 Bringuier became a delegate to the Student Revolutionary Directorate,[32] whose Dallas supporters included General Edwin A. Walker,[33] whom Oswald supposedly attempted to assassinate. Oswald himself showed up at one meeting of the directorate, when Walker was also in the audience. The notebook Oswald was carrying when he was arrested on November 22 contained Bringuier's name and business address,[34] along with the name "Cuban Student Directorate,"[35] as well as the name and phone number of General Walker.[36]

Oswald clearly knew his way around anti-Castro Cubans at least as well as, if not better than, he did with pro-Castro types, with whom, apart from a few letters to New York, he seemed to have had almost no contact.

When Oswald took a bus to Mexico City in September 1963, he advised two of his fellow passengers to stay at the Hotel Cuba, which he described as "clean and cheap."[37] Oswald added that he had stayed there once himself. A number of Cuban exiles also stayed at the Hotel Cuba. Oswald, however, could not have been one of them. He had never been to Mexico City before September 1963—or so the Warren Commission reported.[38]

Curiously, Oswald failed to take his own advice. He stayed instead at the Hotel del Comercio,[39] a hangout and meeting place for anti-Castro exiles. His performance at the Cuban embassy was even more curious. To Silvia Duran, the secretary of the consul, Oswald showed proof of his having resided in Russia, as well as identification stating that he was director of the New Orleans chapter of the Fair Play for Cuba Committee, credentials, Oswald said, which qualified him as a "friend" of the Cuban revolution.[40] Later, though, when Oswald met the consul himself, Eusebio Azque, he got into an angry shouting match. Azque informed Oswald that because of a delay in processing his Soviet visa application, it would be a minimum of four months before he could get a Cuban visa. Oswald thereupon exploded, proclaiming his deeds on behalf of Marxism and the Cuban revolution and lambasting the Cuban for his "ingratitude." Oswald's outburst angered Azque, who told Oswald that people like him were harming the Cuban revolution rather than helping it, and as far as he, Azque, was concerned, Oswald would never get a visa.[41]

Oswald left Mexico City a week later. His adventure with Cuba, whatever it might have been, was at an end.

Oswald's travels back and forth between the competing Cuban camps were suspicious to say the least. With the trouble and expense he invested, including forging credentials, traveling to Mexico City, and attempting to "infiltrate" the violent anti-Castro right, it was hard to imagine him as a free-lance provocateur. Either he was completely irrational (and there was no evidence for that; on the contrary, those who came in contact with him in the course of his Cuban activities were impressed with his poise and seeming sophistication) or there was some unknown method in his madness. David Slawson and William Coleman, two Warren Commission lawyers who were detailed to investigate Oswald's Cuban ties, came away from sifting the evidence suspecting that Oswald, rather than being the pro-Castro partisan he tried to seem, might on the contrary have been an agent of the anti-Castro exiles. Slawson and Coleman set down their thesis in a 111-page memorandum which was withheld from the Warren Commission's volumes of testimony and evidence. Even today parts of the Coleman-Slawson memorandum remain classified, but enough has been recently revealed to show that the "double agent" hypothesis was far from a crackpot suggestion. The memo reads in part:

> The evidence here *could* lead to an anti-Castro involvement in the assassination on some sort of basis as this: Oswald could have become known to the Cubans as being strongly pro-Castro. He made no secret of his sympathies, and so the anti-Castro Cubans must have realized that law enforcement authorities were also aware of Oswald's feelings and that, therefore, if he got into trouble, the public would also learn of them. The anti-Castro group may

> even have believed the fiction Oswald tried to create that he had organized some sort of large, active Fair Play for Cuba group in New Orleans. Second, someone in the anti-Castro organization might have been keen enough to sense that Oswald had a penchant for violence that might easily be aroused. This was evident, for example, when he laughed at the Cubans and told them that it would be easy to kill Kennedy after the Bay of Pigs. On these facts, it is possible that some sort of deception was used to encourage Oswald to kill the President when he came to Dallas. Perhaps "double agents" were even used to persuade Oswald that pro-Castro Cubans would help in the assassination or in the get-away afterwards. The motive of this would of course be the expectation that after the President was killed Oswald would be caught or at least his identity ascertained, the law enforcement authorities and the public would then blame the assassination on the Castro government, and the call for its forceful overthrow would be irresistible. A "second Bay of Pigs invasion" would begin, this time, hopefully, to end successfully.[42]

"The foregoing is probably only a wild speculation," Coleman and Slawson concluded. "But the facts that we already know are certainly sufficient to warrant additional investigation." [43] None, however, was ever undertaken.

The Coleman-Slawson memorandum was speculation; informed speculation, certainly, convincing speculation, perhaps, but still no more than that. As Oswald's own life had demonstrated, there were two sides to the Cuban coin. An argument could be made that Oswald was what he wished people to believe: a backer of Castro. From there it was not too great a leap to suggest that Castro had ordered Kennedy's assassination.

Such reports were circulating in Dallas within days of the assassination. Nearly all the information, predictably, came from anti-Castro sources, in some cases from people who themselves later came under suspicion. One tale, recounted to the Secret Service three weeks after the assassination, emanated from the same Alonzo Hudkins who claimed that Oswald had been a paid informer for the FBI.[44] The Secret Service account of the interview with Hudkins, classified until 1975, reports:

> Alonzo Heidt Hudkins III, a reporter for the *Houston Post,* advised the writer confidentially that he had received information from Felton West, the *Houston Post* Washington Bureau representative, to the effect that citizens of the United States had entered into an agreement or a plot to assassinate Premier Castro of Cuba and that Lee Harvey Oswald, who went to Mexico City on September 26 and allegedly returned October 1–3, learned of this plot, which infuriated him. Mr. Hudkins inferred that this was a possible reason for Oswald assassinating the President. . . . [Hudkins] states that Felton West, *Post* Washington Bureau, has more specific information as to the plot to assassinate Castro and the fact that President Kennedy and Vice-President Johnson were informed of same by a former Cuban premier.[45]

West later disclaimed any knowledge of such a plot.[46] Hudkins, who obviously relished the attention both of his stories brought him, embellished some of the details when reporters queried him about it in 1975. According to Hudkins he had once been a part of an abortive plan to smuggle one thousand guns to anti-Castro Cubans around the time of the Bay of Pigs.[47] He added that the CIA had approached him in late 1962 or early 1963, while he was working as an engineer for Hunt Oil in Houston, with a proposal that he join an Agency "contract team" that was supposed to assassinate Castro.[48] This venture was abandoned as too risky, Hudkins claimed, and instead the team switched its attentions to Cheddi Jagan, the former Marxist premier of Guyana and the reported target of at least one CIA-engineered assassination plot.[49] According to Hudkins, this attempt, too, was called off "when it got close to nutcracking." [50]

While it is hard to imagine the CIA recruiting a reporter like Hudkins to plot anything, his story was typical of the reports coming in to the FBI and the Warren Commission as they began their investigation. They did little to shed light on the assassination or

Oswald, but they did have the effect of further muddying already murky waters. Which, on reflection, may have been exactly their purpose.

One story the Warren Commission pursued with considerable vigor, for instance, came from a source identified only as "D," who was said to be a young Latin-American secret agent. According to the Report, which devotes almost two pages to recounting "D" 's story:

> "D" . . . approached U.S. authorities in Mexico shortly after the assassination and declared that he saw Lee Harvey Oswald receiving $6,500 to kill the President. Among other details, "D" said that about noon on September 18, waiting to conduct some business at the Cuban consulate, he saw a group of three persons conversing in a patio a few feet away. One was a tall, thin Negro with reddish hair, obviously dyed, who spoke rapidly in both Spanish and English, and another was a man he said was Lee Harvey Oswald. A tall Cuban joined the group momentarily and passed some currency to the Negro. The Negro then allegedly said to Oswald in English, "I want to kill the man." Oswald replied, "You're not man enough, I can do it." The Negro then said in Spanish, "I can't go with you, I have a lot to do." Oswald replied, "The people are waiting for me back there." The Negro then gave Oswald $6,500 in large-denomination American bills, saying, "This isn't much." After hearing this conversation, "D" said that he telephoned the American Embassy in Mexico City several times prior to the assassination in an attempt to report his belief that someone important in the United States was to be killed, but was finally told by someone at the Embassy to stop wasting his time.[51]

Alas, "D" 's story, intriguing as it sounds, never checked out. The day he saw Oswald plotting on the patio of the Cuban embassy the real Lee Harvey Oswald was engaged in much more mundane pursuits, namely visiting the Louisiana State Unemployment Commission in New Orleans.[52] "D" subsequently retracted his story, saying that he cooked up the hoax to get to the

United States so he could have a hand in anti-Castro action,[53] then recanted his retraction, and finally was adjudged a liar by a polygraph machine. (*Report*, p. 285)[54]

Once again the source of the story turned out to be more interesting than the story itself. The report on "D" originally came to the Commission's attention in the form of a memo from Richard Helms at the CIA.[55] Helms, however, provided few details and made no mention of "D" 's actual identity. That was left to the FBI, which named him as Gilberto Alvarado, an agent for the Nicaraguan intelligence service.[56] Alvarado said he was in Mexico City in September 1963 to get a visa for travel to Cuba, on a "penetration mission for the Nicaraguan Intelligence Service."[57] Not surprisingly, the Nicaraguans denied that Alvarado had been sent on such an assignment.[58] There *was*, however, a Nicaraguan anti-Castro conspiracy afoot, including a plan to assassinate Castro. The operation, according to journalist Tad Szulc, was dubbed Second Naval Guerrilla.[59] Among its leading actors were three names later to become familiar to Americans: Bernard Barker, James McCord, and E. Howard Hunt.* [60]

"D" was not the end of the stories from Nicaragua. Fernando Penabaz, a Cuban with his own Nicaraguan connections and a friend of Carlos Bringuier, claimed that Oswald had had contact with a Cuban intelligence agent in Nicaragua.[62] A check of Penabaz's story revealed that his information had come from Sixto Mesa and Miguel de Leon, two Cuban exile leaders[63] associated with Manuel Artime, who would later organize a defense fund for his friend Howard Hunt and the other Watergate defendants.[64]

---

* The linchpin of Second Naval Guerrilla, according to Szulc, was the assassination of Castro. At the moment Castro was shot, 750 armed exiles were supposed to wade ashore. Their invasion and the death of Castro would supposedly be the end of the Cuban revolution. Szulc writes that the assassination part of the scheme was cooked up by the Agency during meetings in Paris and Madrid (where Hunt was assigned), and continued even after the invasion was aborted in 1965. The assassin-to-be was a bearded Cuban physician and former Cuban Revolutionary Army major named Rolando Cubela. When Cubela was arrested by Cuban authorities in February 1966 he was equipped with a small arsenal of weapons, including an FAL automatic rifle equipped with telescopic sights and a silencer, obligingly provided by the CIA.[61]

In the cases of Penabaz and Alvarado the connection to Watergate figures was at least once removed. That was not true of the stories coming from Miami, which also claimed that Oswald was a Cuban agent. Two Miami area reporters, brothers Jerry and James Buchanan, published several stories alleging that Oswald had been in Miami (which was news to everyone who tracked his movements), and had been in contact with Cuban intelligence.[65] The Buchanan brothers were reported members of the International Anti-Communist Brigade.[66] An attorney for one of the brigade's members described it as "financed by dispossessed hotel and gambling room operators who operated under Batista." [67] The leader of the brigade was also the source of the Oswald stories. His name was Frank Fiorini, or to give his better-known alias, Frank Sturgis, one of the burglars arrested in the Watergate.[68]

Sturgis and his Latin-American friends all had their axes to grind. More to the point, the stories they spread were studded with so many factual errors that even the Warren Commission was able to see through them. The charge that Oswald was a Castro agent was easily discredited; the stories simply lacked a credible source.

Then in 1967 a source of a wholly different kind appeared: Jack Anderson.

On March 3, 1967, Anderson, on information "from sources whose credentials are beyond question," detailed for the first time six alleged CIA-organized crime attempts to assassinate Castro between March 1961 and January 1963. The next day Anderson raised "some ugly questions that high officials would rather keep buried." "Could the plot against Castro have backfired against President Kennedy?" Anderson wondered. "The late President was murdered nine months after the last assassination team was caught on a Havana rooftop with high-power rifles. Former associates recall that Robert Kennedy, deeply despondent, went into semi-seclusion after the assassination. . . . Could Bob Kennedy have been plagued by the terrible thought that the CIA plot, which he must at least have condoned, put into motion forces that may have led to his brother's martyrdom?" [69]

Kennedy was enraged by Anderson's column. He told two of his aides, Adam Walinsky and Peter Edelman, that some of Anderson's facts were true: the Agency and the mob had contemplated assassinating Castro. But Kennedy insisted, "When I found out about it, I turned it off." [70]

In the beginning John and Robert Kennedy were in no mood to turn anything off. They had inherited a scheme from the Eisenhower administration to overthrow Castro by force of arms: one quick, violent thrust at the Cuban homeland by a handful of exiles, an invasion that would touch off rebellion from Oriente to Escambray. The setting of 1200 ragtag exiles against a trained army and air force of 200,000 men did not seem the likeliest of match-ups, and it had not been Kennedy's idea. But in time Kennedy adopted the plan as if it had been his own. There had been pressure, the CIA had encouraged and cajoled and warned of the dark consequences of, as Allen Dulles put it, "the disposal problem . . . we can't have them wandering around the country telling everyone what they have been doing," [71] but in the end the President had given the order. It was his decision. His responsibility. And, when the exile brigade was cut to pieces on the beaches of the Bay of Pigs, his shame.

No President likes losing. But John Kennedy seemed to take the humiliation of the Bay of Pigs personally. His wrath had two targets: the man who had defeated him, and the adviser who had urged him into battle. Of the latter, Kennedy told Arthur Schlesinger:

> I probably made a mistake in keeping Dulles on. It's not that Dulles is not a man of great ability. He is. But I have never worked with him, and therefore I can't estimate his meaning when he tells me things. . . . Dulles is a legendary figure, and it's hard to operate with legendary figures. . . . I must have someone there [at CIA] with whom I can be in complete and intimate contact—someone from whom I know I will be getting the exact pitch. I made a mistake in putting Bobby in the Justice Department. He is wasted there. Byron White could do that job perfectly well. Bobby should be in CIA.[72]

The President was true to his word. Dulles and Richard Bissell, his chief deputy, were soon sacked. John McCone, a Wall Street lawyer and friend of the President's, was installed as CIA director. But to Robert Kennedy fell responsibility for overseeing the Agency's clandestine operations, particularly the operations directed against Cuba.[73] As for the Agency itself, Kennedy told some of his aides he would like to "splinter [it] . . . into a thousand pieces and scatter them to the winds." [74]

Castro, too, would be dealt with. The newly constituted agency, with Kennedy's blessing, set out to undermine the regime with virtually every weapon at its disposal. Cuba was isolated economically. Shipments of critically needed machinery and spare parts were sabotaged.[75] And, most ominously, the surviving exiles were organized, trained, armed, equipped, and sent out on what for a time were almost nightly raids on the Cuban homeland.[76]

The CIA's exile operations were run out of the campus of the University of Miami, a spot that the CIA code-named JM WAVE.[77] Even by the CIA's standards JM WAVE was a massive operation. Its budget ran to more than $50 million.[78] Three hundred American agents were assigned to it, working under the cover of more than fifty dummy corporations.[79] JM WAVE had its own medical staff, its own polygraph teams, its own psychologists, and its own cavernous logistical warehouse that included, as one former official boasted, "everything from machine guns to caskets." [80] George Crile and Taylor Branch, two journalists who chronicled JM WAVE, reported that the exiles' exploits included shelling the Cuban coast, blowing up a sugar mill, and in one memorable raid, strafing a beachfront hotel in downtown Havana itself.[81] On August 24, 1962, Crile and Branch wrote, six young CIA-trained Cubans, attached to both JM WAVE and Bringuier's Revolutionary Student Directorate, "piloted a boat to within 200 yards of the shore near Havana and shelled the Blanquita Hotel. . . . [They] got so close that Bates [one of the raiders] remembers seeing lights in the ballroom and the uniforms of the soldiers.

His companions opened up with a five minute barrage at point-blank range, inflicting heavy damages on the hotel before returning to Miami at reckless speed." [82]

Two exiles who went along on other operations were Bernard Barker and Eugenio Martinez, both of whom were later arrested at the Watergate. Martinez told Crile and Branch that the Agency and the exiles wanted to inflict more than pinpricks on the Castro regime. They wanted to bring down the man himself. "I can tell you there were plots," Martinez said. "I took a lot of weapons to Cuba. Some of them were very special weapons for very special purposes. They were powerful rifles with sophisticated scopes—Springfields with bolt actions, rifles used only by snipers. They were not sent to shoot pigeons or kill rabbits. Everyone in the underground was plotting to kill Castro, and the CIA was helping the underground. I was with the underground, as well as with the CIA, so you could say I was involved in the plots, too, but that is all so obvious." [83]

That there were plots and that they included assassination attempts on Castro is, after the Church committee's investigation of CIA, as Martinez says, "obvious." By the end of 1961, Crile and Branch report, "several men affiliated with CIA had already been foiled in attempts to kill him, among them Luis Toroella (executed), Eloy Gutierrez Menoyo (still imprisoned), William Morgan (executed), and Antonio Veciana (escaped to the United States)." [84] The idea was not a new one. In the closing days of the Eisenhower administration one of the chief CIA contact men with the exiles made perhaps the first Castro assassination proposal: that was Howard Hunt.[85]

Castro, of course, was not unaware of what was going on. In July 1975 Castro sent Senator George McGovern an "uninclusive" list detailing twenty-four separate assassination attempts engineered by the exiles and/or the CIA.[86] Castro may have been exaggerating for effect, but certainly there was a lot of plotting going on. The question is who sanctioned it.

So far there has been no credible evidence to link President Kennedy or his brother to approving any assassination plot against Castro. There have been informed *surmises* from a number of sources, including General Edwin Lansdale, who oversaw much of the anti-Castro activity, that Robert Kennedy must have known about the attempts and given at least tacit approval to them.[87] Various senior members of the Kennedy administration discussed the possibility of killing Castro, and at least one cabinet member, Secretary of Defense Robert McNamara, urged it on the President.[88] The President himself told several friends, including Florida Senator George Smathers,[89] who himself was anxious to be rid of Castro, and at least one journalist, Tad Szulc, then of the *New York Times,* that he was under great pressure to approve such a plan.[90]

As Szulc later recounted the incident, he had been invited to the Oval Office in November 1961, seven months after the Bay of Pigs, to chat generally about Cuba. At one point in the conversation, Szulc says, "Kennedy leaned forward in his rocking chair and hurled a question at me: 'What would you think if I ordered Castro to be assassinated?' " Szulc was startled by the query and blurted out that he was against political assassinations as a matter of principle, and to be cold-blooded about it, killing Castro probably wouldn't solve the Cuban problem anyway. "Kennedy leaned back in his chair, smiled and said he had been testing me because he was under great pressures from advisers in the Intelligence community (whom he did not name) to have Castro killed," Szulc remembered. "But that he himself was violently opposed to it on the grounds that for moral reasons the United States should never be a party to political assassinations. 'I'm glad you feel the same way,' he said." [91]

Former presidential assistant Richard Goodwin, who chaired a White House task force on Cuba, confirms Szulc's recollections and insists that neither Kennedy brother gave the go-ahead for the Castro assassination. Yet there were numerous attempts, with considerable American assistance. The CIA, Goodwin thinks, may have proceeded on its own, taking what it assumed was a cue from Robert Kennedy. As Goodwin explained:

"To the extent that Bobby was involved in anything, it would have been like Henry II asking rhetorically, 'Who will free me of this turbulent priest?' and then the zealots going out and doing it." [92]

If the Kennedys were indeed blameless, Castro might not have known it. Since a number of American agents were doing their best to kill him and seemed to possess unlimited resources to carry out the project, Castro might logically have assumed that they had to be taking orders from the President. Castro then could have decided to stop the orders at their source. Lyndon Johnson evidently believed this was the case when he was interviewed by Leo Janos, one of his former staff members, not long before his death. Writing in the *Atlantic Monthly,* Janos reported that Johnson—

> . . . expressed the belief that the assassination in Dallas had been part of a conspiracy . . . Johnson said that when he had taken office, he found that "we were operating a damn 'Murder Inc' in the Caribbean." A year or so before Kennedy's death a CIA-backed assassination team had been picked up in Havana. Johnson speculated that Dallas had been a retaliation for this thwarted attempt.[93]

The flaw in Johnson's logic is that after he took office, whether with or without his approval, the assassination plots continued. By Castro's reckoning there were at least *ten* other plots on his life or the lives of Cuban leaders between the time Kennedy was assassinated and Johnson left office.[94] And according to Castro, there was one additional plot against him in 1971, when Nixon was President.[95] If Castro had Kennedy assassinated in retaliation, as Johnson contended, why did the Cuban stop there? Why didn't he go after LBJ and Nixon as well? Unless, of course, Castro understood that various American presidents had nothing to do with the plots on his life, that they were wholly under the direction and control of the CIA.

In any case, both logic and the available facts point against a Castro-backed assassination of Kennedy. Castro as well as Che Guevara were reported deeply shaken by Kennedy's assassination, and fearful that Oswald had been framed by anti-Castro Cubans as a pretext for a new, and this time decisive, invasion of the island. Ironically, when word of the assassination reached Castro the Cuban leader was talking with Jean Daniel, a French journalist who had only days before met with Kennedy. Kennedy had asked Daniel to feel Castro out to see how interested he was in normalizing relations. "Speak to Castro and come back again here, to Washington, to talk with me," Kennedy had told Daniel.[96] Daniel later reported that Castro appeared "shocked" by the news that Kennedy had been killed. "Es una mala noticia," he said—"This is bad news."[97] Castro's fears were heightened when within hours of the assassination President Johnson put all U.S. forces worldwide on red alert. In Florida troops were moved into position. At bases across the United States, including those in Florida, and on carriers on station in the Caribbean, planes were poised on flight decks, engines whining.[98] The moment passed, and instead the nation lost itself in sorrow. Three days after the assassination, after the alert had been called off, Castro spoke to a crowd in Havana about the assassination, disclaiming any role in it, pointing to Oswald's bizarre behavior at the Cuban embassy in Mexico City, and accusing his enemies of using Kennedy's death to bring the Cuban revolution down.[99]

In later years Castro talked of his grudging admiration, even his affection for Kennedy. During a long series of interviews with former Kennedy aide Frank Mankiewicz and Kirby Jones, Castro proved himself as vulnerable to the Kennedy mystique as anyone. "Kennedy was a bold man," he said, "a man with initiative, a man with imagination. And he was a man of courage. . . . He took many measures against us. But I speak to you in all sincerity and try to give you the opinion that I have of Kennedy. I say that truly he was one of the few men who had enough courage to question a policy and change it."[100] Jones recalled that when the subject of the assassination came up, Castro seemed pained to talk about it, but insisted that neither he nor his regime had had a hand in it. When Jones and Mankiewicz asked the reverse of the question, whether Castro had any information that exiles had been involved, Castro, according to Jones, "paused a long time, as if he were trying to get his thoughts together, so he could be very careful about what he said. Finally, he said that he knew nothing about it. Then he went on to talk about it, about Dallas, about the exiles, with a lot of detail, the kind of detail you would seem to know, only if you knew something about it. I can't put my finger on it. It's just the way he spoke, the look on his face, that convinced me that, in fact, he knew a lot and was holding back." [101]

What Castro did say was significant. "We were in conflict with Kennedy politically. We had nothing against him personally, and there was no reason to wish him personal harm," he insisted. "Besides, Kennedy could be followed by someone worse. I always used to say that at least we knew Kennedy, that we had fought against him during the Bay of Pigs incident, the missile crisis, and all that. He was a known enemy. But let me repeat that the Kennedy who was assassinated in Dallas was a much more experienced man than the one who had assumed the Presidency two years before." Finally, Castro added: "I ask myself, why would a man [Oswald] who commits such an act try to come here? Sometimes we ask ourselves if someone did not wish to involve Cuba in this." [102]

In mid-1975, during a visit to Cuba, Senator George McGovern again raised the subject of Kennedy's assassination with Castro. The point came up while Castro and the South Dakota senator were returning to Havana in a jeep from inspecting the provinces. As McGovern recalled their conversation:

> We discussed a number of subjects on the long drive back to Havana. I told him of speculation in the United States that Cuban agents may have been involved in the assassination of President Kennedy. He responded in disbelief. "We had troubles with the Kennedy administration, but it is monstrous even to contemplate that we would murder the head of state of any nation, to say nothing as to be so foolish as to incur the wrath of a great power like the United

> States." Then he added, "Before that man Oswald killed President Kennedy, he tried to get a visa in our embassy in Mexico City to visit Cuba. The application was refused. I have often thought that if we had admitted him many people might have blamed us for what he later did." [103]

McGovern was impressed by Castro's sincerity, to say nothing of his logic.[104]

Castro, in fact, had reason to be thankful to Kennedy. For shortly after the Cuban missile crisis in the fall of 1962, the JM WAVE operation was disbanded at Kennedy's command. Henceforth the exiles were prohibited from launching attacks on Cuba from American soil. Moreover, the CIA was forbidden to provide the exiles with any armed assistance larger than a pistol. Army intelligence took over the Agency's liaison role with the exiles. Most dramatically of all, the President pledged to the Russians that the United States would never again undertake an invasion of Cuba.[105]

The turning point had been the missile crisis. Coming eyeball to eyeball with the Soviet Union—and seeing the other side blink—had given Kennedy a new appreciation of the realities of power, his own ability to cope with them, and how, if used unwisely, they could send both sides skittering over the edge of nuclear extinction. There had been ample opportunity, indeed ample provocation, for use of force. Most of the President's aides—including, predictably, the CIA—had been clamoring for it. But Kennedy had drawn back. His brother, once so enamored of "all that covert stuff, counter-insurgency and all the garbage that went with it," [106] as George Ball said in disgust, was the most eloquent dove of all. At one point during the crisis meetings, when a proposal for a preemptive air strike was on the table, Bobby had quietly passed his brother a note. "I know," it said, "how Tojo felt when he was planning Pearl Harbor." [107] In the end Kennedy stood firm. There was no sellout and no Pearl Harbor. He came away from the experience with confidence in his own instincts and renewed distrust of CIA. In many ways the missile crisis was the pinnacle of his presidency. And Kennedy sensed it. As his brother left the

White House, the crisis now over, the President referred to Lincoln and said jokingly, "This is the night I should go to the theatre." Robert replied: "If you go, I want to go with you." [108]

The peaceful resolution of the missile crisis was not without its critics. Among the JM WAVE exiles there was excited anticipation that the missile crisis would provide a new excuse for yet another invasion of Cuba.[109] The CIA fostered that impression, and at one point agents in Florida alerted the exiles to stand by for an imminent invasion.[110] The military, too, were unhappy that the moment had passed. In his memoirs Khrushchev recounts a key meeting in the midst of the crisis, between Robert Kennedy and Soviet Ambassador Anatoly Dobrynin. "The President is in a grave situation," Kennedy, according to Khrushchev, told Dobrynin. "We are under very severe stress. In fact we are under pressure from our military to use force against Cuba. . . . That is why the President is appealing directly to Chairman Khrushchev for his help in liquidating the conflict. If the situation continues much longer, the President is not sure that the military will not overthrow him and seize power. The American army could get out of control." [111]

We have, of course, only Khrushchev's word that Kennedy said any such thing. Even if Kennedy was quoted accurately, he could have been raising a specter of military intervention simply as a ploy to induce the Soviets to make concessions. Against these arguments, though, is independent evidence that the President took most seriously the possibility of some sort of coup (see chapter 10).[112] Whether or not this fear was justified, there is no question that Kennedy's relationship with the defense and intelligence communities was strained and that Cuba played an important role in straining it. Kennedy, however, was determined to press on.

The groping toward détente with the Soviet Union was symbolized best by the President's speech at American University on June 10, 1963. Gone was the cold war rhetoric, the threats Kennedy had made shortly after the Bay of Pigs. Instead of talk of "the insidious nature of this new and deeper struggle," of exile flags flying "in a free Havana," the President addressed himself to "the most important topic on earth: peace." Not "a Pax Americana enforced on the world by American weapons of war," Kennedy said, but a peace patiently worked out by former adversaries. "We must re-examine our own attitude—as individuals and as a nation," he said, "for our attitude is as essential as theirs." No government or social system, he added, "is so evil that its people must be considered as lacking in virtue. . . . The tide of time and events will often bring surprising changes in the relations between nations." [113]

One of the changes Kennedy envisioned was in relations with the Soviet Union. The other was with Castro. Castro was more than amenable to the idea. In September the Guinean Ambassador to Havana approached William Attwood, a personal friend of the President's and adviser on African affairs to the U.S. United Nations delegation. The Guinean told Attwood that Castro was unhappy with Cuba's satellite status, and if an accommodation with the United States could be arranged he would be willing to make major concessions.[114] Attwood told UN Ambassador Adlai Stevenson of the conversation and Stevenson relayed it to Kennedy.[115] Kennedy gave Attwood the go-ahead for further contacts.[116] Subsequently Attwood met with the Cuban delegate to the UN, who informed him that there was a good chance that Castro would invite Attwood to Cuba. Now Robert Kennedy was alerted.[117] Once again Attwood was told to proceed. Meanwhile Castro's personal aide, Dr. Rene Vallejo, sent word to the White House that Castro wanted "to talk personally to us about improving relations and was pleased to find out that we were ready to listen." [118] Attwood telephoned Vallejo at a private number in Havana and confirmed that Castro was interested in a settlement.[119] On November 19 Attwood relayed this information to McGeorge Bundy, Kennedy's national security adviser. Attwood later recalled that Bundy told him that "the President would want to see me. . . . The

President, he said, would not be leaving Washington except for a brief trip to Dallas."[120] On November 23 Attwood heard from the Cuban delegate to the United Nations that Castro wanted to begin informal talks. The word came one day too late.[121]

The sudden turnabout in Kennedy's policy toward Castro, as well as toward the Soviet Union, met sharp resistance from the State Department and the CIA, not to mention from the exiles themselves.[122] John McCone remained unconvinced that accommodation with Castro was possible. Whether the CIA director ordered them or merely looked the other way, the exile raids against Cuba continued, although far less frequently than before. In March Alpha 66, the most rabid of the exile groups, reportedly attacked a Soviet military post in Cuba and two Soviet freighters.[123] The raid brought a stiff protest from Cuba and the Soviet Union. In response, State and Justice announced in a joint statement that they "would take every step necessary to insure that such raids are not launched, manned, or equipped from U.S. territory."[124] The FBI raid on the Louisiana dynamite cache followed a few months later. In September the federal government issued "strong warnings" to six Americans to stop their anti-Castro activities.[125] One of the six was Frank Sturgis, who was then piloting a B-25 on raids over Cuba.[126] The FAA promptly lifted Sturgis's authorization to fly the plane.[127] That did not put an end to the exiles' violence. In late October Castro announced that his forces had captured two motor launches from an exile mother ship, the *Rex*.[128] Castro also produced an exile captive who publicly confessed that he had landed on the island with a boatload of arms from the *Rex*, and that "the CIA organized all arms shipments."[129] Reporters from the *New York Times* investigated the story and discovered that, true enough, two launches were missing from the *Rex*'s davits. The *Times* also learned that the *Rex* had been bought by J. A. Belcher of the Belcher Oil Company[130] in Miami from a Nicaraguan firm owned by the family of that country's CIA-supported dictator, Luis Somoza. At the time of the raid the boat had been leased for "electronic and oceanographic research" to the international division of the Collins Radio Company of Dallas, Texas.[131]

Angered by the *Rex* raid and other incidents, Kennedy in mid-November began planning yet another shake-up of the Agency. As he left for Dallas, a task force was already being created to, as one report described it, "survey the global intelligence and other activities of the United States to improve coordination and efficiency."[132]

Kennedy might try to bring the CIA to heel. There was little to be done about the exiles. The crackdown on raids against Cuba was to many of them only the final proof of what the legendary "Eduardo" called Kennedy's "betrayal."[133] Kennedy's failure to provide additional air support to the Bay of Pigs invaders had, they believed, doomed the invasion from the start, resulting in the killing or imprisonment of hundreds of sons, brothers, and husbands. E. Howard Hunt, the invasion's CIA political officer better known to his exiles by his code name "Eduardo," reflected their bitterness. "No event since the communization of China in 1949 has had such a profound effect on the United States and its allies as the defeat of the US-trained Cuban invasion brigade at the Bay of Pigs in April 1961," Hunt recalled in his Cuban memoirs.[134] "Out of that humiliation grew the Berlin Wall, the missile crisis, guerilla warfare throughout Latin America and Africa, and our Dominican Republic intervention. Castro's beachhead triumph opened a Pandora's box of difficulties."[135] For Kennedy Hunt had nothing but scorn. The President, he said, tried "to whitewash the New Frontier by heaping guilt on the CIA."[136] Hunt sarcastically recalled Kennedy's appearance before the ransomed exile brigade in Miami on December 29, 1962. "Watching the televised ceremony, I saw Pepe San Román give JFK the Brigade's flag for 'temporary safekeeping.' In response the President said, 'I can assure you that this flag will be returned to this Brigade in a free Havana.' One wonders what time period he had in mind."[137]

Actually, Hunt reveals, the flag presented to Kennedy in the Orange Bowl was merely a replica of the brigade banner, and that "the Brigade feeling against Kennedy was so great that the presentation nearly did not take place." [138]

The feelings increased throughout the spring and summer of 1963. The statements of the exile leaders, as collected by Peter Dale Scott, showed the growing frustration. In June Dr. Miro Cardona, the exiles' chief, complained angrily that he and his key lieutenants had been forbidden to travel outside the Miami area.[139] "In Florida, where we were once welcome, we must now operate like guerillas in the hills of Escambray," said one of the brigade survivors. "We are watched like criminals." [140] Cardona himself resigned as head of the CIA-supported Cuban Revolutionary Council, accusing the United States of going back on an alleged promise to support a new invasion.[141] In May the Citizens Committee for a Free Cuba demanded a new national policy to liberate Cuba "by all necessary means." [142] Other right-wing exile supporters called for "an overwhelming invasion of Cuba" as soon as possible.[143] In mid-April Cubans living in Miami received a flier with the most radical proposal of all. "Only through one development will you Cuban patriots ever live again in your homeland as free men," it said. "[Only] if an inspired Act of God should place in the White House within weeks a Texan known to be a friend of all Latin Americans." [144]

The exiles, shorn of official American support, turned to the radical right for help. One of the men arrested in the FBI raid on the dynamite cache in Louisiana was Richard Lauchli, a reported member of the Minutemen.[145] The Minutemen were active elsewhere in securing arms for the exiles. One place was Dallas, where in late 1963 U.S. Treasury agents arrested a local gunshop owner and Minutemen member who was supplying the exiles with guns.[146] The exiles were members of Alpha 66. With their leader Manuel Rodriguez, they met regularly at the house on Hollandale Street in Dallas.[147] After the assassination police received a report that Oswald too had attended the meetings. Like many such reports it turned out to be incorrect. But then another report came in from Oklahoma saying that Oswald had been spotted there. The witness was again mistaken. He had only seen someone who closely resembled Oswald. The police nonetheless checked out the report, and eventually discovered the identity of the Oswald look-alike who had been in Oklahoma. He was Manuel Rodriguez. (C.D. 23.4)[148]

Rodriguez was described by one of the Dallas FBI's informers as "violently anti-Kennedy." (C.D. 1085)[149] Evidently the Secret Service perceived him as a threat of some sort, for on March 18, 1964, four months after the assassination, a "Protective Research Referral Memorandum"—an alert on persons judged to present a potential danger to the President—was filed on Rodriguez. (C.D. 853)[150]

Rodriguez began his revolutionary career on the side of Castro. He had fought against the Batista regime and been imprisoned by it. When Castro came to power Rodriguez was released from prison and for a time became one of Castro's provincial chiefs. Like many others, however, Rodriguez turned against his former *jefe* and fled to the United States, where he helped found Alpha 66. Eventually he wound up in Dallas. Sometime after the assassination he moved to Puerto Rico. (C.D. 853) [151–53]

Alpha 66 itself was linked to the assassination by two separate reports, both of which were discarded. They were contained in an FBI document filed from Miami. One of them reported that "another government agency which conducts intelligence and personnel investigations, advised that one of their sources stated that he heard one Dora Causa relate that Eloy Gutierrez Menoyo had stated on November 21, 1963, that 'something very big would happen soon that would advance the Cuban cause.' " [154] Causa later denied that the story related to the assassination.[155] The other report came from the wife of John Klinner, identified by the FBI as an ex-convict [156] who had been imprisoned by Castro after being shipwrecked off the Cuban coast. On the day of the assassination Mrs. Klinner said that she and her husband were in a large Miami department store. When they heard the word that the President had been shot she said her husband immediately went to a telephone and called someone identified only as "the Major." Klinner reportedly asked: "Was it us?" or "Was it one of our boys or was it one of our group that did it?" [157] Mrs. Klinner could not be positive of the precise wording. She was sure, though, that her husband had begun speculating about the possibility of arrests in Florida. When the FBI contacted Klinner he denied any knowledge of the assassination or the stories to which the witnesses were referring.[158] There the investigation of Alpha 66 ended.

John Kennedy did not have to have been killed *by* Cubans *for* Cubans to have been involved, or for Cuba itself to have been a motive. The peculiar overlapping of interests that existed among the anti-Castro exiles, organized crime, and the Central Intelligence Agency amounted in the autumn of 1963 to a tripartite pact. Each had individual motives: the mob, greed and revenge; the exiles, a longing for their homeland; and the Agency, a twisted kind of patriotism. Cuba fused those motives in common cause. Each group helped the other. In their free-floating association, members drifted out of one group and into another and then back again. When it came to Cuba the demarcation between organized crime, the exiles, and intelligence was fuzzy, if not meaningless. An offense against one was an offense against all. The President's Cuban policy offended all of them.

Quite on their own the exiles had the means (courtesy of the CIA and the mob) and the murderous temperament necessary to commit the assassination. Their links with Oswald and their presence in New Orleans, Mexico City, and Dallas gave them the opportunity. The Odio story alone, which was never disproved and continued to haunt members of the Commission even after the submission of the final Report, is reason enough to be suspicious of the exiles. Add to it the lengths to which the exiles went to *disprove* the incident and the story takes on even darker overtones. Moreover, the fanaticism of the exiles was well known. So was their hatred of Kennedy. So was their disposition to use violence, even assassination, to achieve their ends. Castro was the intended victim of at least a dozen substantiated attempts. All of them, of course, were bungled. Ironically, the exiles' congenital clumsiness is perhaps their best defense in the Kennedy murder. The assassination was committed with such lethal efficiency it is hard to imagine the gang-that-couldn't-shoot-straight being involved. Though, by the Warren Commission's standards, if a demonstrated poor shot like Oswald on his own managed such a feat, why not the Cubans?

Why not indeed. Assassins might have been recruited from among the exiles; the CIA's "Operation 40" [159] was supposedly created for the explicit purpose of turning exiles into assassins, who were then to be unleashed, reportedly, not only against Castro and the members of his regime, but against the anti-Castro left, the so-called exponents of *Fidelismo sin Fidel,* like Manuel Ray's MRP, who were hated as much as if not more than Castro by the exiles and their CIA tutors, among them E. Howard Hunt.[160] And therein lies the hitch. The exiles were so thoroughly infiltrated by the CIA (and after Kennedy ordered a crackdown on the exiles' activities, by the FBI) that it would have been virtually impossible for the exiles to mount an assassination without the Agency knowing about it. The question then is whether the Agency was actively implicated in the killing or merely permitted it to happen.

It seems doubtful that the exiles played the leading role. Exile politics are so bizarre and Byzantine, with friends one day blood enemies the next, as to raise serious questions about their reliability in an undertaking so sensitive. If the exiles did have a role in the conspiracy, more probably it was as members of the supporting cast. To judge from the available evidence that is precisely the part they seem to have played, both before the assassination, with Sylvia Odio; and after, during extraordinary energetic efforts to link Oswald to the Castro cause. The reason is plain enough. If Oswald were firmly established as a Castro agent, it would be a powerful inducement for a new invasion. Possibly the exiles were merely capitalizing on a national tragedy. Possibly, too, they had a hand in helping the tragedy occur.

They need not have. The exiles were merely symptomatic of a larger madness, an intensity so passionate, so engulfing, that it swept all reason before it. There was no simple explanation for the obsession. Today it seems incredible that so small an island, so removed from day-to-day concern, so preposterously irrelevant, could have been the trigger that nearly loosed the holocaust. Only Cuba could.

The obsession that seized the exiles infected others: people who, for their own reasons, were as bound up in the Cuban cause as the romantics who plotted revolution in Miami restaurants and went to war in tiny boats. These were more accomplished men. They did not fumble at murder. Their expertise was different. Their obsession was the same. It all traced back to Cuba.

10

The Gentlemen from Langley

> The National Security Act of 1947 . . . has given Intelligence a more influential position in our government than Intelligence enjoys in any other government in the world.
>
> —Allen Dulles

E. HOWARD HUNT had a bad memory.

He had thought about it, racked his brain, asked his friends, checked his notes, but for the life of him he could not remember what he was doing on November 22, 1963, when John Kennedy was murdered in Dallas.

He wasn't in Dallas, that much Hunt did remember.[1] No, he was in Washington somewhere, doing what just slipped his mind. At first he thought he might have been having lunch with some friends from the Agency and the Pentagon, but they didn't remember seeing him. He didn't go to his CIA office in Langley, Virginia, either. The CIA records showed he was probably absent that day, taking "sick leave." [2] Hunt was sure he was at home with his wife and family.[3] Just what he was doing at the moment John Kennedy was killed remained a puzzle.

Hunt's remarkable absentmindedness may seem suspicious. But there *are* a few Americans who simply don't recall where they were or what they were doing when John Kennedy was killed. Take Richard Nixon, for instance. He thought he was in New York the morning of November 22. That at least is what he told the Warren Commission.[4] But Mr. Nixon was mistaken. Early that morning he had gotten on an airplane at Love Field, which is an airport in Dallas, Texas.

Oh, well.

Poor Howard Hunt. After Watergate people were ready to blame him for just about everything, and considering his background—spy, burglar, devotee of plots and assassinations—it wasn't really surprising. The cruelest charge, of course, was that he and his friend Frank Sturgis (who Hunt said wasn't all that good a friend, since they had only met in 1972, although Sturgis put the beginning of their acquaintance in 1961) had been two of the "tramps" arrested by the Dallas police behind the grassy knoll shortly after the assassination.[5] The accusation received considerable publicity, especially after comedian Dick Gregory repeated it on national television.[6] David Belin and the Rockefeller CIA commission went to great pains to prove there was nothing to it. Belin really didn't mind the effort; indeed he was delighted, since the accusation was so patently preposterous. Photo experts were called in, measurements taken, witnesses interviewed, and in the end the Rockefeller commission was able to report what virtually everyone knew from the beginning: whoever the "tramps" were, they were not Howard Hunt and Frank Sturgis. The height was all wrong. So was the age. As a matter of fact, except to Gregory and a few others, they didn't look like Hunt and Sturgis at all.[7]

Such, however, typifies the investigation of whether the Central Intelligence Agency was involved in the murder of President Kennedy. There was, there has never been, any investigation at all.

The CIA was an inevitable suspect. Kennedy and the Agency had long been at loggerheads. The CIA's failure to correctly estimate the resistance of Castro's forces at the Bay of Pigs was only one of a number of incidents. Almost on the eve of the missile crisis the Agency, without the President's authority, pulled off one of its patented anti-Castro capers which had at first amused Kennedy. Kennedy did not find this one funny; nor did the Russians. What the men from Langley did was sabotage a shipment of Cuban sugar bound for the Soviet Union. The opportunity presented itself in late August 1962, when a British freighter filled with sugar bound for Russia sailed into San Juan harbor for repairs. The CIA managed to contaminate 14,000 of some 80,000 sacks of sugar by injecting them with an allegedly harmless substance that would give the sugar a foul taste. The purpose was to undermine the Russians' confidence in Cuba's chief export crop. When Kennedy found out what had happened he warned the Russians, prevented the ship from sailing, and excoriated the Agency for creating "a dreadful precedent for chemical sabotage." [8] The Russians, who were busily installing missiles in Cuba, strongly protested the incident in a series of diplomatic notes. After the missile crisis and the growing rapprochement with Castro and the Soviet Union, the Agency defied Kennedy's orders to turn off exile raids on the Cuban homeland—just as it had prepared to defy him at the Bay of Pigs. Before the invasion the Agency prepared a plan for the operation to go forward *even if* Kennedy got cold feet at the last moment and tried to stop it.[9] The President's orders had also been disobeyed in Vietnam, where, three weeks before his own death, Ngo Dinh Diem had been overthrown and murdered, apparently with the active complicity of the CIA. Kennedy welcomed Diem's departure from the scene, and when rival Vietnamese generals informed the American embassy that they were planning to oust him, the U.S. had raised no objections, which, in Vietnam, was tantamount to sanctioning the coup d'etat. But Diem's murder had, on instructions from the President, been explicitly ruled out. Nonetheless, Diem and his brother-in-law had been shot to death in the back of an armored personnel carrier after Vietnamese officers consulted with the CIA's liaison man on the project, Lucien Conein.[9a] Diem's death shocked Kennedy.[10]

The disobedience, at whatever level, enraged the President. At the time of his death he was planning a full-scale review of the Agency's activities. He did not like being embarrassed, and the Agency embarrassed him not only in Cuba and in Vietnam but in the Soviet Union, where in 1963 the Russians arrested a Yale history professor and charged him with committing espionage against the Soviet Union. Kennedy, after receiving assurances from the Agency that the professor was "clean," had personally appealed to Khrushchev to release him, and Khrushchev, as a gesture of his esteem for Kennedy, had agreed. But when the professor returned and met with Kennedy in the oval office, he reportedly admitted that he had indeed been spying for the Agency. Kennedy was livid.[11]

The President had already sacked Dulles and Bissell and installed his own brother to honcho the Agency's covert operations, but apparently more shake-ups were required. His desire to splinter the CIA into a thousand pieces and scatter it to the winds did not escape the attention of the Agency.[12]

The Agency had grievances against the President as well. Hunt was not the only CIA man to believe that Kennedy had betrayed the Agency and its people at the Bay of Pigs. The bitterness was increased by what Hunt termed Kennedy's "heaping guilt on the CIA." [13] Even McCone, whom Kennedy had appointed, and who was supposedly his ally, deeply disagreed with the President's moves to normalize relations with Cuba. The Agency was also fearful of a whole range of Kennedy initiatives that grew out of the American University speech, from arms control to the banning of atmospheric testing of nuclear weapons to accommodation with the Communists in Laos to the reevaluation of the entire American commitment to Southeast Asia.[15] Shortly before his death Kennedy had approved the first withdrawal from South Vietnam of American advisers. A thousand advisers were to be called home by the end of the year—a token number perhaps, but a clear sign of where Kennedy was heading.[16] On his return from Texas he had said he would conduct a full-scale policy review of U.S. relations with South Vietnam. One of the first moves was meeting with Ambassador to Saigon Henry Cabot Lodge. He and Kennedy were to have lunched at the President's Virginia estate on November 24.[17] CIA liked none of it.

If the Agency had a motive it also had the means. The Agency's budget was counted in the hundreds of millions of dollars, a sum for which it had to provide no accounting. The employees, including "contract agents" and part-timers, numbered in the tens of thousands. No one man, not even the President, knew just how many, or who they all were. But it was common knowledge that the ranks of American intelligence agents included not a small number of thugs, thieves, and murderers,[18] men, as Dulles himself conceded, "of the worst moral character." [19] The CIA had its own army, of which the exiles were only one brigade. There were other brigades and divisions strung out around the world from Katanga to Laos to the hills of Burma.[20] The CIA had airplanes and the pilots to fly them. It had naval vessels and the crews to man them. As Roger Hilsman, who worked closely with the Agency during the Kennedy administration, said of the CIA: "Political leverage is power. Information is power. Secrecy is power. Speed in communications is power. Ability is power. And the sheer number of people is power. CIA had all these." [21]

Or as David Wise and Thomas B. Ross, two respected journalists for the *New York Herald Tribune,* put it:

> There are two governments in the United States today. One is visible. The other is invisible. The first is the government that citizens read about in their newspapers and children study in their civics books. The second is the interlocking, hidden machinery that carries out the policies of the United States in the Cold War. This second, invisible government gathers intelligence, conducts espionage, and plans and executes secret operations all over the globe. . . . To an extent that is only beginning to be perceived, this shadow government is shaping the lives of 190,000,000 Americans. Major decisions involving peace or war are taking place out of public view. An informed citizen might come to suspect that the foreign policy of the United States often works publicly in one direction and secretly through the Invisible Government in just the opposite direction.[22]

An invisible government, with uncontrolled, incalculable powers. It was more than just two journalists' imagination. Harry Truman, the man who created the

CIA, was frightened by what it had become. "For some time I have been disturbed," he said a month after the President's assassination, "by the way CIA has been diverted from its original assignment. It has become an operational and at times a policy-making arm of the government. . . . This quiet intelligence arm of the President has been so removed from its intended role that it is being interpreted as a symbol of sinister and mysterious foreign intrigue. . . . We have grown up as a nation respected for our free institutions and for our ability to maintain a free and open society. There is something about the way the CIA has been functioning that is casting a shadow over our historic position." [23]

The public came to share Truman's perceptions. In 1962 a novel called *Seven Days in May* was written by Fletcher Knebel and Charles W. Bailey. The book told what seemed to be a fanciful tale of a cabal of right-wing generals, unhappy about what they regarded as "appeasement of the Communists," plotting to seize the government and depose the President. Most reviewers dismissed Knebel and Bailey's book as irresponsible sensationalism. The book nonetheless became a big bestseller and was eventually made into a popular movie. John Kennedy probably would have liked it. He had asked that the movie be made.* [24]

Nothing was impossible with the CIA, no fiction too remote. Assassination? The CIA was a specialist. The Agency recruited killers, armed and trained them, and with or without the President's authorization sent them against their target. Castro was only one. There was Duvalier in Haiti, Trujillo in the Dominican Republic, Diem in Vietnam, Lumumba in the Congo.[27] And, if persistent reports were to be believed, Schneider in Chile, Jagan in Guyana, even de Gaulle in France. Assassination was one of the CIA's "assets," to be used like other assets against what CIA deemed

* Historian Arthur Schlesinger, who was Kennedy's special assistant, says the President wanted the film made "as a warning to the nation." [25] John Frankenheimer, the film's director, recalls: "Those were the days of General Walker and so on. . . . President Kennedy wanted *Seven Days in May* made. Pierre Salinger conveyed this to us. The Pentagon didn't want it done. Kennedy said that when we wanted to shoot at the White House he could conveniently go to Hyannis Port that weekend." [26]

to be enemies of the United States, or—for they were not always the same—of the Agency itself.

So inbred was the Agency's desire to get rid of troublesome opponents that a small team of specialists in such tasks was pulled together and given a home in the Langley bureaucracy. The unit, according to the Church committee, which revealed its existence in late 1975, was dubbed the "Executive Action Group." A "former high official of the intelligence agency" later told the *New York Times* that the group probably included no more than three persons, who "developed methods for the removal of unfriendly foreign leaders." The group, which supposedly "petered out" sometime in 1963, was, according to another intelligence official, intended to "maintain an 'assassination capability' " within the Agency. There was no evidence, Senator Church added, that President Kennedy knew of or approved the group.[27a]

Indeed John Kennedy was one of the Agency's opponents, potentially its most dangerous adversary. The CIA had a motive. It had the means. It had the experience. It had the disposition. The Agency could have killed him, and far better than anyone else covered its crime. But did it?

If Oswald was the assassin (or a member of an assassination conspiracy), and *if* he was still an intelligence agent (as he certainly seemed to have been during his sojourn in the Soviet Union) on November 22, 1963, and *if,* finally, he was acting with the Agency's approbation when he killed Kennedy, then, of course, the answer is self-evident. But there are a number of hurdles to cross before reaching that conclusion. It is by no means certain, in the first place, that Oswald was an assassin. Much of the evidence, along with his casual behavior immediately after the shots were fired, points to the contrary. However cool and calculating killers are supposed to be, it is difficult to imagine someone who has just shot the President of the United States pausing to drink a Coke,[28] then strolling outside in no evident hurry, getting on a bus,[29] getting off, hailing a cab, offering it up to a little old lady,[30] and finally, as the police and FBI closed in, making good his escape, which turns out to be to a local movie theater.[31] Oswald's excuse for "fleeing" the scene of the crime was that he thought that, because of the assassination, work would be suspended for the rest of the day.[32] The assumption was not illogical. Work, as it happens, was suspended for the rest of the day, and besides Oswald eleven other workers left the Book Depository after the assassination.[33] There may have been a conspiracy, but it wasn't *that* big. Some critics have found Oswald's going to the movie theater suspicious, a sign perhaps that Oswald was an intelligence agent. George O'Toole, a former CIA man who suggests that the FBI may have been involved in Kennedy's killing (a not surprising contention, considering the Bureau's and the Agency's mutual detestation),[34] points out that movie theaters are a favored rendezvous for agents. O'Toole quotes a Soviet intelligence manual which describes them thus:

> Intelligence Officers can make extensive use of movie theaters when organizing agent communications by spending a certain amount of time in them before a meeting. The fact is that there are few people in most movie theaters, especially on weekdays during working hours. Movie theaters located away from the center of the city are often practically empty. Thus, by arriving at a designated time at a previously predetermined movie theater and taking advantage of many empty seats, the intelligence officer and the agent can hold a meeting right in the theater.[35]

The Texas Theatre was, just as the Soviet manual predicted, virtually empty when Oswald entered it, and there was at least one other man in the theater who knew him—the person who fingered him for the police and then disappeared during the ensuing melee. Oswald might well have gone there either to kill time until a getaway plan could be arranged or to meet a contact. Why, otherwise, would he carry a revolver with him?

Assuming that Oswald was part of a conspiracy, whether or not he fired any shots, that still leaves open the questions of what kind of conspiracy it was, who sponsored it, what was Oswald's role in it, and whether it had the Agency's backing. Unfortunately it is not merely a matter of going to Langley, walking to the file drawer marked A, and seeing if Oswald's name is listed under Assassins. There are, as Dulles told the Commission, no written records of many of the CIA's agents, let alone its assassins.[36] Until someone comes forward with convincing evidence that Oswald was a paid killer for the CIA one can only look to the available facts and draw one's own conclusions. After that it is a matter of faith. As Richard Helms put it on one occasion, "We are honorable men. You simply have to trust us." Despite the source's credibility, that is sadly the case.

Moreover, Oswald's apparently having been an agent does not necessarily mean he was a CIA man. Part of the common misunderstanding of the nature of intelligence derives from the assumption that all spies work for the CIA. The CIA, in fact, is only one member of a much larger intelligence community, and when compared to such giants as the National Security Administration (whose chief stated function is the monitoring of intelligence gained from ELINT, COMINT, and "spy-in-the-sky" satellite sources), the Defense Intelligence Agency, the Office of Naval Intelligence, army intelligence, and air force intelligence, a relatively weak sister at that. Army intelligence,* in particular,

* One army intelligence officer who has asserted that he had contacts with Oswald before the assassination is Captain Richard Case Nagell (ret.).[37] According to Nagell he worked for army intelligence during the Korean War and after, and also took on assignments for the Agency.[38] During the late 1950s and early '60s Nagell's assignments for army intelligence reportedly involved infiltration and spying on domestic dissident groups, especially those supporting the Castro regime. In the course of this work Nagell supposedly came in contact with Oswald. Nagell says that when he learned of the conspiracy he used an alias and wrote J. Edgar Hoover a letter in mid-September 1963 warning him that the President would be assassinated on September 26, 1963.[39] The same month Nagell walked into an El Paso, Texas, bank, whipped out a .45 automatic, and pumped two shots into the ceiling, and walked out again, waiting to be arrested. Federal authorities were only too glad to oblige. Nagell is quoted by Edward J. Epstein as saying he took the action to put himself under federal protection at the time of the assassination.[39a] It all makes for a fascinating story until one checks on Nagell's background and finds that while he was indeed in the army, and apparently working for army intelligence, he was also in a plane crash in 1954 that left him with organic brain damage.[40] After his arrest and conviction for the incident in the El Paso bank Nagell was committed to a federal mental institution. He was released in 1967.[41] Despite his mental state Nagell has produced substantiation for many of his claims. The single most important piece of evidence, however—the letter he allegedly wrote Hoover, warning of the plot and mentioning Oswald by name—has not turned up in FBI files.

has nearly as large a budget as the Agency, and more than three times as many agents. Long before the CIA ever dreamed up Operation CHAOS, army intelligence was busy spying on thousands of Americans. The army paid particular attention to domestic dissidents like Lee Harvey Oswald. Moreover, in June 1961 Kennedy, in a memorandum to the Joint Chiefs of Staff, set new rigid guidelines for the Agency's covert operations. Theoretically, at least, the Agency was supposed to clear and coordinate with the Defense Department its paramilitary activities against Cuba, a requirement that brought the army into the picture.[42] Finally, far better than the CIA, army intelligence was in a position to know the arrangements of the President's trip to Dallas, as well as the security precautions the Secret Service was taking to ensure his safety. Chronically short-handed, the Secret Service worked with army intelligence as a matter of routine. Years after the assassination Peter Dale Scott collected information that showed that Dallas was no exception.

The coincidences Scott encountered are extraordinary. Secret Service Agent Winston Lawson, who was responsible for the choice of the motorcade route, had been a member of the army intelligence reserve.[43] So was Captain W. P. Gannaway, the head of the Dallas police special service bureau, which used Ruby as an informer.[44] So was James W. Powell, who was present on the sixth floor of the School Book Depository when the Mannlicher-Carcano was found, and was later "trapped inside . . . after the Depository doors had been sealed."[45] The police pilot car which preceded the motorcade contained the commander of the local army intelligence reserve and possibly one other agent.[46] The morning of the assassination another army intelligence officer met with James Hosty, the FBI man whose name appeared in Oswald's notebook.[47] There was yet another army intelligence agent who drove from the assassination site with Dallas Police Lieutenant Jack Revill.[48] The night of the assassination a secret cable (finally declassified in 1973) went out from the 4th Army Command in Texas to the U.S. Strike Command at MacDill Air Force Base in Florida. USSTRICOM, as it is known, was an army-air force operation set up in 1961 and designed to be a quick-reaction strike force. Its location in Florida, as Scott notes, would have made it the logical vehicle for any attack on Cuba. And the cable that went from Texas to USSTRICOM the night of November 22 seemed to favor just such an eventuality. It read:

> Don Stringfellow, Intelligence Section, Dallas Police Department, notified 112th Intelligence Group, this headquarters, that information obtained from Oswald revealed that he had defected to Cuba in 1959 and is a card carrying member of the Communist Party.[49]

All of which was untrue. But at that moment, with U.S. forces on worldwide alert and the Secret Service fearful of a Communist conspiracy, few people knew it was untrue. If pressure was building for a postassassination invasion of Cuba, the incendiary cable from Texas was an important element in furthering the plot. Perhaps it was all innocent coincidence: the cable, the army's ties with the exiles, the spying on dissidents, the agents who just happened to be in and around the Book Depository, the Secret Service, the FBI, and the Dallas police. But if the coincidence truly was innocent it was no more so than Oswald's own links to the CIA.

For Oswald was almost surely an intelligence agent of some sort. While in Dallas, New Orleans, and Mexico City he was in close, even intimate contact with other intelligence agents or contract employees of the Agency. On November 22, however, he could just as well have been operating *without* the Agency's sanction, or, though this seems less likely, without its prior knowledge. There are numerous instances when the Agency has lost control of its own people, and, one presumes (though the Agency has yet to admit it), when one of its agents has been turned against it. Another possibility is that Oswald was "taken over" by an extremist faction within the Agency, or a group close enough to it to be aware of Oswald's background. Again, there are a number of cases when this has happened, when individual agents have acted not only contrary to the orders of the President but those of the leadership of CIA. One longtime observer of the Agency says:

> That sort of thing is inevitable, given the sort of people CIA recruits. CIA looks for guys who are bright, tough, naturally competitive. Ideology does not mean nearly as much as the instinct to win. If you take one of these guys, hell, maybe he's even idealistic, and put him out somewhere like the Bolovens Plateau, and give him a job, well, he's going to do it, whatever it takes. He gets close to the people he is working with. Cares about them. Identifies with them. And he does his damnedest to help them. Maybe there are things the Agency doesn't want him to do—tells him he *can't* do. But he does them anyway. How will the Agency ever find out? It's just part of winning. These guys are trained to win.[50]

Cuba produced that feeling in many agents, of whom Howard Hunt is merely the best known. The cause of the exiles came in time to be the cause of the Americans who worked with them. Idealistic, fiercely, even naively patriotic, the exiles were easy to like. They were gambling everything, including their lives, on the word Americans gave them. Sometimes the promises were extravagant. Pepe San Román, the leader of the exile brigade, later recalled: "What we were told was, 'If you fail *we* will go in.' "[51] When the moment came, and the pledges were not kept, the men who worked with the exiles, came to know them as friends, and sent many of them off to die were naturally moved. Only moved is not the word for it. "Guilty" perhaps comes closer, "bitter," as Howard Hunt was bitter, "determined" that the sacrifice would not be in vain. Sometimes comradeship led the CIA men to perform acts of personal bravado for the sake of the exiles that were in direct contravention of Agency orders.

George Crile and Taylor Branch recount the story of one such American named Rip Robertson. Robertson was close to fifty by the time he started running JM WAVE guerrilla operations, but neither his age nor orders from his superiors could keep him from the thick of the action. Once when a group of Robertson's commandos were adrift in a motorless raft just yards from Castro's guns, Robertson personally charged in to save them. He also paid his men fifty dollars for every ear of a Castro soldier they brought back. "Rip was a patriot, an American patriot," one of his commandos told Crile and Branch. "Really, I think he was a fanatic. He'd fight anything that came against democracy. He fought with the Company [the CIA] in Korea, in Cuba, and then he went to Vietnam. He never stopped, but he also went to church and he practiced democracy." [52]

There were many Rip Robertsons. E. Howard Hunt was only a milder version. He was not an "operations man," someone who manned a machine gun or stormed a beach. He was more at home with a typewriter than with a Walther P-38. As far as is known the only blood he ever spilled was in the pages of the pulp spy novels he pumped out by the dozen. Hunt only planned murders, and then from a safe remove.

Yet there was something about "Eduardo" that inspired fanatical loyalty from the Cubans with whom he came in contact. "Eduardo represents to the Cuban people their liberation," Bernard Barker told the Senate Watergate committee, explaining why he "could not deny" Hunt's request for help in burglarizing the Watergate.[53] Hunt returned the feeling in kind. Artime, the Cuban exile leader, became Hunt's closest friend. Hunt was the godfather of one of Artime's children. When Hunt was arrested after the Watergate break-in, Artime organized a defense fund for him. Hunt had his own way of raising money. "The Watergate bugging is only one of a number of highly illegal conspiracies engaged in by one or more of the defendants at the request of White House officials," Hunt warned in a memo to back up his demand for a million dollars in "support money" for the Watergate defendants' families and legal fees. "These as yet undisclosed crimes can be proved." [54] Nixon hardly needed reminding. Even before Hunt's arrest, Nixon warned H. R. Haldeman: "You open that scab there's a hell of a lot of things and we just feel that it would be very detrimental to have this thing go any further. This involves these Cubans, Hunt and a lot of hanky-panky that we have nothing to do with ourselves." [55] Two days before Hunt's sentencing, Nixon told Dean and Haldeman, "Hunt . . . is most vulnerable in my opinion, might blow the whistle." [55a] Several hundred thousand dollars were paid, but in the end the money did no good and Hunt went off to jail, leaving three motherless children behind. He entrusted them to the care of Manuel Artime.

Hunt's life and the lives of the Cuban exiles were always crossing. In that nexus many strange people would meet, including Lee Harvey Oswald. Some of the Fair Play for Cuba leaflets Oswald distributed in New Orleans, for instance, bore the address 544 Camp Street.[56] Subsequent investigation revealed that neither Oswald nor anyone from the Fair Play for Cuba Committee had ever kept an office at that address, though at one time, a year before Oswald came to New Orleans, an anti-Castro group had. The group was the Cuban Revolutionary Council. The CRC was an umbrella organization under which all the exiles, whatever their political coloration, could gather. Like many of the exile organizations it had been a CIA creation. The CIA liaison officer was E. Howard Hunt.[57]

A coincidence, perhaps, to go with the coincidence of Hunt not being able to prove—or even remember—what he was doing on November 22. There was one other coincidence. According to Hunt's biographer, Tad Szulc, for a brief period in 1963 Hunt was acting CIA station chief in Mexico City.[58] Hunt's incumbency included the month of September, when Lee Oswald came looking for a Cuban visa, and managed the unique feat of escaping detection by the CIA's surveillance cameras. Instead, of course, someone else was photographed and identified by the CIA as Oswald, someone who clearly was not Oswald. Hunt has denied that he was in Mexico City at all during 1963 in any capacity,[59] and David Phillips, an ex-CIA man who resigned in 1975 to rally support for the beleaguered agency, and says he *was* in Mexico City during Oswald's stay, confirms Hunt's story.[60] Maybe so. In any case, Hunt's biography, which is quite detailed about the 1940s and '50s, as well as the later '60s and the '70s, is quite skimpy for the period between 1961 and 1964.[61] In Szulc's book the years are reduced to less than a page.[62] In Hunt's autobiography the year 1963 is not mentioned at all.

Hunt, wherever he was, whatever he was doing, is not so interesting in himself as in the mentality he represents. He was a rigid anti-Communist, a hater of President Kennedy, a man at home with violence and assassination as a "political option," * a romantic about the Cuban exile cause, someone who was ready to use all means necessary to help the exiles regain their homeland.

At that Hunt was far from the worst. He represented the Agency's old school. He was a throwback to the days when the CIA seemed a gentlemanly calling, a vocation for the thin-lipped and well turned-out, the products of good families and the right schools who wished to serve their country and fight communism without getting their hands dirty. They were, like E. Howard Hunt (Brown, class of '39), tweedy, civilized sorts, in the best traditions of the "Oh So Social" OSS. And certainly there were many who fit that mold. The quiet men of Langley's seventh-floor executive suite—the analysts, the OSS veterans who went into business and publishing and wrote their memoirs of derring-do with the French maquis—they were like that. But they were never the men on whom CIA relied, who were a

---

* Hunt is reported to have planned or recommended at least three assassination attempts. Two were against Castro: a proposal in 1960 that was rejected by the Eisenhower administration,[63] and the Cubela plot that was foiled by Castro in 1966.[64] The third Hunt assassination proposal was reportedly drafted after he allegedly retired from the Agency and went to work in the Nixon White House. In 1971, according to *Newsweek* magazine, Hunt had an assassination team in Mexico ready to kill the president of Panama, a nationalist who was demanding that the United States give up sovereignty over the Canal Zone. The assassination was never attempted.[65]

different sort. Harrison Salisbury, who used to visit with Allen Dulles regularly, remembered them from the old days:

> Usually there would be one man in the small group who was silent through the polite talk. His suit did not come from Brooks. It came off the rack. And his face did not come from the Ivy League. It was not relaxed or handsome. It was harsh-featured and there was likely to be the look of the weasel in it. This man would sit through the whole conversation, his back to the wall, saying nothing, ignored by the others. When the conversation was over and Allen Dulles was shaking hands and expressing his deep appreciation, the silent man would slide into the background, saying nothing, not offering to shake hands; as you were walking out, you would remember that you had never been introduced.[66]

"I remember the first time I ran into them," adds a former senior official of the New York police department. "And I remember the jolt I got. I expected Yale blue-bloods. And you know what they were? Animals. Just animals." [67]

The problem, of course, was the nature of the job. The real work of CIA, the sleaziness that went with it, was not for blue bloods. It was for those rather less squeamish about the unpleasant necessities of intelligence work—the dope running and blackmailing and "hits" of men gone sour. Thus from the beginning there was always a duality in CIA, a cleavage between what it wished to seem, even to itself, and what, given the nature of the world it worked in, it had to be. CIA men were killers, Salisbury wrote, but always "gentleman killers." [69]

It was inevitable, then, that gentlemen wishing to be killers would gravitate to killers wishing to be gentlemen. And in their meeting would be the most macabre alliance in the history of the United States: the Central Intelligence Agency and organized crime.

From the beginning it was a natural affinity. According to the jaunty memoir of Miles Copeland, a former agent, General William "Wild Bill" Donovan, the founder and wartime chief of OSS, decided it would be useful to have a "corps of skilled safecrackers, housebreakers, and assassins" on hand "who might be put to constructive purposes in wartime." [70] And so, as the connoisseur of fine things that he was, General Donovan went out and got the best: the best in this case being Mr. Salvatore C. Luciana, more familiarly known as Charles "Lucky" Luciano, the boss of all bosses, the smartest and most ruthless man La Cosa Nostra—the Mafia—has ever seen.[71]

Those who know the CIA, the heir of the OSS, are not surprised. In many respects the Agency and La Cosa Nostra are remarkably alike. "Like the Mafia, the agency forms a true brotherhood—one for all and all for one—except that, in the clutch, alas, everyone is expendable," recounted Salisbury. "But up to that final point, the members of the Company will do anything for each other—lie, cheat, steal, kidnap, suborn perjury, bribe, corrupt, subvert, kill and kill again. If you are of the blood, the CIA will take care of you." [72] It is not personal; as they say in *The Godfather*, it is strictly a business relationship. The CIA gets something, and so does the mob. "From the CIA's standpoint, the arrangement makes good sense," explains John Marks, a former State Department intelligence official and coauthor of *The CIA and the Cult of Intelligence*. "There are things which organized crime can do which CIA either cannot or chooses not to do. They [the Mafia] have intelligence contacts all over the world. And their dealings are entirely secret. In fact, they are about the only people as secret as CIA." [73] That secrecy—the vow of omertà—still shrouds much of the nature and extent of CIA's dealings with La Cosa Nostra. But incident by incident the truth is slowly dribbling out, some of it connected with the Kennedy assassination. When the incidents are put together they form a mosaic of cooperation in everything from drug pushing to attempted murder. All done in what the Agency likes to call "the national interest."

Thirty years ago there was no quarrel about the national interest: it was winning the war. There is also little doubt that at the behest of OSS the Mafia contributed greatly to the war effort. The reason was not so much patriotism as self-interest. In the United States Luciano, who had been convicted in 1936 of forced prostitution, was moldering in New York's Dannemora prison on a thirty-to-fifty-year sentence.[74] Meanwhile, in Italy and Sicily, the Mafia was being brutally uprooted by Mussolini, who regarded its sway over the rural countryside as a threat to Fascist rule.[75] From his cell Luciano let it be known that the mob could play a valuable role in protecting East Coast ports from Axis saboteurs. As a demonstration of what he was talking about, the French liner *Normandie,* then the largest vessel in the world, was burned at its moorings in February 1942, the day before its scheduled commissioning as a troopship.[76] A deal was quickly struck between the mob and the Office of Naval Intelligence, with Meyer Lansky acting as broker.[77] In the years that followed American ports, now under the benign protection of the mob, never again suffered a serious incident of sabotage.

Luciano again put his talents to use when the Allies invaded Sicily in July 1943. On Luciano's instructions the Mafia came out of the hills to clear the way for the American and British invaders, going so far as to organize welcoming demonstrations for the advancing troops.[78] In gratitude, the Allies appointed local Mafia chieftains as mayors of a number of Sicilian towns.[79] When the invasion spread to Italy and Luciano again proved useful, the American military government expressed its thanks by appointing one of his lieutenants as translator/liaison officer in U.S. Army headquarters. The officer's name was Vito Genovese.[80]

Luciano's own reward did not come until six months after the end of the war, when in January 1946 New York Governor Thomas E. Dewey, the man who had sent him to prison, granted him executive clemency.[81] Luciano was deported and in the succeeding months so were more than a hundred of his brother mafiosi.[82] Together in Italy, they resurrected their international heroin ring. By 1952 the number of U.S. addicts had tripled.[83]

Much of the heroin that came into the United States

moved through Marseilles,[84] where within a few years after the war the CIA was once again calling on the Mafia for help. Marseilles was a traditional stronghold of the French left, and in mid-November 1947 the city's docks were hit by wildcat strikes organized by Communist-dominated unions. The labor unrest spread quickly throughout the rest of the country. In response the CIA struck a deal with the large Corsican Mafia in Marseilles. In return for CIA-supplied money and arms Corsican gangs would break the strikes. This they proceeded to do with brutal efficiency. In the ensuing weeks a number of strikers were murdered, until finally the dockers called it quits.[85]

Trouble flared again in Marseilles in 1950, this time over the shipment of men and material to Indochina, and once more the CIA turned to the Mafia.[86] Again the Mafia's terror squads went into operation, supplied as usual by the CIA. Back in Washington syndicated columnist Tom Braden, then an Agency official, wrote out a check to finance the operation with a certain sense of satisfaction. "It was my idea to give $15,000 to Irving Brown" (an AFL official), Braden recalled. "He needed it to pay off his strong-arm squads in the Mediterranean ports, so that American supplies could be unloaded against the opposition of Communist dock workers." [87]

Whatever Langley wanted Langley got, even if in the case of Indochina the ends produced some highly questionable means. Throughout the 1950s and into the '60s, as U.S. involvement in Indochina deepened, the CIA was increasingly hard-pressed to contain the growing Communist insurgency in Southeast Asia. With only a handful of American advisers on hand and no combat troops, the CIA had to strike alliances where it could. The result was an informal tripartite pact between the Agency, the "secret armies" that fought for it, and organized crime. What held the unlikely alliance together was expediency, money, and heroin.

The CIA's "secret army" was actually a ragtag collection of irregulars—hill tribes in Laos and Vietnam and leftover battalions of Nationalist Chinese in Burma and Thailand. As vividly documented in Alfred McCoy's *The Politics of Heroin in Southeast Asia,* the Agency provided its army with a steady infusion of money and arms and looked the other way while commanders put their men to work cultivating and gathering opium.[88] Pragmatism was the great excuse. In Indochina, one agent noted, opium was the coin of the realm.[89] In the Agency's view, if the job were to be done there was no choice but to spend it.

By the early sixties CIA money was indirectly financing a vast opium industry. CIA-employed troops grew it, harvested it, and shipped it to Vientiane and Saigon aboard planes of Air America, the CIA airline. Dozens if not hundreds of CIA operatives were enriched in the process, and few better than Vang Pao, the general of the CIA's Armée Clandestine that operated in Laos into the seventies.[90]

The opium that flowed into Vientiane and Saigon was sold to the Corsican Mafia. The Corsicans cut the opium into heroin, shipped it out to Marseilles and other ports, and from there to its final destination, the streets of the United States.[91] The Corsicans, allies of the Sicilian Mafia that operated in the United States, were a powerful factor in Vietnamese politics, and over the years were courted assiduously by French intelligence and later by the CIA.[92] Many CIA men worked with the Corsican Mafia, but none more closely than Lucien Conein, a CIA hand in Saigon who reportedly had a hand in the overthrow and assassination of President Ngo Dinh Diem.[93] When after years of service Conein left Vietnam in 1970, the Corsicans presented him with a heavy gold medallion embossed with the Napoleonic eagle and the Corsican crest, and engraved with the inscription *"Per Tu Amicu, Conein."*[94] Conein subsequently went to work for the U.S. Drug Enforcement Administration, an intelligence organization that reportedly had its own ties to the mob.[95] Other agents were quick to excuse Conein, for quite clearly his methods were the Agency's methods. "Look," says a prominent former CIA man who operated in Latin America, "the name of this game is getting intelligence, and you go about getting it as best you can from whomever you can. When the information is good, you don't ask any questions about the people who give it to you. You are damn glad to get it. Sometimes, getting intelligence from a source leads to a source doing things for you, and you doing things for the source. Maybe it's not nice, but it's what happens." [96]

The logical question is how far such favors go. In the late fifties a young investigator for the Senate Rackets Committee named Robert Kennedy discovered that they extended to immunity for certain Las Vegas mobsters. Kennedy, according to two of his aides, didn't believe it when a Cosa Nostra figure told him he had "immunity" from the CIA. But Kennedy checked and found the mobster was telling the truth.[97] In New York, according to a high-ranking former police official, the favors CIA bestows include "protection" for some suggested drug couriers. For instance, in 1973 a Thai national was arrested in New York City and charged with attempting to smuggle narcotics into the United States. According to federal authorities, the man was one of the most important heroin figures in the world. But the Agency intervened with the Justice Department, and prosecution was dropped to protect CIA's "intelligence sources and methods." [98] At least twenty other similar cases have recently come to light. One of them involved a murder that took place outside the United States. In that instance, two CIA men helped dispose of the body.[99] When these cases were revealed during the Rockefeller commission investigation of the Agency, the CIA insisted that it had an "agreement" with the Justice Department to avoid prosecutions in cases where its agents were involved.[100] No one at the Department of Justice, including two former attorney generals of the United States, could recall such an arrangement.[101]

Occasionally the CIA's relationship with the mob surfaces. One notable example was in 1969: shortly after the inauguration of Richard Nixon, then pending deportation charges against Johnny Roselli were dropped when government lawyers argued in court that Roselli had performed unspecified "valuable services to national security." [102] Roselli was not the only beneficiary of the Agency's largess. In 1971 Gabriel Mannarino was on trial in federal court in New York along with a number of other defendants—chief among them John Sebastian LaRocca, Mafia boss of the Pittsburgh organized crime family—for charges growing out of a Teamsters-connected kickback scheme.[103] When it came time for the defense to present its case, one of the star witnesses turned out to be the head of the local CIA.[104] According to a source close to the FBI, the FBI men in the courtroom were stunned at the agent's appearance, and when the court recessed for the day, physically hustled him out of the courthouse and into a waiting car. The CIA man was sped to the airport for a flight to Washington and from there on to Italy to "cool off," as the source puts it, until the conclusion of the trial.[105] Mannarino and the other defendants were acquitted.[106]

By far the weirdest by-product of the CIA-organized crime alliance was the burglary of comedian Dan Rowan's Las Vegas hotel room. Rowan was becoming overly friendly with singer Phyllis McGuire, a long-time romantic interest of Chicago Mafia boss Sam "Momo" Giancana.* [107] During a Las Vegas engagement, Rowan returned to his hotel room to find two burglars rummaging through his belongings. He summoned hotel security men, who in turn summoned the Las Vegas sheriff. After a few days in jail the burglars informed the FBI that they had been hired by a private detective agency in Miami. The proprietor of the detective agency (himself a former FBI man) told the FBI that his contract had come from the CIA. Eventually the CIA confirmed that it had engineered the break-in as a "favor" for Giancana.[109]

In July 1975 investigators from Senator Henry Jackson's Permanent Investigations Committee produced affidavits detailing an operation that made the CIA's previous favors for its allies look minuscule by comparison. According to members of Jackson's staff these

---

* In June 1975, shortly before he was scheduled to testify before the Church committee on the CIA's assassination attempts on Fidel Castro, Giancana was shot in the head seven times in the kitchen of his Chicago home. His killers are still at large.[108]

affidavits told of a CIA counterfeiting scheme in which organized crime had a direct cut. The operation (which was denied by the CIA) involved the use of actual U.S. currency plates from the U.S. Bureau of Printing and Engraving. The plates were shipped to three locations in Southeast Asia, where counterfeit U.S. dollars were turned out by the billions, by one estimate some $20 billion in all. The mob was cut in on the operation and took away an unspecified share of the bogus cash. The rest was used to finance the Agency's covert operations as well as the purchase of opium in Southeast Asia and Turkey in an attempt to keep it off the market and away from the U.S. What happened to the opium after the Agency bought it, along with most other details of the alleged counterfeiting operation, remained cloudy.[110]

Fantastic as the counterfeiting story sounds it would simply be another step, albeit a long one, down the road the Agency and organized crime had trod together for more than three decades. The Mafia is an important CIA "asset," one the Agency is delighted to have. Former agents such as Miles Copeland make no apologies about the morality of the arrangement. The fact is that it works. Of the original alliance with organized crime, Copeland writes:

> At that time, cooperation between the OSS and the Mafia was successful in stemming the tide. No serious historian, left or right, who is familiar with the situation at that time can deny that had it not been for the Mafia the Communists would now be in control of Italy, and the world balance of power would be decisively in favor of the Soviets.[111]

The name of the game is self-interest. "To understand how it works," explains Fletcher Prouty, a retired air force colonel who served as a liaison officer between the Pentagon and the CIA, "you have to think of CIA and organized crime as two huge concentric circles spread all over the world. Inevitably, in some places, the circles overlap." [112]

As in Cuba.

The coming to power of Fidel Castro was a disaster not only for the United States foreign policy but for organized crime. The mob (see chapter 11) was anxious to see Castro removed from the scene at the earliest possible moment. So was the CIA. During the Agency's planning of the Bay of Pigs invasion one of the sources it turned to for intelligence information on the disposition of Castro's forces was the mob,[113] which at the time still maintained a considerable apparatus on the island. Before and after the invasion the mob was also trying to secure Castro's assassination, sometimes with the Agency's help, sometimes without it. Frank Sturgis, who as a casino operator in Havana had lines to both the CIA and the mob,[114] was twice approached shortly after the Cuban revolution by organized crime figures wishing to enlist him as an assassin. On one occasion, according to Sturgis in an interview in the *New York Daily News,* a Lansky associate who was an acquaintance of Sturgis casually remarked that it would be "worth a million" to the Cosa Nostra to get rid of Castro.[115] Later, when Castro was visiting in New York, Sturgis was again contacted, this time by an unnamed stranger who identified himself as a member of the Havana gambling mob. The stranger offered Sturgis $100,000 to assassinate Castro, with whom Sturgis was then on very good terms. Sturgis declined, but reported the conversations to CIA friends in Havana.[116]

The CIA itself had been talking of eliminating Castro since the closing days of the Eisenhower administration, and Sturgis's report may have freshened interest in the project. A mob hit rather than an assassination by the Agency itself would provide the CIA with what was known in the trade as "plausible deniability" if, as ultimately turned out, the attempt went askew.

By early 1961 the Agency and organized crime were deep into discussions on how best to eliminate their common foe. Reports vary on how the initial contacts were made. One version has it that Norman "Roughhouse" Rothman, a syndicate figure in both Miami and Havana, was selected as the go-between. Rothman, according to the *New York Daily News,* consulted leading mafiosi, including Santo Trafficante, Jr., of Tampa, Sam Mannarino of Pittsburgh, and John "Don Giovanni" Roselli of Las Vegas, about the feasibility of the project.[117] Another story, from a source close to the FBI, identifies the contact man as an attorney, himself a former agent, who had several important mobsters as clients.[118] In still another scenario, spun out by Jack Anderson, the person who made the necessary introductions was a former FBI agent and private investigator named Robert Maheu,* who would later go on to become boss of Howard Hughes's Nevada empire. What the stories agree on is that after protracted discussion Roselli, the suavely vicious Mafia *capo* of Las Vegas,[119a] agreed to recruit a team of hit men for the CIA.[120]

In March 1961 Roselli flew to Miami to iron out the final details of the project in separate meetings with Trafficante, whose specialty was drug traffic on the East Coast, and the CIA. Though accounts differ, the Agency apparently agreed to supply Roselli with money, weapons, and transportation for the assassination attempt. Roselli volunteered to accompany one of the missions to Cuba.[121]

For all the elaborate preparations the Roselli hit men turned out to be the gang that couldn't shoot straight. The first group of assassins were successfully landed on the Cuban coast, but they simply disappeared.[122] Another time a landing party was driven off in a running gun battle with a Cuban patrol boat.[123] On a third occasion a Roselli operative tried to kill Castro with a CIA-supplied poison capsule which had been slipped into the Cuban leader's daily chocolate

---

* In July 1975 during closed-door testimony before the Senate committee investigating the CIA, Maheu admitted that he had recruited Roselli for the assassination assignment. To reporters afterward Maheu revealed that he had been a paid operative for the Agency between 1954 and 1960. In 1960, Maheu said, he was approached by James O'Connell, a CIA official and Maheu's "project officer," who "asked me if in connection with a planned invasion in Cuba I would contact a Mr. John Roselli in Los Angeles, asking if Mr. Roselli would be inclined to help in a program for removing Mr. Castro from the scene or eliminating him in connection with the invasion of Cuba." Maheu claimed he found the whole business rather distasteful. Roselli, Maheu related, was "very reluctant to participate," but at length Maheu prevailed upon his patriotism. He agreed, Maheu said, "when it was explained to him that this was on behalf of this government, and that as unpleasant as it may have sounded . . . this was a necessary ingredient so as to effectuate a successsful invasion in a country which was . . . located less than 100 miles" from the United States.[119]

malted. The attempt went awry when the waiter bearing Castro the fated malted started shaking in terror and aroused Castro's suspicions.[124]

All of this was unknown to all but one of the men of the Warren Commission in 1964. The exception was Allen Dulles,* and he was hardly talking. The mob, after all, worked for him. Or was it he who worked for it? It was still unknown two years later when Jim Garrison began indicting strange characters by the odd lot. Through the years there had been vague stories about Lucky Luciano somehow helping the Allies during the war, but then, everyone had been enlisted in the war effort. No one could have guessed or imagined that Luciano's "patriotism" was actually the first step down one of the darkest corridors in American history.

Even now the full truth about the Company and the mob is far from clear. What the few brief glimpses down the corridor have provided is chilling enough: the two most secret and powerful organizations in America working hand and glove in a relationship so intimate that for all practical purposes there has ceased to be a distinction between what is done in the name of intelligence and what is done in the name of crime. Everything, even murder, comes together under a simple heading: "the national interest." †

The melding together of American intelligence and organized crime is the key to understanding John Ken-

---

* In July 1975 Richard Bissell, who served as Dulles's deputy at the CIA and was head of the Agency's clandestine services during the first thirteen months of the Kennedy administration, said that the Agency's relationship with the Mafia was so secret that reports of all the Mafia's activities, including assassination attempts against Castro, went only to one man. That man was Allen Dulles.[125]

† In March 1975 *New York Times* reporter Seymour Hersh reported that during a series of interviews in 1974 a former undercover agent for the CIA in New York City conceded that the Agency and the mob worked together in the United States, and that sometimes their projects included murder. Wrote Hersh:

> The former CIA man, who told of monitoring the activities of radicals and other dissidents in the late nineteen sixties and early nineteen seventies and whose knowledge of the CIA seemed extensive, said that the Mafia was relied upon for exchanges of information and also *to assault targets selected by the CIA.* [Italics added.]
>
> The former CIA man refused to name any such victims or to permit his name to be used. . . .
>
> A number of high-ranking present and former Justice Department officials with close involvement in organized crime activities also expressed the belief in interviews last week that the full story of alleged CIA involvement with the Mafia was not known.[126]

nedy's murder. Without that understanding the conspiracy is like the jumbled pieces of a puzzle, each of them odd-shaped, impossible to connect. But lay in that keystone and suddenly what has all seemed so bizarre for so many years makes terrifying sense.

One way or another all the major figures connected to the assassination are also linked to the Agency and the mob.

There is Oswald, the apparent agent, in constant contact with other CIA men, many of whom have their own ties to the mob. He lists as the address for his fictitious pro-Castro organization a building whose tenants include both mob and intelligence figures.[127] After the assassination a large quantity of Oswald's literature turns up in the office of one of those tenants, Guy Banister, a private investigator employed by Carlos Marcello who in the past worked on CIA operations.[128] One of his close friends in New Orleans is David Ferrie, an identified agent who also works for the mob.[129] Another reported associate is Clay Shaw, like Ferrie an identified agent.[130]

After the assassination Oswald is shot to death by Jack Ruby, a man with numerous connections to Cosa Nostra figures, who is also involved with Cuba and Cuban exiles. When a story arises that Oswald has met with a prominent exile figure to plan the assassination, the man who conveniently appears to debunk it turns out to be a reported gunrunner for an Agency-backed organization. (11 H. 367; C.D. 1553.9)[131] Later, an Oswald look-alike is found to be one of the leaders of an exile organization reportedly backed by both the Agency and the mob. (C.D. 23.4; C.D. 1085; C.D. 853)[132]

Finally, when the pressures for a new investigation of the assassination are boiling over, the man who announces he has solved the case is a district attorney who by his own admission has numerous contacts with Cosa Nostra figures.[133] During the trial he dismisses all references to the Cosa Nostra and fixes blame on an odd-lot assortment of conspirators. The trial ends in farce and the prospects for a new investigation are obliterated. In the process the CIA gains sympathy.

Just how many coincidences can be piled atop one another before one has to wonder? One especially wonders when the groups involved are neither Boy Scouts nor, as Garrison once put it, "retired circus clowns." [134] They are two secret violent societies whose fates are inextricably intertwined. Many things bring them together. One of them is Cuba. Another is hatred of John Kennedy.

Few people know of their alliance, and only one is in a position to do anything about it. He has sworn that he will. Before he can, he is murdered in Dallas, Texas, on November 22, 1963.

Coincidence.

11

Organization Men

TOMMY HAGEN: Mike, it's impossible. He'll be met by the Internal Revenue, the Customs Service, and half the FBI. . . . It would be like trying to kill the President. There's no way we can get at him.

MICHAEL CORLEONE: I'm surprised at you, Tom. If there's anything certain; certain in life; if history has taught us anything; it's you can kill . . . it's you can kill *anybody.*

—*The Godfather, Part II*

ON APRIL 4, 1961, an inconspicuous little man was walking to the United States Immigration Office in New Orleans. There was little to set him apart from any of the other people who walked by that day. Well tailored and silvery-haired, he could have been a successful businessman, as in a sense he was. Suddenly several men rushed toward him. They were federal agents. There was a brief scuffle and handcuffs were placed on the little man's wrists. A waiting black limousine pulled up next to the curb and the little man was bundled inside, hurling oaths. The car raced to the airport, where a special jet was waiting on the tarmac. The little man would be the only passenger. When the flight ended a few hours later and the little man stepped out into the bright sunshine, he was in Guatemala.[1]

Thus did Robert Kennedy deal with enemies of the United States. For the little man was no ordinary New Orleans businessman, he was Calogero Minacori, otherwise known as Carlos "the Little Man" Marcello, organized crime boss of New Orleans.[1a] Kennedy had personally arranged Mr. Marcello's sudden trip to Guatemala. The attorney general had been looking for an excuse to get rid of Marcello, whose various operations in New Orleans were reckoned by the head of the city's crime commission to bring in $1.114 billion per year, and he found one when Marcello filled in a phony place of birth on his immigration records, which was technically perjury. The American Civil Liberties Union condemned what it called the "totalitarian tactics" [2] in disposing of Marcello, but Kennedy did not seem overly concerned.

Neither did Marcello. After his arrival in Guatemala Marcello became a local celebrity. According to one account he was "wined and dined by the local aristocracy . . . flown to the finest resort areas in the private plane of the country's President, Miguel Ydigoras Fuentes." [3] Marcello's stay was a brief one. Within two months he was back in the United States, where he surrendered himself to federal agents. One story, which Marcello himself liked to tell, was that he returned to Louisiana by shrimp boat. A more plausible tale, one which many federal agents believed, is that he was flown back to the United States in a private plane with David Ferrie at the controls.[4]

The Justice Department subsequently indicted Marcello for perjury and a host of related charges. Marcello and Ferrie were in a New Orleans courtroom listening to a jury announce its not guilty verdict at the moment John Kennedy was murdered in Dallas.

After the assassination Marcello became a prime suspect. Several of Robert Kennedy's aides at the Justice Department conducted a brief, quiet investigation of Marcello but were unable to turn up hard evidence.[5] Later an unidentified associate of Marcello's told Ed Reid, an investigative reporter and Cosa Nostra specialist, a highly unlikely story: that Marcello had in fact been behind the assassination. The source said that at a meeting in September 1962 at Churchill Farms, a plantation Marcello owned outside New Orleans, Marcello had sworn vendetta against the Kennedys. *"Livarsi na petra di la scarpa!"* Marcello is supposed to have yelled—"Take the stone out of my shoe." "Don't worry about that little Bobby son of a bitch," he shouted. "He's going to be taken care of!" [6]

It sounds like something out of the movies. And that is the trouble with La Cosa Nostra—it all sounds like something out of the movies. Swarthy men in shiny suits and white-on-white ties, swearing Sicilian oaths of revenge. They are all so familiar. How many times have we seen them, in "The Untouchables," *The Godfather, The Brotherhood, The Sicilian Gang, The Valachi Papers*—the books and TV shows and movies about those ridiculous people with funny nicknames who love their families and only kill each other. Someone who seems so familiar, so grotesque, so much part of pop culture cannot possibly be serious. "When the average American citizen thinks about the Mafia, he usually contemplates scenes of action and violence, of dramatic intrigue and million dollar schemes, of big black limousines screeching around corners with bullets spraying the sidewalk," Gay Talese wrote. "This is the Hollywood version and it widely exaggerates reality; ignoring the dominant mood of Mafia existence: endless waiting, tedium and hiding, excessive smoking, overeating, lack of physical exercise, reclining in rooms behind drawn shades, being bored to death while trying to stay alive." [7] Somehow the mundane world that Talese paints seems more real than an international conspiracy involving thousands of men sworn to secrecy while they manipulate lives and governments and rake in billions every year. J. Edgar Hoover himself officially proclaimed that the Mafia did not exist. Then, in 1963 a tired capo named Joseph Valachi appeared before a Senate committee and stated not only that it did exist, but that it pervaded virtually every facet of American life. Valachi named places, dates, and hundreds of names, told of payoffs and rub-outs and skims and of politicians and lawmen bought by the gross.[8] His story checked out. The FBI no longer said that the Mafia was a fantasy.

Even now there is only a dim perception of organized crime's power. What is known from investigations, wiretaps, and the rare turncoats like Valachi is that gambling, prostitution, and drugs, the organization's three traditional mainstays, account for only a fraction of the mob's revenues. Much more comes from the penetration of legitimate businesses and labor unions such as the Teamsters, whose Central States, Southeast, Southwest Areas Pension Funds—a Hoffa-controlled kitty worth an estimated $1.4 *billion*—is shot through with organized crime connections.[9] Ralph Salerno, formerly an organized crime analyst for the New York City police department's central intelligence bureau and perhaps the most knowledgeable authority on organized crime in the country, reckons that, *conservatively,* organized crime turns a yearly profit of $40 billion, more than the profit of United States Steel, Ford, Standard Oil, General Electric, and General Motors combined.[10]

As the CIA came to appreciate, organized crime's operations stretch around the world in a complex network of production, distribution, and investment. What runs the network is dope. It runs most efficiently and profitably in places ruled by friendly dictators: Haiti, the Dominican Republic, Taiwan, and, until the success of socialist revolutions in both countries, Cuba and South Vietnam. The mob's interest in such places dovetails nicely—and far from coincidentally—with the interests of the United States. Because the mob stays healthy only so long as it has a protector whose interests coincide with its own. In some cases the protector is a Batista, a Duvalier, or a Ky. In others, it is the Central Intelligence Agency.

Of all the countries where La Cosa Nostra has operated, Cuba was perhaps the most important. The Cuban connection was "discovered" by Meyer Lansky in the mid-thirties, shortly after Batista came to power. Lansky, who as Maeir Suchowljansky had come to the United States from Poland in 1911, is by all accounts the most gifted of the mob's organization men. Gray-haired, short, thin, even ascetic in appearance, Lansky, writes one reporter who has followed his career, might well pass for a "successful investment broker on a two week Miami Beach vacation from Scarsdale." He drives rented Chevrolets, lives in a modest home, wears conservatively cut clothes, brags about his grandchildren, walks his dog, and comes home every night. In short, he is a family man, only in Lansky's case, the family is spelled with a capital *F.* It was Lansky who organized what were rival gangs into the national crime syndicate, Lansky who moved the mob away from such traditional pastimes as murder and extortion and into banking, investment, and real estate, Lansky who began the practice of buying governments wholesale. Lansky's own past, according to federal authorities, includes murder and kidnapping,[11] but first and foremost he has always been an organization man.

Miami has been home base for Lansky since 1933. He quickly took over illegal off-track betting and a variety of hotels and casinos, and designated Miami as an "open city," a place free from the mob's usual rules of territorial monopoly.[12] After the groundwork in Miami had been laid Lansky moved to Havana for three years. There he managed the rackets like a well-run corporation. His first move was to eliminate possible competition. He had finagled the passage of a law "which allowed gambling in hotels worth $1 million or more, and proceeded to build the only hotels that would qualify.[13] He also had Cuban immigration regulations adjusted so his dealers, pit bosses, and stickmen would be classified as 'valuable technicians.' "[14] When Lansky's host Fulgencio Batista was ousted from power, Lansky arranged his comeback by providing the money necessary to fix the 1952 election.[15] By the beginning of World War II Lansky owned a major casino and was leasing the municipal racetrack from a reputable New York bank. Lansky brought in partners to handle some of the Cuban operations, which were growing enormously. The most important of them was Santo Trafficante, Sr., a Sicilian-born Tampa gangster. "Trafficante had earned his reputation as an effective organizer in the Tampa gambling rackets and was already a figure of some stature when Lansky first arrived in Florida," writes Alfred McCoy.

> By the time Lansky returned to New York in 1940, Trafficante had assumed responsibility for Lansky's interests in Havana and Miami. By the early 1950's Trafficante had himself become such an important figure that he in turn delegated his Havana concessions to Santo Trafficante, Jr., the most talented of his six sons. Santo, Jr.'s official position in Havana was that

> of manager of the Sans Souci Casino, but he was far more important than his title indicates. As his father's financial representative, and ultimately Meyer Lansky's, Santo, Jr. controlled much of Havana's tourist industry and became quite close to the pre-Castro dictator, Fulgencio Batista. Moreover, it was reportedly his responsibility to receive bulk shipments of heroin from Europe and forward them through Florida to New York and other major urban centers, where the distribution was assisted by the local Mafia bosses.[16]

Havana was the hub of this network. For nearly twenty years, until Castro came to power, it remained under the guidance of Messrs. Lansky, Trafficante, and Luciano, who thanks to his service for the OSS was now free to resume his former career. Luciano arrived in Havana in 1947. He summoned a council meeting of various underworld chieftains and declared Havana an open city.[17] To keep it open the local Cuban officials, including Batista himself, were paid off handsomely.

The sudden convergence on Cuba did not go unnoticed. Harry Anslinger, then director of the Federal Bureau of Narcotics, later recalled:

> I had received a preliminary report through a Spanish-speaking agent I had sent to Havana, and I read this to the Cuban ambassador. The report stated that Marcello had already become friendly with a number of high Cuban officials through the lavish use of expensive gifts. Luciano had developed a full-fledged plan which envisioned the Caribbean as his center of operations. . . . Cuba was to become the center of all international narcotics operations.[18]

U.S. narcotics agents might be well aware of Luciano's presence in Havana but they made no move to evict him until vacationing newspaper correspondent Robert Ruark spotted Luciano one day having lunch with a recently divorced New York socialite. Ruark started writing columns about Luciano, suggesting that his presence in Havana and the sudden increase in drug traffic in southeastern U.S. cities was more than innocent coincidence. The articles prompted the Narcotics

Bureau to demand that the Cubans oust Luciano. The Cubans simply ignored the American request. The U.S. retaliated by announcing that since Luciano was a long-time narcotics wholesaler it was cutting off shipments of medicine and narcotics to the island. At length the Cubans capitulated and Luciano was put on a boat for Genoa, where he continued to keep close tabs on the Cuban operation.[19]

In the meantime all manner of interesting people began buying up large hunks of prime Havana real estate. The Tropicana Hotel was snapped up by the brothers Lansky, Meyer and Jake, and another Miami mobster named Norman "Roughhouse" Rothman.[20] Rothman would eventually send an emissary to Frank Sturgis (who himself was a casino operator) with a proposal to assassinate Castro.[21] Still later Rothman would be tried and acquitted for unlawfully pledging $8.5 million worth of stolen bonds, taken in what the FBI called "the biggest burglary in the world." [22] Lewis J. McWillie, the gambler whom Jack Ruby "idolized," became the boss of the Tropicana's casino. During Ruby's first visit to Havana in 1959 he met with McWillie's employers, two brothers who Ruby said were "the greatest" of all the hoods who were later thrown out of Cuba. The brothers talked to Ruby about "collecting a debt" in Dallas. Ruby identified them (at least according to the stenographic transcription of his interview) as "the Fox brothers." [23] No one knew of any "Fox" brothers who owned anything in Havana, but the Lansky brothers did own the Tropicana. And they were foxy indeed.

Down the way from the Tropicana was the Sans Souci, owned by the ubiquitous Santo Trafficante, Jr., and the brothers Mannarino of Pittsburgh. Sam Mannarino was arrested along with Rothman (who also managed the Sans Souci) on the bonds caper.[24] Brother Gabriel turned up at the famous Mafia conclave in Apalachin, New York, in the company of Trafficante.[25] Years later Gabriel was arrested for a union kickback scheme, put on trial in New York, and acquitted.[26] It was that trial where the CIA came riding to the rescue.

Cuba was not an end in itself. The heroin that came

into its ports did not stay there. Neither did the cash that was generated by casinos like the ones at Sans Souci and the Tropicana. The island was merely an enormous funnel through which the cash and heroin poured, bound for its next destination, the city of New Orleans. The McClellan committee, whose hearings on organized crime were among the first to trace the extent of the syndicate's power, named New Orleans as the key distribution point for heroin and syndicate cash.[27] That came as no news to the New Orleans Crime Commission. The commission had long been suspicious of the massiveness of Marcello's holdings, which were far too large to be controlled by a single don, even one as powerful as Marcello. "There is too much money here," said a New Orleans chief assistant district attorney. "We feel that it's flowing in from other Cosa Nostra organizations in other parts of the country for investment by the local mob. This could be their financial center, with a lot of nice safe places where campaign contributions and outright bribery have pretty well insulated them from the law." [28]

Carlos Marcello could take credit for making New Orleans a syndicate safe haven. With a personal worth estimated at $40 million Marcello had the wherewithal to attract friends in high places. Jim Garrison was only one. Frank Landridge, the district attorney of neighboring Jefferson Parish, Marcello's home ground, managed in eighteen years to avoid prosecuting Marcello or any of his senior lieutenants.[29] Landridge's chief investigator was Joseph "Zip" Chimento, whose law enforcement credentials included a conviction for bribing a witness to help two Cosa Nostra defendants, and previous employment as a collector for a jukebox company owned by Marcello.[30] Marcello shared his wealth. He once contributed $100.000 to victims of a hurricane. Another time he gave $10,000 to the Girl Scouts. And every year he sent $25,000 to a senior official in the Italian government to ensure that he would never be deported back to Italy.[31] He was especially generous toward the law. At a peace officers' convention in 1966 one of his hoods accompanied a visiting sheriff and picked up the sheriff's tabs.[32] Marcello's offer to pay for the entire meeting was graciously turned down. Even Marcello's enemies couldn't help but be impressed by such brazenness. Aaron Kohn, who came from Chicago to head the New Orleans Metropolitan Crime Commission, once remarked in awe: "In Chicago, people are generally on one side of the fence or the other—honest or crooked. But in Louisiana, there just isn't any fence." [33]

The "little man" (he stands 5′2″) whom Estes Kefauver called "one of the worst criminals in the country" [34] was also one of the most successful. Among his holdings were hotels, restaurants, a sightseeing bus service, $16 million worth of undeveloped land, and tourist attractions throughout Louisiana—not to mention control of gambling, prostitution, and narcotics in a region stretching from Florida to California.[35] Among the far-flung fiefdoms under his control, as it happened, were the rackets in Dallas, Texas. In 1970 the *Wall Street Journal* paid businessman Marcello the ultimate accolade of a long profile on the front page. He was, the *Journal* concluded, "the undisputed patriarch of the Cosa Nostra in Louisiana and the Gulf Coast area." [36]

The patriarch protected his investments. In April 1970 *Life* reported:

> People who cross the Little Man still get killed. In 1967, for example, Harry Bennett, a Marcello syndicate gambler, was gunned down 13 hours after he was seen approaching a federal prosecutor with an offer to testify against the boss. Last fall Donald ("Jimmie") James, who had been Bennett's partner in a Gulf Coast gambling casino, also ran afoul of Marcello. James' sin was to swindle a Marcello gang member out of $10,000. When he learned of it, Marcello found James and got the money back. In January, James was found shot to death in almost the exact spot where Bennett had been killed two years earlier.[37]

To be a friend of Marcello—that rated entirely different treatment. Take Jimmy Hoffa. In 1967 Hoffa was languishing in a federal penitentiary after being convicted of mail fraud and jury tampering. The chief witness against Hoffa had been Edward Grady Partin, a

Baton Rouge Teamster official. According to *Life*, Partin was offered a $1 million bribe to encourage him to change his testimony. The bribe offer, the magazine said, came via a complicated series of telephone calls from "cheesebox" phones, used by bookies to hide their location. Some of the calls, according to *Life* (which had been provided transcripts from wiretaps conducted by the FBI), went to the governor's offices in the state capitol in Baton Rouge, after being diverted from a nearby motel owned by a Marcello associate. Other calls went out to at least six Mafia chieftains across the United States: Mike Miranda and Thomas Eboli of New York, Nick Civella of Kansas City, Joe Civello of Dallas, James Lanza of San Francisco, and Santo Trafficante of Florida. Partin, who was under even greater pressure from the government not to change his testimony, turned down the bribe.[38]

Marcello and his fellow mafiosi could afford to offer million-dollar bribes, because the years had been good. They had been especially good when Fulgencio Batista was in the presidential palace in Havana, and the heroin and gambling skim flowed in from the Caribbean undisturbed. It seemed it would never end, not when the entire American foreign policy was arrayed in its defense, and the only cloud on the horizon was an unlikely guerrilla named Castro who had gone into the hills with all of a dozen followers. La Cosa Nostra had been slow to perceive the potential threat posed by Castro's insurgency. When it increased after 1955, casino operators like Norman Rothman sought to curry the revolution's favor by quietly providing a small quantity of aid, including guns,[38a] even as a large share of the proceeds from the hotel slot machines went into Batista's coffers.[39] Even when the Fidelistas rolled into Havana on New Year's Day 1959 there was no immediate panic. Meyer Lansky fled Havana the same day as Batista, but left behind brother Jake to oversee his operations. Castro ungraciously kept Jake hostage for twenty-five days before allowing him to return to Miami.[40] Still the mob tried accommodation, and for a time Castro seemed to welcome it. Castro installed a liaison man to work out problems between his regime and the American casino operators. He chose someone with ties to both: Frank Sturgis, who was named Minister for Games of Chance. But the honeymoon was destined to be short-lived. Before the year was out Lansky had called a syndicate board meeting and persuaded his fellow dons to put a $1 million price tag on Castro's head.[41] Soon thereafter the syndicate was approaching Sturgis with a proposal to assassinate his boss. Castro in turn began expropriating American properties, including the casinos. By the time of the Bay of Pigs invasion the last remnants of the Cosa Nostra had been driven from Cuba.

The Castro revolution, Jack Anderson wrote, dealt the mob "a financial body blow . . . as hard as the 1929 stock market crash rocked Wall Street."[42] The loss was reckoned in the hundreds of millions; the disappearance of the gambling skim alone, according to Sturgis, amounted to $100 million in cash per year.[43] By contrast, *Fortune* magazine placed the largest loss from expropriation for an individual U.S. corporation at $272 million.[44]

With the blind fury of a gored ox the syndicate struck back at its tormentor. Johnny Roselli was only too anxious to lend the Agency a hand in "dumping" Castro. When those attempts failed the syndicate invested considerable sums in various exile schemes. Arms, ammunition, boats, even aircraft were purchased out of Cosa Nostra funds and put at the disposal of the exiles. Sturgis's International Anti-Communist Brigade was a reported front for dispossessed casino operators.[44a] The dynamite cache raided by the FBI outside New Orleans was also supplied by the mob.[45] The mob even lent "advisers" to train the exiles in guerrilla warfare. One of them was David Ferrie, who was running a guerrilla warfare school near New Orleans when Lee Harvey Oswald approached Carlos Bringuier with an identical proposal.[46] In these and all its other anti-Castro endeavors the mob had at least tacit encouragement from the Central Intelligence Agency. Given the Agency's support, and the ends to which the syndicate was willing to go in recovering its lost investment, eventually the project might well have succeeded/ There were only two problems: John and Robert Kennedy.

The Kennedy brothers were no strangers to the mob. They had been on the McClellan committee that probed the links between organized labor and organized crime, John as a senator, Robert as chief counsel. For Bobby especially, the pursuit of racketeers was more than a job, it became a personal obsession. The single-mindedness with which he went about his task—the quality that came to be called "ruthlessness"—was evident in the treatment meted out to Marcello, not to mention the nearly decade-long pursuit of James Riddle Hoffa. A story former White House press secretary Pierre Salinger (who also worked as an investigator on the committee with the Kennedys) recounts in his memoirs is instructive. "One night," Salinger writes, "Bob and I left our offices in the Senate Office Building after one o'clock in the morning. He offered to drive me home, but as we passed the Teamsters' Washington headquarters, which is just across the street from the SOB, he saw a light burning in Jimmy Hoffa's office. 'If he's still at work, we ought to be,' said Bob. And we went back for another two hours."[47]

Kennedy and Hoffa made no secret of their mutual loathing. During the televised hearings that thanks to Kennedy's investigation portrayed a union riddled with graft, theft, bribery, and extortion, the two men would stare at one another like a mongoose and a cobra. Kennedy seemed to relish the confrontation:

> I noticed that he was glaring at me across the counsel table with a deep, strange, penetrating expression of intense hatred. I suppose it must have dawned on him about that time that he was going to be the subject of a continuing probe—that we were not playing games. It was the look of a man obsessed by his enmity, and it came particularly from his eyes. There were times when his face seemed completely transfixed with this stare of absolute evilness.[48]

Kennedy, needless to say, had a look of his own: pure contempt. "They have the look of Capone's men," he said of Hoffa and his cronies. "They are sleek, often bilious and fat, or lean and hard. They have the smooth faces and cruel eyes of gangsters: they wear the same rich clothes, the diamond rings, the jeweled watch, the strong, sickly-sweet-smelling perfume." About Jimmy Hoffa, Robert Kennedy could act and sound positively evangelical, like a Jesuit, someone said, determined to stamp out the last vestige of sin. Under Hoffa, he said, the Teamsters were "a conspiracy of evil." [49] "Quite literally, your life—the life of every person in the United States—is in the hands of Hoffa and his Teamsters," Kennedy wrote.[50] John Kennedy's rhetoric was not far behind. Once when a committee investigator informed him that a probe into labor racketeering in Gary, Indiana, would likely lead to one of the most powerful Democrats in the state, Kennedy snapped, "Go back and build the best case against him that you can. We have only one rule around here. If they're crooks, we don't wound 'em, we kill 'em." [51]

John Kennedy made good on his promise after his election to the presidency. With brother Robert installed as attorney general the Department of Justice began attacking organized crime on a scale and with a vigor never before seen in Washington, oftentimes to the discomfiture of J. Edgar Hoover. Hoover was strangely unworried by the mob. In 1958 he had an FBI report on the Mafia recalled, terming it "baloney," denying that there was a need for "special groups" to fight the imaginary organized crime conspiracy.[52] At the Justice Department antimob efforts were at a virtual standstill. Kennedy changed all that. In his first press conference as attorney general he announced that he was giving organized crime his top priority.[53] Henry E. Petersen, a career government attorney who as head of the Justice Department's criminal division would later become embroiled in the Watergate scandal, told Kennedy biographer Victor Navasky: "When you talked about organized crime, people would ask you to define what you meant. Robert Kennedy came in and said, 'Don't define it, do something about it.' His instructions were: 'Don't let anything get in your way. If you have problems, come see me. Get the job done, and if you can't get the job done, get out.' " [54]

Kennedy moved to get the job done fast. He personally lobbied to secure a package of five anticrime bills, including laws which made it a crime to travel in interstate commerce in aid of racketeering or gambling enterprises, to transport gambling paraphernalia in interstate commerce, and to transport gambling information by wire in interstate commerce.[55] The new attorney general assigned sixty lawyers to the organized crime and racketeering section, in one stroke increasing the section's size by 400 percent.[56] The section coordinated the activities of the twenty-seven separate investigative agencies that had formerly chipped away at mob activities. A "hit list" was gathered of important Cosa Nostra figures for prosecution. The list started at 40; by the time Kennedy left the Justice Department, it stood at 2300.[57]

The activity began to have results. The year before Kennedy took over, criminal division attorneys spent 283 days in court and 1963 days in the field; the year after, they were in court 809 days and 7359 days in the field.[58] Kennedy and Jack Miller, the man he chose to head the criminal division (He "would not hesitate to indict a man for spitting on the sidewalk if he thought that was the best he could get," said one of his colleagues)[59] were not picky about how they nailed the mob, just so they did it. Joey Aiuppa, number six on the hit list, was arrested and convicted for violating provisions of the migratory bird act. Lou Gallo was busted for filling out false statements on a VA loan application for a house. Chicago mobster Moses Joseph was prosecuted for perjury for failing to list a previous criminal conviction on an application with the FCC.[60]

Kennedy had already written of the need of "weapons and techniques" as effective as the mob's. One of his favorites as attorney general was electronic surveillance. Wiretaps and bugs were installed in mob hangouts with only slight attention to legal niceties. More than once FBI agents burglarized the homes and offices of Cosa Nostra capos, carrying away evidence and leaving electronic calling cards behind. Nearly all the evidence thus gained was inadmissable in court. But, with Kennedy's blessing, it had a way of surfacing in friendly publications. The documentation of the mob's activities, oftentimes in their own words, stripped away some of the mystery of the mob, made it real to the doubters, and, ripplelike, triggered off smaller investigations of Cosa Nostra activity in big and small cities across the country.

For all his success in harassing and prosecuting the mob, Kennedy, far better than anyone, knew that the source of mob's power remained untouched. The money that financed the mob's operations, that bought the judges and politicians and cops, that made it possible for the Cosa Nostra to cut out a larger slice of legitimate businesses every year, had to be dried up if the syndicate was to be dismembered. He had to go after the mob on its home ground, and that was Las Vegas. By the fall of 1963 the attorney general had begun laying plans for a massive, frontal assault on the entire state of Nevada. No weapon would be spared. All the investigative resources of the federal government, from FBI to IRS, would be enlisted in the effort. Nevada was to be a test case. If the mob could be taken on and beaten there, it could be defeated anywhere.[61]

But first there was Hoffa.

The Teamsters were not the only labor union to be infested by organized crime. But the Teamsters were the biggest, the most corrupt, the most vital, not only to the mob but to a country which depended on trucks to move the goods that were its life.* Nor was Jimmy Hoffa the first Teamster leader to have done business

---

* With 2.2 million members, the Teamsters are the nation's biggest, richest, and most aggressive union, and the one union with the power to totally paralyze the nation. *Time* summed up the Teamsters' clout in 1975:

> Teamsters today are almost literally everywhere. They include brewers in Memphis, drawbridge operators in New York City, pipeline workers in Alaska, telephone answering service employees in Boston. In Chicago, Teamster locals take up two full columns in the Yellow Pages of the telephone directory; they represent armored-car drivers, newspaper deliverers, gas-station employees, airline stewardesses and meat packers. The city's Local 727 goes by the somewhat unbelievable official name of "The Auto Livery, Chauffeurs, Embalmers, Funeral Directors, Apprentice Ambulance Drivers and Helpers, Taxi Cab Drivers, Miscellaneous Garage Employees, Car Washers, Greasers, Polishers and Wash Rack Attendants Local." In Michigan recently, state police sergeants and lieutenants voted for Teamster affiliation—and got it. In California, the Teamsters net covers scientists, nurses, firemen, even district attorneys. . . . The Teamsters lately have sought respectability through a magazine and billboard advertising campaign that proclaims: TEAMSTERS—A PART OF THE AMERICAN LIFE.[62]

with the mob. Hoffa's predecessor, Dave Beck, had resigned from the union presidency only because he was about to be convicted of fraud and sentenced to the penitentiary.[63] But compared to Hoffa and his operation, Beck and his lieutenants were minor leaguers.

Jimmy Hoffa was seventeen years old when he participated in his first strike. His rise in the Teamster hierarchy and in the esteem of the mob was a rapid one. By 1933 Hoffa was head of Teamster local 299 in Detroit, the largest Teamster local in the city. By 1947 he was boss of all the Teamsters in Michigan. In the next few years he extended and consolidated his influence south, east, and west through the heartland of the country. His technique was crude but effective. He simply bullied his way to power, with, as Walter Sheridan records, skilled practitioners in such fields:

> Hoffa decided early in the game that he would have more muscle than the other guy. He obtained his own racketeers. Some of his business agents . . .were recruited right out of prison. Many of the others had criminal records. But the real muscle that everyone feared and understood was the mob—the Detroit Purple Gang and the Mafia. Hoffa formed working relationships with both.[64]

By 1952 Hoffa had sufficient influence and friends (who by now included New York gangster Johnny Dio)[65] to demand and get an international vice-presidency from the Teamsters. Hoffa's power continued to expand. At its base was control of the union's Central States Pension Fund, then worth $200 million.[66] Hoffa used the fund to make loans to various mob enterprises (many of which were merely covers for Cosa Nostra coffers), and in return won new friends, like Joey Glimco, the boss of the cabdrivers' union in Chicago (thirty-six arrests on various charges, including extortion, assault with a deadly weapon, and, twice, murder);[67] Tony Provenzano, a Mafia-connected Teamster boss of New Jersey (who would later wind up with Hoffa in Lewisburg penitentiary);[68] Tony "Ducks" Corallo, a senior Mafia capo in New York;[69] and Paul "the Waiter" Ricca, one of the two organized crime chiefs of Chicago.[70] Hoffa's was the kind of power that could not be denied. Those who tried were threatened, beaten, firebombed, and murdered.

Hoffa's first encounter with the Kennedys came during the McClellan hearings. Despite the exposure of his methods that came during the hearings, despite two criminal trials (both ending in acquittals), Hoffa took office as Teamster president in January 1958. He did his best to head off a similar promotion for John Kennedy. On September 7, 1960, as the presidential campaign was swinging into high gear, the executive board of the International Brotherhood of Teamsters voted to oppose Kennedy.[71] Within weeks Hoffa embarked on a nationwide speaking tour, urging Teamster rallies in twelve cities to split their tickets, voting for Nixon for President and Democratic candidates friendly to labor for lesser offices.[72] The outgoing Eisenhower administration reciprocated Hoffa's efforts by calling off a federal investigation of Hoffa in Florida, which was on the verge of indicting him for defrauding the Teamsters pension funds.[73] When Kennedy won the indictment went forward.[74]

It was only the beginning. Robert Kennedy named Walter Sheridan to assemble a special task force to look into labor racketeering, beginning with Hoffa.[75] Within the year, Hoffa complained "that there were twenty-nine special grand juries around the country out to get him, and that half the attorneys in the Department of Justice and half the agents of the FBI were involved in the effort." [76] The Kennedy effort was massive, but not quite that massive. There were, Sheridan dryly noted, only thirteen grand juries, sixteen attorneys, and thirty FBI men after him.[77] They caught up to him in the spring of 1962. Hoffa was indicted in Nashville for allegedly receiving hundreds of thousands of dollars in payoffs through a trucking company set up in his wife's maiden name.[78] His trial ended later that year in a hung jury, after what one investigator described as "one of the most massive efforts to tamper with a jury in history." [79] Hoffa was promptly indicted again on jury-tampering charges and was eventually convicted.[80] There was one other present from Kennedy to Hoffa.

In 1962 a Chicago grand jury indicted the Teamster boss for having defrauded the pension fund of almost $2 million.[81] Hoffa would be convicted of that charge,[82] too, but John Kennedy would not live to see it.

Jimmy Hoffa was in Miami on November 22, 1963. When his Washington office reached him and told him the news, adding that the Teamster building had been closed and the flag lowered to half-staff in mourning, Hoffa flew into a rage, yelling at his secretary for crying, saying that they had been "hypocrites" to lower the flag.[83] Hoffa knew it even then; John Kennedy's murder changed everything. Two days later, when a Nashville reporter asked him about the attorney general, Hoffa gloated, "Bobby Kennedy is just another lawyer now."[84] Later Hoffa told a meeting of Teamsters: "Bobby Kennedy is out. He will no longer have the veto power of the presidency behind him." He was, Hoffa said, an ordinary cabinet member now, "just one of nine men."[85]

In a letter to Robert Kennedy a few months after the assassination, a Teamster official who had been indicted by the Kennedy administration put the union's and Hoffa's feelings more plainly:

> Sir:
>
> This is for your information.
>
> The undersigned is going to solicit from the membership of our union that each one donate whatever they can afford to maintain, clean, beautify and supply with flowers the grave of Lee Harvey Oswald.
>
> You can rest assured contributions will be unanimous.
>
> Sincerely,
> Frank Chavez*
> Secretary-Treasurer
> Teamsters Local 901 [90]

---

* Chavez, the boss of the Teamsters in Puerto Rico, was twice named by the FBI as a would-be assassin of Robert Kennedy. According to the Bureau, Chavez traveled to New York in March 1964, armed and in the company of two bodyguards, for the purpose of killing Kennedy, who was then campaigning for the U.S. Senate.[86] The attempt was aborted at the personal orders of Hoffa, who was fearful that killing Kennedy would complicate his already intricate legal problems.[87] The other Chavez plot was hatched after Hoffa lost his final appeal to the Supreme Court.[88] Once again Hoffa intervened, and the plan was aborted. Chavez himself was murdered a year later, shot down by one of his own bodyguards.[89]

Violence was endemic to the Teamsters. As more than one enemy of Jimmy Hoffa's was to discover, no means were unthinkable, not even murder. Fittingly Hoffa himself was to meet an apparently bloody end in July 1975, when in the midst of a bitter struggle to regain the Teamster presidency he went to a rendezvous with a leading organized crime figure in Detroit and never returned.[91] Such occurrences were not unexpected in the rough-and-tumble trucking industry. With hundreds of millions on the line and the likes of Dio, Corallo, Glimco, and Ricca in the background, opponents of the Teamsters had good cause to be worried. The Teamsters did not deal with their enemies, they crushed them. To both his credit and his peril Robert Kennedy was the most dangerous enemy of all.

In 1962 Edward Grady Partin, the Baton Rouge Teamster official whose testimony eventually put Hoffa in jail, revealed that Hoffa had decided to do something about his pursuer. As Partin told the story, that summer while Partin was at the Teamsters' Washington headquarters Hoffa called him into his office and asked if he could lay his hands on some plastic explosive.[92]

"Something has to be done about that little S.O.B., Bobby Kennedy," Partin quoted Hoffa as saying. "He'll be an easy target, always driving around Washington in that convertible with that big black dog. All we need is some plastic explosives tossed in with him, and that will finish him off." [93] Later Partin heard that the plot had been altered to blowing up Kennedy in his home along with everyone inside.[94] When Justice Department aides heard this story they were skeptical. But Partin offered to take a lie detector test. When the test showed he was telling the truth, and other elements of Partin's story checked out, the aides were skeptical no longer.[95] Kennedy refused to be accompanied by bodyguards and the attack on the Teamsters continued.[96]

Rumors, a history of violence, even a clear desire to want John and Robert Kennedy out of the way are a long way from proof that Hoffa or his lieutenants were actual participants in a murder conspiracy against the President. Just as clearly, though, Hoffa had a motive, and with his friends in the mob, the means and the opportunity to kill the President. It would not be unthinkable. After the assassination, close aides of Robert Kennedy suspected that the Teamsters or Hoffa had to have been involved. Their suspicions were not allayed when Ruby's friends and acquaintances were found to read like a Who's Who of the Teamsters. However, neither they—not anyone else—have ever been able to translate the suspicions into fact.

It will be surprising if anyone ever does. Jimmy Hoffa's best alibi was that his enmity with the Kennedys was so public. If Kennedy were murdered attention would naturally focus on Hoffa as a prime suspect. Against that logic was Hoffa's historic brazenness, his conviction that his power and that of his 1,700,000 members made him untouchable. And for decades he was right. The 1940s, '50s, and '60s, are filled with examples of Hoffa's open disdain for the law. Yet he managed to keep beating the rap. Prosecutions were headed off, officials bribed, juries fixed, witnesses threatened, virtually out in the open. Finally, of course, Hoffa did go to jail. But only for a time. The record of the efforts to get him released—including, according to the sworn deposition of a former assistant director of the FBI, an offer of $100,000 to J. Edgar Hoover [97] —is even more remarkable than the crimes that put him in prison. At length the efforts were successful. Hoffa was released from prison at the direction of no less than the President of the United States, Richard M. Nixon. In return, as Hoffa himself conceded (and the White House never denied), the Teamsters supported Richard Nixon's successful bid for reelection.[98]

Hoffa might well have expected similar treatment from Lyndon Johnson. At the 1960 Democratic convention in Los Angeles Hoffa met with John Connally, then Johnson's chief political strategist, and promised to support Johnson if he won the nomination. The reception from Connally was warm and friendly.[99] Later, when Hoffa was locked in battle with the Justice Department, a number of Democrats from the Johnson wing of the party took the floor of Congress to denounce Robert Kennedy for his "persecution" of Hoffa.[100] The speeches, in some cases, appeared to have been composed by the Teamsters' chief lobbyist on Capitol Hill.[101] Johnson and Hoffa shared a number of mutual friends. In 1959, then Senate majority leader Johnson was one of the guests of honor at the opening of the Stardust Hotel in Las Vegas.[102] The Stardust had been the dream of Antonio Cornero Stralla, a California mafioso who pioneered in the mob's efforts to settle Las Vegas.[103] Cornero died before the project could be completed and control of the Stardust passed to others, among them Morris "Moe" Dalitz.[104] Dalitz, a prominent figure in the Cleveland and Detroit underworld before World War II,[104a] also played a major role in developing the Rancho La Costa country club not far from San Clemente, California, where, on one memorable occasion, John Dean, John Ehrlichman, and H. R. Haldeman met to plot strategy for how to cope with the Senate Watergate investigation.[105] Dalitz was most sensitive about his business partners. So sensitive that in 1975, he, his three partners, and the five corporations they set up to run La Costa, sued *Penthouse* magazine for an article *Penthouse* had run about the Teamster-financed project. The complaint, filed in Los Angeles Superior Court, charged that the magazine had falsely stated that La Costa was founded by the syndicate, and controlled and frequented by mobsters, including a horde of underworld types under surveillance by law enforcement officials.[105a] According to papers filed by *Penthouse,* Dalitz had good reason to be sensitive. The papers maintain that Dalitz, a close associate of Jimmy Hoffa, used $57 million of Teamster pension fund loans to create La Costa,[105b] and that all the magazine's charges were true.[105c] As for Dalitz, the papers say, there is "overwhelming documentation" of his "critical role as the architect in the organization of crime in this country."[106] And then there was Johnson's right-hand man in the Senate—"one of my trusted friends, a man who will go far"—Bobby Baker, the so-called "101st senator."[107] Before his conviction in 1967 on seven counts of tax evasion, larceny, and conspiracy,[108] Baker maintained numerous ties with mob-Teamster enterprises, not only in Texas but in Nevada and the Caribbean (where the Teamsters in 1962 were reportedly involved in a Cosa Nostra-backed gunrunning operation to the Dominican Republic).[109] He was, in fact, their man in Washington. And, as became acutely embarrassing during Senate hearings into Baker's activities in 1963, Baker was also Lyndon Johnson's man.

Hoffa, of course, was proved wrong. However undiscriminating Johnson may have been in the choice of his friends, the prosecution of the Teamster boss went forward, ultimately with success. Still, with Kennedy's removal, the intensity of the harassment diminished dramatically.

Organized crime had considerable cause for relief; for with Kennedy's murder the Justice Department's Nevada Project (see p. 317) was abandoned entirely. Soon the rest of the effort began to slip away. Within four years of the assassination the number of days spent in the field by Justice Department organized crime investigators had been cut nearly in half: the days before grand juries declined by 72 percent, the days in court by more than 56 percent. The number of federal court briefs filed by Justice Department lawyers in organized crime cases was slashed by 83 percent.[110] What the statistics added up to was a quiet, largely unnoticed surrender in the war Robert Kennedy had declared. It had cost only one casualty: the life of his brother.

Hoffa himself need not have been involved in the assassination. His closeness to the mob was such that his grievances automatically became its grievances, his enemies its enemies. The Teamsters were vital to the mob. Under Hoffa the union provided the Cosa Nostra with tens of millions of dollars in "loans" (many of which were never repaid),[111] not to mention jobs, respectability, and a further handhold on the nation's jugular. In New York "paper locals" awarded by Hoffa to Johnny Dio, federal investigators discovered forty union "officials" who were actually members of the syndicate. Among them, they had seventy-seven convictions for crimes including theft, narcotics, forgery, possession of stolen mail, robbery, and accessory to murder.[112] The Hoffa-controlled Central States Pension Fund, which one federal investigation characterized as "a lending agency for the Mob,"[113] has hundreds of millions of dollars tied up in Las Vegas casinos and hotels operated by the mob.[114] In Florida, more millions in Teamster funds have financed apartment buildings, hospitals, condominiums, hotels, motels, and country clubs, many of which, according to Florida law enforcement officials, are controlled by the mob.[115] The Kennedy assault on Hoffa was an attack on a key mob subsidiary. The mob defended its interests—all of them.

And in 1963, because of Kennedy, all of those interests were threatened not only at home but overseas. Kennedy had not been responsible for the Cuban debacle. He had, though, prevented the mob from righting it. Even at the height of the Kennedy vendetta against Castro, Robert Kennedy had specifically forbidden mob participation in any CIA ventures. The ventures had gone in in any case under Agency-provided cover. The cover was stripped away when Kennedy banned exile raids from the United States. From the mob's standpoint Cuba was only the beginning. Kennedy was also friendly with non-Communist democrats in the Caribbean, notably Juan Bosch of the Dominican Republic, where the mob had transferred much of their gambling operations after the Castro takeover.[116] Bosch was hostile to the mob. If with Kennedy's support his nonviolent social revolution was successful, the mob would face the same situation it had in Havana.

The Caribbean was bad enough. But Kennedy was also making peace overtures in Southeast Asia, where CIA-supported dictators had allowed the syndicate to flourish. The Mafia's interest in Southeast Asia was heroin, the lifeblood of its operations.

Since the 1950s the so-called Golden Triangle in Burma, Thailand, and Laos had provided much of the heroin that flowed into the United States, and the percentage was rising steadily each year.[117] The opium moved out of the hills and onto oceangoing freighters bound for Marseilles, where it was processed and sent on to the United States (until the Castro takeover, via Cuba) beginning by two routes.[118] One ran from Burma into downtown Bangkok.[119] The other stretched from northern Laos to Tan Son Nhut Air Base outside Saigon.[120] On the receiving ends in both locations were the Corsican Mafia, close allies of the Sicilian mob that operated in the United States.[121] The Corsicans, CIA man Lucien Conein once boasted, were "smarter, tougher, and better organized than the Sicilians. They are absolutely ruthless and are the equal of anything we know about the Sicilians." [122] The Corsicans' supposed edge over the Sicilians did not prevent them from doing business with their Mediterranean cousins. It was a profitable arrangement for both syndicates, as well as succeeding generations of South Vietnamese government, from Diem through Thieu.[123] By contrast, the puritanical Communists took a decidedly dim view of the opium traffic, and had successfully eliminated it from areas under their control, including the whole of China, which had once been the world's major supplier.[124] The Communists' opposition explained the mob's alliance with French intelligence and later with the CIA. The fact was that each Communist victory cut into the syndicate's profits. Kennedy had already arranged a shaky coalition government in Laos. By 1963, he was moving toward an ultimate settlement in South Vietnam. From the mob's standpoint the possible consequences were ominous.

The planned phaseout of advisers was only one step in a large-scale process. Peter Dale Scott's essay on the war cites a number of other indicators. In November 1963 UN Secretary General U Thant had presented the United States with a proposal for a neutralist coalition in South Vietnam, one including some Vietnamese exiles living in Paris.[125] The Communists themselves seemed amenable. The radio of the National Liberation Front "began in November a series of appeals for negotiations aimed not only at the Vietnamese people, but also at their new leaders in the junta that succeeded Diem."[126] In late October Kennedy told General James Gavin, one of his military aides, that he would soon meet with de Gaulle to sound out his ideas on the subject.[127] Before his trip to Dallas

Kennedy had ordered his own administration to conduct "a complete review of U.S. policy in Southeast Asia to confront the new set of conditions which developed with the overthrow of President Diem."[128]

The evidence was overwhelming. And so was the motive. The mob, if not beleaguered at the end of 1963, could hardly regard the coming years under Kennedy with anything less than acute anxiety. Cuba was gone. As long as Kennedy was in the White House there was no chance of getting it back. Their most important ally in the whole of organized labor, the single most powerful labor leader in the United States, was under indictment. Nevada was threatened. From coast to coast their activities were under investigation and harassment as never before. And now even the Indochina connection was coming undone. The potential loss from that source of revenue alone could be figured in the billions. If the mob was not fighting for its life it soon would be. The question was whether organized crime could survive another five years of the brothers Kennedy.

In many respects Robert Kennedy was the larger threat. It was he who directed the Justice Department with such single-minded intensity, he who counseled caution in both South Vietnam and Cuba, he who pursued Hoffa. But there was no easy way to turn Robert Kennedy off. Killing Robert Kennedy would only unleash the furies. All the resources of the federal government would still be at his enraged brother's command. Kill John Kennedy, though, and the equation, as Hoffa had immediately perceived, was altogether different. How well could the right arm function without a head?

Others might hate Kennedy. The mob was in a unique position to do something about it. Unlike Kennedy's other enemies, the Minutemen or the exiles, the Cosa Nostra was not a small band of fanatic zealots. It was a cool, well-disciplined conspiracy of enormous dimensions. It could call on some of the finest minds in the country, along with the most experienced killers. Virtually unlimited resources were at its disposal. The syndicate maintained its own intelligence operation from coast to coast, and through its connections with CIA and the exiles could tap into their networks as well. At least two mob associates—Banister and Ferrie—had had personal contact with Oswald. There may well have been others, though there need not have been. The Cosa Nostra could just as easily come upon Oswald through information supplied by the exiles, who were in daily intimate contact with the syndicate, or by the CIA. Once Kennedy was killed, the mob (assuming it was not working with either the CIA or the exiles) could keep its participation secret. The CIA, which could hardly be saddened at Kennedy's demise, might easily be deflected with the threat of blackmail.* The Agency had been before, it would be again. Of course, if the CIA itself, or some of its agents, were involved or implicated in the conspiracy, not even blackmail would be necessary.

In sum La Cosa Nostra had everything to gain by Kennedy's assassination and very little to lose. Witnesses were no problem. There were men who could handle such tasks. One of them was Jack Ruby.

In recent years two stories have circulated not only linking the mob to the assassination, but naming names. The first, implicating Carlos Marcello, appeared in reporter Ed Reid's account of life inside the mob, *The Grim Reapers*. Reid, quoting from an unidentified "former associate" of Marcello's, recounted the meeting at Churchill Farms outside New Orleans, where Marcello is supposed to have sworn a blood oath against the Kennedys. "No one at the meeting had any doubt

---

* It was fear of similar Mafia blackmail that prompted FBI Director J. Edgar Hoover to oppose cooperation between the Agency and the mob, specifically in the effort to get rid of Castro. According to former FBI officials, during a conversation with then Attorney General Robert F. Kennedy in late 1963 or 1964, Hoover learned that the Agency had recruited Chicago mobster Sam "Momo" Giancana in a Castro assassination plot.[129] Kennedy himself had found out about the plot from the Agency. According to a former senior Agency official, Kennedy was told of the plan in late 1962. "We gave Kennedy the facts and said 'Here's the problem,'" the official said. "Mr. Kennedy said, 'The next time you deal with the Mafia, come to me first,' but he didn't voice any other objection."[130] When Kennedy told Hoover, the FBI director spelled out his fears in a memorandum which was later turned over to the Rockefeller commission investigating the CIA.[131] "Mr. Hoover was deeply concerned that this put Giancana in the position to blackmail the United States Government," one source said later.[132] If there was a blackmail attempt, it didn't succeed. After Kennedy left the Justice Department, his former aides successfully prosecuted Giancana and put him behind bars.[133]

about Marcello's intentions when he abruptly arose from the table," Reid reported.[134] "Marcello did not joke about such things. In any case, the matter had gone beyond being mere 'business'; it had become an affair of honor, a Sicilian vendetta. Moreover, the conversation at Churchill Farms also made clear that Marcello had begun to plan a move. He had, for example, already thought of using a 'nut' to do the job."[135]

The "nut," evidently, was Lee Harvey Oswald. Like the other members of the Cosa Nostra, Reid's informant is reflexively patriotic. He seems to swallow the Warren Commission whole.

A more serious but also dubious account appeared in 1973 in a little-noticed book entitled *Legacy of Doubt*, written by Peter Noyes, a television newsman in Los Angeles. Noyes fastened on the never satisfactorily explained presence of Eugene Hale Brading, an associate of several powerful organized crime figures,[136] in the Dal-Tex building immediately after the assassination. Brading (also known by one of his aliases, "Jim Braden"),[137] was the kind of person who would arouse anyone's suspicions. He had been jailed the first time in 1934 for a burglary in Kansas.[138] In 1941 he was arrested and fined in Miami for running a gambling house.[139] Three times during the war years he was busted for selling gasoline ration coupon booklets on the black market.[140] With peace Brading moved on to even more auspicious endeavors. In 1951 FBI agents arrested Brading in New York on a Texas warrant charging him with embezzlement of $50,000.[141] Brading was eventually found guilty of fraud and related charges and sentenced to a dozen years in prison.[142] Still later Brading moved on to Denver and Los Angeles, where he became involved in oil deals and associated with a number of leading Cosa Nostra figures.[143]

On November 18, 1963, Brading received permission from his parole officer in Los Angeles to go to Dallas.[144] He checked in at the Dallas sheriff's office on November 21 and announced that he was in town to talk some deals with local oilmen, including Lamar Hunt.[145] By chance, Brading insisted—by design,

Noyes and other critics suspected—Brading found himself in Dealey Plaza during the assassination. Brading was picked up for questioning and released that afternoon. In a voluntary statement he made for the Dallas sheriff, Brading explained how he came to be in the Dal-Tex Building shortly after 12:30 p.m.:

> I . . . was walking down Elm Street trying to get a cab and there wasn't any. I heard people talking, saying "My God, the President has been shot." . . . I moved on up to the building across the street from the building which was surrounded and I asked one of the girls if there was a telephone I could use and she said, "Yes, there is one on the third floor of the building where I work." I walked through a passage to the elevator where they were getting on [the freight elevator] and I got off at the third floor of the building with all the other people. . . . The colored man who ran the elevator said, "You are a stranger in this building and I was not supposed to let you up," and he ran outside to an officer.[146]

Thus the truth according to Brading. Despite the source it sounds plausible. There is such a thing as innocent coincidence. If Brading were going to Dallas to shoot the President it hardly seems likely that he would advertise his itinerary to his parole officer in Los Angeles. Being in the Dal-Tex Building (from which some of the shots may well have been fired) after the shooting is understandable. Going to a phone to call someone and inform them of the tragedy was the reaction of tens of millions of Americans on November 22; the phone lines across the country were jammed. Even Brading identifying himself to the sheriff by his alias, and making no mention of his criminal record, is what one would expect from a paroled ex-con anxious to stay out of trouble. In this caper, at least, Brading seems to be innocent.

At best Brading was a functionary, a high-level errand boy for organized crime. The Warren Commission did not take him seriously. Nor did it take seriously the men he worked for. The Commission, however halfheartedly, considered many possible suspects and groups in John Kennedy's assassination; organized crime was not one of them. The one known criminal conspiracy in the United States, the group with the best motive, means, and opportunity to murder John Kennedy, managed uniquely to avoid investigation.

Blinded, misled, with an understanding of organized crime seemingly taken from the movies, the Report talks only of "gambling acquaintances"[147] who were somehow everywhere, and yet meant nothing. They were just "Family" men, odd little characters with funny-sounding names who walked their dogs, loved their grandchildren, and only killed each other.

12

Toward a New Investigation

> Because of the difficulty of proving negatives to a certainty the possibility of others being involved with either Oswald or Ruby cannot be rejected categorically, but if there is any such evidence it has been beyond the reach of all investigative agencies and resources of the United States and has not come to the attention of this Commission.
>
> —Report of the President's Commission on the Assassination of President Kennedy

> To the living, one owes consideration; to the dead, only the truth.
>
> —Voltaire

ON MARCH 8, 1975, a story appeared in the *New York Times* which seemed on first reading to have momentous consequences. The commission investigating the domestic activities of the Central Intelligence Agency, appointed by President Ford and chaired by Vice-President Nelson Rockefeller, would according to informed sources close to the investigation probe charges of "possible CIA involvement in the assassination of President Kennedy." [1] More than a decade after the assassination, no less than a commission appointed by the President of the United States was finally investigating the most haunting rumor of all. Or so it seemed.

The surviving members of the Warren Commission (among them President Ford) and the Central Intelligence Agency need not have worried. The investigation was in the capable hands of the Rockefeller commission's executive director, David Belin, a former staff lawyer for the Warren Commission and perhaps the most vociferous of the Report's defenders. Belin's performance as expected.

"Two different theories have been advanced," the Rockefeller report said of the CIA and the assassination. "One theory is that E. Howard Hunt and Frank Sturgis, on behalf of the CIA, personally participated in the assassination. The other is that the CIA had connections with Lee Harvey Oswald or Jack Ruby or both of them and that these connections somehow led to the assassination."[2]

In the course of the next eighteen pages Belin neatly demolished the first theory, whose proponents consisted of comedian Dick Gregory; the *National Tattler;* A. J. Weberman, a self-described "garbologist" whose specialty is poking through celebrities' trash cans; and a West Coast woman who among other things is convinced that Mark Lane is a Bulgarian secret agent with the code name "Boris."[3] Belin then turned his attentions to the second, more serious notion. The report ticked through a series of allegations about Oswald's and Ruby's background (many of which, the report conceded in a footnote, were true),[4] and then stated:

> Even if the individual items contained in the foregoing recitations were assumed to be true, it was concluded that the inferences drawn must be considered to be farfetched speculation insofar as they purport to show a connection between the CIA and either Oswald or Ruby.
>
> Even in the absence of denials by living persons that such connections existed, no weight could be assigned to such testimony. Moreover, Sturgis was never an employee or agent of the CIA. . . .
>
> Hunt and Sturgis categorically denied that they had ever met or known Oswald or Ruby. They further denied that they ever had any connection whatever with either Oswald or Ruby.
>
> . . . On the basis of the staff's investigation, the Commission concluded there was no credible evidence of any CIA involvement.[5]

So ended the Rockefeller commission's investigation of the CIA and the assassination of John Fitzgerald

Kennedy—on the word of two of the suspects, both convicted felons. In many respects, the Rockefeller commission's investigation of CIA involvement in the assassination of President Kennedy was a far more blatant and malicious cover-up than that of the Warren Commission. With one exception, Dr. Cyril Wecht, the Rockefeller commission took testimony only from the most sensational and irresponsible Warren Commission critics. Sober, thoughtful critics like physicist Paul Hoch who wanted to testify or submit evidence were ignored. Hoch submitted a twenty-five-page single-space typed memorandum to the commission detailing a number of instances when the Agency apparently withheld vital information from the Warren Commission, including Oswald's contacts with the Albert Schweitzer College in Switzerland (where Oswald was enrolled as a student, and to which he was supposed to be going when he departed for the Soviet Union), files on Marina Oswald, data on Sylvia Odio's father (he had been imprisoned by Castro because he harbored two fugitives in an assassination plot; moreover, Manuel Rodriguez, the Oswald look-alike and Dallas Alpha 66 leader [C.D. 23.4], belonged to the same group as Odio's father), and the Agency's apparent lie to the FBI the day of the assassination that it had no CIA-originated material in its file on Oswald.[6] After Hoch sent his material to the Rockefeller commission he was contacted by Belin, who asked only if Hoch agreed that Oswald shot Kennedy and Tippit. Belin promised that a commission counsel would be in touch with Hoch about his memo. It was the last Hoch heard from the commission.[7] Instead Hoch was apparently included among those who were described by the Rockefeller report as "a witness, a telephone caller and a mail correspondent" who "tendered additional information of the same nature. None of it was more than a strained effort to draw inferences of conspiracy from facts which would not fairly support the inference."[8] Wecht, the one responsible critic who was allowed to testify before the Rockefeller commission, emerged incredibly in the commission's report as a *defender* of the Warren Commission. Said the Rockefeller report:

"Dr. Wecht testified that the available evidence all points to the President being struck only by two bullets coming from the rear, and that no support can be found for theories which postulate gunmen to the front or right front of the Presidential car." [9] When the report containing this statement was released Wecht charged that Belin had "twisted and distorted the substance and meaning of my testimony," [10] and demanded that the full transcript of his testimony be released. Said Wecht: "If that transcript shows in any way that I have withdrawn or revised my thought of the Warren Commission Report, I'll eat the transcript on the steps of the White House." [11] The Rockefeller commission denied Wecht's request.

The Church committee will probably not fare much better. Its chairman, Senator Frank Church of Idaho, is a cautious man with a well-deserved reputation among his colleagues for steering clear of overly controverial issues. And Church has presidential ambitions. There is ample cause for his prudence. Still, through the summer and fall of 1975, information from diehard conspiracy buffs flowed into the Church committee, some of it serious, most of it simply scurrilous, including the "confession" of a Puerto Rican former soldier in Castro's army who told, under hypnosis, how he had been programmed Manchurian candidate-style to be a member of the assassination team.[12] Meanwhile, public pressure for a new investigation mounted, spurred by continuing disclosures of both the CIA and FBI withholding evidence from the Warren Commission. In the fall of 1975 the disclosures, the rallies, the petition drives, the new spate of national publicity, finally began to have an impact. In the House, a resolution calling for a new investigation of *all* the political assassinations that occurred during the sixties was introduced by Henry Gonzalez, a Democratic representative from San Antonio who rode in the fatal motorcade.[13] The Gonzalez resolution picked up several dozen congressional cosponsors and endorsement from a number of leading conservatives, including columnist William F. Buckley and former Senate Watergate committee chairman Sam Ervin.

More important than the Gonzalez resolution, though, was the work of two congressional subcommittees, one in the House, the other in the Senate, that in the fall of 1975 began limited reexaminations of the assassination. On the House side, California Representative Don Edwards, chairman of the Civil and Constitutional Rights Subcommittee, announced that his panel would not repeat all the work of the Warren Commission, but would try, on a small scale, to "set the record straight on just what went on." Edwards, a former FBI man, was particularly interested in Ruby's and Oswald's relationships with the FBI, as well as in evidence that the FBI kept from the Warren Commission. At the same time, Senator Richard Schweiker, Republican from Pennsylvania, and Senator Gary Hart, Democrat of Colorado, both members of the Church committee's CIA investigation, were designated to sort out Oswald's connections to American intelligence, as well as to go over what evidence the Agency withheld from the Warren Commission. Schweiker said that the "Warren Commission report is like a house of cards. It's going to collapse." He added that his subcommittee had developed "very significant leads" about the murder and wanted to investigate three possibilities: that President Kennedy was the victim of a Communist plot originating in the Soviet Union; that the assassination was the result of a right-wing plot hatched in the United States, and, finally, that anti-Castro Cubans, angry over diminishing support from the Kennedy administration, planned the murder. As Schweiker, a no-nonsense conservative, put it: "During the last few years we came very close to having Big Brother take over with very many of our intelligence operations. We're only learning now how close, and it was frighteningly close."

If the full truth about John Kennedy's murder is ever to be learned, the new probes will have to be markedly different from the old. Past experience has shown that mounting a new investigation does not guarantee results. The members of the Warren Commission all had impressive credentials. Jim Garrison had the law enforcement powers of an entire state at his disposal. The results in both cases were disastrous. The problem is not in wanting to investigate, but in how to go about it. Good intentions are not enough.

The immediate difficulty, of course, is the credibility of the investigators. Mark Lane tells the story of his recent appearance at Purdue University in Lafayette, Indiana. At the end of his talk he asked the 6000 students listening to him how many favored a new investigation. Seemingly all the hands in the hall went up. When Lane asked if there were any dissenters a lonely hand appeared. When Lane asked why the dissenter didn't want a new congressional investigation, the student replied: "I don't trust Congress." [14]

The polls confirm that the overwhelming majority of Americans agree with him. Congress has shown itself ill equipped to deal with ordinary problems, much less the complexities of unraveling a criminal conspiracy. The Senate's Watergate investigation is a case in point. The hearings made for compelling daytime television drama, but as a probe into a conspiracy they were something less than adequate. The senators' questions were often ill prepared or meandering. Many items were taken on faith, notably the CIA's lack of involvement in the break-in, a remarkable grant of confidence considering that at least four of the figures later arrested were CIA men, two of them—Hunt and McCord—important operatives. The most notable achievement of the Watergate committee was its discovery of the existence of the White House taping system, and that came quite by chance during preparatory questioning of Alexander Butterfield by a committee junior counsel.[15] No, the members of the Senate are nothing like Sam Spade.

All the same, the Congress, in the absence of a special prosecutor, is the logical place for a probe of the Kennedy case. It has subpoena powers and can grant witnesses immunity from prosecution (something which the Warren Commission failed to do). Selecting the members of an investigating committee and proper staffing are crucial elements in ensuring the investigation's integrity. The Warren Commission demonstrated that the busiest men make the worst investigators, and congressmen are by the nature of their jobs busy men. But to the extent possible, assignment on the Kennedy assassination committee should be a full-time occupation for the committee members, and certainly the members of the staff. Conflicts of interest, while they should be minimized as much as possible, are probably unavoidable. Given the diversity of Congress, some members of an investigating committee inevitably will be open to the charge that they are too close to the intelligence community, too close to the mob, too close even to the Kennedys—a factor that should not be dismissed, since conceivably an investigation, even one limited in scope, could lead to the discovery of facts that could prove embarrassing to the Kennedy family. (The President's autopsy report, for instance, fails to mention the results of inspection of the adrenal glands, a violation of standard autopsy procedure,[16] leading to speculation that the President, as long rumored, was a victim of Addison's disease.) The suspicions will be inevitable. But Congress need not be deterred. The task it has to perform is a relatively simple one.

The Congress should confine itself to the investigation of two areas: the existence of a conspiracy, and the purpose and extent of the cover-up that followed. The "who-done-it" aspect of the case, while intriguing for armchair private detectives, ought to be left to professionals, specifically a special prosecutor of the kind that functioned during the Watergate investigation.

Congress need not repeat all the steps the Warren Commission stumbled through to prove the existence of a conspiracy. Eyewitness testimony is not only conflicting, but after twelve years is likely to be at substantial variance with first recollections. Nor are Oswald's movements that important. Quite unintentionally the Warren Commission proved that it is impossible to fix with certainty where he was at the time the shots rang out, much less whether he had a rifle in his hands. For the sake of the initial investigation it can be assumed that he was somehow connected to the conspiracy, performing whatever role matters little. Congress should focus instead on the two sine qua nons of conspiracy: ballistics tests and autopsy results.

A number of ballistics tests have already been performed, so in part the solution lies in prying them loose from the FBI and the vaults of the National Archives. Thanks to Freedom of Information Act lawsuits filed by Harold Weisberg and others, the "bench notes" from the neutron activation analysis run on the "magic bullet" and fragments taken from Governor Connally are now available.[17] These notes, while they indicate some differences in composition between the fragments that were recovered from Connally and C.E. 399,[18] neither prove nor disprove that the bullets came from different weapons. Some items are missing from the data, however, and there is no report summing up the FBI's conclusions. If this material exists, the first order of business should be securing its release.

New tests will also have to be run. The state of the art in neutron activation analysis has advanced considerably since 1963. Technicians today are able to make much finer measurements of the compositions of various pieces of matter.[19] The "magic bullet" and the fragments should be subjected to these new tests. Also the bullet Oswald allegedly fired at General Walker, supposedly too mangled for positive identification, should be bombarded with NAA radiation. This has not been done.

Autopsy results go hand in hand with ballistics tests. For once a distinguished panel of the country's leading pathologists (not veterinarians and urologists), with no axes to grind or affiliations with government or military agencies which would make their credibility suspect, should be appointed and given free access to *all* the autopsy data, X rays, and pictures. If, as seems to be the case, some of the data is missing, a rigorous accounting should be demanded. Commander Humes should be asked *why* he burned his "preliminary notes" of the autopsy results the Sunday after the assassination, and if it was at someone's direction, *whose* direction. Colonel Finck should be asked why he failed to probe the path of the President's back wound and if, as he stated at the Garrison trial, his failure came from obedience to a senior officer, the officer who told him not to should be called to state why he gave the order.

The Dallas doctors should be summoned to explain their original contention that the small hole in the President's throat was an entry wound, and more to the point, why they changed their story when they appeared before the Warren Commission. All the autopsy doctors should be compelled to testify under oath about the most remarkable aspect of the autopsy of all: how the wound in the President's back managed to "move" several inches higher six months after his death.

Finally Congress must resolve the grisliest mystery of the autopsy: how the President's brain came to be missing. The brain was saved after the autopsy and "set" in formalin for future autopsy study. The study was never performed. According to a "memorandum of transfer" at the National Archives, various autopsy material, including a small stainless steel box containing gross material, was turned over to the archives by representatives of the Kennedy family for safekeeping.[20] The "gross material" in the stainless steel box is almost certainly the President's brain. But the brain is not at the archives, and so far everyone connected with the case has been most reluctant to say where it is. It seems highly unlikely that the brain has been truly stolen. A more reasonable explanation is that it is being withheld by representatives of the Kennedy family in the interests of taste. That is certainly an understandable motive after the trauma the Kennedys have experienced during the last twelve years. Taste, however, must be weighed against the truth. Once the brain is recovered, a distinguished team of pathologists should, following standard autopsy procedure, "section" it surgically to determine, once and for all, the path of the bullets that took John Kennedy's life.

If these procedures are followed, the conspiracy will be revealed; not its nature or its motive, or who was behind it, or even how many gunmen were involved, but simply that there were men "breathing together" in a criminal act. That finding, in itself, will do much to relieve the anxiety of the last decade. At that point a special prosecutor should be appointed, someone with ties neither to the Warren Commission or the

Kennedy family (a requirement that eliminates all three special Watergate prosecutors, Leon Jaworski, Archibald Cox, and Henry Ruth), a seasoned law enforcement professional, ideally someone possessed of the same zeal that Robert Kennedy's critics called ruthlessness. To solve a crime of this sort a prosecutor will need to be ruthless and tough and uncaring of the political consequences of the truth. He will face enormous difficulties. The first will be assembling an investigative team of his own; for, unlike the Warren Commission, a special prosecutor will be unable to rely on the resources and goodwill of the Federal Bureau of Investigation and the Central Intelligence Agency. Not when they themselves, unfairly or not, are prime suspects in the crime and cover-up.

Meanwhile Congress should do its best to unravel the cover-up. Such an effort should not be a punitive expedition, but an honest attempt to uncover and learn from the mistakes of our past. There are three possibilities:

1. All the investigative resources of the federal government simply overlooked the conspiracy, an explanation which, whatever one thinks of the efficiency of the FBI and CIA, strains even the most innocent imagination (and which, moreover, is contradicted by a number of suspicious circumstances).

2. The cover-up was undertaken by accomplices in the actual crime, an explanation that by extension implicates the Dallas police, the Secret Service, the FBI, the CIA, and even President Johnson in the most sinister undertaking, and which, whatever the record of the last twelve years, strains even the sinister imagination.

3. The most probable explanation, a benign cover-up, either in whole or in part, undertaken to safeguard what was perceived to be the national interest, with the Warren Commission its unwitting accomplice.

It is easy to see how such a benign cover-up could have happened. There would have been little difficulty in effectively sidetracking the Warren Commission, however intense the Commission's desire to seek out the truth. Apart from the Commission's built-in limitations—the pressure of deadlines, the predisposition to find a single assassin, the hectic schedule of the commissioners—the Commission depended almost entirely on what the FBI and CIA chose to tell it. There are numerous instances of both the Bureau and the Agency ignoring Commission requests, half-fulfilling them, or delaying even partial compliance, as the CIA did with the Commission's repeated questions about Ruby's background until the Report was already being written. The commissioners themselves voiced suspicions about the Bureau's instant readiness to blame the crime on Oswald during their famous secret sessions of January 22 and 27, 1964. At one point in the discussions on the twenty-seventh, the following exchange occurs:

> RANKIN: They [the FBI] have no problem. They have decided that it was Oswald who committed the assassination, they have decided that no one else was involved, they have decided—
>
> RUSSELL: They have tried the case and reached a verdict on every count.
>
> BOGGS: You have put your finger on it.
>
> MC CLOY: They are a little less certain in the supplementals than they were in the first.
>
> RANKIN: Yes, but they are still there. They have decided the case, and we are going to have maybe a thousand further inquiries that we can say the Commission has to know all these things before it can pass on this.
>
> And I think their reaction would probably be, "Why do you want all that. It is clear."
>
> RUSSELL: You have our statement. What else do you want?
>
> MC CLOY: Yes, "We know who killed cock robin." That is the point. It isn't only who killed cock robin. Under the terms of reference we have to go beyond this.[21]

Of course the Commission was unable to go on, because it was never able to devise a way of getting around the CIA and the Bureau, even to answer so central a question as whether Oswald was an agent of the CIA or the FBI.

If Oswald was, or even once had been an agent it

would have provided powerful motive for both agencies to cover up not only Oswald's background but Ruby's and those of others involved in the conspiracy; for if the Commission had discovered that Oswald had been part of a conspiracy, it would not have stopped there, but would have probed deeper into his background to discover just who he was and how he happened to join a conspiracy to murder the President. Seen in that light, the withholding of the 1960 Hoover memorandum about the possibility of an Oswald impostor is not surprising. Nor is it surprising that the FBI, which knew full well the background of Ruby's associates and his own links to the Bureau, should blandly report an interview with the likes of Dave "Yeres," making no mention of the fact that he was a Teamster gangster and, on information developed by the Bureau's own surveillance devices, a professional hit man for the mob.[22] "There are two kinds of FBI interviews," says a former senior official in the Department of Justice, and himself a former FBI agent. "The first kind is where you simply sit down with a source and come away with nothing. The second kind is where you really dig into him, check everything about him and his friends. In this case [the assassination], it looks like the Bureau used the first kind of interview."[23] Attempts by Kennedy men in the Department of Justice to push further were blunted by the Bureau. Jack Miller, who served as Robert Kennedy's chief in the Criminal Division, went to Dallas immediately after the assassination and, according to one of his former senior aides, "was totally frozen out by the Bureau."[24] "The relationship with Hoover changed overnight," recalls a former organized crime investigator in the Justice Department. "They wouldn't have anything to do with us anymore. Just read their reports. You can see the kind of investigation they conducted."[25]

Embarrassment alone is sufficient reason for the FBI's participation in the conspiracy cover-up. The CIA, on the other hand, is a different story.

The revelation of Oswald's participation in an intelligence operation in the Soviet Union would have put the Agency in a highly uncomfortable position. Similarly, the full disclosure of Oswald's background would have compromised several of the Agency's most sensitive operations, including the attempts on Castro's life, its alliance with organized crime, and the Agency's "domestic operations," whose uncovering a dozen years later has, by the Agency's own admission, left it shaken and disarrayed. The Agency thus was presented with a choice: either it presented the full facts about Oswald (which, in any case, would not have brought John Kennedy back to life) and in the process disclosed a whole range of its own illegal activities, or it kept its mouth shut. History shows which option the Agency chose.

That is the "best case" scenario. The "worst case" scenario, involving the Agency's own participation in the assassination, or more likely, participation by conspirators closely allied to the Agency, namely organized crime, various Cuban exile figures, or some employees of the Agency itself, presents the most powerful motive for a cover-up of all. This last possibility —a murderous faction within the Agency—is not as unlikely as it seems. Excess of zeal or plain criminality can, as the Rockefeller and Church commissions have amply demonstrated, set the CIA off on an uncontrolled charge—"like a rogue elephant," [26] to use the words of Senator Frank Church. Kennedy himself found it impossible to rein in the entire Agency, which continued to defy his express orders before, during, and after the Bay of Pigs invasion. If the CIA as a whole is impossible to control, it makes it far more likely that a faction within it could get loose. One can easily imagine such a revanchist clique plotting and executing the President's murder. It is far less easy to imagine John McCone and his senior deputies planning the death of their chief. Not that it is impossible. It is simply one of those things which, even now, one hopes could not be true. The circumstantial evidence of Oswald's ties to CIA, or some other branch of U.S. intelligence, is nonetheless overwhelming. What one wants to make of those ties—whether they involve a "worst case" or a "best case" scenario—depends on how much personal faith one has in the workings of the Central Intelligence Agency.

The only other possible rationale for a cover-up was the fear or actual knowledge that, in killing the President, Oswald was working at the behest of a foreign power, Soviets or Cubans—or, a possibility Allen Dulles raised at one executive session, the Chinese. Clearly President Johnson was worried that such was the case. Through his assistant, Clifton Carter, he took steps the very night of the assassination to ensure that Oswald would not be charged by Dallas authorities with being part of "an international Communist conspiracy." [27] Reportedly Johnson himself on November 23 called Dallas Police Captain Will Fritz to personally request that the police investigation of Oswald's links to foreign governments be terminated.[28] Whether or not this story is true, it is certain that Johnson raised the specter of World War III in convincing Earl Warren to head up a blue-ribbon commission that would lay all the rumors of Oswald's involvement in a foreign-inspired conspiracy to rest. Shortly before his death Johnson repeated his conviction that Oswald was a member of a "Communist conspiracy," and that Cuba was probably its source.[29]

Credible evidence linking Oswald to such a conspiracy has so far been lacking. On the contrary there are strong indications that the conspiracy of which he may have been a part was domestically based. Various theories have been advanced about the identity of these domestic conspirators, everyone from the Minutemen to Texas oil millionaires to southern racists. None of these theories hold up, if only for the reason that the alleged conspirators lacked the power to turn off an investigation of their crime. If the murder had been plotted by any of these groups, even if it had been plotted by Cuban exiles or organized crime acting on their own, the federal government would have pursued the crime to its source. The conspirators had to be sure they would have protection. They could only be sure if they had the power to blackmail the government, or were, in fact, part of the government. Who possessed such power? Who had the motive, the means, the opportunity? The answer keeps coming back to Langley.

As with Watergate, the unraveling of the cover-up may tell us more than the crime itself. Congress can begin the process by subpoenaing former senior officials of the CIA and FBI, many of whom are now retired, and some of whom have lately been talking about all manner of things that once were the most closely held secrets. A number of possible questions spring to mind.

To Richard Helms: How is it that the Agency photographed the wrong "Lee Henry Oswald" as outside the Cuban and Soviet embassies in Mexico City? Who is the man in the pictures? If Oswald was not photographed, how did he manage to avoid detection? Does the voiceprint of the Oswald conversations taped in Mexico City match the voiceprint of the tapes of Oswald in Dallas and New Orleans? Who is the "Harvey Lee Oswald" carried in the Agency's files? Why wasn't Oswald interviewed on his return from the Soviet Union? Why weren't Oswald's letters from the Soviet Union intercepted? Who, in fact, went to the Soviet Union using the name Lee Harvey Oswald? What connections, if any, has the Agency ever had with the following people: Marina Oswald, George De Mohrenschildt, Clay Shaw, David Ferrie, William G. Gaudet, Richard Snyder, Richard Case Nagell, Sergio Arcacha Smith, Guy Banister, Loran Eugene Hall, Lee Harvey Oswald? What security clearance did Oswald have in the Marine Corps? What was his mission at Atsugi, Japan?

To E. Howard Hunt: Where were you on November 22, 1963? When did you first meet Frank Sturgis? Were you acting station chief in Mexico City in September 1963? If not, where were you? What other "numerous and illegal conspiracies" were you referring to in your note to President Nixon?

To Richard Bissell: Who authorized the assassination attempts on Fidel Castro's life? How much did President Kennedy and his brother know about them? What was the nature and extent of organized crime's relationship with the Agency during the early 1960s? Why weren't the exile raids on Castro halted, as ordered by the President of the United States?

To James Jesus Angleton: What did you mean when after your resignation from the Agency you told reporters, "A mansion has many rooms. . . . I'm not privy to who struck John"?[30] Who in the mansion would be privy?

To FBI Director Clarence Kelley: Why does the Federal Bureau of Investigation refuse to release all of Lee Harvey Oswald's file? Where are the "302" files of each of the nine interviews with Jack Ruby when he was an informer for the Bureau? If you have them, why won't you release them? (Release of both the Oswald and Ruby files are exempted under provisions of the Freedom of Information Act. Congress, however, could presumably subpoena them or pressure President Ford for their release.)

To Charles Flynn (the Dallas FBI man who recruited Ruby as a Bureau informer; now retired): What led you to believe that Ruby would have knowledge of "the criminal element in Dallas"?[31] What knowledge did he provide? If none, why did you see him nine times in the space of eight months?

To James Hosty (the FBI man whose name was in Oswald's notebook): Just how did Lee Harvey Oswald get your name, telephone number, and auto license number and put it in his notebook? What was the extent of your contacts with the Oswald family, other than those reported in official FBI reports? Was Oswald recruited as an informer on the Cuban exiles? If so, was his code name A. J. Hidell? Why did you tell the Dallas police shortly after the assassination that Oswald was in the Bureau's "Communist file," that he had had contact with two subversives two weeks before the assassination, and that he was "capable of committing this assassination"?[32] Who were the "subversives" with whom Oswald was in contact? If the Bureau knew that Oswald was a potential danger to the President, why wasn't this information turned over to the Secret Service? What was contained in the note

Oswald left with the Bureau only days before the assassination? Who ordered you to destroy the note? *

Answers to these questions should provide a much fuller understanding of who Oswald was, and if, as seems to be the case, he was an intelligence agent and/or a Bureau informer, partial insight into why the cover-up was undertaken. That is the first layer of the onion. The second is more difficult to peel away: Why was Oswald wanted by the police in the first place?

The police decided that a man matching Oswald's description was their prime suspect before his arrest for the murder of Officer Tippit.[36] The explanation Dallas Police Chief Jesse Curry provided the Warren Commission is that the police began looking for Oswald after a roll call of the Book Depository disclosed that he was the only person missing.[37] We know now that this is not true. There was no roll call. There *was* a memorandum, listing some fifty-five employees of the Depository, twelve of whom are marked "not home," [38] among them a man with a police record. The name at the very top of the list is "Harvey Lee Oswald." [39] There are other puzzles. The description of Oswald that went out over the police radio—5′10″, 150 pounds, gray eyes—corresponds closely to the description carried by the FBI.[40] Yet the FBI and the Dallas police were not in contact until *after* Oswald was arrested.[41] How, then, did the police come up with such an accurate description, one almost identical to the FBI's? And how did the police know Oswald's address—1026 North Beckley, Oak Cliff? [42] Oswald concealed that address from his employers, and the police claim to have had no knowledge about him until after his arrest for the murders of Kennedy and Tippit.[43] The address was known only by the FBI. How did the police get the address from the FBI if the Bureau did not join the case until after Oswald's arrest? Even more strangely, the police came up with yet another address for Oswald shortly after the assassination, this one 605 Elsbeth Street.[44] Oswald had

---

* Hosty denied under oath that he said any of these things to the Dallas police department.[33] Lieutenant Jack Revill, the man whom Hosty saw immediately after Oswald's arrest, swore that he did.[34] Moreover, Revill's story is corroborated by several witnesses, including a Secret Service agent.[35]

lived at *602* Elsbeth, but had moved out more than a year before the assassination. The Elsbeth Street address was not known to Oswald's employers,[45] so the police could not have gotten it from the Book Depository. The address *was* known by the FBI.[46] However, at the time the police listed the Elsbeth Street address, the Bureau had not yet arrived on the scene. The only possible explanation seems to be that the police *did* know about Oswald well before the assassination, and lied about this knowledge to the Warren Commission. But why? Finally, when the police arrived at Oswald's rooming house, they told his housekeeper that they were seeking "Harvey Lee Oswald." This transposition of first and middle names would seem to be an honest mistake, were it not for the identical transpositions carried in various reports and files of U.S. intelligence agencies. Congress should find out how this mistake was made. One possibility is that the unidentified army intelligence agent who accompanied Lieutenant Jack Revill from Dealey Plaza provided the name, as well as Oswald's address and description. But who was this man? And if he was the source of the data about Oswald, how did he happen to have such information at his fingertips?

While Congress is questioning the army it should also ask about James W. Powell, the intelligence officer who was on the sixth floor of the Book Depository when the Mannlicher-Carcano was found, and who was later "trapped inside" [47] when the building was sealed. How did he happen to be in Dealey Plaza on November 22? Congress should also inquire whether the army included Oswald among the thousands of dissidents in its computer banks. If so, did the army contact him? By the same token, was army intelligence in touch with any of Oswald's friends and acquaintances, especially among the Cuban exiles? What exactly was the army's role with the exiles? Did army intelligence have agents among any of the groups, notably Alpha 66 and the 30th of November Group, which were later linked to the assassination? How is it that a message stating that Oswald had been to Cuba and was a card-carrying Communist was flashed to

USSTRICOM the night of the assassination? Who was the source of this disinformation? What action, if any, did USSTRICOM take in response to the cable? Was there a plan for an invasion of Cuba in the works after the assassination? If so, who ordered it, and who finally countermanded the order?

There are also some questions for the marines, the Department of Defense, and the Office of Naval Intelligence to answer. Namely, in the cable from the naval attaché in Moscow, describing Oswald's defection, what are the forty-three spaces which are blanked out, and which describe whatever else Oswald was besides an ordinary marine? What was Oswald's exact mission at Atsugi? What access did he have to classified information about the U-2? Did he pass this information on to the Russians? If there was a suspicion that he did, why wasn't he arrested or at least questioned when he returned from the Soviet Union? How did Oswald, who had been twice convicted in court-martials, secure a minimum security clearance of "secret"? What was Oswald's exact security clearance? What was Oswald's mission on Taiwan? Why were the records of Oswald's service that were turned over to the Warren Commission falsified? How did Oswald secure such a speedy "hardship discharge" from the Marine Corps when there was clear evidence that there was no hardship at all? Was Oswald recruited for an intelligence assignment while he was stationed overseas? If so, what was the nature of that assignment? What accounts for the variations in height in Oswald's medical examinations?

And to Captain Alexis Davison: why did you invite Oswald to visit your mother if he were ever in Atlanta? Did you first tell the Secret Service you could not recall meeting Oswald? [47a] If so, did you later admit to the FBI that indeed you had, and, in fact, had invited him to your home? What connection, if any, do you have to U.S. intelligence? What was your role in the Penkovskiy affair?

If Congress is successful in getting answers to even some of these questions if may help flush out the mystery of Oswald and why he was wanted by the police.

Then, of course, another mystery remains: How did the police know where to look for him?

The Warren Commission explained that the capture of Oswald grew out of the shooting of Police Officer J. D. Tippit. According to the Commission Oswald shot Tippit at 1:15 p.m. approximately one mile from Oswald's rooming house.[48] Since Oswald's housekeeper said he left the house a few minutes after one, this would have given him just enough time to walk to the spot where Tippit was murdered. (Even then, he would have to have jogged; walking, it would have taken Oswald eighteen minutes to cover the distance.)[49] The entire scenario hinges, however, on the exact time of Tippit's death. If Tippit was shot earlier, say sometime between 1:08 and 1:10, when T. F. Bowley recalls arriving on the scene,[50] Oswald would not have had sufficient time to walk—or even run—to the scene of the crime. While there were a number of eyewitnesses to the killer's escape, only two eyewitnesses got a good look at the killer. One was Acquila Clemmons. But Mrs. Clemmons told independent investigators, including Mark Lane, that the man she saw shoot Tippit was *not* Oswald; moreover, he was not alone.[51] The Warren Commission never called Mrs. Clemmons to testify. Instead it relied on the testimony of other eyewitnesses. Several could not identify Oswald. Those who could either saw him after the shooting, were first unsure that the man they saw was Oswald, or picked him out of highly questionable lineups. Domingo Benavides, who was the closest witness to the murder, observing it from fifteen feet away, was unable to identify Oswald as the killer.[52] Warren Reynolds, the owner of the used-car lot who saw a man fleeing from the scene of the crime with a pistol in his hand, at first told the FBI that the man he saw was not Oswald.[53] The day after his interview Reynolds was shot in the head. After he recovered, he decided that the man he had seen was Oswald after all.[54]

Tippit's murder was a crucial occurrence. It was the event which brought the Dallas police, sirens screaming, into the neighborhood were Oswald was soon discovered. But if Oswald did not kill Tippit, who did and why? Why, also, was Tippit brought to what would be the scene of his death from his regular patrol post miles away?

Until a new investigation comes up with some answers one can only look at the available facts and speculate. The series of radio calls that drew Tippit to the scene are certainly odd. Some critics have suggested that Tippit was lured to his death deliberately, that his killing was a necessary prelude to snaring Oswald. In support of this contention critics point to the fact that Tippit moonlighted from his police job in a restaurant owned by a member of the John Birch Society.[55] Considering the political climate in Dallas, however, this does not seem unusual. Other critics point to the statements of two of Ruby's employees, Andrew Armstrong and Larry Crafard, who said that after Tippit was shot Ruby exclaimed that he knew Tippit.[56] Again, if Armstrong and Crafard are correct (Ruby said they weren't),[57] that would not be unusual. Ruby seemed to know hundreds of police officers. Still another witness, Mary Dowling, a waitress at a local restaurant, told the Commission that two days before the assassination Oswald caused a small scene in the restaurant, and Tippit, a regular customer who happened to be in the restaurant at the time, "shot a glance at Oswald." [58] Again possible, and perhaps yet another coincidence. The difficulty in evaluating these stories is that Tippit's background is largely unknown. It is possible that he was somehow connected to the conspiracy, if only unwittingly; there is no evidence that proves that he was, and no evidence that proves that he wasn't. One of the things Congress should investigate is Tippit's life, and whether it contains anything that links him either to the far right, or as has also been suggested, organized crime.[59]

In the absence of such connections Tippit still could have been chosen by the luck of the draw. An even more likely possibility, especially in view of the fact that a close friend of Tippit's was making the radio calls to him on November 22, is that the story the Dallas police tell of Tippit just happening to be on the scene when his killers came by is the truth. The description Mrs. Clemmons provided of one of the killers (a tall, skinny man, wearing a light shirt and khaki pants) [60] at least approximates that of Oswald. As it happens it is even closer to the description provided by several witnesses who spotted a man fleeing from Dealey Plaza. Possibly Oswald was supposed to be fingered some other way, and Tippit merely blundered into two men who were acting suspiciously and was killed for his troubles.

The most searching analysis should be of the events *after* the killing. Why, for instance, did the police fail to search the fundamentalist church? Why, instead, did they concentrate on the Texas Theatre, where a man matching Oswald's description was said to have run in without buying a ticket? The ticket seller and one other witness both identified Oswald as that man, but the ticket taker, Mrs. Julia Postal, seemed shaken and not entirely certain of her identification.[61] Oswald had money on him at the time of his arrest. If he was escaping from by what was now two murders why, after his cool performance in the Book Depository immediately after assassinating the President, would he do something that was bound to call attention to his presence? The only other explanation is that Oswald *did* buy a ticket, and that someone else ran into the theater to draw the police to the scene. This other person could either have run out the back or remained, becoming the mysterious man in the front row who informed the police where the man they were looking for was sitting. As N. M. McDonald, the officer who arrested Oswald, remembered him: "A man sitting near the front, and I still don't know who it was, tipped me the man I wanted was sitting in the third row from the rear, not in the balcony." [62]

McDonald then advanced on Oswald, *gun drawn.*[63] When he reached him, Oswald, according to McDonald, struck him in the face and reached for the revolver stuck in the waist of his own trousers.[64] Oswald, McDonald, and several other officers grappled, and there was a click of a gun misfiring.[65] The Warren Commission said that the click came from Oswald's gun. However, an FBI firearms expert told the Commission: "We found nothing to indicate that this weapon's firing pin had struck the primer of any of these cartridges." [66] The pity is that the FBI didn't have the opportunity to inspect the cartridges carried by the police officers who arrested Oswald. Then the firearms experts might well have discovered a dented primer. Once Oswald was in custody and yelling to everyone in the theater that he was not resisting arrest he could hardly be disposed of on the spot. That would have to wait for two more days.

While twelve years have passed, there is an outside chance that a determined investigation would uncover the full circumstances of what exactly occurred in the dark of the Texas Theatre. The accent, however, must be on determination. Unlike the Warren Commission, which was only too glad to accept testimony at face value so long as it complied with the single-assassin thesis, congressional investigators must demonstrate a readiness to use coercive means to extract testimony. Congress must begin skeptically and stay that way. Immunity plus the threat of prosecution for possible perjury, as the Watergate investigation showed, has a way of making the most reluctant witnesses talk. If the true facts of what occurred in the theater and beforehand are at variance with the Warren Commission's version of events, these tools might bring some answers. Certainly it is worth the effort. Accordingly, the present and former members of the Dallas police involved in sending out the alert for Oswald's arrest, the pursuit that followed, and the ultimate capture should be summoned to testify. William Alexander, the assistant district attorney who apparently waited outside the theater while the police went in to get Oswald,[67] should be asked to explain how he happened to be there. He also should account for his eagerness to indict Oswald as part of an "international Communist conspiracy." [68] Clifton Carter, who called Henry Wade the night of the assassination to express the White House's concern about "conspiracy" appearing in the indictment,[69] is now dead. But other former officials of the Johnson administration might be able to explain his calls, and who asked him to make them.

We also need to know far more about Jack Ruby. His links with the Teamsters should be probed, as well as his numerous connections with organized crime. All the men he called during the month before the assassination should be investigated. The investigation should start with Barney Baker and Dusty Miller of the Teamsters. Once and for all it must be determined how Ruby managed to slip into the police basement at precisely the right moment. Lieutenant George E. Butler, the Ruby chum who later said that Oswald was Ruby's illegitimate son, and that Ruby had been in Mexico at the same time as Oswald,[70] should be asked how and why he dreamed these stories up. He should also be questioned anew about Ruby's role in the attempted bribe of the Dallas County sheriff.

That, then, is the task for Congress: the establishment of the conspiracy and the partial unraveling of the cover-up that followed. The rest of the job is for a special prosecutor. The investigation he must undertake is so massive and complex that one hardly knows where to begin. One obvious place to start, though, is with Sylvia Odio. Her story of the three men who came to visit seeking aid for a violent conspiracy is, at the moment, the most substantial confirmation of the assassination plot. It would be nice to know the identity and whereabouts of "Angelo" and "Leopoldo," not to mention "Leon Oswald," assuming he was not the Lee Oswald who was murdered in the basement of the Dallas jail. However, the identity of Loran Eugene Hall and of William Seymour is known, and they both may be able to provide important clues, if not the actual identity of "Angelo" and "Leopoldo." Hall should be given special attention. Why did he tell the FBI that he was at Sylvia Odio's, and then deny it?[71] If he was not at Sylvia Odio's, where was he that evening? What are his connections to the exiles, organized crime, and the Central Intelligence Agency? Many of the same questions should be asked of Carlos Bringuier, Manuel Rodriguez, and Sergio Arcacha Smith.

With a crime such as the murder of John Kennedy the investigation must proceed carefully, a step at a time, beginning at the bottom, where the suspects are most vulnerable to pressure, and working upward, one link leading to another and another until finally the identity of the ultimate conspirators is revealed. There are certain clues that stand out: the station wagon, for instance, that was seen leaving the parking lot behind the grassy knoll immediately after the assassination. Reportedly, the Dallas police know to whom this car belonged. Obviously the owner should be questioned, his background investigated, his associations probed. Likewise a concerted effort should be made to ascertain the actual identity of the "Clay Bertrand" who asked Dean Andrews to defend Oswald.[72] The twists and turns in Andrews's story do not necessarily mean that he was lying. There is independent confirmation that there was, indeed, a Clay Bertrand, and that he accompanied Oswald into Andrews's law office while Oswald was in New Orleans. If Andrews is frightened about testifying, protection can be made available. It was not offered during the Garrison investigation.

The lack of *positive* evidence of conspiracy surely hampers an investigation of John Kennedy's death; it need not deter it. Oftentimes *negative* information is almost as important. Thus, each bit of conscious disinformation that was put out after the assassination should be followed to its source. All attempts to deflect the original investigators from the truth should be rigorously followed up. Once more Ruby is crucial. If it can be determined for whom he was working, who gave him the orders to kill Oswald, we will be that much closer to discovering who killed Kennedy. The use of "cutouts"—third parties who shuttle information back and forth between its source and its recipient—is standard intelligence procedure. We would expect to discover numerous cutouts in the Kennedy case. The trick is getting by them. The anxiety to find the killers should not decrease the investigators' wariness. The most ironic tragedy would be if we were to repeat the mistakes of 1963 and once again find guilty someone who was only part of a plot, and a minor part at that.

Who, then?

Over the years critics of the Commission have fastened on numerous figures who were, they said, somehow part of the plot, if not the actual assassination, then the "framing" of Oswald that followed. The darkest suspicions are cast on those who were closest to Oswald. Closest of all was his wife, Marina. Her testimony to the Commission provided more damaging evidence against her husband than that of any other witness. Much of that testimony is also riddled with errors, distortions, contradictions, and outright lies. Was it because she was a frightened young widow, alone in a strange country, in the midst of the most sensational murder of the century, or did the lies spring from some more culpable motives? Marina is remarried now, living the quiet life of a suburban Texas housewife. Despite the fact that she has lived in this country almost fifteen years she has yet to take out citizenship. "I haven't had time to memorize all those questions about the Constitution," [73] she has explained. So long as Marina is subject to deportation and the kind of intimidation to which she apparently fell victim in 1963 she will remain an incredible source. The doubts about her will persist. The obvious solution is a grant of immediate citizenship and absolute immunity for her testimony. Even then, of course, there will be no certainty that she will tell the truth. A woman who, as a Commission lawyer put it, "has lied numerous times about matters of crucial concern" [74] can be expected to lie again. Her testimony, however, is vital. If proper safeguards are taken, if her inquisitors are more skeptical judges of human nature than Earl Warren was, she may provide much valuable information, if not about the assassination, then at least about the shadowy man who was her husband.

George De Mohrenschildt is another key witness. He too still lives in Dallas. He should be subjected to the most intensive grilling. Whatever his background is, it should be known. If it includes an intelligence capacity, that role should be made clear. How was it that he just happened to be in Guatemala at the moment of the Bay of Pigs invasion? [75] To what government agency did he make a report of his trek through Central America? Was he, as many critics have suggested, the

CIA's "baby-sitter" for Oswald? If so, why, and to whom was he reporting?

It will be surprising if Marina or De Mohrenschildt or any of Oswald's close friends knows much more about who committed the assassination than any other American. What they do know—what they have never fully revealed—is Lee. Guilty or innocent, Oswald, "this miserable creature," as more than one person remembered him, remains the central figure in the murder of John Fitzgerald Kennedy. If he was guilty, then others worked with him. If he was innocent, then somehow he was singled out. Why Lee Harvey Oswald? What was it about this unhappy, solitary man that put him at the center of this most infamous crime? Who were his friends? For whom did he work? What was his obsession with Cuba? The answers did not die with Oswald. There are those who know. These are the men who murdered Kennedy.

They will never be found, and questions about the assassination will remain unanswered, unless there is a new investigation. Congress will not launch that investigation on its own. It must be pressured, much as it was pressured into investigating Watergate. Citizen protest, and private lobbying such as that being conducted by a number of ad hoc assassination committees and commissions around the country, can play a valuable role in applying that pressure. But, because of their interested nature, such committees are automatically suspect. The professional Warren Commission critics are easily written off, however compelling the case they present. In the final analysis, it is up to the press—not the *National Tattler* or *Rolling Stone* or any of the various underground publications that have been calling for a new investigation, but the established media, the *New York Times,* the *Washington Post,* the newsmagazines and television networks—to do the kind of digging that will, as in Watergate, not solve the crime, but so arouse public indignation as to leave Congress and the Justice Department no other choice but to reopen the investigation of John Kennedy's murder.

One critic of the Warren Commission said recently:

"We are one Seymour Hersh story away from a new investigation." Would that it were that simple. A Hersh would be a help; so would a Woodward and Bernstein—so, in fact, would any anonymous reporter with the full backing of a news organization behind him. The old argument that all the facts have been gone over time and time again no longer washes, if indeed it ever did. The truth is that the press has never given the murder of the President of the United States the kind of attention it routinely accords to politicians it suspects of having their hands in the public purse. Some of these investigations consume months and the full-time energies of whole teams of reporters. The murder of the century merits at least that. Furthermore, since the time the press lost interest in the Kennedy case (namely, when Jim Garrison began investigating it), vast quantities of new information have been turned up, and more documents continue to be declassified every month. It is fair to say that with tiny exceptions none of this material has been scrutinized by the representatives of any major news-gathering organization. The reasons, of course, are plain: reporters don't like the smell of the Kennedy story, especially the people who push it. Seymour Hersh is right when he says that many of the critics are "extremely vituperative,"[76] quick to assume that anyone who doesn't see the conspiracy must therefore be part of it. That should hardly deter a tough reporter.

What the press can do is bring the new facts of the Kennedy case to light. It can pursue the leads that grow out of it, interview witnesses, use its contacts with law enforcement agencies to pry loose still more information. One of the handicaps of most critics is that they are more talmudic scholars than private detectives. They are confined to meticulous exegesis of the facts they find on paper. They are not, by and large, doorbell ringers and buttonholers. The press, however, is. Reporters may not be able to subpoena witnesses, grant immunity, and gain access to autopsy data and classified files (at least on most occasions), but they can begin to provide answers to some of the long unanswered questions. One place to start is with the available photographic record. United Press International still has in its possession the original copy of the Orville Nix film. The original print—not a second-generation copy—should be subjected to photoanalysis and image enhancement, and not by a company run by the Central Intelligence Agency. The same is true of the Abraham Zapruder film, a clear copy of which is still in the possession of Time Inc. (the original print was sold back to Zapruder's heirs in 1975, and they are withholding it from public viewing until a lucrative "commercial opportunity" presents itself),[77] as well as a movie film taken of the area in front of the Book Depository after the assassination (and which reportedly shows the famous light-colored station wagon leaving the scene of the crime), which is locked up in the vaults of CBS.[78] Possibly none of these films will reveal anything. Possibly, too, they may reveal something quite startling, even the presence of a second assassin. Their withholding from professional and public scrutiny is indefensible.

There is no guarantee that an "exhaustive"[79] investigation (the word the *Times* chose to describe the Warren Commission's labors) of the assassination by the press will bring results. Investigative reporting often brings in a dry hole. It is certain, though, that the press will never know until it tries.

Why try at all? Is it really worth the effort for anyone, press, Congress, or private citizens?

Twelve years have passed since John Kennedy was assassinated in Dallas. The truth of what happened on November 22, 1963, is, if only because of the passage of time, more obscured than ever. Many important witnesses have died, or been murdered. Those who planned the killing and those who carried it out may well be dead too. The likelihood of apprehending the actual assassins is exceedingly remote. If Oswald was murdered for fear that he would talk, the same fear would hold for the other members of the conspiracy. Simple prudence would seem to dictate that they are long since in their graves. If organized crime was involved, that possibility can be regarded as near certainty. The mob is not in the habit of leaving witnesses.

What is the value, then, of a new investigation, except to satisfy a lingering, morbid curiosity?

If it were only to sate curiosity, that would be reason enough. Curiosity, though, does not describe the gnawing that Americans have had in the pit of their stomachs since November 1963. The "dirty rumors" that the Warren Commission tried so desperately to squelch have become all too true. Little would surprise most Americans today, even the revelation that an agency of their government had a hand in killing the President of the United States. There is no integrity to be damaged. Somewhere between Dallas and Watergate it evaporated quite on its own. What the full facts about the Kennedy assassination might provide is a basis on which Americans' shattered confidence in themselves and their institutions can be rebuilt.

If institutions of government were involved in the assassination, or acted to cover it up, then those institutions ought to be exposed and reconstituted. There is a need for intelligence, as there is a need for an effective national law enforcement agency. Such agencies can only function efficiently if they have the people's trust. They do not warrant that trust unless the full facts of this, the most heinous crime in our recent history, are known. The CIA's alliance with organized crime has to end. Quite apart from the moral questions raised by a relationship with elements outside the law, so long as CIA relies on organized crime to do its bidding, organized crime will forever have the power of blackmail. The nation's security ought not to be entrusted to the likes of Johnny Roselli and Meyer Lansky. To end that reliance the CIA itself may have to end, to be replaced by a new agency that carries out the functions Harry Truman envisioned for the CIA in the National Security Act of 1947.

Those are the remedial reasons for a new investigation. There are also darker questions that need answering. John Kennedy is not the only American leader to have been assassinated in the last decade. Without stating that there were conspiracies involved in their deaths, Robert Kennedy and Martin Luther King both died under suspicious circumstances. In 1972 George

Wallace was gunned down by another supposed lone, deranged assassin. Wallace himself, however, continues to believe that he was the intended victim of a conspiracy. It is conceivable. A plot worked successfully once can be worked a second and a third time. The plots need not be linked, but they may be. However remote the possibility of such an occurrence, it needs the closest scrutiny, if only, someday in the future, to prevent a fourth killing.

Which brings us to the final reason for a new investigation: Edward M. Kennedy. In the past one of the most powerful arguments against the existence of a conspiracy in the murder of President Kennedy is that if one had existed, Robert Kennedy would surely have found it out. Various suppositions are offered on why he didn't. His grief, certainly, was overwhelming. According to his friends he functioned almost not at all while he remained in Johnson's cabinet. Others have suggested that it was fear for his own family that prevented Robert from pursuing his brother's killers, or that he was merely biding his time, waiting to gain the presidency and the power that would be his to root them out. None of these answers, true as they may be, are wholly satisfactory. Friends and close associates of the Kennedy family have from time to time encouraged various assassination investigators, and in private many of them make no secret of their contempt for the Warren Commission. Still, the surviving Kennedy brother has held back. As perhaps he should. Whatever Edward Kennedy's personal feelings about the death of his brother, though, they should have no bearing on a new investigation. John Kennedy's murder was more than a death in the family. He was the President of every American. He belonged to us all.

If one day Edward Kennedy should follow in his brothers' footsteps and seek the presidency, we should know the full facts of his brother's murder. What we know now only endangers him. For years the press has been full of predictions of how another lone, deranged assassin would find the temptation of killing the final Kennedy irresistible. This is nonsense, but no more nonsensical than the Warren Commission Report.

By believing it, we provide a future assassin with an alibi and a motive even before the act. For Edward Kennedy's sake and our own, there must be a new investigation.

The search for John Kennedy's killers has been a long and lonely one. Some of those who have done the best research, the deepest digging, are also the least confident that his murderers will ever be found. They are strangely obsessed people, many of them, as they should be after working in a grave the last dozen years. They have cause for their obsession as well as their pessimism. Each day that the assassination recedes in time further diminishes the prospects that the truth will ever be found. It would be easy to let go, to settle back, to forget, to resume John Kennedy's pledge "to move America forward." If his death were merely a murder, perhaps we could. The killing of a man, however, is not what brings people to Dealey Plaza and keeps the rest of us wondering. We are not pursuing death and deceit; we are searching for a bit of ourselves.

America today is a different country than it was in 1963. More of our leaders have been cut down. The red menace in Havana is now a benevolent curiosity. The dirty rumors have become fact. We ourselves are an altered people. What hasn't changed is the loss. We need to know why.

Source Notes

All references to "C.D." and "C.E." indicate that the text is reporting information contained in a document or exhibit filed with the Warren Commission.

INTRODUCTION

1. *New York Times,* April 26, 1974.
2. "A Matter of Reasonable Doubt," *Life,* Nov. 25, 1966.
3. Edward Jay Epstein, *Inquest* (New York: Viking Press, 1966), p. 43.
4. Ibid., pp. 149–50.
5. Interview with Dallas District Attorney Henry Wade, Dallas, Tex., July 1, 1975.
6. George O'Toole, *The Assassination Tapes* (New York: Penthouse Press, 1975), pp. 6–7.
7. Mark Lane, *Rush to Judgment* (New York: Holt, Rinehart and Winston, 1966), p. 37.
8. Edward Jay Epstein, *Counterplot* (New York: Viking Press, 1968), p. 148.
9. Cambridge Survey Research, July 1975.
10. *Report to the President by the Commission on CIA Activities Within the United States,* June 1975, pp. 134–49. (Hereafter referred to as *CIA Commission Report.*)
11. Ibid., pp. 101–16.
12. *New York Times,* Aug. 31, 1975.
13. *CIA Commission Report,* pp. 240–50.
14. *The Senate Watergate Report, Volume I* (New York: Dell Publishing Co., 1974), pp. 53–55.
15. *New York Times,* March 10, 1975.
16. Ibid., Sept. 7, 1975.
17. Arthur Schlesinger, *The Imperial Presidency* (New York: Popular Library, 1974), p. 167.
18. *New York Times,* May 9, 1974.
19. Ibid., June 8, 1974; May 17, 1975.
20. *Congressional Quarterly,* "Report of Impeachment Proceedings," July 27, 1974.
21. *New York Times,* May 24, 1975.
22. *The Watergate Hearings: Break-in and Cover-up* (New York: Bantam Books, 1973), p. 521.
23. William Attwood, *The Reds and the Blacks* (New York: Harper & Row, 1967), p. 146.
24. Ibid., p. 147.
25. White House Statement, October 2, 1963, in *Public Papers of the Presidents, John F. Kennedy, 1963* (Washington, D.C.: U.S. Government Printing Office, 1964), pp. 759–60; cited by Peter Dale Scott, "The Dallas Conspiracy" (unpublished ms.), chap. 10, p. 1.
26. Tom Wicker, *JFK and LBJ: The Influence of Personality on Politics* (New York: William Morrow & Co., 1968), p. 183.
27. Ibid., p. 185.
28. Roger Hilsman, *To Move a Nation* (Garden City, N.Y.: Doubleday & Co., 1967), p. 68.
29. Harry Rowe Ransom, "Containing Central Intelligence," *New Republic,* Dec. 11, 1965.
30. Interview with Frank McCulloch, managing editor, *Sacramento Bee,* Sacramento, Calif., April 11, 1975.

31. Robert F. Kennedy, *The Enemy Within* (New York: Harper & Row, 1960), p. 265.
32. Harold Willens memorandum to J. Lee Rankin, Feb. 26, 1964 (National Archives, Washington, D.C.)

CHAPTER 1

1. Jesse Curry, *Assassination File* (Dallas: American Printing & Poster Co., 1969), p. 7.
2. Ibid., p. 23.
3. Arthur Schlesinger *A Thousand Days* (Boston: Houghton Mifflin, 1965), pp. 1021–22.
4. *Report of the Warren Commission on the Assassination of President Kennedy* (New York: Bantam Books, Inc., 1964), pp. 47–48. (Hereafter referred to as *Report.*)
5. Ibid., pp. 54–55.
6. Ibid., p. 48.
7. Ibid.
8. Curry, *Assassination File*, pp. 10–11.
9. Schlesinger, *A Thousand Days*, p. 1020.
10. Ibid., p. 1021.
11. Curry, *Assassination File*, p. 19.
12. Schlesinger, *A Thousand Days*, p. 1024.
13. Ibid.
14. *Report*, p. 125.
15. Ibid., p. 372.
16. Ibid., p. 375.
17. Ibid., p. 392.
18. Ibid., p. 379.
19. Ibid., p. 397.
20. Ibid., p. 125.
21. Ibid.
22. 3 H. (Hearings) 20. (I.e., p. 20 of vol. 3, *Hearings Before the President's Commission on the Assassination of President Kennedy* [Washington, D.C.: Government Printing Office, 1964, 26. vol.])
23. *Report*, p. 145.
24. 19 H. 483; cited by Mark Lane in *Rush to Judgment*, p. 29.
25. Interview with Jones Harris, New York City, Aug. 3, 1975. (Harris worked in New Orleans with Garrison during the Shaw investigation.)
26. *Report*, p. 132.
27. C.D. 735, pp. 296–97.
28. *Report*. p. 132.
29. Curry, *Assassination File*, p. 25.
30. *Report*, pp. 57–60.
31. Ibid., p. 56.
32. C.D. 5.
33. 6 H. 286.
34. Ibid.
35. 24 H. 201.
36. 7 H. 570; cited by Josiah Thompson, *Six Seconds in Dallas* (New York: Bernard Geis Associates, 1967), p. 3.
37. Thompson, *Six Seconds in Dallas*, p. 5.
38. 24 H. 522.
39. 6 H. 193.
40. Ibid.
41. 2 H. 169.
42. *Report*, pp. 63–65.
43. William Manchester, *The Death of a President* (New York: Harper & Row, 1967), p. 154.
44. 5 H. 179.
45. 4 H. 147.
46. "A Matter of Reasonable Doubt," *Life*, Nov. 25, 1966.
47. Ibid., p. 47.
48. 4 H. 147.
49. 24 H. 542.
50. Ibid.
51. 4 H. 473.
52. *Report*, p. 79.
53. Ibid.
54. Ibid.
55. 2 H. 155–65; 19 H. 517; 24 H. 117.

56. 2 H. 159.
57. Thompson, *Six Seconds in Dallas*, p. 6.
58. 24 H. 150–202.
59. 21 H. 548.
60. 18 H. 762; 2 H. 118, 76, 44; cited by Thompson in *Six Seconds in Dallas*, pp. 97, 82.
61. Manchester, *The Death of a President*, p. 160.
62. Ibid., p. 161.
63. *New York Daily News*, Nov. 24, 1963.
64. Thompson, *Six Seconds in Dallas*, p. 126.
65. 7 H. 555.
66. Thompson, *Six Seconds in Dallas*, p. 83.
67. 6 H. 244.
68. Interview by Josiah Thompson, Nov. 30, 1966; cited in *Six Seconds in Dallas*. p. 122.
69. 19 H. 492.
70. 7 H. 535.
71. C.D. 205.
72. 7 H. 535.
73. 18 H. 722–99.
74. 6 H. 287.
75. Ibid.
76. Lane, *Rush to Judgment*, p. 32.
77. Maurice Schoenfeld, "The Shadow of a Gunman," *Columbia Journalism Review*, July–Aug. 1975.
78. The "umbrella man" appears in a number of films and pictures taken before, during, and after the assassination, most notably in the Zapruder film, beginning at frame 210. See Robert Groden, "A New Look at the Zapruder Film," *Rolling Stone*, April 24, 1975, p. 36.
79. Thompson, *Six Seconds in Dallas*, pp. 227–28.
80. The *Report* states that Oswald bought the Coke after being accosted by the police officer (*Report*, pp. 141–42). However, this scenario is contradicted by the account given to reporters on Nov. 23, 1963, by Dallas Police Chief Jesse Curry. See Sylvia Meagher, *Accessories After the Fact* (Indianapolis: Bobbs-Merrill Co., 1967), pp. 73–74.
81. *Report*, p. 141.
82. C.E. 2168.
83. *Report*, pp. 147–51.
84. Ibid., pp. 151–52.
85. Ibid., p. 152.
86. 22 H. 632–86.
87. 20 H. 499.
88. Thompson, *Six Seconds in Dallas*, p. 132.
89. Peter Noyes, *Legacy of Doubt* (New York: Pinnacle Books, 1973), pp. 33–36.
90. Statement by "Jim Braden" to Dallas Sheriff's Office. Nov. 22, 1963; cited by Noyes, *Legacy of Doubt*, pp. 21–22.
91. Noyes, *Legacy of Doubt*, p. 30.
92. Ibid., p. 22.
93. *Report*, p. 84.
94. Ibid.
95. C.D. 354.
96. Ibid.
97. 16 H. 959.
98. C.D. 385.
99. Ibid.
100. Ibid.
101. C.D. 5.
102. Manchester, *The Death of a President*, p. 162.
103. Statement of Texas State Trooper Hurchel Jacks, Nov. 28, 1963.
104. Manchester, *The Death of a President*, p. 171.
105. *Report*, p. 66.
106. Ibid.
107. Curry, *Assassination File*, p. 34.
108. Ibid.
109. Ibid.
110. Ibid., p. 35.
111. *Dallas Times Herald*, Nov. 24, 1963.
112. *Report*, p. 68.
113. 15 H. 80.
114. 7 H. 439.
115. 6 H. 439.
116. 6 H. 443–44.
117. Meagher, *Accessories After the Fact*, p. 264.

118. C.E. 705.
119. Ibid.
120. Ibid.
121. Ibid.
122. *Report*, p. 155.
123. Lane, *Rush to Judgment*, p. 194.
124. Ibid., p. 124.
125. 6 H. 477.
126. Ibid.
127. 6 H. 450.
128. Ibid.
129. 6 H. 452.
130. Testimony of William Scoggins to the Warren Commission; cited by David Belin, *November 22, 1963: You Are the Jury* (New York: Quadrangle Books, 1973), pp. 54–60.
131. Ibid.
132. Ibid.
133. Ibid.
134. 24 H. 202.
135. 6 H. 393.
136. Ibid.
137. C.E. 1974, p. 59.
138. Ibid.
139. Belin, *November 22, 1963: You Are the Jury*, p. 28.
140. *Report*, p. 165.
141. Belin, *November 22, 1963: You Are the Jury*, p. 24.
142. *Report*, p. 165.
143. Ibid.
144. Ibid.
145. Ibid.
146. Belin, *November 22, 1963: You Are the Jury*, p. 25.
147. Ibid.
148. Ibid., p. 26.
148a. O'Toole, *The Assassination Tapes*, p. 230n.
149. Manchester, *The Death of a President*, p. 287.
150. Belin, *November 22, 1963: You Are the Jury*, p. 28.
151. Ibid., p. 32.
152. N. M. McDonald, "Officer Recalls Capture," *Dallas Morning News*, Nov. 24, 1963, p. 13.
153. Ibid.
154. Ibid.
155. *Report*, p. 165.
156. Belin, *November 22, 1963: You Are the Jury*, p. 33.
157. N. M. McDonald, "Officer Recalls Capture," *Dallas Morning News*, Nov. 24, 1963, p. 13.
158. *Report*, p. 165.
159. Ibid., p. 166.
160. Ibid.
161. Ibid.
162. Belin, *November 22, 1963: You Are the Jury*, p. 27.

CHAPTER 2

1. Melvin Eisenberg memo, Feb. 17, 1964; cited by Harold Weisberg, *Whitewash IV* (privately published at Frederick, Md., 1975), p. 24.
2. *New York Times*, Sept. 28, 1964.
3. Eisenberg memo, Feb. 17, 1964.
4. Ibid.
5. *Report*, p. 450.
6. Interview with Murray Kempton, New York City, April 12, 1975.
7. *Transcript*, Warren Commission Executive Session, Dec. 5, 1963.
8. Epstein, *Inquest*, p. 33.
9. Ibid.
10. Ibid., p. 7.
11. *Report*, pp. 451–52.
12. Epstein, *Inquest*, p. 8.
13. *Transcript*, Warren Commission Executive Session, Jan. 22, 1964.
14. Ibid.
15. Ibid.
16. Ibid.
17. Ibid.

18. Ibid.
19. *Rolling Stone,* April 24, 1975, p. 30; *New York Times,* Nov. 6, 1973, p. 22.
20. Ibid.
21. 5 H. 13.
22. Epstein, *Inquest,* p. 38.
23. Ibid.
24. Ibid., p. 29.
25. Ibid., p. 33.
26. Ibid., p. 12.
27. FBI Summary Report on the Assassination of President Kennedy, Dec. 9, 1963.
28. *Report,* p. 112.
29. Thompson, *Six Seconds in Dallas,* p. 78.
30. Epstein, *Inquest,* p. 115.
31. *Report,* p. 178–79.
32. KGB file on Lee Harvey Oswald provided by Yuri Nosenko (National Archives, Washington, D.C.).
33. *Report,* p. 181.
34. Ibid.
35. Ibid.
36. Epstein, *Inquest,* p. 45.
37. 3 H. 444.
38. 3 H. 441–51.
39. Thompson, *Six Seconds in Dallas,* p. 152.
40. C.E. 856.
41. "A Matter of Reasonable Doubt," *Life,* Nov. 25, 1966.
42. *Report,* p. 109.
43. Ibid.
44. 24 H. 542; 18 H. 744; 2 H. 143.
45. C.E. 59; C.E. 60.
46. C.E. 397.
47. Epstein, *Inquest,* p. 55; Thompson, *Six Seconds in Dallas,* pp. 222–23.
48. Epstein, *Inquest,* pp. 149–50.
49. Ibid., p. 149.
50. Ibid., p. 150.
51. *Report,* pp. 38–39.
52. Lane, *Rush to Judgment,* p. 37.
53. Ibid., p. 32.
54. 20 H. 163.
55. 20 H. 245–46.
56. *Report,* p. 82.
57. 5 H. 255; cited by Lane, *Rush to Judgment,* p. 392.
58. 5 H. 255–56.
59. 5 H. 256.
60. Lane, *Rush to Judgment,* p. 37.
61. Ibid.
62. Ibid., pp. 29–30.
63. Epstein, *Inquest,* pp. 69–71.
64. *Report,* p. 49.
65. 5 H. 35; C.E. 709; 17 H. 495.
66. *Report,* p. 417.
67. Ibid., p. 423.
68. Ibid., p. 424.
69. Ibid.
70. Ibid., p. 423.
71. Ibid., p. 424.
72. Ibid.
73. Interview with Col. Fletcher Prouty, USAF (ret.), Washington, D.C., April 1, 1975.
74. *Report,* p. 426.
75. Ibid.
76. Ibid., p. 427.
77. The position of the Secret Service follow-up car as the motorcade drove up Houston Street is clearly shown in the Mary Muchmore film (National Archives, Washington, D.C.) taken at the time of the assassination.
78. The position of the Secret Service follow-up car as the motorcade headed down Elm Street is clearly shown in the Zapruder film.
79. *Report,* p. 429.
80. Groden, "A New Look at the Zapruder Film," *Rolling Stone,* April 24, 1975, p. 36.
81. Ibid.

82. Ibid.
83. *New York Herald Tribune*, May 22, 1964; cited by Lane in *Rush to Judgment*, p. 275.
84. *New York Herald Tribune*, May 22, 1964.
85. Belin, *November 22, 1963: You Are the Jury*, p. 466.
86. Lane, *Rush to Judgment*, p. 176.
87. *Report*, p. 155; 3 H. 320.
88. 3 H. 307.
89. 6 H. 456–59; 7 H. 272, 273–74.
90. Lane, *Rush to Judgment*, p. 180.
91. 7 H. 252.
92. *Report*, p. 157.
93. Comment by Commission lawyer Joseph Ball, Beverly Hills, Calif., Dec. 4, 1964; quoted by Lane in *Rush to Judgment*, p. 190.
94. *Report*, p. 581.
95. Ibid., p. 157.
96. C.E. 705, p. 30.
97. C.D., 5, p. 329.
98. Sylvia Meagher, "The Curious Testimony of Mr. Givens," *Texas Observer*, Aug. 13, 1971.
99. 6 H. 345–56.
100. C.D. 735; Meagher, "The Curious Testimony of Mr. Givens," *Texas Observer*, Aug. 13, 1971.
101. *Report*, p. 370.
102. Ibid., p. 626.
103. Ibid., pp. 674–75.
104. 1 H. 32.
105. 5 H. 594.
106. 1 H. 119.
107. 5 H. 611.
108. *Report*, p. 174.
109. C.D. 344.
110. 1 H. 16.
111. 1 H. 16; 5 H. 387–88.
112. 1 H. 123.
113. 18 H. 641.
114. 5 H. 607.
115. Epstein, *Inquest*, p. 97.
116. Ibid., p. 96.
117. Ibid.
118. Ibid.
119. Ibid., pp. 96–97.
120. Ibid., p. 96.
121. Ibid., pp. 129–130.
122. Ibid., p. 137.
123. Ibid., pp. 138–39.
124. Ibid., pp. 141–46.
125. Ibid., p. 139.
126. Ibid., pp. 135–36.
127. Ibid., p. 136.
128. Ibid., pp. 135–36.
129. Ibid., p. 136.
130. Ibid., pp. 135, 136.
131. Ibid., p. 135.
132. Ibid.
133. Ibid., pp. 137–38.
134. Ibid., pp. 146–47.
135. Ibid., p. 147.
136. Ibid.
137. Stuckey Exhibit 3.
138. 2 H. 408.
139. 5 H. 610.
140. Epstein, *Inquest*, p. 152.
141. Ibid.
142. Ibid.
143. *Report*, p. 399.
144. Statement of Lee Harvey Oswald to CBS reporter, Nov. 22, 1963; cited by O'Toole, *The Assassination Tapes*, p. 125.
145. *Report*, p. 399.
146. Ibid.
147. Ibid.
148. Manchester, *The Death of a President*, p. 104.
149. Hartogs Exhibit 1.
150. 10 H. 60–1.

151. 5 H. 105.
152. C.E. 2146.
153. Meagher, *Accessories After the Fact,* p. 246.
154. C.E. 2162.
155. 7 H. 330.
156. Statements on Oswald's mental competence cited by Meagher, *Accessories After the Fact,* p. 246.
157. Lane, *Rush to Judgment,* p. 194.
158. Meagher, *Accessories After the Fact,* p. 293.
159. Ibid., pp. 293–94.
160. Ibid., p. 299.
161. Ibid.
162. Ibid.
163. Ibid.
164. Ibid.
165. Ibid.
166. Ibid.
167. Ibid.
168. Ibid.
169. Ibid.
170. Ibid.
171. Ibid.
172. Ibid.
173. Ibid., p. 301.
174. *London Sunday Times,* Feb. 26, 1967; cited by Meagher, *Accessories After the Fact,* p. 302.
175. Epstein, *Inquest,* p. 24.
176. *New York Times,* June 1, 1964.
177. Epstein, *Inquest,* p. 177.
178. Ibid., p. 26.
179. Ibid., pp. 101–3.
180. Ibid., pp. 93–95.
181. Ibid., p. 26.
182. Ibid.
183. *Report,* p. 27.
184. Epstein, *Inquest,* p. 27.
185. Ibid., pp. 24, 27.
186. *New York Herald Tribune,* Dec. 18, 1964.

CHAPTER 3

1. Interview with Jean Highland, Bantam Books, New York City, Aug. 14, 1975.
2. Telephone interview with Government Printing Office, Oct. 20, 1975.
3. Harrison Salisbury, "An Introduction to the Warren Commission Report," *Report,* p. xxiv.
4. Ibid.
5. Ibid.
6. Ibid., p. xxv.
7. Ibid.
8. Ibid.
9. Interview with Mark Lane, Washington, D.C., Aug. 22, 1975.
10. Ibid.
11. Mark Lane, *A Citizen's Dissent/Mark Lane Replies* (New York: Holt, Rinehart and Winston, 1968), p. 4.
12. Ibid., p. 9.
13. Ibid., p. 183; Markham Deposition Exhibit 1; 7 H. 499–506.
14. Ibid.
15. 5 H. 53.
16. Lane, p. 182.
17. Declassified correspondence from Lewis W. Powell to J. Lee Rankin, April 17, 1964, Mark Lane file (National Archives, Washington, D.C.).
18. Lane, *Rush to Judgment,* p. 183; Markham Deposition Exhibit 1; 7 H. 499–506; *Report,* pp. 157, 582.
19. Harold Willens memorandum to J. Lee Rankin, Feb. 26, 1964 (National Archives, Washington, D.C.).
21. *Washington Post,* Jan. 21, 1975.
22. Interview with Warren Commission critic, Washington, D.C., Aug. 26, 1975.
23. Interview with Mark Lane, Washington, D.C., Aug. 22, 1975.
24. Lane, *A Citizen's Dissent/Mark Lane Replies,* p. 43.

25. Epstein, *Inquest*, p. xviii.
26. *Report*, p. 114.
27. Ibid.
28. Ibid.
29. C.E. 2694.
30. *Report*, p. 86.
31. 4 H. 29.
32. John P. Conlon, letter to the editor of *Analog*, June 1964; cited by Meagher, *Accessories After the Fact*, p. 101.
33. Jack O'Connor, *The Rifle Book* (1949), p. 62; cited by Lane, *Rush to Judgment*, p. 133.
34. C.E. 2974.
35. *Report*, p. 181.
36. Lane, *Rush to Judgment*, p. 116.
37. Letter from H. J. Gebelein, assistant sales service manager, Winchester-Western Division, Olin Mathieson Chemical Corp., East Alton, Ill., to Stewart Galanor, Riverdale, N.Y., July 14, 1965.
38. Letter from H. J. Gebelein, Winchester-Western Division, Olin Mathieson Chemical Corp., to Sylvia Meagher, April 20, 1965.
39. 26 H. 104.
40. *Report*, p. 182.
41. C.E. 2560.
42. C.E. 2562; cited by Meagher, *Accessories After the Fact*, p. 105.
43. Meagher, *Accessories After the Fact*, p. 48.
44. C.E. 1303.
45. 5 H. 611.
46. 3 H. 25.
47. *Report*, pp. 116–18.
48. 4 H. 81.
49. C.E. 2003.
50. C.E. 1403.
51. C.E. 2694.
52. C.E. 2003.
53. 3 H. 479.
54. 4 H. 253, 258–60.
55. C.E. cited by Thompson, *Six Seconds in Dallas*, p. 144.
56. Thompson, *Six Seconds in Dallas*, pp. 143–45.
57. Ibid., p. 145.
58. C.E. 2003, p. 63.
59. Ibid.
60. 7 H. 108.
61. 5 H. 560–61.
62. *Report*, pp. 174–75.
63. C.E. 1953.
64. *Dallas Morning News*, April 11, 1963, p. 1; *New York Times*, April 12, 1963, p. 12; *Newsweek*, April 22, 1963; cited by Peter Dale Scott in "The Dallas Conspiracy" (unpublished ms.).
65. C.E. 133A; C.E. 133B.
66. *Report*, p. 120.
67. *Life*, Feb. 21, 1964.
68. *Report*, p. 545.
68a. Ibid., p. 168.
69. 1 H. 16.
70. Interview with Rusty Rhoades, Committee to Investigate Political Assassinations, Bronx, N.Y., March 29, 1975.
71. Letter to author from Edward Tatro, Braintree, Mass., April 11, 1975.
72. Meagher, *Accessories After the Fact*, p. 208.
73. Ibid.
74. Interview with Rusty Rhoades, Bronx, N.Y. March 10, 1975.
75. Lewis (Aubrey L.) Exhibit 1.
76. Interview with Rusty Rhoades, Bronx, N.Y., March 29, 1975.
77. Meagher, *Accessories After the Fact*, p. 208.
78. Ibid.
79. *Report*, pp. 543–47.
80. Ibid., pp. 84–112; C.E. 399.
81. *Report*, pp. 101–12.
82. Ibid., p. 85.
83. 6 H. 126–31.
84. 6 H. 129.
85. *Report*, p. 85.
86. Ibid., pp. 108–9.
87. Interview with Dr. Cyril Wecht, New York City, April 26, 1975.
88. Cf. C.E. 572.

89. Thompson, *Six Seconds in Dallas,* p. 151.
90. C.E. 856; C.E. 853; CE. 857.
91. 2 H. 376; 4 H. 113; 2 H. 374–75; 4 H. 114.
92. 2 H. 374–75.
93. C.E. 392; Jones (Dr. Ronald) Exhibit 1.
94. 6 H. 54.
95. 2 H. 73; 18 H. 724.
96. 2 H. 74–75.
97. *New Times,* May 11, 1975.
98. Ibid.
99. Statement by George Hunt, managing editor of *Life;* cited by Thompson, *Six Seconds in Dallas,* pp. 217–18.
100. Ibid.
101. Ibid.
102. Thompson, *Six Seconds in Dallas,* p. 90.
103. *Report,* p. 62.
104. Meagher, *Accessories After the Fact,* p. 22.
105. Thompson, *Six Seconds in Dallas,* pp. 178–95.
106. Bernard Geis, Introduction to *Six Seconds in Dallas,* p. xviii.
107. Interview with Robert Groden, New York City, March 15, 1975.
108. *Report,* p. 62.
109. Ibid., p. 112.
110. Ibid.
111. Ibid., pp. 110–11.
112. Ibid., p. 102.
113. "A Matter of Reasonable Doubt," *Life,* Nov. 25, 1966.
114. Thompson, *Six Seconds in Dallas,* p. 70; 4 H. 114, 128.
115. *Life,* Nov. 25, 1966.
116. *Report,* p. 109.
117. Ibid., pp. 108–9.
118. 4 H. 104.
119. Thompson, *Six Seconds in Dallas,* p. 77.
120. *Life,* Nov. 25, 1966.
121. Thompson, *Six Seconds in Dallas,* p. 111.
122. 2 H. 76, 118; 18 H. 762; 6 H. 207.
123. Dr. A. J. Riddle, assistant professor of physics, University of California at Los Angeles; cited by Thompson, *Six Seconds in Dallas,* p. 94.
124. *CIA Commission Report,* p. 262.
125. *Boston Globe,* June 29, 1975.
126. *CIA Commission Report,* p. 262.
127. 3 H. 429, 499–500.
128. C.E. 842.
129. *Report,* p. 87.
130. Letters from J. Edgar Hoover to J. Lee Rankin, July 8, 1964; cited by Cyril Wecht, "JFK Assassination: 'A Prolonged and Willful Coverup,'" *Modern Medicine,* Oct. 28, 1974.
131. Ibid.
132. Wecht, "JFK Assassination: 'A Prolonged and Willful Coverup,'" *Modern Medicine,* Oct. 28, 1974.
133. Telephone interview with Robert Lifton, Sept. 22, 1975.
134. Howard Roffman, *Presumed Guilty* (Cranbury, N.J.: Associated University Presses, 1975), pp. 108–20.
135. C.D. 5.
136. Ibid.
137. C.D. 7.
138. C.D. 5.
139. 5 H. 172–73.
140. Thompson, *Six Seconds in Dallas,* p. 55.
141. *Report,* pp. 69–70.
142. Ibid.
143. Marshall Houts, *Where Death Delights* (New York: Coward-McCann, 1967), p. 64.
144. *Report,* p. 67.
145. *New York World-Telegram and Sun,* Nov. 23, 1963; *New York Times,* Nov. 24, 1963; *New York Post,* Nov. 24, 1963; cited by Meagher, *Accessories After the Fact,* p. 134.
146. *Report,* p. 91.
147. 2 H. 348.
148. Cyril H. Wecht, "A Critique of President Kennedy's Autopsy," Appendix D, Thompson, *Six Seconds in Dallas,* p. 278.
149. Ibid.
150. Interview with Dallas District Attorney Henry Wade, Dallas, Tex., July 1, 1975.

151. Quoted by Cyril H. Wecht, interview with Wecht, New York City, April 26, 1975.
152. Houts, *Where Death Delights*, p. 55.
153. Interview with Cyril Wecht, New York City, April 26, 1975.
154. C.D. 7, p. 4.
155. James Kirkwood, *American Grotesque* (New York: Simon and Schuster, 1968), p. 381.
156. C.E. 397.
157. C.E. 59; C.E. 60.
158. 2 H. 127, 81; 24 H. 542.
159. 18 H. 744; 2 H. 143.
160. C.D. 7.,
161. *Transcript*, Warren Commission Executive Session Jan. 27, 1964.
162. *Report*, p. 573.
163. C.E. 397.
164. Meagher, *Accessories After the Fact*, p. 141.
165. *New York Times*, Nov. 25, 1966.
166. C.E. 397, p. 47.
167. 2 H. 365.
168. Cited by Meagher, *Accessories After the Fact*, p. 139.
169. *CIA Commission Report*, pp. 259–61.
170. *New York Times*, Aug. 27, 1972.
171. Ibid.
172. Ibid.
173. Ibid.
174. Ibid.

CHAPTER 4

1. Rosemary James and Jack Wardlaw, *Plot or Politics* (New Orleans: Pelican Books, 1967), p. 34.
2. Ibid.
3. *Report*, pp. 645–47.
4. *New York Times*, Feb. 25, 1967.
5. 10 H. 33–34, 82–83.
6. "Interview: Jim Garrison," *Playboy*, Oct. 1967.
7. *Garrison* v. *Louisiana*, 379 U.S. 64 (1964).
8. Warren Rogers, "The Persecution of Clay Shaw," *Look*, Aug. 26, 1969.
9. William W. Turner, "The Garrison Commission on the Assassination of President Kennedy," *Ramparts*, Jan. 1968, p. 46.
10. Epstein, *Counterplot*, p. 43.
11. Ibid., p. 46.
12. Paris Flammonde, *The Kennedy Conspiracy* (New York: Meredith Press, 1969), p. 19.
13. *Playboy*, Oct. 1967.
14. *New York Times*, March 26, 1974; Dec. 15, 1973.
15. Epstein, *Counterplot*, p. 74.
16. Ibid., p. 23.
17. Noyes, *Legacy of Doubt*, p. 96.
18. Ibid., p. 30.
19. Epstein, *Counterplot*, p. 35.
20. Richard H. Popkin, "Garrison's Case," *New York Review of Books*, Sept. 14, 1967, p. 28.
21. Interview with Mark Lane, Washington, D.C., April 20, 1975.
22. James and Wardlaw, *Plot or Politics*, p. 72.
23. Epstein, *Counterplot*, p. 35.
24. *Playboy*, Oct. 1967, p. 59.
25. Epstein, *Counterplot*, p. 37.
26. *New York Times*, April 6, 1961.
27. Epstein, *Counterplot*, p. 37.
28. Turner, "The Garrison Commission on the Assassination of President Kennedy," *Ramparts*, Jan. 1968, p. 46.
29. Ibid., p. 47.
30. Ibid., p. 46.
31. *New Orleans Times-Picayune*, Feb. 27, 1967.
32. Epstein, *Counterplot*, p. 37.
33. Turner, "The Garrison Commission on the Assassination of President Kennedy," *Ramparts*, Jan. 1968, p. 47.
34. James A. Autry, "The Garrison Investigation: How and Why It Began," *New Orleans*, April 1967, p. 8.
35. Epstein, *Counterplot*, p. 39.

36. 9 H. 326–39.
37. 9 H. 331.
38. Epstein, *Counterplot,* p. 41.
39. Ibid.
40. Ibid., p. 42.
41. 22 H. 826.
42. 8 H. 14; 22 H. 826–27.
43. Epstein, *Counterplot,* p. 40.
44. Turner, "The Garrison Commission on the Assassination of President Kennedy," *Ramparts,* Jan. 1968.
45. Epstein, *Counterplot,* p. 40.
46. Ibid.
47. Ibid.
48. Ibid., p. 44.
49. Ibid., p. 111.
50. Interview with Gordon Novel, Dallas, Tex., July 9, 1975.
51. Transcript of Preliminary Hearing, Russo Testimony, p. 188.
52. Epstein, *Counterplot,* pp. 48–49.
52a. Ibid., p. 49.
53. Ibid.
54. James Phelan, "Rush to Judgment in New Orleans," *Saturday Evening Post,* Aug. 26, 1969.
55. Epstein, *Counterplot,* p. 50.
56. Ibid., p. 57.
57. Ibid., p. 49.
58. Ibid., p. 46.
59. *New Orleans Times-Picayune,* Feb. 26, 1967.
60. Epstein, *Counterplot,* pp. 67–69.
61. *New Orleans Times-Picayune,* June 24, 1967.
62. Interview with Mark Lane, Washington, D.C., April 20, 1965.
63. Kirkwood, *American Grotesque,* p. 179.
64. "Lane: I Know the Assassin," *New York Post,* March 21, 1967, p. 14.
65. Epstein, *Counterplot,* p. 68.
66. Interview with Jones Harris, New York City, June 12, 1975 (Harris was present at the dinner with Popkin and Garrison).
67. Dick Russell, "'Dear President Ford: I Know Who Killed JFK . . .,'" *Village Voice,* Sept. 1, 1975.
68. Interview with Penn Jones, New York City, April 26, 1975; Epstein, *Counterplot,* p. 68.
69. Interview with Jones Harris, New York City, June 12, 1975.
70. Ibid.
71. Ibid.
72. Epstein, *Counterplot,* p. 38.
73. *Playboy,* Oct. 1967, p. 59.
74. *Chicago Tribune,* Dec. 30, 1967.
75. Ibid.
76. Interview with Mark Lane, Washington, D.C., April 20, 1975.
77. Epstein, *Counterplot,* p. 45.
78. Kirkwood, *American Grotesque,* p. 26.
79. Epstein, *Counterplot,* p. 71.
80. Ibid., p. 70.
81. Ibid., p. 96.
82. Ibid., p. 133.
83. *New Orleans Times-Picayune,* Sept. 5, 1967.
84. Rogers, "The Persecution of Clay Shaw," *Look,* Aug. 26, 1969, p. 56.
85. Ibid., p. 54.
86. *New York Times,* May 5, 1967.
87. Kirkwood, *American Grotesque,* p. 20.
88. Ibid., p. 21.
89. Ibid.
90. Ibid., p. 22.
91. Ibid., p. 158.
92. Phelan, "Rush to Judgment in New Orleans," *Saturday Evening Post,* Aug. 26, 1969.
93. Popkin, "Garrison's Case," *New York Review of Books,* Sept. 14, 1967.
93a. Walter Sheridan, *The Fall and Rise of Jimmy Hoffa* (New York: Saturday Review Press, 1973), p. 377.
94. Ibid., p. 420.
95. NBC, "The JFK Conspiracy: The Case of Jim Garrison," June 19, 1967.
96. Edward Jay Epstein, "The Final Chapter in the Assassination Controversy?" *New York Times Magazine,* April 20, 1969.
97. *Washington Post,* Feb. 11, 1969.

98. Ibid.
99. *Los Angeles Times,* Feb. 27, 1969.
100. *New York Times,* Aug. 14, 1974.
101. Ibid.
102. Kirkwood, *American Grotesque,* p. 232.
103. Ibid.
104. Ibid., p. 235.
105. Ibid., p. 240.
106. Ibid.
107. Ibid., p. 649.
107a. Jack Anderson column, Feb. 23, 1970.
108. *New York Times,* Sept. 28, 1973.
109. Ibid., March 27, 1974.
110. Ibid., Dec. 15, 1973.
111. Ibid., Aug. 14, 1974.
112. Kirkwood, *American Grotesque,* p. 379.
113. Ibid., p. 380.
114. Ibid.
115. Ibid., p. 381.
116. Ibid.
117. Ibid.
118. Ibid., p. 383.
119. Ibid.
120. Ibid., p. 213.
121. Ibid., p. 214.
122. Ibid.
123. Ibid.
124. Ibid., p. 215.
125. Ibid., p. 216.
126. Warren Rogers, "The Persecution of Clay Shaw," *Look,* Aug. 26, 1969.
127. Transcript, Bernard Fensterwald interview with William G. Gaudet, Waveland, Miss., May 13, 1975.
128. Ibid.
129. Telephone interview with Victor Marchetti, former executive assistant to the director, Central Intelligence Agency, June 25, 1975.
130. Ibid.
131. Harold Weisberg, *Oswald in New Orleans* (New York: Canyon Books, 1967), p. 175.
132. Commission Document, cited by Weisberg, *Oswald in New Orleans,* p. 184.
133. Ibid.
134. Epstein, *Counterplot,* p. 36.
135. James and Wardlaw, *Plot or Politics,* p. 45.
136. Epstein, *Counterplot,* p. 36.
136a. Michael J. Canfield and Alan J. Weberman, *Coup d'État in America* (New York: Third World Press, 1975), p. 36; C.D. 87, p. 3.
137. E. Howard Hunt, *Give Us This Day* (New York: Arlington House, 1973), pp. 44, 183.
138. Epstein, *Counterplot,* pp. 36–37.
139. Ibid.
140. Ibid., p. 37.
707. Turner, "The Garrison Commission on the Assassination of President Kennedy," *Ramparts,* Jan. 1968, p. 48.
142. Ibid., p. 47.
143. Epstein, *Counterplot,* p. 10.
144. Ibid.
145. Turner, "The Garrison Commission on the Assassination of President Kennedy," *Ramparts,* Jan. 1968, p. 47.
146. Ibid.
147. *New Orleans States-Item,* April 25, 1967.
148. Canfield and Weberman, *Coup d'État in America,* p. 36.
149. Turner, "The Garrison Commission on the Assassination of President Kennedy," *Ramparts,* Jan. 1968, p. 47.
150. Ibid.
151. Ibid.
152. Ibid.
153. Scott, "The Dallas Conspiracy (unpublished ms.), chap. 2, p. 12.
154. E. Howard Hunt, *Undercover* (New York: Berkley Putnam, 1974), pp. 96–97.
155. Scott, "The Dallas Conspiracy" (unpublished ms.), chap. 2, p. 12.
156. Turner, "The Garrison Commission on the Assassination of President Kennedy," *Ramparts,* Jan. 1968, p. 48.

157. Ibid.
158. C.D. 75.
159. Rogers, "The Persecution of Clay Shaw," *Look,* Aug. 26, 1969.
160. Ibid.
161. Sheridan, *The Fall and Rise of Jimmy Hoffa,* p. 417.
162. *Life,* Sept. 8, 1967, p. 96; Sheridan, *The Fall and Rise of Jimmy Hoffa,* p. 431.
163. Ed Reid, *The Grim Reapers* (Chicago: Henry Regnery Co., 1969), p. 153.
164. James Phelan, "The Vice Man Cometh," *Saturday Evening Post,* June 8, 1963.
165. Sheridan, *The Fall and Rise of Jimmy Hoffa,* p. 417.
166. *Life,* Aug. 10, 1970.
167. Ibid., Sept. 1, 8, 1967.
168. Rogers "The Persecution of Clay Shaw," *Look,* Aug. 26, 1969.
169. Ibid.
170. *Life,* Sept. 1, 1967.
171. Ibid., Aug. 10, 1970.
172. Epstein, *Counterplot,* p. 47.

CHAPTER 5

1. Manchester, *The Death of a President,* p. 168.
2. Salisbury, "An Introduction to the Warren Commission Report," p. xx.
3. Ibid., p. xvi.
4. *New York Times,* Sept. 27, 1964.
5. Ibid.
6. 6 H. 12–14.
7. *New York Times,* Nov. 23, 1963.
8. *Esquire,* Nov. 1973.
9. Paul Mandel, "An End to Nagging Rumors," *Life,* Dec. 6, 1963.
10. Ibid.
11. Telephone interview with Dan Rather, Sept. 10, 1975.
12. "The Evolution of an Assassin," *Life,* Feb. 21, 1964.
13. *New York Times,* March 19, 1975.
14. Hartogs Exhibit 1.
15. "The Evolution of an Assassin," *Life,* Feb. 21, 1964, p. 72.
16. Ibid. p. 80.
17. Meagher, *Accessories After the Fact,* p. 461.
18. Ibid., p. 208.
19. *Report,* p. 121.
20. 1 H. 16.

20a. Priscilla Johnson, "The Stuff of Which Fanatics Are Made," *Boston Sunday Globe,* Nov. 24, 1963.

21. Ibid.
22. Johnson (Priscilla) Exhibit No. 6.

23.-24. Priscilla Johnson testimony before the Warren Commission, July 25, 1964; C.E. 911.

25. Telephone interview with Evan Thomas, New York City, May 6, 1975.
26. *New York Times,* March 13, 1969.
27. *Washington Star,* March 12, 1967; *Washington Post,* March 21, 1967.
28. *New York Times,* Nov. 23, 1973.
29. Ibid., Oct. 19, 1972.
30. C.D. 49, p. 24.
31. *Ramparts,* Nov. 1966, p. 32.
32. Ibid.
33. Ibid., p. 41.
34. Ibid.
35. Ibid.
36. *New York Times,* June 1, 1964.
37. CBS, "The Warren Report," Sept. 27, 1964.
38. Jerry Policoff, "The Media and the Assassination of President Kennedy," *New Times,* Aug. 8, 1975; *Life,* Oct. 2, 1964.
39. *Life,* Oct. 2, 1964.
40. *New Times,* Aug. 8, 1975.
41. *Life,* Oct. 2, 1964.
42. Salisbury, "An Introduction to the Warren Commission Report," p. xxix.
43. Ibid., p. xvi.
44. Jerry Policoff, "How All the News About Political Assassination in

the United States Has Not Been Fit to Print in the New York Times," *Realist,* Oct. 1972, p. 28.
45. Ibid.
46. *New York Herald Tribune* (Paris ed.); cited by Lane, *A Citizen's Dissent/Mark Lane Replies,* p. 144.
47. Charles Roberts, *The Truth About the Assassination* (New York: Grosset & Dunlap, 1966), pp. 118–22; cited by Lane, *A Citizen's Dissent/Mark Lane Replies,* p. 177.
48. Lane, *A Citizen's Dissent/Mark Lane Replies,* p. 177.
49. *New Times,* Aug. 8, 1975.
50. *New York Times,* Nov. 25, 1966.
51. *Newsweek,* Dec. 12, 1966.
52. *Realist,* Oct. 1972, p. 30.
53. *New Times,* Aug. 8, 1975.
54. Ibid.
55. CBS, "The Warren Report," June 25–26–27–28, 1967.
56. Ibid.
57. Ibid.
58. Ibid.
59. Ibid.
60. Ibid.
61. Ibid.
62. *Life,* Nov. 25, 1966.
63. CBS, "The Warren Report,'" June 25–26–27–28, 1967.
64. Ibid.
65. *Report,* p. 100.
66. CBS, "The Warren Report," June 25–26–27–28, 1967.
67. Ibid.; *New Times,* Aug. 8, 1975.
68. CBS, "The Warren Report," June 25–26–27–28, 1967.
69. *New Times,* Aug. 8, 1975.
70. Ibid.
71. Lane, *A Citizen's Dissent/Mark Lane Replies,* pp. 76, 80.
72. Ibid., p. 83.
73. CBS News press release, June 29, 1967; cited by Lane, *A Citizen's Dissent/Mark Lane Replies,* p. 98.
74. Ibid. (Note: Several Commission critics have skillfully demolished the CBS documentaries. See Policoff, "The Media and the Assassination of President Kennedy," *New Times,* Aug. 8, 1975; Lane, *A Citizen's Dissent/Mark Lane Replies;* and Thompson, *Six Seconds in Dallas.*)
75. "A Matter of Reasonable Doubt," *Life,* Nov. 25, 1966.
76. Schoenfeld, "The Shadow of a Gunman," *Columbia Journalism Review,* July–Aug. 1975, p. 47.
77. Ibid.
78. Ibid.
79. Ibid.
80. Ibid., p. 48.
81. Ibid., p. 50.
82. Ibid.
83. Letter from Alan Gillespie to Richard Sprague, Aug. 8, 1975.
84. Schoenfeld, "The Shadow of a Gunman," *Columbia Journalism Review,* July–Aug. 1975, p. 50.
85. Epstein, "The Final Chapter in the Assassination Controversy?" *New York Times Magazine,* April 20, 1969.
86. Ibid.
87. Belin, *November 22, 1963: You Are the Jury,* introduction by Harrison Salisbury, p. xiii.
88. *New York Times Book Review,* Nov. 18, 1973.
89. *New York Times,* Dec. 1, 1970.
90. Ibid.
91. *New Times,* Aug. 8, 1975.
92. *National Tattler,* June 15, 1975.
93. Ibid.
94. Ibid.
95. *Newsweek,* April 28, 1975, p. 36.
96. *New Times,* Aug. 8, 1975.
97. Ibid.
98. Interview with Dallas District Attorney Henry Wade, Dallas, Tex., July 1, 1975.
99. *Rolling Stone,* April 11, 1975.
100. Interview with Frank McCulloch, managing editor, *Sacramento Bee,* Atherton, Cal., June 28, 1975.
101. Gay Talese, *The Kingdom and the Power* (New York: New American Library, 1966), p. 5.

102. Letter from Clifton Daniel to J. Lee Rankin, May 21, 1964; cited by Policoff, "The Media and the Assassination of President Kennedy," *New Times,* Aug. 8, 1975.
103. *Rolling Stone,* April 24, 1975.

CHAPTER 6

1. *Transcript,* Warren Commission Executive Session, Jan. 27, 1964.
2. Ron Rosenbaum and George O'Toole, "Was Fidel on the Grassy Knoll?" *New Times,* July 11, 1975.
3. Ibid.
4. Ibid.
5. O'Toole, *The Assassination Tapes,* p. 216.
6. Manchester, *The Death of a President,* p. 287.
7. *Newsweek,* April 28, 1975.
8. Rosenbaum and O'Toole, "Was Fidel on the Grassy Knoll?" *New Times,* July 11, 1975.
9. *Report,* p. 589.
10. Ibid., p. 607.
11. Ibid., pp. 596–607.
12. Ibid., p. 360.
13. Ibid., p. 608.
14. Ibid.
15. Ibid., p. 609.
16. Ibid.
17. Interview with Fletcher Prouty, Washington, D.C., April 1, 1975.
18. Ibid.
19. 8 H. 298.
20. *Report,* p. 609.
21. Ibid.
22. Ibid., p. 610.
23. Ibid., p. 611.
24. Ibid.
25. Ibid.
26. Ibid., pp. 610–11.
27. Ibid., p. 611.
28. Ibid., p. 612.
29. Ibid.
30. Ibid., pp. 613–14.
31. Ibid., p. 614.
32. Robert Oswald, *Lee* (New York: Coward-McCann, 1967), p. 93.
33. *Report,* p. 613.
34. 16 H. 337; cf. C.D. 107, p. 37.
35. 8 H. 257.
36. Coleman/Slawson Memorandum to J. Lee Rankin (unpublished Commission Document), p. 14.
37. *Report,* p. 610.
38. Ibid.
39. C.E. 3099; 26 H. 715.
40. 26 H. 713, 719, 721, 723; cited by Scott, "The Dallas Conspiraacy" (unpublished ms.), chap. 2, p. 6.
41. C.E. 3099; 26 H. 715.
42. *Report,* p. 589; Scott, "The Dallas Conspiracy" (unpublished ms.), chap. 2, p. 3.
43. *Report,* p. 614.
44. Ibid., p. 615.
45. Ibid.
46. Ibid.
47. Ibid.
48. Ibid.
49. Ibid.
50. Ibid.
51. Ibid., p. 367.
52. C.E. 1150; 22 H. 180.
53. *Report,* p. 240.
54. C.E. 2676; 26 H. 32.
55. 18 H. 162; cited by Meagher, *Accessories After the Fact,* p. 331.
56. *Report,* p. 615.
57. Ibid., p. 616.
58. Ibid.
59. Ibid.
60. Ibid.

61. Ibid.
62. Ibid.
63. Ibid., p. 617.
64. Ibid.
65. Ibid., pp. 617–18.
66. Ibid., p. 618.
67. Ibid.
68. Ibid.
69. C.E. 941; 18 H. 155.
70. *Report*, p. 618.
71. Ibid., p. 255.
72. Ibid.
73. Ibid., p. 367.
74. Ibid., p. 621.
75. Ibid.
76. *New York Times*, June 20, 1959; cited by Scott, "The Dallas Conspiracy" (unpublished ms.).
77. Ibid.
78. Scott, "The Dallas Conspiracy" (unpublished ms.), chap. 2, p. 2.
79. Ibid.
80. John Barron, *KGB* (New York: Reader's Digest Press, 1974), p. 452.
81. Ibid.
82. Nosenko File (National Archives, Washington, D.C.).
83. *Report*, p. 622.
84. Ibid., p. 625.
85. Ibid.
86. Ibid., p. 626.
87. Ibid.
88. Ibid.
89. Ibid.
90. Ibid.
91. *Transcript*, Warren Commission Executive Session, Jan. 27, 1964.
92. *Report*, p. 649.
92a. Ibid.
93. Stuckey Exhibit 3.
94. *Report*, p. 667.
95. Ibid.
96. Ibid.
97. Meagher, *Accessories After the Fact*, pp. 332–33.
98. Ibid.
99. *Transcript*, Warren Commission Executive Session, Jan. 22, 1964.
100. Scott, "The Dallas Conspiracy" (unpublished ms.), chap. 2, p. 20.
101. *Transcript*, Warren Commission Executive Session, Jan. 22, 1964.
102. *Report*, p. 303.
103. Ibid., p. 666.
104. 26 H. 40.
105. *Report*, p. 253.
106. Ibid.
107. Ibid.
108. Ibid.
109. Ibid., p. 633.
110. Ibid., p. 674.
111. Ibid., p. 671; cf. p. 669.
112. Ibid., p. 634.
113. C.D. 87SS569; C.D. 235; C.D. 409, p. 3; C.D. 11, p. 15, XIII, item 103.
114. C.D. 87SS569; C.D. 235; C.D. 409, p. 3.
114a. C.E. 18; 16 H. 50.
115. 16 H. 616; 18 H. 16.
116. *The Penkovskiy Papers* (New York: Avon Books, 1966), p. 24.
117. Ibid.
118. Ibid., p. 359.
119. Ibid., p. 360.
120. Ibid., p. 366.
121. Ibid.
122. Ibid., p. 367.
123. Ibid., p. 359.
124. *Report*, p. 624.
125. Ibid., p. 634.
126. C.E. 29; 16 H. 144.
127. C.E. 9.
128. *Report*, p. 634.
129. 18 H. 615.
130. *Transcript*, Warren Commission Executive Session, Jan. 27, 1964.

131. *Report*, p. 635.
132. Ibid.
133. Ibid.
134. Ibid.
135. Ibid.
136. *Free China and Asia* (Taipei), Aug. 1959, p. 28; cited by Scott, "The Dallas Conspiracy" (unpublished ms.), chap. 2, p. 23.
137. Telephone interview with Spas T. Raikin, June 1, 1975.
138. Ibid.
139. Ibid.
140. C.E. 917.
141. *New York Times*, Dec. 5, 1963.
142. Folsom Exhibit 1, p. 10; 19 H. 665.
143. C.E. 917.
144. 18 H. 281.
145. Telephone interview with CBS producer Harry Moses, Aug. 28, 1975.
146. *New York Times*, May 2, 1960.
147. Francis Gary Powers, *Operation Overflight* (New York: Holt, Rinehart and Winston, 1970), p. 374.
148. *CIA Commission Report*, pp. 102–6.
149. Ibid.
150. C.D. 692.
150a. 5 H. 57.
151. Peter Dale Scott, "Oswald's Ties with U.S. Intelligence" (unpublished monograph).
152. 18 H. 616.
153. Ibid.
154. 9 H. 5.
155. Scott, "The Dallas Conspiracy" (unpublished ms.), chap. 3, p. 9.
156. 8 H. 358; 9 H. 3, 5.
157. 9 H. 22.
158. Scott, "The Dallas Conspiracy" (unpublished ms.), chap. 3, p. 6.
159. *Report*, pp. 261–62.
160. Ibid., p. 643.
161. Ibid., p. 640.
162. Ibid., p. 261.
163. C.D. 534, p. 16.
163a. 9 H. 96.
164. *Report*, p. 262.
165. Ibid.
166. 9 H. 183.
167–70. C.E. 537, p. 21, 9 H. 186; C.D. 777a, p. 3, National Archives, Washington, D.C.
171. *Report*, p. 262.
172. Ibid., pp. 393–94.
173. Ibid., p. 639.
174. Ibid., p. 646.
175. 10 H. 33–34, 82–83.
177. *Report*, p. 269–70.
178. Ibid., pp. 266–67.
179. Lee (V. T.) Exhibit 1; 20 H. 511.
180. 17 H. 33.
181. Telephone interview with Victor Marchetti, June 25, 1975.
182. 10 H. 33–34, 82–83.
183. *Report*, p. 649.
183a. Canfield and Weberman, *Coup d'état in America*, p. 41.
183b. Ibid.
184. *Report*, pp. 648–49.
185. 4 H. 432; 17 H. 758.
186. *Report*, p. 279.
187. C.D. 75; C.D. 588; C.D. 613; C.D. 652.
188. Transcript of Bernard Fensterwald interview with William G. Gaudet, Waveland, Miss., May 13, 1975; C.D. 75; pp. 588, 613, 652.
189. C.D. 75, pp. 588, 613, 652, National Archives, Washington, D.C.
190. Transcript of Fensterwald interview with William G. Gaudet, May 13, 1975.
191. Ibid.
192. Ibid.
193. 5 H. 34, 37.
194. C.D. 349.
195. 5 H. 34, 37.
196. 4 H. 238.
197. *New York Times*, Sept. 2, 1975.
198. *Report*, p. 548.

199. 1 H. 409–10.
200. *Report,* pp. 304–5.
201. *New York Times,* Sept. 16, 1975.
202. C.E. 833, p. 15; 5 H. 112.
203. 2 H. 103.
204. 1 H. 79–80.
205. 1 H. 410.
206. C.D. 1, *FBI Summary Report, Investigation of Assassination of President John F. Kennedy,* Dec. 9, 1963.
207. *Transcript,* Warren Commission Executive Session, Jan. 22, 1964.
207a. *New York Times,* Oct. 22, 1975, p. 25.
208. Ibid., Sept. 1, 1975.
209. Ibid., Sept. 17, 1975; Oct. 22, 1975, p. 25.
210. 1 H. 57; 3 H. 18–19; cited by Meagher, *Accessories After the Fact,* p. 216.
211. 1 H. 57.
212. William Turner, *Hoover's FBI* (Los Angeles: Sherbourne Press, 1970); telephone interview with William Turner, Sept. 22, 1975.
213. Interview with former senior official, Department of Justice, Washington, D.C., Aug. 25, 1975.
214. C.D. 294B.
215. Telephone interview with Spas T. Raikin, June 1, 1975.
216. 4 H. 420.
217. Ibid.
218. O'Toole, *The Assassination Tapes,* pp. 206–35; *Transcript,* Warren Commission Executive Session, Jan. 22, 27, 1964.
219. 4 H. 429.
220. 4 H. 437; 17 H. 758–62.
221. Comment of Lee Harvey Oswald to unidentified reporter, Nov. 22, 1963, recorded by *Probe;* cited by O'Toole, *The Assassination Tapes,* p. 125.
222. A full discussion of polygraphs and the Psychological Stress Evaluator is contained in O'Toole, *The Assassination Tapes,* pp. 41–87.
223. O'Toole, *The Assassination Tapes,* p. 221.
224. C.D. 1052.
225. *Transcript,* Warren Commission Executive Session, Jan. 27, 1964.

CHAPTER 7

1. 6 H. 270.
2. 24 H. 729–34.
3. *Report,* p. 652.
4. 10 H. 353.
5. 26 H. 685.
6. 26 H. 577.
7. *Report,* p. 298.
8. Ibid.
9. 22 H. 524, 534–36, 546–49.
10. 22 H. 525, 531.
11. 16 H. 178–79; 10 H. 327–40.
12. 10 H. 309–27.
13. *Report,* p. 294.
14. Ibid., p. 297.
15. Meagher, *Accessories After the Fact,* p. 260.
16. *Report,* p. 295.
17. Ibid., p. 296.
18. 11 H. 371.
19. 11 H. 372.
20. C.E. 3147.
21. C.D. 1553.
22. 11 H. 381.
23. 11 H. 382.
24. 26 H. 595.
25. *Report,* p. 324.
26. C.D. 1553.
27. *Report,* pp. 299–300.
28. Epstein, *Inquest,* p. 103.
29. Ibid.
30. Coleman/Slawson Memorandum, p. 110.
31. *New York Times,* April 22, 1959; July 4, 1959; July 9, 1959.
31a. Ibid., July 9, 1959.
32. Ibid.

33. Ibid.
34. Ibid., July 9, 1959.
35. C.E. 3146; 26 H. 834.
36. Harold Weisberg, *Whitewash II* (Hyattstown, Md.: Harold Weisberg, 1966), p. 53.
37. Meagher, *Accessories After the Fact*, p. 387.
38. William Turner, *Power on the Right* (Berkeley: Ramparts Press, 1971), p. 106.
39. C.D. 1553.9.
40. C.D. 1179.
40a. Noyes, *Legacy of Doubt*, p. 29; Canfield and Weberman, *Coup d'état in America*, p. 191.
41. Canfield and Weberman, *Coup d'état in America*, p. 192.
42. C.E. 2980; 26 H. 421–73; cited by Scott, "The Dallas Conspiracy" (unpublished ms.).
43. 26 H. 472.
44. Ed Reid and Ovid Demaris, *Green Felt Jungle*, p. 87; cited by Scott, "The Dallas Conspiracy" (unpublished ms.)
45. Reid and Demaris, *Green Felt Jungle*, p. 87; *McClellan Hearings*, p. 16442; Hank Messick, *Syndicate Abroad* (New York: Macmillan Publishing Co., 1969), p. 86; cited by Scott, "The Dallas Conspiracy" (unpublished ms.).
46. Telephone interview with Jack Tobin, Oct. 15, 1975; Messick, *Syndicate Abroad*, p. 87.
47. William W. Turner, "The Garrison Commission on the Assassination of President Kennedy," *Ramparts*, Jan. 1968, p. 58.
48. *Miami News*, Feb. 2, 1967; cited by Meagher, *Accessories After the Fact*, p. 89.
49. Ibid.
50. Meagher, *Accessories After the Fact*, p. 89.
51. Ibid.
52. *New York Times*, Feb. 23, 1975.
53. Ibid.
54. Ibid.
55. Ibid.
56. C.D. 294B.
57. Ibid.
58. C.D. 294J.
59. *Report*, p. 669.
60. Ibid., p. 634.
61. Ibid., p. 673.
62. Coleman/Slawson Memorandum, p. 20.
63. Ibid., p. 21.
64. James and Wardlaw, *Plot or Politics*, pp. 44, 46.
65. Office of Naval Intelligence file on Lee Harvey Oswald (National Archives, Washington, D.C.).
66. Folsom Exhibit.
67. U.S. Code, Title 18, Section 1544.
68. *Report*, p. 618.
69. Johnson (Priscilla) Exhibit 6.
70. Johnson, "The Stuff of Which Fanatics Are Made," *Boston Sunday Globe*, Nov. 24, 1963.
71. *Report*, p. 307.
72. Oswald, *Lee*, p. 105; *Report*, p. 618.
73. Ibid.
74. Coleman/Slawson Memorandum, pp. 58–59.
75. C.E. 183; 16 H. 1537.
76. Interview with Dena Birnback (educational psychologist specializing in learning disorders), New York City, Sept. 28, 1975.
77. *Report*, p. 627.
78. Lee (V. T.) Exhibit 4.
79. *Transcript*, Warren Commission Executive Session, Jan. 27, 1964.
80. Coleman/Slawson Memorandum, p. 22.
80a. *New York Times*, Oct. 10, 1975, p. 19.
81. Ibid., p. 87.
82. Gore Vidal, "The Art and Arts of E. Howard Hunt," *New York Review of Books*, Dec. 13, 1973.
83. C.E. 2613; C.E. 2609; C.E. 2891; C.E. 2892.
84. Interview with Jones Harris, New York City, June 24, 1975.
85. C.E. 1392.
86. C.E. 23.
87. Interview with Priscilla Johnson MacMillan, New York City, May 11, 1975.
88. 18 H. 161.

89. Donabedian Exhibit 1; 19 H. 615.
90. Donabedian Exhibit 1; 19 H. 584.
91. Interview with Douglas Gasner, Brooklyn, N.Y., Aug. 17, 1975.
92. C.E. 1981, C.E. 3002.
93. Telephone interview with Spas T. Raikin, May 1, 1975.
94. Ibid.
95. Interview with Jones Harris, New York City, June 24, 1975. (Harris interviewed Bogard and his fellow employees shortly after the assassination.)
96. Interview with Jones Harris, New York City, June 24, 1975. (Harris interviewed the motelkeepers after the assassination.)
97. Cited by James Grady, *Six Days of the Condor* (New York: Dell Publishing Co., 1975), p. 29.
98. C.D. 75.
99. Interview with Jones Harris, New York City, June 24, 1975.
100. 20 H. 216.
101. Oswald, *Lee*, p. 117.
102. 4 H. 415.
103. Miles Copeland, *Without Cloak or Dagger* (New York: Simon and Schuster, 1974), p. 141.
104. Telephone interview with John Marks, May 20, 1975.
105. *Report*, pp. 280–82.
106. Ibid., pp. 280–81.
107. C.D. 963.
108. Philip Agee, *Inside the Company: CIA Diary* (Harmondsworth, England: Penguin Books, 1975), p. 528.
109. C.D. 631.
110. Ibid.
111. "A Primer of Assassination Theories," *Esquire*, Dec. 1966, p. 208.
112. Telephone interview with Dallas County Medical Examiner's Office, Oct. 13, 1975; *National Tattler*, July 13, 1975.
113. 4 H. 245.
114. *Report*, p. 235.

CHAPTER 8

1. Frank Mankiewicz and Kirby Jones, *With Fidel* (Chicago: Playboy Press, 1975), p. 167.
2. 4 H. 196.
3. C.E. 1467.
4. *Report*, p. 710.
5. Ibid., pp. 706–7.
6. Ibid., p. 349.
7. Ibid., p. 350.
8. Ibid., p. 313.
9. Ibid.
10. Kantor Exhibit 8.
11. C.E. 2249, p. 14.
12. *Report*, p. 317.
13. Ibid., p. 318.
14. Ibid.
15. Ibid., p. 319.
16. Ibid., p. 320.
17. Ibid., p. 321.
18. Ibid., p. 322.
19. Ibid.
20. Ibid.
21. Ibid., p. 323.
22. Ibid., p. 326.
23. Ibid.
24. Ibid., pp. 331–32.
25. Ibid., p. 209.
26. Ibid., pp. 209–10.
27. 13 H. 17.
28. *New York Post*, Jan. 20, 1964, p. 4.
29. Interview with Dallas District Attorney Henry Wade, Dallas, Tex., July 1, 1975.
30. *New York Journal-American*, March 15, 1964.
31. Kantor Exhibit 8; C.E. 2290.
32. 15 H. 348–51; Jenkins Exhibit 1; C.E. 2249, p. 14; 15 H. 617.
33. *Report*, p. 711.
34. Ibid., p. 331.

35. Ibid., p. 350.
36. Ibid., p. 343.
37. Ibid., p. 341.
38. Ibid., p. 709.
39. Ibid., p. 707.
40. Ibid.
41. Meagher, *Accessories After the Fact,* p. 442.
42. Ibid.
43. C.E. 1288.
44. U.S. Congress, Senate, Committee on Government Operations, *Organized Crime and Illicit Traffic in Narcotics, Hearings,* 88th Cong., 2d Sess. p. 508, Chart 2; 14 H. 444; the various spelling errors are cited in Scott, "The Longest Cover-up," *Ramparts,* Nov. 1973.
45. 25 H. 244; 5 H. 200.
46. C.E. 1288.
47. Ovid Demaris, *Captive City* (New York: Lyle Stuart, 1969), pp. 5, 17, 169.
48. *Report,* p. 695.
49. *Chicago Tribune,* Dec. 9, 1939.
50. *Report,* p. 703.
51. 5 H. 200.
52. Interview with former official, Department of Justice, Washington, D.C., August 25, 1975.
53. C.E. 2303, p. 30; 25 H. 246.
53a. *Time,* Aug. 25, 1975, p. 55.
54. Ibid.
54a. Judy Klemesrud, "Clyde," *New York Times Magazine,* Feb. 16, 1975.
55. C.E. 2303, p. 30; 25 H. 247.
56. Kennedy, *The Enemy Within,* p. 60.
57. Ibid., p. 88.
58. Scott, "The Dallas Conspiracy" (unpublished ms.), chap. 6, p. 16.
59. *Newsweek,* March 27, 1967.
60. *Report,* p. 348.
61. Ibid., p. 203.
62. C.E. 2050; cf. Meagher, *Accessories After the Fact,* p. 405
63. *Report,* p. 349.
64. Ibid., p. 688.
65. Ibid., p. 689.
66. Ibid., p. 691.
67. Ibid., p. 689.
68. Ibid., p. 690.
69. Ibid., p. 694.
70. C.E. 1288.
71. Ibid.
72. Ibid.
73. U.S. Congress, Senate, Committee on Government Operations, *Organized Crime and Illicit Traffic in Narcotics, Hearings,* 88th Cong., 2d Sess., p. 508, Chart 11.
74. Demaris, *Captive City,* p. 130.
75. Ibid.
76. U.S. Congress, Senate, Select Committee on Improper Activities in the Labor or Management Field, *Hearings,* 85th Cong., 2d Sess., p. 12522.
77. 22 H. 372.
78. *Life,* May 30, 1969, pp. 45–47.
79. *Report,* p. 694.
80. Ibid., p. 695.
81. Ibid.
82. C.E. 1292.
83. *Report,* p. 695.
84. Ibid.
85. Ibid.
86. Ibid.
87. Ibid.
88. Kennedy, *The Enemy Within,* p. 84.
89. Ibid., pp. 84–85.
90. *Report,* p. 701.
91. Ibid., p. 700.
92. Ibid., p. 699; Kefauver Hearings, part 5, p. 1177; McClellan Hearings, p. 12520.
93. C.E. 1184.
94. Demaris, *Captive City,* p. 27.
95. *Report,* p. 700.

96. Ibid.
97.–98. C.E. 1798; 23 H. 203–4; C.E. 1271; 22 H. 374; cited by Scott, "The Dallas Conspiracy" (unpublished ms.), chap. 5, p. 9.
99. *Report*, p. 707.
100. C.E. 2887; 26 H. 342.
101. C.E. 2249; 25 H. 166.
102. C.E. 2002; 24 H. 69.
103. Penn Jones, *Forgive My Grief* (Midlothian, Tex.: Midlothian Mirror), pp. 160–61; Meagher, *Accessories After the Fact*, p. 425.
104. 15 H. 593–95.
105. Ibid.
106. Ibid.
107. 22 H. 302.
108. *Report*, pp. 701–2.
109. Ibid., p. 707.
110. 23 H. 78; 25 H. 290.
111. Scott, "The Longest Cover-up," *Ramparts*, Nov. 1973.
112. 13 H. 183; cited by Scott, "The Longest Cover-up," *Ramparts*, Nov. 1973.
113. C.E. 1761, Item 3; 23 H. 369.
114. 23 H. 369; cited by Scott, "The Longest Cover-up," *Ramparts*, Nov. 1973.
115. C.D. 1052.
116. Ibid.
117. Ibid.
118. Interview with former official, Department of Justice, Washington, D.C., Aug. 25, 1975.
119. C.D. 1052.
120. Harry Anslinger, *The Murderers* (New York: Farrar, Straus and Co., 1961), p. 106; cited by Alfred McCoy, *The Politics of Heroin in Southeast Asia* (New York: Harper & Row, 1972), p. 26.
121. McCoy, *The Politics of Heroin in Southeast Asia*, p. 26.
122. *New York Daily News*, April 23, 1975.
123. McCoy, *The Politics of Heroin in Southeast Asia*, p. 26.
124. *Report*, p. 346; C.E. 1693, Item 4, 23 H. 166.
125. *Report*, p. 346.
125a. C.D. 686, p. 2.
126. C.E. 1693, Item 4, 23 H. 166.
127. 5 H. 201.
128. C.E. 1697; 23 H. 166.
129. *Report*, p. 708.
130. C.E. 1442; C.E. 1443.
131. *Report*, p. 708.
132. 23 H. 163; cited by Scott, "The Longest Cover-up," *Ramparts*, Nov. 1973.
133. C.E. 1697; 23 H. 166.
134. C.E. 1586.
135. Scott, "The Longest Cover-up," *Ramparts*, Nov. 1973.
136. *Report*, p. 346.
137. Ibid., p. 708.
138. Ibid., p. 345.
139. C.E. 1689; 23 H. 157, 159.
140. 23 H. 158–59.
141. 23 H. 159.
142. Ibid.
143. Ibid.
144. 23 R. 159–60.
145. Ibid.
146. 14 H. 350.
147. 12 H. 340–43.
148. 26 H. 467; cited by Lane, *Rush to Judgment*, pp. 302–3.
149. 26 H. 470; cited by Lane, *Rush to Judgment*, p. 303.
150. 26 H. 466.
151. Meagher, *Accessories After the Fact*, p. 453.
152. *New York Times*, June 29, 1971.
153. Ibid.
154. 5 H. 210.
155. *New York Times*, Jan. 4, 1967.
156. Ibid.

CHAPTER 9

1. 26 H. 441.
2. Ibid.
3. Ibid.
4. Ibid.
5. C.D. 1085.
6. *Hispano-American Report,* 1963, p. 449.
6a. *New York Times,* March 12, 1962; March 14, 1962; Oct. 23, 1962; March 7, 1963; April 19, 1970; April 21, 1970; April 26, 1970; May 14, 1970.
7. C.D. 1085.
8. Press release of Senator George McGovern, July 30, 1975.
9. Ibid.
10. Manchester, *The Death of a President,* p. 326.
11. Lyndon Johnson, *The Vantage Point* (New York: Holt, Rinehart and Winston, 1971), p. 26.
12. *Report,* p. 365.
13. Ibid., p. 388.
14. C.E. 261Z.
15. Ibid.
16. C.E. 32; 16 H. 152.
17. *Report,* p. 382.
18. Ibid., p. 383.
19. Ibid.; Canfield and Weberman, *Coup d'état in America,* p. 41.
20. 10 H. 33–34, 82–83.
21. 10 H. 43; C.D. 984B.
22. *New York Times,* Aug. 1, 1963.
23. Associated Press, March 4, 1967; cited by Harold Weisberg, *Oswald in New Orleans,* p. 69; William Turner, "The Garrison Commission on the Assassination of President Kennedy," *Ramparts,* Jan. 1968, p. 52.
24. *Report,* p. 384.
25. 11 H. 353.
26. C.E. 1414.
27. David Wise and Thomas Ross, *The Invisible Government* (New York: Bantam Books, 1965), pp. 26, 42.
28. *Report,* p. 318.
29. 22 H. 831.
30. Milton E. Brener, *The Garrison Case: A Study in the Abuse of Power* (New York: Clarkson N. Potter, 1969), p. 47.
31. Ibid., pp. 48–49; cited by Scott, "The Dallas Conspiracy" (unpublished ms.), chap. 4, p. 2.
32. Scott, "The Dallas Conspiracy" (unpublished ms.), chap. 4, p. 9.
33. 11 H. 425.
34. 16 H. 67.
35. Ibid.
36. Ibid.
37. *Report,* p. 653.
38. Ibid.
39. Ibid.
40. Ibid., pp. 653–54.
41. Ibid., p. 654.
42. Coleman/Slawson Memorandum, p. 110–11.
43. Ibid., p. 111.
44. *Transcript,* Warren Commission Executive Session, Jan. 22, 1964.
45. Cited by Rosenbaum and O'Toole, "Was Fidel on the Grassy Knoll?" *New Times,* July 11, 1975.
46. Rosenbaum and O'Toole, "Was Fidel on the Grassy Knoll?" *New Times,* July 11, 1975.
47. Ibid.
48. Ibid.
49. Ibid.
50. Ibid.
51. *Report,* p. 284.
52. Ibid., p. 285.
53. Ibid.
54. Ibid.
55. 26 H. 857–58.
56. C.D. 1084.
57. Ibid.

58. 26 H. 857–58.
59. Tad Szulc, *Compulsive Spy* (New York: Viking Press, 1974), p. 97.
60. Ibid.
61. Ibid.; Tad Szulc, "Cuba on Our Mind," *Esquire*, Feb. 1974, p. 90.
62. 26 H. 302.
63. C.D. 770.8–9; cited by Peter Dale Scott, "Government Documents and the John F. Kennedy Assassination," 1975 (unpublished monograph).
64. *New York Times*, June 9, 1973.
65. C.D. 59; C.D. 395.
66. Scott, "The Longest Cover-up," *Ramparts*, Nov. 1973.
67. Hans Tanner, *Counter-Revolutionary Agent* (G. T. Foulis, 1962), p. 167; cited by Scott, "The Longest Cover-up," *Ramparts*, Nov. 1973.
68. Scott, "The Longest Cover-up," *Ramparts*, Nov. 1973.
69. Jack Anderson column, March 3, 1967.
70. *New York Times*, March 10, 1975.
71. Schlesinger, *A Thousand Days*, p. 242.
72. Ibid., p. 276.
73. Taylor Branch and George Crile III, "The Kennedy Vendetta," *Harper's*, Aug. 1975.
74. Ibid.
75. Ibid.
76. Ibid.
77. Ibid.
78. Ibid.
79. Ibid.
80. Ibid.
81. Ibid.
82. Ibid.
83. Ibid.
84. Ibid.
85. Szulc, *Compulsive Spy*, p. 81.
86. Press release of Senator George McGovern, July 30, 1975.
87. *New York Post*, May 21, 1975, p. 22.
88. Branch and Crile, "The Kennedy Vendetta," *Harper's*, Aug. 1975.
89. Tad Szulc, "Cuba on Our Mind," *Esquire*, Feb. 1974.
90. Ibid.
91. Ibid.
92. Branch and Crile, "The Kennedy Vendetta," *Harper's*, Aug. 1975.
93. *Atlantic*, July 1973.
94. Press release of Senator George McGovern, July 30. 1975.
95. Ibid.
96. Mankiewicz and Jones, *With Fidel*, p. 161.
97. Schlesinger, *A Thousand Days*, p. 1029.
98. Manchester, *The Death of a President*, p. 193.
99. *New York Times*, Nov. 25, 1963.
100. Mankiewicz and Jones, *With Fidel*, pp. 163–64.
101. Telephone interview with Kirby Jones, July 20, 1975.
102. Mankiewicz and Jones, *With Fidel*, p. 167.
103. Letter to author from John Holum, legislative assistant to Senator George McGovern, Aug. 5, 1975.
104. Ibid.
105. Schlesinger, *A Thousand Days*, p. 834.
106. Branch and Crile, "The Kennedy Vendetta," *Harper's*, Aug. 1975.
107. Robert F. Kennedy, *Thirteen Days* (New York: Signet Books, 1969), p. 31.
108. Ibid., p. 110.
109. Branch and Crile, "The Kennedy Vendetta," *Harper's*, Aug. 1975.
110. Ibid.
111. *Khrushchev Remembers* (New York: Bantam Books, 1971), pp. 551–52.
112. Arthur Schlesinger, *The Imperial Presidency*, p. 198.
113. Schlesinger, *A Thousand Days*, p. 901.
114. Attwood, *The Reds and the Blacks*, p. 142.
115. Ibid.
116. Ibid., p. 144.
117. Ibid., p. 142.
118. Ibid., p. 143.
119. Ibid.
120. Ibid., p. 144.
121. Ibid.
122. Stewart Alsop, "CIA: The Battle for Secret Power," *Saturday Evening Post*, July 27, 1963.
123. Scott, "The Dallas Conspiracy" (unpublished ms.), chap. 8, p. 11.

124. U.S. Department of State, *Bulletin*, April 22, 1963.
125. *New York Times*, Sept. 16, 1963.
126. Associated Press wirephoto, May 12, 1960; Canfield and Weberman, *Coup d'état in America*, p. 96.
127. Ibid.
128. *New York Times*, Nov. 1, 1963.
129. Ibid., Nov. 3, 1963.
130. Ibid., Nov. 1, 1963.
131. Ibid.
132. Ransom, "Containing Central Intelligence," *New Republic*, Dec. 11, 1965, p. 13.
133. Howard Hunt, *Give Us This Day;* cited by Vidal, "The Art and Arts of E. Howard Hunt," *New York Review of Books*, Dec. 12, 1973.
134. Ibid.
135. Ibid.
136. Ibid.
137. Ibid.
138. Ibid.
139. *New York Times*, April 16, 1963.
140. H. H. Martin, *Saturday Evening Post*, June 8, 1963, p. 28.
141. *New York Times*, April 16, 1963.
142. Ibid., June 4, 1963; cited by Scott, "The Dallas Conspiracy" (unpublished ms.), chap 8, p. 14.
143. *New York Times*, May 8, 1963.
144. Manchester, *The Death of a President*, p. 53.
145. *New York Times* Aug. 1, 1963, p. 6.
146. Memorandum to J. Lee Rankin from Burton Griffin, April 16, 1964.
147. C.D. 1085U.4.
148. C.D. 23.4.
149. C.D. 1085; cited in Canfield and Weberman, *Coup d'état in America*, p. 118.
150. C.D. 853 (under seal at the National Archives, Washington, D.C.); cited by Canfield and Weberman, *Coup d'état in America*, p. 119.
151–53. Canfield and Weberman, *Coup d'état in America*, p. 120; C.D. 853 (under seal at the National Archives, Washington, D.C.); C.D. 1085U.1; Canfield and Weberman, *Coup d'état in America*, p. 120, p. 119.
154. FBI File MM 89–35; cited by Canfield and Weberman, *Coup d'état in America*, p. 121.
155. Ibid.
156. Ibid.
157. Ibid.
158. Ibid.
159. *New York Daily News*, April 24, 1975.
160. Hunt, *Give Us This Day*, pp. 90–97, 156.

CHAPTER 10

1. *CIA Commission Report*, p. 254.
2. Ibid.
3. Ibid.
4. C.E. 1973.
5. *CIA Commission Report*, pp. 255–57.
6. ABC, "Good Night, America," March 6, 1975.
7. *CIA Commission Report*, pp. 256–57.
8. *Washington Post*, March 27, 1967.
9. Haynes Johnson, *The Bay of Pigs*, (New York: W. W. Norton & Co., 1964), p. 76.
9a. McCoy, *The Politics of Heroin in Southeast Asia*, p. 211.
10. Schlesinger, *A Thousand Days*, p. 997.
11. *Nation*, Dec. 7, 1963; *Time*, June 12, 1964, p. 47.
12. Branch and Crile, "The Kennedy Vendetta," *Harper's*, Aug. 1975.
13. Hunt, *Give Us This Day;* cited by Vidal, "The Art and Arts of Howard Hunt," *New York Review of Books*, Dec. 13, 1973, p. 14.
15. Scott, "The Dallas Conspiracy" (unpublished ms.), chap. 8, pp. 6–19.
16. *Public Papers of the Presidents, John F. Kennedy, 1963*, White House Statement, Oct. 2, 1963.
17. Wicker, *JFK and LBJ*, p. 183.
18. Copeland, *Without Cloak or Dagger*, p. 235; Harrison Salisbury, "The Gentlemen Killers of the CIA," *Penthouse*, May 1975, pp. 48, 53.

19. *Transcript*, Warren Commission Executive Session, Jan. 27, 1964.
20. McCoy, *The Politics of Heroin in Southeast Asia*, p. 248.
21. Hilsman, *To Move a Nation*, p. 67.
22. Wise and Ross, *The Invisible Government*, pp. 3–4.
23. Harry S. Truman, Dec. 22, 1963; cited by Hilsman, *To Move a Nation*, p. 63.
24. Charles Higham and Joel Greenberg, *The Celluloid Muse: Hollywood Directors Speak* (New York: Signet Books, 1972), p. 92.
25. Schlesinger, *The Imperial Presidency*, pp. 198, 417.
26. Higham and Greenberg, *The Celluloid Muse*, p. 92.
27. *Time*, March 17, 1975; *New York Times*, Sept. 7, 1975.
27a. *New York Times*, Oct. 4, 1975.
28. Meagher, *Accessories After the Fact*, p. 74.
29. *Report*, p. 147.
30. Ibid., p. 152.
31. Ibid., pp. 164–66.
32. Ibid., p. 170.
33. C.E. 2003, pp. 127–28.
34. O'Toole, *The Assassination Tapes*, pp. 234–35.
35. *The Penkovskiy Papers*, p. 129.
36. *Transcript*, Warren Commission Executive Session, Jan. 27, 1964.
37. Epstein, *Counterplot*, p. 76.
38. Interview with Jones Harris, New York City, June 24, 1975.
39. Epstein, *Counterplot*, p. 76.
39a. Ibid.
40. Ibid.
41. Ibid., pp. 76–77.
42. Telephone interview with John Marks, Sept. 26, 1975.
43. 4 H. 318.
44. C.D. 1426.
45. C.D. 354 (National Archives, Washington, D.C.); cf. Thompson, *Six Seconds in Dallas*, p. 312.
46. Stevenson Exhibit 5053; 21 H. 578.
47. 4 H. 461.
48. 5 H. 57.
49. Scott, "Government Documents and the John F. Kennedy Assassination" (unpublished monograph).
50. Interview with Frank McCulloch, Atherton, Calif., June 28, 1975.
51. Johnson, *The Bay of Pigs*, p. 68.
52. Branch and Crile, "The Kennedy Vendetta," *Harper's*, Aug. 1975, p. 58.
53. *The Watergate Hearings: Break-in and Cover-up*, p. 205.
54. *New York Times*, Sept. 15, 1973.
55. *The End of a Presidency* (New York: Bantam Books, 1974), p. 330.
55a. *The White House Transcripts* (New York: Bantam Books, 1974), p. 160.
56. *Report*, p. 384.
57. E. Howard Hunt, *Give Us This Day*, p. 183.
58. Szulc, *Compulsive Spy*, p. 96.
59. *CIA Commission Report*, p. 269.
60. Telephone interview with David Phillips, June 19, 1975.
61. Hunt, *Undercover*, pp. 132–33.
62. Szulc, *Compulsive Spy*, p. 96.
63. Szulc, "Cuba on Our Mind," *Esquire*, Feb. 1974, p. 91.
64. Ibid.
65. *Newsweek*, May 18, 1973.
66. Salisbury, "The Gentlemen Killers of the CIA" *Penthouse*, May 1975, p. 48.
67. Interview with former official, New York Police Department, New York City, July 3, 1975.
69. Salisbury, "The Gentlemen Killers of the CIA," *Penthouse*, May 1975, p. 144.
70. Copeland, *Without Cloak or Dagger*, p. 235.
71. Thomas Sciacca, *Luciano* (New York: Pinnacle Books, 1975), p. 180.
72. Salisbury, "The Gentlemen Killers of the CIA," *Penthouse*, May 1975, p. 53.
73. Telephone interview with John Marks, May 25, 1975.
74. McCoy, *The Politics of Heroin in Southeast Asia*, p. 19.
75. Ibid.
76. Martin A. Gosch and Richard Hammer, *The Last Testament of Lucky Luciano* (Boston: Little, Brown and Co., 1975), pp. 261–62.
77. Sciacca, *Luciano*, p. 181.
78. Michael Pantaleone, *The Mafia and Politics* (London: Chatto & Windus, 1966), p. 59.

79. Ibid., p. 58.
80. McCoy, *The Politics of Heroin in Southeast Asia*, p. 22.
81. Ibid., p. 23.
82. Ibid., p. 24.
83. Ibid.
84. Ibid., p. 29.
85. Ibid., pp. 42–43.
86. Ibid., pp. 45–46.
87. Thomas W. Braden, "I'm Glad the CIA Is 'Immoral,'" *Saturday Evening Post*, May 20, 1967, p. 10.
88. McCoy, *The Politics of Heroin in Southeast Asia*, p. 248.
89. Ibid., p. 298.
90. Ibid., p. 281.
91. Ibid., p. 210.
92. Ibid., p. 211.
93. Ibid.
94. Ibid.
95. *New York Post*, May 21, 1975.
96. Interview with former CIA agent, New York City, June 5, 1975.
97. *New York Times*, March 10, 1975, p. 49.
98. Ibid., July 23, 1975, p. 16.
99. Ibid.
100. Ibid.
101. Ibid.
102. *New York Daily News*, April 23, 1975.
103. Telephone interview with former U.S. Attorney Robert Morgenthau, June 6, 1975.
104. Ibid.
105. Telephone interview with source close to the FBI, June 7, 1975.
106. Telephone interview with former U.S. Attorney Robert Morgenthau, June 6, 1975.
107. *Time*, June 30, 1975, p. 26.
108. *New York Times*, June 20, 1975.
109. *Time*, March 17, 1975.
110. CBS, "The CBS Morning News," correspondent Daniel Schorr, July 28, 1975.
111. Copeland, *Without Cloak or Dagger*, p. 236.
112. Interview with Col. Fletcher Prouty, USAF (ret.), Washington, D.C., April 1, 1975.
113. *New York Times*, March 10, 1975, p. 49.
114. *New York Daily News*, April 23, 1975.
115. Ibid.
116. Ibid.
117. Ibid.
118. Telephone interview with source close to the FBI, June 7, 1975.
119. *New York Times*, July 31, 1975, pp. 1, 31.
119a. Kefauver Hearings, part V, p. 404.
120. Jack Anderson column, Jan. 18, 1971; *New York Daily News*, April 23, 1975.
121. *New York Daily News*, April 23, 1975.
122. Ibid.
123. Ibid.
124. Ibid.
125. *New York Post*, July 31, 1975.
126. *New York Times*, March 10, 1975, p. 49.
127. *Report*, p. 384.
128. Canfield and Weberman, *Coup d'état in America*, p. 36.
129. Telephone interview with Victor Marchetti, June 25, 1975.
130. Ibid.
131. 11 H. 367; C.D. 1553.9.
132. C.D. 23.4; C.D. 1085; C.D 853; cited by Canfield and Weberman, *Coup d'état in America*, pp. 118–20.
133. Rogers, "The Persecution of Clay Shaw," *Look*, Aug. 26, 1969.
134. Interview with Mark Lane, Washington, D.C., April 20, 1975.

CHAPTER 11

1. Reid, *The Grim Reapers*, p. 150.
1a. Sheridan, *The Fall and Rise of Jimmy Hoffa*, p. 389.
2. *New York Times*, April 6, 1961, p. 14.
3. Reid, *The Grim Reapers*, p. 150.
4. Rogers, "The Persecution of Clay Shaw," *Look*, Aug. 26, 1969, p. 56.

5. Interview with former official, Justice Department, Washington, D.C., Aug. 25, 1975.
6. Reid, *The Grim Reapers,* p. 158.
7. Gay Talese, *New York Times;* cited by Noyes, *Legacy of Doubt,* pp. 149–50.
8. Reid, *The Grim Reapers,* p. 8.
9. *Time,* Aug. 25, 1975, p. 55.
10. Ralph Salerno and John S. Tompkins, *The Crime Confederation* (Garden City, N.Y.: Doubleday & Co., 1969), p. 225.
11. Nicholas Gage, "The Little Big Man Who Laughs at the Law," *Atlantic,* July 1970, p. 69.
12. Ibid., p. 68.
13. Ibid.
13. Ibid.
15. Ibid.
16. McCoy, *The Politics of Heroin in Southeast Asia,* p. 27.
17. Ibid., p. 26.
18. Anslinger, *The Murderers,* p. 106.
19. Sciacca, *Luciano,* p. 198.
20. *New York Daily News,* April 23, 1975; Hank Messick, *Lansky* (New York: Berkley Books, 1971), p. 189; McClellan Hearings, p. 12432.
21. *New York Daily News,* April 23, 1975.
22. *New York Times,* July 4, 1959, p. 5; March 3, 1962.
23. 5 H. 205; C.E. 1691; C.D. 686d; cited in Canfield and Weberman, *Coup d'état in America,* pp. 293–94.
24. *New York Times,* July 4, 1959, p. 5.
25. McClellan Hearings, p. 16598.
26. Telephone interview with former U.S. Attorney Robert Morgenthau, June 1, 1975.
27. U.S. Congress, Senate, Committee on Government Operations, *Organized Crime and Illicit Traffic in Narcotics, Hearings,* 88th Cong., 2d Sess., p. 801.
28. Reid, *The Grim Reapers,* p. 153.
29. *Life,* Sept. 8, 1967, p. 96.
30. Ibid.
31. Ibid., pp. 94–96.
32. Ibid., p. 96.
33. Ibid., p. 94.
34. Cited by Noyes, *Legacy of Doubt,* p. 153.
35. Reid, *The Grim Reapers,* p. 149; *Wall Street Journal;* cited by Noyes, *Legacy of Doubt,* pp. 152–53.
36. Cited by Noyes, *Legacy of Doubt,* pp. 152–53.
37. *Life,* April 10, 1970, p. 31.
38. Ibid., Sept. 29, 1967, pp. 34–35.
38a. *New York Times,* March 21, 1959, Feb. 5, 1960.
39. Jack Anderson, *Parade,* April 28, 1963.
40. Gage, "The Little Big Man Who Laughs at the Law," *Atlantic,* July 1970, p. 68.
41. Ibid.
42. Jack Anderson, *Parade,* April 28, 1963, p. 4.
43. *New York Daily News,* April 23, 1975.
44. Cited by Scott, "The Dallas Conspiracy" (unpublished ms.), chap. 7, p. 5.
44a. Tanner, *Counter-Revolutionary Agent,* p. 127; cited by Scott, "The Longest Cover-up," *Ramparts,* Nov. 1973, p. 15.
45. Scott, "The Longest Cover-up," *Ramparts,* Nov. 1973.
46. 10 H. 36, 82–83.
47. Pierre Salinger, *With Kennedy* (Garden City, N.Y.: Doubleday & Co., 1966), p. 19.
48. Kennedy, *The Enemy Within,* p. 74.
49. Ibid., p. 162.
50. Ibid.
51. Salinger, *With Kennedy,* p. 26.
52. Victor S. Navasky, *Kennedy Justice* (New York: Atheneum Publishers, 1971), p. 44.
53. Ibid., p. 48.
54. Ibid., p. 46.
55. Ibid., p. 48.
56. Ibid., p. 53.
57. Ibid., p. 55.
58. Ibid., p. 49.
59. Ibid., p. 53.
60. Ibid., p. 57.
61. Interview with Frank McCulloch, Sacramento, Calif., June 28, 1975.

62. *Time*, Aug. 25, 1975, pp. 52, 57.
63. *New York Times*, Feb. 20, 1959.
64. Sheridan, *The Fall and Rise of Jimmy Hoffa*, pp. 14–15.
65. Kennedy, *The Enemy Within*, p. 42.
66. Sheridan, *The Fall and Rise of Jimmy Hoffa*, p. 6.
67. Kennedy, *The Enemy Within*, p. 87.
68. Sheridan, *The Fall and Rise of Jimmy Hoffa*, p. 28.
69. Ibid., p. 27.
70. Ibid., p. 28.
71. Ibid., p. 157.
72. Ibid.
73. Ibid., p. 5.
74. Ibid.
75. Ibid.
76. Ibid., p. 193.
77. Ibid.
78. Ibid., p. 7.
79. Ibid.
80. Ibid.
81. Ibid.
82. Ibid.
83. Ibid., p. 300.
84. Ibid.
85. Ibid., p. 301.
86. Ibid., p. 407.
87. Ibid., pp. 407–8.
88. Interview with former official, Justice Department, Washington, D.C., Aug. 25, 1975.
89. Ibid.
90. Sheridan, *The Fall and Rise of Jimmy Hoffa*, p. 356.
91. *Newsweek*, Aug. 18, 1975, p. 14.
92. Clark Mollenhoff, *Tentacles of Power* (New York: World Publishing Co., 1965), pp. 374–75.
93. Ibid., p. 374.
94. Ibid., pp. 374–75.
95. Ibid., pp. 375–77.
96. Interview with former official. Justice Department, Washington, D.C., Aug. 25, 1975.
97. Sheridan, *The Fall and Rise of Jimmy Hoffa*, p. 401.
98. *Time*, Aug. 25, 1975, p. 55.
99. Sheridan, *The Fall and Rise of Jimmy Hoffa*, p. 156.
100. Ibid., p. 151.
101. Ibid., p. 214.
102. Reid, *The Grim Reapers*, p. 169.
103. Ibid., p. 168.
104. Sheridan, *The Fall and Rise of Jimmy Hoffa*, p. 528; *Newsweek*, Aug. 18, 1975, p. 16.

104a. *New York Times*, Oct. 10, 1975, p. 11.

105. *The Watergate Hearings: Break-in and Cover-up*, p. 97.

105a. Papers filed in *Rancho La Costa, Inc., et al. vs. Penthouse International, Ltd., et al.*, No. C 124 901; *New York Times*, Oct. 10, 1975, p. 11.

105b. Affidavit of Alan M. Gelb, filed in *Rancho La Costa vs. Penthouse*, p. 15.

105c. Answers filed by Penthouse defendants in *Rancho La Costa vs. Penthouse*.

106. Affidavit of Alan M. Gelb, filed in *Rancho La Costa vs. Penthouse*, p. 6.
107. Reid, *The Grim Reapers*, p. 130.
108. *New York Times*, Jan. 30, 1967.
109. Reid, *The Grim Reapers*, p. 130.
110. Navasky, *Kennedy Justice*, p. 49.
111. *Time*, Aug. 25, 1975, p. 55.
112. *New York Times*, Aug. 19, 1975, p. 34.
113. *Time*, Aug. 25, 1975.
114. *Newsweek*, Aug. 18, 1975, p. 17.
115. Ibid.
116. *New York Times*, Feb. 9, 1963, p. 8.
117. McCoy, *The Politics of Heroin in Southeast Asia*, pp. 244–45.
118. Ibid., p. 152.
119. Ibid.
120. Ibid., p. 153.
121. Ibid., p. 210.
122. Ibid., pp. 211–12.

123. Ibid., pp. 153–56.
124. Ibid., pp. 367–75.
125. *New York Times,* March 9, 1965, p. 4.
126. Franz Schurmann, Peter Dale Scott, and Reginald Zelnik, *The Politics of Escalation* (New York: Fawcett World Library, 1966), p. 189.
127. Schlesinger, *A Thousand Days,* p. 871.
128. Edward Weintal and Charles Bartlett, *Facing the Brink* (New York: Charles Scribner's Sons, 1967), p. 71.
129. *New York Times,* May 22, 1975, p. 23.
130. *New York Post,* May 21, 1975, p. 22.
131. Ibid.
132. *New York Times,* May 22, 1975, p. 23.
133. Ibid.
134. Reid, *The Grim Reapers,* p. 159.
135. Ibid.
136. Noyes, *Legacy of Doubt,* pp. 30, 47, 49.
137. Ibid., p. 28.
138. Ibid., p. 39.
139. Ibid., p. 40.
140. Ibid.
141. Ibid., p. 41.
142. Ibid., p. 43.
143. Ibid., pp. 47, 49, 66.
144. Ibid., p. 71.
145. Ibid.
146. Ibid., pp. 21–22.
147. *Report,* p. 707.

CHAPTER 12

1. *New York Times,* March 8, 1975.
2. *CIA Commission Report,* p. 251.
3. Interview with Mark Lane, Washington, D.C., Aug. 22, 1975.
4. *CIA Commission Report,* p. 267.
5. Ibid., p. 268.
6. Paul Hoch, "Relevant Kennedy Assassination Material Avoided by the Rockefeller Commission," July 1975 (unpublished monograph).
7. Interview with Paul Hoch, Berkeley, Calif., July 8, 1975.
8. *CIA Commission Report,* p. 268.
9. Ibid., p. 264.
10. *New York Times,* June 12, 1975.
11. *Saturday Evening Post,* Sept. 1975.
12. Russell, "Dear President Ford: I Know Who Killed JFK . . .," *Village Voice,* Sept. 1, 1975.
13. *Saturday Evening Post,* Sept. 1975.
14. Interview with Mark Lane, Washington, D.C., Aug. 22, 1975.
15. *New York Times,* July 17, 1973.
16. Cyril H. Wecht, "A Critique of President Kennedy's Autopsy"; published in Thompson, *Six Seconds in Dallas,* p. 279.
17. FBI report on neutron activation analysis (NAA), declassified 1975.
18. Ibid.
19. *Boston Globe,* May 30, 1975.
20. *New York Times,* Aug. 27, 1972.
21. *Transcript,* Warren Commission Executive Session, Jan. 27, 1964.
22. *Life,* May 30, 1969.
23. Interview with former official, Department of Justice, Washington, D.C., Aug. 25, 1975.
24. Ibid.
25. Ibid.
26. *New York Times,* Sept. 7, 1975.
27. Interview with Dallas District Attorney Henry Wade, Dallas, Tex., July 1, 1975.
28. Interview with Mary Ferrel, Dallas, Tex., June 30, 1975.
29. *New York Times,* April 26, 1975.
30. Ibid., Dec. 25, 1974.
31. C.D. 2305.
32. 5 H. 35; C.E. 709, 17 H 495.
33. 4 H. 463; 17 H. 783.
34. 5 H. 34, 37.
35. C.D. 349 (National Archives, Washington, D.C.).
36. 23 H. 843; 24 H. 7.
37. 24 H. 820.

38. C.E. 2003, p. 127.
39. Ibid.
40. FBI file DL 105–967; C.E. 821; 17 H. 706 (first Dallas file).
41. Meagher, *Accessories After the Fact,* p. 96.
42. 4 H. 207.
43. 4 H. 181.
44. C.E. 709.
45. Meagher, *Accessories After the Fact,* p. 93.
46. Ibid., p. 96.
47. C.D. 354SS1009.
47a. C.D. 87SS569; C.D. 235; C.D. 409, p. 3; C.D. 11, p. 15, XIII, item 103.
48. *Report,* p. 147.
49. 6 H. 434.
50. C.E. 2003.
51. Lane, *Rush to Judgment,* pp. 193–94.
52. Meagher, *Accessories After the Fact,* p. 256.
53. Ibid., p. 258.
54. Ibid.
55. Ibid., p. 254.
56. 25 H. 530.
57. *Report,* pp. 591–92.
58. C.E. 3001.
59. *Transcript,* Warren Commission Executive Session, Jan. 27, 1964; interview with Mary Ferrel, Dallâs, Tex., June 29, 1975.
60. Lane, *Rush to Judgment,* pp. 193–94.
61. Interview with Jones Harris, New York City, July 23, 1975 (Harris interviewed Mrs. Postal in Dallas shortly after the assassination).
62. First-person story by N. M. McDonald, *Dallas Morning News,* Nov. 24, 1963.
63. Ibid.
64. *Report,* p. 166.
65. Ibid.
66. 3 H. 463.
67. O'Toole, *The Assassination Tapes,* p. 230n.
68. Manchester, *The Death of a President,* p. 287.
69. Interview with Dallas District Attorney Henry Wade, Dallas, Tex., July 1, 1975.
70. C.E. 2249; 25 H. 166.
71. Meagher, *Accessories After the Fact,* p. 387.
72. 11 H. 331, 326–29.
73. Thomas Thompson, "Marina Oswald: A Casualty of History Recovers," *People,* March 4, 1974.
74. Epstein, *Inquest,* p. 97.
75. *Report,* p. 262.
76. *Rolling Stone,* April 10, 1975.
77. Time Inc. press release, April 9, 1975.
78. Telephone interview with Richard Sprague, May 22, 1975.
79. *New York Times,* Sept. 28, 1964.

Index